Microsoft® Windows™ 3.1

Guide to Programming

Microsoft
P R E S S

PUBLISHED BY
Microsoft Press
A Division of Microsoft Corporation
One Microsoft Way
Redmond, Washington 98052-6399

Library of Congress Cataloging-in-Publication Data
Microsoft Windows guide to programming / Microsoft Corporation.
     p. cm.
   Includes index.
   ISBN 1-55615-452-6
   1. Microsoft Windows (Computer program) I. Microsoft
Corporation.
QA76.76.W56M5315 1992
005.4'3--dc20   91-37510
                                           CIP

Printed and bound in the United States of America.

2 3 4 5 6 7 8 9 MLML 7 6 5 4 3

Distributed to the book trade in Canada by Macmillan of Canada, a division of Canada Publishing Corporation.

Distributed to the book trade outside the United States and Canada by Penguin Books Ltd.

Penguin Books Ltd., Harmondsworth, Middlesex, England
Penguin Books Australia Ltd., Ringwood, Victoria, Australia
Penguin Books N.Z. Ltd., 182-190 Wairau Road, Auckland 10, New Zealand

British Cataloging-in-Publication Data available.

Contents

Part 2   Programming Windows Applications

Part 3   Advanced Programming Topics

Introduction

This introduction provides some background information that you should review before using this guide, including the following topics:

- The manuals that come with the Microsoft® Windows™ 3.1 Software Development Kit (SDK)
- What you should know before you start
- The purpose and contents of this guide
- The tools you need to create applications for the Windows operating system
- The code samples described in this guide
- The document conventions used throughout this guide

Software Development Kit Documentation Set

Throughout this documentation set, "SDK" refers specifically to the Microsoft Windows 3.1 Software Development Kit and its contents. The SDK includes the following manuals:

Microsoft Windows 3.1 Software Development Kit Getting Started provides an orientation to the SDK, explains how to install the SDK software, and highlights the changes for Windows 3.1.

The *Microsoft Windows Guide to Programming* (this manual) explains how to write Windows applications and provides code samples that you can use as templates for writing your own applications. This manual also addresses some advanced Windows programming topics.

Microsoft Windows Programming Tools explains how to use the tools you will need to develop Windows applications. These tools include debuggers and specialized SDK editors.

The *Microsoft Windows Programmer's Reference* is a comprehensive guide to all the details of the Microsoft Windows application programming interface (API). The four volumes of this reference list in alphabetic order all the current functions, macros, messages, data types, and structures of the API, and provide extensive overviews on how to use the API.

Before You Start

To start using this guide, you need the following:

- Experience using Windows and an understanding of the Windows user interface.

  Before starting any Windows application development, you should install Windows version 3.1 on your computer and learn how to use it. Be sure to learn the names, purposes, and operation of the various parts of a Windows application (such as windows, dialog boxes, menus, controls, and scroll bars). Because your Windows applications will incorporate these features, it is important for you to understand them so that you can implement them properly.

- An understanding of the Windows user-interface style guidelines.

  One goal of Microsoft Windows is to provide a common user interface for all applications. This ultimately helps your application's user by reducing the effort required to learn the user interface of a Windows application; it helps you, the programmer, by clarifying the choices you have to make when designing an interface.

- Experience writing C-language applications and using the standard C run-time functions.

  The C programming language is the preferred development language for Windows applications. (Although you can develop Windows applications in Pascal and assembly language, these languages present additional challenges that you typically bypass when writing applications in the C language.)

About This Guide

This guide is intended to help the experienced C programmer make the transition to writing applications that use the Windows version 3.1 API. It explains how to use Windows functions, messages, and structures to carry out useful tasks common to all Windows applications and illustrates these explanations with code samples that you can compile and run with Windows version 3.1.

This guide consists of three parts, each containing several chapters.

Part 1, "Programming in the Windows Environment," presents an overview of the Windows operating system and programming environment and provides an in-depth look at a sample Windows application. Part 1 contains the following chapters:

- Chapter 1, "Overview of the Windows Environment," compares Windows to the Microsoft® MS-DOS® programming environment, provides a brief overview of Windows, describes the elements of a Windows application, and outlines the Windows application-development process.

- Chapter 2, "Generic Windows Application," shows how to create a simple Windows application called Generic. This application is the basis for subsequent examples in this guide.

Part 2, "Programming Windows Applications," explains basic Windows programming tasks, such as creating menus, printing, and using the clipboard. Each chapter covers a specific topic and provides code samples that illustrate that topic. Part 2 contains the following chapters:

- Chapter 3, "Output to a Window," introduces the graphics device interface (GDI) and shows how to use GDI tools to create your own output.

- Chapter 4, "Keyboard and Mouse Input," shows how to process input from the mouse and keyboard.

- Chapter 5, "Icons," shows how to create and display icons.

- Chapter 6, "Cursors," shows how to create and display cursors.

- Chapter 7, "Menus," shows how to create menus for your applications and how to process input from menus.

- Chapter 8, "Controls," explains how to create and use controls, such as push buttons and list boxes.

- Chapter 9, "Dialog Boxes," explains how to create and use dialog boxes and how to fill them with controls.

- Chapter 10, "File Input and Output," explains how to use the **OpenFile** function and provides rules about reading from and writing to disk files.

- Chapter 11, "Bitmaps," shows how to create and display bitmaps.

- Chapter 12, "Printing," explains how to use a printer with Windows.

- Chapter 13, "Clipboard," explains the clipboard and shows how to use it.

Part 3, "Advanced Programming Topics," introduces and explains some advanced topics, such as memory management and dynamic data exchange (DDE). Each chapter covers a specific topic. Part 3 contains the following chapters:

- Chapter 14, "C and Assembly Language," presents some guidelines for writing C-language and assembly-language Windows applications.

- Chapter 15, "Memory Management," shows how to allocate global and local memory.

- Chapter 16, "More Memory Management," provides a more in-depth look at how your application can efficiently manage memory. This chapter also explains how Windows manages memory under different memory configurations.

- Chapter 17, "Print Settings," explains how to tailor printer settings (such as page size and orientation).

- Chapter 18, "Fonts," shows how to create and load fonts and how to use them in the **TextOut** function.

- Chapter 19, "Color Palettes," shows how to use Windows color palettes to make the most effective use of color.

- Chapter 20, "Dynamic-Link Libraries," explains how to create and use Windows dynamic-link libraries (DLLs).

- Chapter 21, "Multiple Document Interface," explains how to create an application that uses the Windows multiple document interface (MDI) so that users can work with more than one document at a time.

- Chapter 22, "Dynamic Data Exchange," explains how to pass data from one application to another by using the message-based DDE protocol.

Suggested Tools

To build most Windows version 3.1 applications, you need the following tools:

- Microsoft® C Optimizing Compiler (CL)
- Microsoft Segmented Executable Linker (LINK)
- Microsoft Windows Resource Compiler (RC)
- Microsoft Image Editor (IMAGEDIT.EXE)
- Microsoft Dialog Editor (DLGEDIT.EXE)

To build Windows libraries and font resource files, you need the following additional tools:

- Microsoft® Macro Assembler (ML)
- Microsoft Windows Font Editor (FONTEDIT.EXE)

The following tools may also be useful in building and debugging Windows applications:

- Microsoft Program Maintenance Utility (NMAKE)
- Microsoft® CodeView® for Windows™ (CVW)
- Microsoft Windows Profiler
- Microsoft Windows Heap Walker (HEAPWALK.EXE)
- Microsoft Windows Spy (SPY.EXE)

The SDK includes all of these tools except for CL, LINK, ML, and NMAKE. All are described more fully in *Microsoft Windows Programming Tools*.

For a list of Windows 3.1 software and hardware requirements, see *Microsoft Windows 3.1 Software Development Kit Getting Started*.

Code Samples

The code samples in this guide are written in the C language and conform to the user-interface style recommended by Microsoft for Windows applications.

Document Conventions

The following conventions are used throughout this manual to define syntax:

Convention	Meaning
Bold text	Denotes a term or character to be typed literally, such as a resource-definition statement or function name (**MENU** or **CreateWindow**), a command, or a command-line option (**/nod**). You must type these terms exactly as shown.
Italic text	Denotes a placeholder or variable: You must provide the actual value. For example, the statement **SetCursorPos**(X,Y) requires you to substitute values for the X and Y parameters.
[ ]	Enclose optional parameters.
|	Separates an either/or choice.
...	Specifies that the preceding item may be repeated.
BEGIN . . . END	Represents an omitted portion of a code sample.

In addition, certain text conventions are used to help you understand this material:

Convention	Meaning
SMALL CAPITALS	Indicate the names of keys, key sequences, and key combinations—for example, ALT+SPACEBAR.
FULL CAPITALS	Indicate filenames and paths, type names and most structure names (which are also bold), and constants.
monospace	Sets off code examples and shows syntax spacing.

Programming in the Windows Environment

Part 1

Overview of the Windows Environment

This chapter provides an overview of programming in the Microsoft Windows 3.1 operating system and covers the following topics:

- A comparison of Windows applications and standard MS-DOS applications
- Elements of a Windows application
- Windows libraries
- Processes and tools you use to develop and build Windows applications

1.1 Windows and MS-DOS Compared

Windows has many features that the standard MS-DOS environment does not. For this reason, Windows applications may, at first, seem more complex than standard MS-DOS applications. This is understandable when you consider some of the additional features that Windows offers:

- A graphical user interface featuring windows, menus, dialog boxes, and controls for applications
- Queued input
- Device-independent graphics
- Multitasking capabilities
- Data interchange between applications

When writing applications for the MS-DOS environment, most C programmers use the standard C run-time libraries to carry out an application's input, output, memory management, and other activities. The C run-time libraries are for the programmer who is working in a standard operating environment consisting of a character-based terminal for user input and output, and exclusive access to system memory as well as to the input and output devices of the computer.

In Windows, these characteristics are no longer valid. Windows applications share the computer's resources, including the CPU, with other applications. Windows applications interact with the user through a graphics-based screen, a keyboard, and a mouse.

1.1.1 User Interface

In a multitasking operating system, it is important to give all applications some portion of the screen so that the user can interact with all applications. Some systems do this by giving one program full use of the screen while other programs wait in the background. With Windows, every application has access to some part of the screen at all times by means of a window for user interaction. A window is a rectangle that provides a combination of useful visual devices, such as menus, controls, and scroll bars, with which the user controls an application.

In the standard MS-DOS environment, the system automatically prepares the screen for an application—typically, by passing a file handle to the application. The application can then use that file handle to send output to the screen by using conventional C run-time functions or MS-DOS function calls. In Windows, an application must create its own window before performing any output or receiving any input. Once the application creates a window, Windows provides the application with a great deal of information about what the user is doing with the window. Windows automatically performs many of the tasks the user requests, such as moving and sizing the window.

Another advantage to developing applications in Windows is that, in contrast to a standard C application, which has access to a single screen "surface," a Windows application can create and use any number of overlapping windows to display information in any number of ways. Windows manages the screen, controls the placement and display of windows, and ensures that no two applications attempt to access the same part of the screen at the same time.

1.1.2 Queued Input

One of the biggest differences between Windows applications and standard C applications is the way in which they receive user input.

Input to an MS-DOS application is typically in the form of 8-bit characters read from the keyboard. The application reads these characters by calling the standard-input functions **getchar** and **fscanf**, which return ASCII or other codes corresponding to the keys pressed. The application can also intercept interrupts from input devices such as the mouse and timer to use information from those devices as input.

In a Windows application, all input from the keyboard, mouse, and timer is intercepted by Windows, which places the input in the appropriate application's message queue. When the application is ready to retrieve input, it simply reads the next input message from its message queue.

A Windows input message contains far more input information than is available in the standard MS-DOS environment. Such a message specifies the system time, the position of the mouse, the state of the keyboard, the scan code of the key (if a key was pressed), the mouse button pressed, as well as the device generating the message. For example, two keyboard messages, WM_KEYDOWN and WM_KEYUP, correspond to the pressing and releasing of a specific key. For each keyboard message, Windows provides a device-independent virtual-key code that identifies the key, the device-dependent scan code generated by the keyboard, and the status of other keys on the keyboard, such as SHIFT, CTRL, and NUMLOCK. Keyboard, mouse, and timer messages all have the same format and are all processed in the same manner.

1.1.3 Device-Independent Graphics

A Windows application has access to a large and varied set of device-independent graphics operations. This means your application can easily draw lines, rectangles, circles, and complex regions. Because Windows provides device independence, applications can use the same functions to draw a circle on either a dot-matrix printer or a high-resolution graphics screen.

Windows requires device drivers to convert graphics-output requests to output for a printer, plotter, screen, or other output device. A device driver is a special executable library that an application can load and connect to a specific output device and port. A device context represents the device driver, the output device, and perhaps the communications port. Your application carries out graphics operations within the context of a specific device.

1.1.4 Multitasking Capabilities

Windows is a multitasking operating system—that is, it can run more than one application at a time. The standard MS-DOS operating system has no particular multitasking capabilities. An MS-DOS application typically operates as though it has exclusive control of all resources in the computer, including the input and output devices, memory, the screen, and even the CPU itself. A Windows application, however, must share these resources with all other applications that are currently running. For this reason, Windows carefully controls these resources and requires Windows applications to use a program interface that guarantees that Windows maintains control of those resources.

For example, an MS-DOS application has access to all memory that has not been taken up by the system, by the application itself, or by terminate-and-stay-resident programs (often called TSRs). This means that applications are free to use all available memory for any purpose and may access it by any method.

In Windows, memory is a shared resource. Since more than one application can be running at the same time, each application must cooperatively share memory to avoid exhausting the resource. Applications may allocate what they need from system memory. Windows provides two sources of memory: global memory, for large allocations; and local memory, for small allocations. To make the most efficient use of memory, Windows often moves or even discards memory objects. This means an application cannot "assume" that objects to which it has assigned a memory location remain where it put them. If several applications are running, Windows may move and discard memory objects often.

Another example of a shared resource is the screen. The system typically grants an MS-DOS application exclusive use of the screen, allowing the application to perform many operations, from changing the color of text and background to changing the video mode from text to graphics. A Windows application, however, must share the screen with other applications and must not take control of the screen.

1.2 Elements of a Windows Application

Most Windows applications use the following elements to interact with the user:

- Windows
- Menus
- Dialog boxes
- Message loops

This section describes these elements in detail.

1.2.1 Windows

A window is the primary input and output device of any Windows application. It is an application's only access to the screen. A window consists of a title bar, a menu bar, scroll bars, borders, and other features that occupy a rectangle on the screen. When creating a window, an application specifies the window features and then draws the window. The following figure shows the main features of a window:

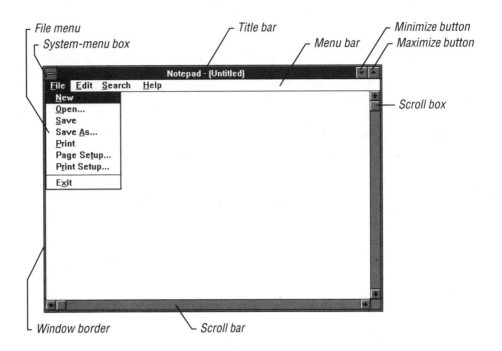

Although an application creates a window, the application and Windows collaborate to manage the window. Windows maintains the position and appearance of the window; manages standard window features such as the border, scroll bars, and title bar; and carries out many tasks initiated by the user that directly affect the window. The application maintains everything else about the window. In particular, it maintains and controls the appearance of the client area of the window (the portion within the window borders).

To manage this collaboration, Windows notifies each window of changes that might affect it. Each window must have a corresponding window procedure, which is a procedure that receives the window-management messages and then responds appropriately. These messages either specify actions for the procedure to carry out or are requests for information from the procedure.

1.2.2 Menus

Menus are the principal means of user input in a Windows application. A menu is a list of items that you supply. To the user, these items are commands that can be viewed or chosen. When creating an application, you create the names of its menus and menu items. Windows then displays and manages the menus, and sends a message to the window procedure when the user makes a choice. The message is the application's signal to carry out the command associated with the menu item.

1.2.3 Dialog Boxes

A dialog box is a temporary window the application displays so that the user can supply more information for a command. A dialog box contains one or more controls. A control is a small window that has a very simple input or output function. For example, an edit control is a simple window in which the user can type and edit text. The controls in a dialog box help the user supply filenames, choose options, and otherwise direct the action of the command.

1.2.4 Message Loops

Since an application receives input through its application queue, the chief feature of any Windows application is its message loop. The message loop retrieves input messages from the application queue and dispatches them to the appropriate windows.

The following figure shows how Windows and applications collaborate to process keyboard-input messages. Windows receives keyboard input when the user presses and releases a key. Windows then copies the keyboard-input messages from the system queue to the appropriate application queue. The message loop retrieves the keyboard-input messages, translates them into the Windows character message WM_CHAR, and dispatches the WM_CHAR message, as well as the keyboard-input messages, to the appropriate window procedure. The window procedure then uses the **TextOut** function to display the character in the client area of the window.

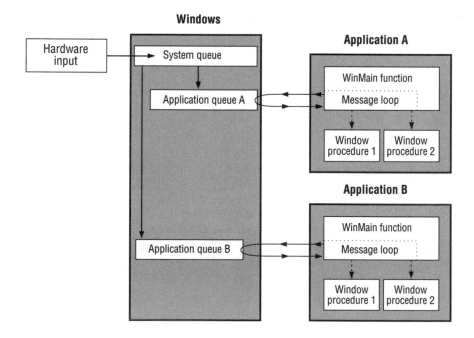

Windows can receive and distribute input messages for several applications at the same time. As shown in the following figure, Windows collects input messages in its system queue and then copies each message to the appropriate application queue. Again, the message loop in each application retrieves messages and dispatches them, through Windows, to each application's appropriate window procedure.

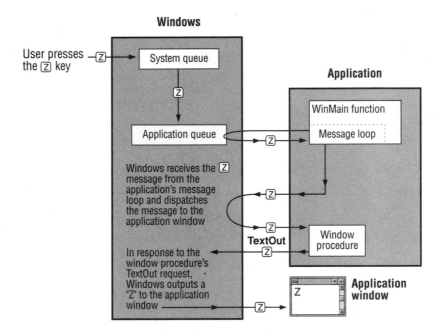

Keyboard-input messages must be retrieved by an application from its message queue. In contrast, window-management messages are sent directly by Windows to the appropriate window procedure. The following figure illustrates this process. After Windows carries out a request to destroy a window, it sends a WM_DESTROY message directly to the window procedure, bypassing the application queue. The window procedure must then signal the main function that the window is destroyed and that the application should terminate. It does this by copying a WM_QUIT message into the application queue by using the **PostQuit-Message** function.

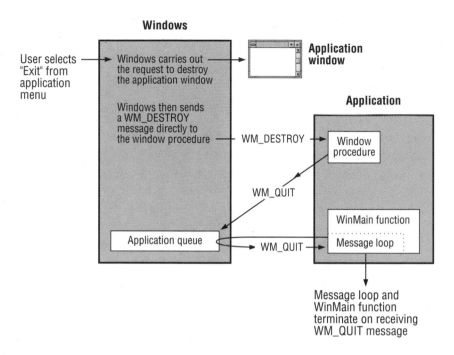

When the message loop retrieves the WM_QUIT message, the loop terminates and the main function exits.

1.3 Windows Libraries

Windows functions, like C run-time functions, are defined in libraries. The Windows libraries, unlike the C run-time libraries, are special dynamic-link libraries (DLLs) that the system links with your application when it loads your application. Dynamic-link libraries are an important feature of Windows because they minimize the amount of code each application requires.

Windows consists of the following three main libraries:

Library	Description
User	Provides window management. This library manages the overall Windows graphical environment, as well as an application's windows.
Kernel	Provides system services, such as multitasking, memory management, and resource management.
GDI	Provides the graphics device interface (GDI).

1.4 Software Development Tools

To create a Windows application, you use many new development tools, as well as some familiar tools with new options. This section briefly describes the tools you will use.

1.4.1 Microsoft C Optimizing Compiler

To compile Windows applications, you use Microsoft C Optimizing Compiler (CL), just as you do for standard C applications. You can use many of the same CL command-line options you use for standard C applications. However, Windows also requires two special options: **/Gw** and **/Zp**. The **/Gw** option adds the Windows prolog and epilog code to each function; this code is required for the application to run with Windows. The **/Zp** option packs structures, ensuring that the structures used in your application are the same size as the corresponding structures used by Windows. Following is a typical CL command for compiling a small-model Windows application:

```
cl /c /AS /Gsw /Os /Zdp test.c
```

The **/c** option instructs the compiler to perform only the C compilation, but not the linking. The **/c** option is necessary if you want to compile multiple C source files separately.

1.4.2 Microsoft Segmented Executable Linker

To produce Windows-format executable files, you use Microsoft Segmented Executable Linker (LINK), which is supplied with CL. Unlike normal C applications, Windows applications require a module-definition (.DEF) file for linking. This file must do the following:

- Define a name for the application.
- Mark the application as a Windows application.
- Specify certain attributes of the application, such as whether a data segment is movable in memory.
- List and name any callback functions in the application.

Following is an example of a module-definition file:

```
NAME      Generic       ;application's module name

DESCRIPTION 'Sample Microsoft Windows Application'

EXETYPE WINDOWS       ;required for all Windows applications
```

```
STUB    'WINSTUB.EXE' ;The "stub" displays an error message if
                      ;the application is run without Windows.

CODE    PRELOAD MOVEABLE      ;code can be moved in memory

;DATA must be MULTIPLE if the program can be invoked more than once.

DATA    MOVEABLE MULTIPLE

HEAPSIZE  1024
STACKSIZE 5120  ;recommended minimum for Windows applications

;All functions that will be called by any Windows function
;MUST be exported.

 EXPORTS
    MainWndProc    @1  ;name of window-processing procedure
    AboutDlgProc   @2  ;name of About processing procedure
```

To link a Windows application, you specify the name of each object file created by the compiler, the name of the Windows import library, the name of the module-definition file, and other options and files. Following is a typical LINK command:

```
link /nod generic, , , slibcew libw, generic.def
```

For more information about LINK and the module-definition file, see *Microsoft Windows Programming Tools*.

1.4.3 Resource Editors

You use the Windows resource editors to create application resources such as cursors, icons, font files, and bitmaps. You must then list these resources in the application's resource-definition file. The resource editors are included in the Microsoft Windows 3.1 Software Development Kit (SDK) and are as follows:

- Microsoft Image Editor (IMAGEDIT.EXE), which creates icons, cursors, and bitmaps.
- Microsoft Windows Font Editor (FONTEDIT.EXE), which creates font files.

Because these editors are Windows applications, you must run them with Windows. For more information about the Windows resource editors, see *Microsoft Windows Programming Tools*.

1.4.4 Microsoft Windows Resource Compiler

Most Windows applications use a variety of resources, each defined in a file called a resource-definition (.RC) file. After creating the resource-definition file, you use Windows Resource Compiler (RC) to compile it and add the compiled resources to the application's executable file. When the application runs, it can load and use the resources from the executable file.

Following is an example of a resource-definition file that defines two resources, a cursor and an icon:

```
Bullseye CURSOR bullseye.cur
Generic ICON generic.ico
```

The first statement defines a cursor resource by naming it (Bullseye), declaring its type (CURSOR), and specifying the file that contains the cursor image (BULLSEYE.CUR). The second statement does the same for an icon resource.

To compile a resource-definition file and add the compiled resources to an executable file, use the RC command. Following is a typical RC command:

```
rc generic.rc
```

For a description of how to use RC, see *Microsoft Windows Programming Tools*. For a description of the resource statements that make up a resource-definition file, see the *Microsoft Windows Programmer's Reference, Volume 4*.

1.4.5 Debugging and Optimizing Tools

The SDK includes several tools you can use to debug your Windows application and to optimize its performance:

- Microsoft CodeView for Windows (CVW) helps you debug Windows applications while your system is running them with Windows in standard mode or 386 enhanced mode. With CVW, you can set breakpoints, view source-level code, and display symbolic information while you are debugging a Windows applications.

- Microsoft Windows Spy (SPY.EXE), monitors the messages that Windows sends to an application. Monitoring can be particularly useful when you are debugging.

- Microsoft Windows Profiler reports the relative times it takes your application's code segments to execute, helping you fine-tune your application's performance.

■ Microsoft Windows Heap Walker (HEAPWALK.EXE) examines the contents of the local or global memory heap.

For more information about these tools, see *Microsoft Windows Programming Tools*.

1.4.6 Microsoft Program Maintenance Utility

The Microsoft Program Maintenance Utility (NMAKE) updates applications by keeping track of the dates of their source files. NMAKE is included with CL version 6.0.

Although NMAKE comes with CL, and not with the SDK, it is especially important for Windows applications because of the number of files required to create a Windows application. This utility uses a text file, called a makefile, that contains a list of the commands and files needed to build a Windows application. The makefile commands compile and link the various files. NMAKE executes the commands only if the files named in those commands have changed. This saves time if, for example, you have made only a minor change to a single file.

The following example shows the content of a typical makefile for a Windows application:

```
# The following line allows NMAKE to use this file as well.
all: generic.exe

# Update the resources if necessary.

generic.res: generic.rc generic.h
    rc /r generic.rc

# Update the object file if necessary.

generic.obj: generic.c generic.h
    cl /AS /c /DLINT_ARGS /Gsw /Oat /W2 /Zped generic.c

# Update the executable file if necessary.
# (If it is necessary, add the resources to it.)

generic.exe: generic.obj generic.def
    link /nod generic, , , slibcew libw, generic.def
    mapsym generic
    rc generic.res
```

```
# If the .RES file is new and the .EXE file is not,
# compile only the resources. Note that you can update
# the .RC file without having to either recompile or
# relink the file.

generic.exe: generic.res
    rc generic.res
```

Typically, a makefile has the same name as the application it builds, although any name is allowed. Following is an NMAKE command that uses the commands in the file GENERIC:

```
nmake generic
```

For more information about NMAKE, see the CL documentation.

1.5 Building a Windows Application

To build a Windows application, follow these steps:

1. Create C-language or assembly-language source files that contain the **Win-Main** function, window procedures, and other application code.

2. Use the resource editors (Image Editor and Font Editor) to create any cursor, icon, bitmap, and font resources the application will require.

3. Create a resource-definition (.RC) file that defines the application's resources. This file lists and names the resources you created in the preceding step. It also defines menus, dialog boxes, and other resources.

4. Create the module-definition (.DEF) file, which defines the attributes of the application modules, such as segment attributes, stack size, and heap size.

5. Compile and link all C-language source files; assemble all assembly-language source files.

6. Use RC to compile the resource-definition file and add it to the executable file.

Some programming practices that work well for C-language or assembly-language applications will not work at all in the Windows environment. For detailed information about using C and assembly language to write Windows applications, see Chapter 14, "C and Assembly Language."

In general, when writing Windows applications, remember the following rules:

- Do not take exclusive control of the CPU—it is a shared resource. Although Windows is a multitasking system, it is nonpreemptive. This means it cannot take control back from an application until the application releases control. A cooperative application carefully manages access to the CPU and gives other applications ample opportunity to run.

- Do not attempt to directly access memory or hardware devices such as the keyboard, mouse, timer, screen, and serial and parallel ports. Windows requires absolute control of these resources to ensure equal, uninterrupted access for all applications that are running.

- Within the application, all functions that Windows can call must be defined with the **PASCAL** keyword; this ensures that the function accesses arguments correctly. Functions that Windows can call are the **WinMain** function, callback functions, and window procedures.

- Every application must have a **WinMain** function. This function is the entry point, or starting point, for the application. It contains statements and functions that create windows and that read and dispatch input intended for the application. The function definition has the following form:

```
int PASCAL WinMain(hinstCurrent, hinstPrevious, lpszCmdLine,
    nCmdShow)
HINSTANCE hinstCurrent;     /* handle of current instance   */
HINSTANCE hinstPrevious;    /* handle of previous instance  */
LPSTR lpszCmdLine;          /* address of command line      */
int nCmdShow;               /* show-window type (open/icon) */
{
        .
        .
        .

}
```

The **WinMain** function must be declared with the **PASCAL** keyword. Although Windows calls the function directly, **WinMain** must not be defined with the **FAR** keyword, since it is called from linked-in startup code.

- When using Windows functions, be sure to check the return values. Do not ignore these return values, because unusual conditions sometimes occur when a function fails.

- Do not use C run-time functions for console input and output. These functions include **getchar**, **putchar**, **scanf**, and **printf**.

- Do not use C run-time file-input-and-output functions to access serial and parallel ports. Instead, use the communications functions, which are described in detail in the *Microsoft Windows Programmer's Reference, Volume 2*.

- You can use the C run-time file-input-and-output functions to access disk files. In particular, use the Windows **OpenFile** function and the low-level, C run-time input-and-output functions. Although you can use the C run-time stream-input-and-output functions, you do not get the advantages that **OpenFile** provides.

- You can use the C run-time memory-management functions **malloc**, **calloc**, **realloc**, and **free**, but be aware that Windows translates these functions to its own local-heap functions, **LocalAlloc**, **LocalReAlloc**, and **LocalFree**. Since local-heap functions do not always operate exactly as do C run-time memory-management functions, you may get unexpected results.

1.6 Related Topics

For information about specific Windows functions and messages, see the *Microsoft Windows Programmer's Reference*, *Volumes 2* and *3*.

For more information about software development tools, see *Microsoft Windows Programming Tools*.

Generic Windows Application

This chapter explains how to create a simple application for the Microsoft Windows 3.1 operating system. Generic demonstrates the concepts explained in Chapter 1, "Overview of the Windows Environment."

This chapter covers the following topics:

- Essential parts of a Windows application
- Initializing a Windows application
- Writing the message loop
- Terminating an application
- Basic steps needed to build a Windows application

The Generic application is used as basic code for all the code samples in Part 2 of this guide.

2.1 A Standard Windows Application: Generic

A standard Windows application is any application that is specifically written to run with Windows, and that uses the Windows application programming interface (API) to carry out its tasks. Every Windows application also has a main function (called **WinMain**) and a window procedure.

Generic is a standard Windows application. It has a **WinMain** function and a window procedure, and it features a main window, a border, an application menu, and Maximize and Minimize buttons. The application menu includes a Help menu with an About command, which, when chosen by the user, displays an About dialog box describing Generic. The following shows the completed Generic application, with an About dialog box:

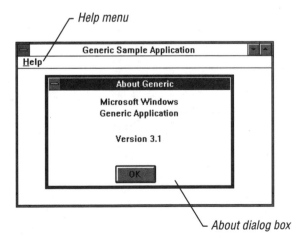

Help menu

Generic Sample Application

Help

About Generic

Microsoft Windows
Generic Application

Version 3.1

OK

About dialog box

Building an application from the Generic template helps you understand how Windows applications are put together and how they work.

2.2 WinMain Function

Much like the main function in standard C-language applications, the **WinMain** function is the entry point for a Windows application. Every Windows application must have a **WinMain** function (it is always named **WinMain**); no Windows application can run without it. In most Windows applications, the **WinMain** function does the following:

- Calls initialization functions that register window classes, create windows, and perform any other necessary initializing

- Enters a message loop to process messages from the application queue

- Terminates the application when the message loop retrieves a WM_QUIT message

The **WinMain** function has the following form:

```
int PASCAL WinMain(hinstCurrent, hinstPrevious, lpszCmdLine, nCmdShow)
HINSTANCE hinstCurrent;     /* handle of current instance   */
HINSTANCE hinstPrevious;    /* handle of previous instance  */
LPSTR lpszCmdLine;          /* address of command line      */
int nCmdShow;               /* show-window type (open/icon) */
{
        .
        .
        .

}
```

The **WinMain** function requires the **PASCAL** calling convention.

When the user starts an application, Windows passes the following four parameters to the application's **WinMain** function:

Parameter	Value passed to application
hinstCurrent	The instance handle of the application.
hinstPrevious	The handle of another instance of the application, if one is running. If no other instances of this application are running, Windows sets this parameter to NULL.
lpszCmdLine	A long pointer to a null-terminated command line.

Parameter	Value passed to application
nCmdShow	An integer that specifies whether to display the application's window as a window or as an icon. The application passes this value to the **ShowWindow** function when calling that function to display the application's main window.

For more information about handles, see Section 2.2.2, "Handles." For more information about the *lpszCmdLine* parameter, see Section 2.2.11, "Application Command-Line Parameter."

2.2.1 Data Types and Structures

The **WinMain** function uses several special data types to define its parameters. For example, it uses the **HANDLE** data type to define the *hinstCurrent* and *hinstPrevious* parameters, and the **LPSTR** data type to define the *lpszCmdLine* parameter. In general, Windows applications use many more data types than are found in a typical C-language application. Although the Windows data types are often equivalent to familiar C-language data types, they are intended to be more descriptive and should help you better understand the purpose of a variable or parameter used in an application.

The Windows data types are defined in the WINDOWS.H header file. This file is an ordinary C-language source file that contains definitions for all the Windows special constants, variables, structures, and functions. To use these definitions, you must include the WINDOWS.H file in each source file. Place the following line at the beginning of your source file:

```
#include <windows.h> /* required for all Windows applications */
```

Following are some commonly used Windows data types:

Type	Meaning
WORD	Specifies a 16-bit, unsigned integer.
LONG	Specifies a 32-bit, signed integer.
HANDLE	Identifies a 16-bit, unsigned integer to be used as a handle.
HWND	Identifies a 16-bit, unsigned integer to be used as a handle of a window.
LPSTR	Specifies a 32-bit address of a character string (of type **char**)
FARPROC	Specifies a 32-bit address of a function.

Following are some commonly used structures:

Structure	Description
MSG	Contains information about an input message from the Windows application queue.
WNDCLASS	Defines a window class.
PAINTSTRUCT	Defines a structure used to paint the client area of a window.
RECT	Defines a rectangle.

For a complete listing and description of Windows data types and structures, see the *Microsoft Windows Programmer's Reference*, *Volume 3*.

2.2.2 Handles

Two of the **WinMain** function parameters (*hinstPrevious* and *hinstCurrent*) are called handles. A handle is a unique integer that Windows uses to identify an object created or used by an application. Windows uses a wide variety of handles, identifying objects such as application instances, windows, menus, controls, allocated memory, output devices, files, and graphics device interface (GDI) pens and brushes.

Most handles are indices into internal tables. Windows uses handle indices to access information stored in these tables. Typically, an application has access only to the handle and not to the information. When the application must examine or change the information, it supplies the handle, and Windows does the rest. This is one way that Windows protects information with its multitasking capabilities.

2.2.3 Instances

Not only can you run more than one application at a time with Windows, you can also run more than one copy, or instance, of the same application at a time. To distinguish one instance from another, Windows supplies a unique instance handle (a unique integer identifying the instance) each time it calls the **WinMain** function to start the application.

With some multitasking systems, to run multiple instances of the same application at the same time the system loads a fresh copy of the application's code and data into memory and runs that copy. With Windows, when a new instance of the application is started only the data for the application is loaded. Windows uses the same code for all instances of the application. This saves as much space as possible for other applications and for data. However, this method requires that the code segments of the application remain unchanged while the application is running. This means that you must not store data in a code segment or change the code while the application is running.

For most Windows applications, the first instance has a special role. Many of the resources an application creates, such as window classes, are generally available to all applications. Consequently, only the first instance of an application creates these resources. All subsequent instances may use the resources without having to create them. To determine which is the first instance, Windows sets the *hinst-Previous* parameter of **WinMain** to NULL if there are no previous instances. The following example shows how to check that a previous instance does not exist:

```
int PASCAL WinMain(hinstCurrent, hinstPrevious, lpszCmdLine, nCmdShow)
HINSTANCE hinstCurrent;     /* handle of current instance  */
HINSTANCE hinstPrevious;    /* handle of previous instance */
LPSTR lpszCmdLine;          /* address of command line     */
int nCmdShow;               /* show-window type (open/icon) */
{
    if (hinstPrevious == NULL)
      .
      .
      .
}
```

To keep the user from starting more than one instance of your application, the application should check the *hinstPrevious* parameter upon starting and should return to Windows if the parameter is not NULL. The following example shows how to do this:

```
if (hinstPrevious)
    return NULL;
```

2.2.4 Registering a Window Class

Before you can create any window, you must have a window class. A window class is a template that defines the attributes of a window, such as the shape of the window's cursor and the name of the window's menu. The window class also specifies the window procedure that processes messages for all windows in the class. Although Windows provides some predefined window classes, most applications define their own window classes in order to completely control how their windows operate.

You must register a window class before you can create a window that belongs to that class. You do this by filling a **WNDCLASS** structure with information about the class and passing it as a parameter to the **RegisterClass** function.

2.2.4.1 Filling a WNDCLASS Structure

The **WNDCLASS** structure provides information to Windows about the name, attributes, resources, and window procedure for a window class. The **WNDCLASS** structure contains the following members:

Member	Description
lpszClassName	Points to the name of the window class. A window class name must be unique; that is, different applications must use different class names.
hInstance	Identifies the application instance that is registering the class.
lpfnWndProc	Points to the window procedure used to carry out work on the window.
style	Specifies the class styles, such as automatic redrawing of the window whenever it is moved or sized.
hbrBackground	Identifies the brush used to paint the window background.
hCursor	Identifies the cursor used in the window.
hIcon	Identifies the icon used to represent a minimized window.
lpszMenuName	Points to the resource name of a menu.
cbClsExtra	Specifies the number of extra bytes to allocate for this class structure. The extra bytes are initialized to zero.
clWndExtra	Specifies the number of extra bytes to allocate for all the window structures created with this class. The extra bytes are initialized to zero.

For more information about these members, see the *Microsoft Windows Programmer's Reference*, *Volume 3*.

Some members, such as **lpszClassName**, **hInstance**, and **lpfnWndProc**, must be assigned values. Other members can be set to NULL. When these members are set to NULL, Windows uses a default attribute for windows created using the class. The following example shows how to fill a window structure:

```
BOOL InitApplication(hinstCurrent)
HINSTANCE hinstCurrent;  /* current instance                       */
{
    WNDCLASS  wc;

    /*
     * Fill in window-class structure with parameters that
     * describe the main window.
     */

    wc.style = NULL;                 /* class style(s)              */
    wc.lpfnWndProc = MainWndProc;    /* window procedure            */
                                     /* for windows of this class   */
```

```
    wc.cbClsExtra = 0;              /* no per-class extra data   */
    wc.cbWndExtra = 0;              /* no per-window extra data  */

    wc.hInstance = hinstCurrent;   /* application that owns class */
    wc.hIcon = LoadIcon(NULL, IDI_APPLICATION);
    wc.hCursor = LoadCursor(NULL, IDC_ARROW);
    wc.hbrBackground = GetStockObject(WHITE_BRUSH);
    wc.lpszMenuName = "GenericMenu";   /* menu name in .RC file   */
    wc.lpszClassName = "GenericWClass"; /* name in CreateWindow   */

    /* Register the window class and return success/failure code.  */

    return (RegisterClass(&wc));
}
```

This example first declares a **WNDCLASS** structure named wc.

The **style** member is set to NULL.

The **lpfnWndProc** member contains a pointer to the window procedure named MainWndProc. This means that the application's MainWndProc procedure will receive any messages that Windows sends to that window and will be the procedure that carries out tasks for that window. To assign the address of MainWndProc to the **lpfnWndProc** member, you must declare the procedure somewhere before the assignment statement. Windows applications should use prototypes for declaring procedures in order to take advantage of the automatic type-checking and casting provided by CL. The following is the correct prototype for a window procedure with the name MainWndProc:

```
LRESULT FAR PASCAL MainWndProc(HWND, UINT, WPARAM, LPARAM);
```

Note that the MainWndProc procedure must be exported in the module-definition file.

The **cbClsExtra** and **cbWndExtra** members are set to zero, so there is no additional storage space associated with either the window class or each individual window. (You can set these members to allocate additional storage space, which you can then use to store information on a per-window basis. For information about using this extra space, see Chapter 16, "More Memory Management."

The **hInstance** member is set to hinstCurrent, the instance handle that Windows passed to the **WinMain** function when the application was started.

The **hIcon** member receives a handle to a built-in icon. The **LoadIcon** function can return a handle to either a built-in icon or an application-defined icon. In this case, the NULL and IDI_APPLICATION arguments specify the built-in application icon. (Most applications use their own icons instead of the built-in application icon. Chapter 5, "Icons," explains how to create and use your own icons.)

The **hCursor** member receives a handle to the standard arrow-shaped cursor. The **LoadCursor** function can return a handle to either a built-in cursor or an application-defined cursor. In this case, the NULL and IDC_ARROW arguments specify a built-in arrow cursor. (Some applications use their own cursors instead of built-in cursors. Chapter 6, "Cursors," explains how to create and use your own cursors.)

The **hbrBackground** member determines the color of the brush that Windows is to use to paint the window's background. In this case, the application uses the **Get-StockObject** function to retrieve the handle of the standard white background brush.

The **lpszMenuName** member specifies the name of the menu for this window class, GenericMenu. This menu then appears for all windows in this class. If the window class has no menu, this member is set to NULL.

The **lpszClassName** member specifies GenericWClass as the class name for this window class.

2.2.4.2 Using the RegisterClass Function

After you assign values to the **WNDCLASS** structure members, you register the class by using the **RegisterClass** function. If registration is successful, the function returns a nonzero value; otherwise, it returns zero. Make sure you check the return value, because you cannot create your windows without first registering the window class.

Although the **RegisterClass** function requires a 32-bit pointer to a **WNDCLASS** structure, in the previous example, the address operator (&) generates only a 16-bit address. This is an example of an implicit cast carried out by CL. The Windows header file contains prototypes for all Windows functions. These prototypes specify the correct types for each function parameter, and the compiler casts to these types automatically.

2.2.5 Creating a Window

You can create a window by using the **CreateWindow** function. This function tells Windows to create a window that has the specified style and belongs to the specified class. **CreateWindow** takes several parameters:

- Name of the window class
- Window title
- Window style
- Window position
- Parent-window handle

- Menu handle
- Instance handle
- 32 bits of additional data

The following example creates a window belonging to the GenericWClass window class (created in the sample code shown in Section 2.2.4.1, "Filling a WNDCLASS Structure"):

```
/* Create a main window for this application instance.      */

hWnd = CreateWindow(
    "GenericWClass",                /* see RegisterClass call */
    "Generic Sample Application",   /* text for title bar     */
    WS_OVERLAPPEDWINDOW,            /* window style           */
    CW_USEDEFAULT,                  /* default horz position  */
    CW USEDEFAULT,                  /* default vert position  */
    CW_USEDEFAULT,                  /* default width          */
    CW_USEDEFAULT,                  /* default height         */
    NULL,              /* overlapped windows have no parent */
    NULL,              /* use window class menu             */
    hinstCurrent,      /* this instance owns this window    */
    NULL               /* pointer not needed                */
);
```

This example creates an overlapped window that has the style WS_OVERLAPPEDWINDOW and that belongs to the window class created by the code in the preceding example.

The first parameter of the **CreateWindow** function specifies the name of the window class Windows should use when creating the window. In this example, the window class name is GenericWClass. The second parameter of **CreateWindow** specifies the window caption as "Generic Sample Application".

The WS_OVERLAPPEDWINDOW style specifies that the window is a normal "overlapped" window, and the next four **CreateWindow** parameters specify the position and dimensions of the window. Since the CW_USEDEFAULT value is specified for the position, width, and height parameters, Windows places the window at a default position and gives it a default width and height. The default position and dimensions depend on the system and on how many other applications have been started. (Note that Windows does not display the window until the application calls the **ShowWindow** function.)

When you create a window, you can specify its parent window (used with control windows and child windows) in the *hwndParent* parameter. Because an overlapped window does not have a parent window, this parameter is set to NULL. If you specify a menu in the *hmenu* parameter when you create a window, the menu overrides the class menu (if any) for the window. Because this window is to use the class menu, this parameter is also set to NULL.

You must specify the instance of the application that is creating the window. Windows uses this instance to make sure that the window procedure supporting the window uses the data for this instance.

The last parameter, *lpvParam*, is for additional data to be used by the window procedure when the window is created. In this case, the window takes no additional data, so the parameter is set to NULL.

When **CreateWindow** successfully creates the window, it returns a handle of the new window. You can then use the handle to carry out tasks, such as showing the window or updating its client area.

If **CreateWindow** cannot create the window, it returns NULL. Whenever your application creates a window, it should check for a NULL handle and respond appropriately. For example, in the **WinMain** function, if the application's main window cannot be created, the application should be terminated—that is, **WinMain** should return control to Windows.

2.2.6 Showing and Updating a Window

Although **CreateWindow** creates a window, it does not automatically display the window. Instead, your application must display the window by using the **Show-Window** function and must update the window's client area by using the **UpdateWindow** function.

The **ShowWindow** function tells Windows to display the new window. For the application's main window, **WinMain** should call **ShowWindow** soon after creating the window and should pass the *nCmdShow* parameter to it. The *nCmdShow* parameter tells the application whether to display the window as an open window or as an icon. After calling **ShowWindow**, **WinMain** should call the **Update-Window** function. The following example illustrates how to show and update a window:

```
ShowWindow(hWnd, nCmdShow);   /* shows the window          */
UpdateWindow(hWnd);           /* sends a WM_PAINT message */
```

Note Normally, the *nCmdShow* parameter of the **ShowWindow** function can be set to any of the constants beginning with SW_ that are defined in the WINDOWS.H header file. The one exception is when the application calls **Show-Window** to display its main window; then, it uses the *nCmdShow* parameter from the **WinMain** function. For a complete list of these constants, see the *Microsoft Windows Programmer's Reference, Volume 2*.

2.2.7 Creating a Message Loop

Once your application has created and displayed a window, the **WinMain** function can begin its primary duty: to read messages from the application queue and dispatch them to the appropriate window. **WinMain** does this by using a message loop. A message loop is a program loop, typically created by using a **while** statement, in which **WinMain** retrieves messages and dispatches them.

Windows does not send input directly to an application. Instead, it places all mouse and keyboard input into an application queue (along with messages posted by Windows and other applications). The application must read the application queue, retrieve the messages, and dispatch them so that the appropriate window procedure can process them.

The simplest possible message loop consists of the **GetMessage** and **Dispatch-Message** functions. This loop has the following form:

```
MSG msg;

    .
    .
    .

while (GetMessage(&msg, NULL, NULL, NULL)) {
    DispatchMessage(&msg);
}
```

In this example, the **GetMessage** function retrieves a message from the application queue and copies it to the message structure named msg. The NULL arguments indicate that all messages should be processed. The **DispatchMessage** function directs Windows to send each message to the appropriate window procedure. Every message an application receives, except the WM_QUIT message, belongs to one of the windows created by the application. Since an application must not call a window procedure directly, it uses the **DispatchMessage** function instead to pass each message to the appropriate procedure.

Depending on what your application does, it may require a more complicated message loop. In particular, to process character input from the keyboard, it must translate each message it receives by using the **TranslateMessage** function. The message loop should then look like this:

```
while (GetMessage(&msg, /* message structure                      */
        NULL,        /* handle of window receiving the message */
        NULL,        /* lowest message to examine              */
        NULL))       /* highest message to examine             */
    {
    TranslateMessage(&msg); /* translates virtual key codes    */
    DispatchMessage(&msg);  /* dispatches message to window     */
```

The **TranslateMessage** function looks for matching WM_KEYDOWN and WM_KEYUP messages and generates a corresponding WM_CHAR message for the window that contains the Windows character code for the given key. This message loop could also contain functions that process menu accelerator keys and keystrokes within dialog boxes. Again, this would depend on what your application does.

Windows places input messages in an application queue when the user moves the cursor in the window, presses or releases a mouse button when the cursor is in the window, or presses or releases a key when the window has the input focus. The window manager first collects all keyboard and mouse input in a system queue and then copies the corresponding messages to the appropriate application queue.

The message loop continues until **GetMessage** returns NULL, which it does only if it retrieves the WM_QUIT message. This message is a signal to terminate the application and is usually posted (placed in the application queue) by the window procedure of the application's main window.

2.2.8 Yielding Control

Windows is a nonpreemptive multitasking system. This means that it cannot take control from an application. Instead, the application must yield control before Windows can reassign control to another application.

To make sure that all applications have equal access to the CPU, the **GetMessage** function automatically yields control when there are no messages in an application queue. This means that if there is no work for the application to do, Windows can give control to another application. Since all applications have a message loop, this implicit yielding of control guarantees that control is shared.

In general, you should rely on the **GetMessage** function to yield for your application. Although a function (**Yield**) is available that explicitly yields control, you should avoid using it. Since there might be times when your application must keep control for a long time, such as when writing a large buffer to a file, you should try to minimize the work and provide a visual clue to the user that a lengthy operation is under way.

2.2.9 Terminating an Application

Your application terminates when the **WinMain** function returns control to Windows. **WinMain** can return control at any time before starting the message loop. Typically, an application checks each step leading up to the message loop to make sure each window class is registered and each window is created. If there is an error, the application can display a message before terminating.

Once the **WinMain** function enters the message loop, however, the only way to terminate the loop is to post a WM_QUIT message in the application queue by using the **PostQuitMessage** function. When the **GetMessage** function retrieves a WM_QUIT message, it returns NULL, which terminates the message loop. Typically, the window procedure for the application's main window posts a WM_QUIT message when the main window is being destroyed (that is, when the window procedure has received a WM_DESTROY message).

Although **WinMain** specifies a data type for its return value, Windows does not currently use the return value. For debugging an application, however, a return value can be helpful. In general, the easiest return-code conventions are those used by standard C-language applications: zero for successful execution, nonzero for error. The **PostQuitMessage** function lets the window procedure specify the return value. This value is then copied to the *wParam* parameter of the WM_QUIT message. To return this value after terminating the message loop, use the following statement:

```
return (msg.wParam);   /* returns value from PostQuitMessage */
```

Although standard C-language applications typically free any allocated resources just prior to terminating, Windows applications should free resources as each window is destroyed. This process is called "cleaning up." Failing to clean up can cause an application to lose some data. For example, when Windows itself terminates, it destroys each window but does not return control to the application's message loop. This means that the loop never retrieves the WM_QUIT message and the statements after the loop are not executed. (Windows does send each application a WM_QUERYENDSESSION message before terminating, so an application does have an opportunity to carry out tasks before terminating. For more information about the WM_QUERYENDSESSION message, see Chapter 10, "File Input and Output."

2.2.10 Initialization Functions

Most applications use two locally defined initialization functions:

- The main initialization function carries out work that must be done only once for all instances of the application (for example, registering window classes).

- The instance initialization function performs tasks that must be done for every instance of the application.

Using initialization functions keeps the **WinMain** function simple and readable; it also organizes initialization tasks so that they can be placed in a separate code segment and discarded after use. The Generic application does not discard its initialization functions.

2.2.10.1 Main Initialization Function

The Generic application's main initialization function looks like the following:

```
BOOL InitApplication(hinstCurrent)
HINSTANCE hinstCurrent;  /* current instance                        */
{
    WNDCLASS  wc;

    /*
     *  Fill in window-class structure with parameters that
     *  describe the main window.
     */

    wc.style = NULL;                    /* class style(s)            */
    wc.lpfnWndProc = MainWndProc;       /* window procedure          */
                                        /* for windows of this class */

    wc.cbClsExtra = 0;                  /* no per-class extra data   */
    wc.cbWndExtra = 0;                  /* no per-window extra data  */

    wc.hInstance = hinstCurrent;    /* application that owns class */
    wc.hIcon = LoadIcon(NULL, IDI_APPLICATION);
    wc.hCursor = LoadCursor(NULL, IDC_ARROW);
    wc.hbrBackground = GetStockObject(WHITE_BRUSH);
    wc.lpszMenuName =  "GenericMenu";   /* menu name in .RC file     */
    wc.lpszClassName = "GenericWClass"; /* name in CreateWindow      */

    /* Register the window class and return success/failure code.  */

    return (RegisterClass(&wc));
}
```

2.2.10.2 Instance Initialization Function

Generic's instance initialization function looks like the following:

```
BOOL InitInstance(hinstCurrent, nCmdShow)
HINSTANCE hinstCurrent; /* handle of current instance              */
int nCmdShow;           /* param for first ShowWindow call          */
{
    HWND hWnd;          /* handle of main window                    */

    /*
     * Save the instance handle in a static variable, which will
     * be used in subsequent calls from this application to
     * Windows.
     */
```

```
hInst = hinstCurrent;

/* Create a main window for this application instance.        */

hWnd = CreateWindow(
    "GenericWClass",              /* see RegisterClass call */
    "Generic Sample Application", /* text for title bar      */
    WS_OVERLAPPEDWINDOW,          /* window style            */
    CW_USEDEFAULT,                /* default horz position   */
    CW_USEDEFAULT,                /* default vert position   */
    CW_USEDEFAULT,                /* default width           */
    CW_USEDEFAULT,                /* default height          */
    NULL,             /* overlapped windows have no parent */
    NULL,             /* use window class menu             */
    hinstCurrent,     /* this instance owns this window    */
    NULL              /* pointer not needed                */
);

/* If the window could not be created, return "failure."      */

if (hWnd == NULL)
    return FALSE;

/*
 * Make the window visible, update its client area, and
 * return "success."
 */

ShowWindow(hWnd, nCmdShow);  /* shows window                  */
UpdateWindow(hWnd);          /* sends WM_PAINT message        */
return TRUE;
}
```

2.2.11 Application Command-Line Parameter

You can examine the command line that starts your application by using the *lpszCmdLine* parameter. The *lpszCmdLine* parameter points to the start of a character array that contains the command exactly as it was typed by the user. To extract filenames or options from the command line, you need to parse the command line into individual values. Alternatively, you can use the **__argc** and **__argv** variables. For more information, see Chapter 14, "C and Assembly Language."

2.3 Window Procedure

A window procedure responds to input and window-management messages received from Windows. The procedure can be short, processing only a message or two, or it can be complex, processing many types of messages for a variety of application windows. In either case, every window must have a window procedure.

A window procedure has the following form:

```
LRESULT FAR PASCAL MainWndProc(hWnd, message, wParam, lParam)
HWND hWnd;       /* window handle              */
UINT message;    /* type of message           */
WPARAM wParam;   /* additional information     */
LPARAM lParam;   /* additional information     */
{
        .
        .
        .

    switch (message) {
        .
        .
        .

        default: /* passes it on if unprocessed   */
            return (DefWindowProc(hWnd, message, wParam, lParam));
    }
    return NULL;
}
```

The window procedure uses the **PASCAL** calling convention. Since Windows calls this procedure directly and always uses this convention, **PASCAL** is required. The window procedure also uses the **FAR** keyword in its definition, since Windows uses a 32-bit address whenever it calls a procedure or function. Also, you must name the window procedure in an **EXPORTS** statement in the application's module-definition file. For more information about module-definition files, see Section 2.5, "Creating a Module-Definition File."

The window procedure receives messages from Windows. These may be input messages that have been dispatched by the **WinMain** function, or they may be window-management messages that come directly from Windows. The window procedure must examine each message; it then either carries out some specific action based on the message or passes the message back to Windows for default processing by the **DefWindowProc** function.

The *message* parameter defines the message type. You use this parameter in a **switch** statement to direct processing to the correct case. The *lParam* and *wParam* parameters contain additional message-dependent information. The window procedure typically uses these parameters to carry out the requested action. If a window procedure does not process a message, it must pass it to **DefWindowProc**. Passing the message to **DefWindowProc** ensures that any special actions that affect the window, the application, or Windows itself can be carried out.

Most window procedures process the WM_DESTROY message. Windows sends this message to the window procedure immediately after destroying the window. The message gives the procedure the opportunity to finish its processing and, if it is the window procedure for the application's main window, to post a WM_QUIT message in the application queue. The following example shows how the main window procedure should process this message:

```
case WM_DESTROY:
    PostQuitMessage(0);
    break;
```

The **PostQuitMessage** function places a WM_QUIT message in the application's queue. When the **GetMessage** function retrieves this message, it terminates the message loop and the application.

A window procedure receives messages from two sources: Input messages come from the message loop, and window-management messages come from Windows. Input messages correspond to mouse input, keyboard input, and sometimes timer input. Typical input messages are WM_KEYDOWN, WM_MOUSEMOVE, WM_KEYUP, and WM_TIMER, all of which correspond directly to hardware input.

Windows sends window-management messages directly to a window procedure without going through the application queue or message loop. These window messages are typically requests for the window procedure to carry out some action, such as painting the client area of its window or supplying information about the window. The messages may also inform the window procedure of changes that Windows has made to the window. Some typical window-management messages are WM_CREATE, WM_DESTROY, and WM_PAINT.

The window procedure should return a 32-bit message-dependent value. For most messages, the return value is arbitrary; cases in which the return value is significant are described in the *Microsoft Windows Programmer's Reference*, *Volume 1*. If the window procedure does not process a message, it should return the **Def-WindowProc** function's return value.

2.4 Creating an About Dialog Box

You should include an About dialog box with every application. A dialog box is a temporary window that displays information or prompts the user for input. The About dialog box displays such information as the application's name and copyright information. The user tells the application to display the About dialog box by choosing the About command from a menu.

You create and display a dialog box by using the **DialogBox** function. This function takes a dialog box template, a procedure-instance address, and a handle of a parent window, and creates a dialog box through which your application can display output and prompt the user for input.

To display and use an About dialog box, follow these steps:

1. Create a dialog box template and add it to your resource-definition file.

2. Add a dialog box procedure to your C-language source file.

3. Export the dialog box procedure in your module-definition file.

4. Add a menu to your application's resource-definition file.

5. Process the WM_COMMAND message in your application code.

Once you have completed these steps, your application will be able to display the dialog box when the user chooses the About command from the application's menu.

2.4.1 Creating a Dialog Box Template

A dialog box template is a description of a dialog box's style, contents, shape, and size. You can create your own custom template or use Microsoft Dialog Editor (DLGEDIT.EXE). In this example, the template is created manually. For information about how to use Dialog Editor to create a dialog box, see *Microsoft Windows Programming Tools*.

You create a dialog box template by creating a resource-definition file. This file contains definitions of resources to be used by the application, such as icons, cursors, and dialog box templates. To create an About dialog box template, you use a **DIALOG** statement and fill it with control statements, as in the following example:

```
AboutBox DIALOG 22, 17, 144, 75
STYLE DS_MODALFRAME | WS_CAPTION | WS_SYSMENU
CAPTION "About Generic"
BEGIN
 CTEXT "Microsoft Windows"        -1, 0,  5, 144,  8
    CTEXT "Generic Application"   -1, 0, 14, 144,  8
    CTEXT "Version 3.1"           -1, 0, 34, 144,  8
 DEFPUSHBUTTON "OK"               IDOK, 53, 59, 32, 14, WS_GROUP
END
```

The **DIALOG** statement starts the dialog box template. The name AboutBox identifies the template when the **DialogBox** function is used to create the dialog box. The box's upper-left corner is placed at the coordinates (22,17) in the parent window's client area. The box is 144 units wide by 75 units high. The horizontal units are $\frac{1}{4}$ of the dialog box's base-width unit; the vertical units are 1/8 of the dialog box's base-height unit. The current base units are computed from the height and width of the current system font. The **GetDialogBaseUnits** function returns the dialog box's base units in pixels.

The **STYLE** statement defines the dialog box style. This particular style is a window with a framed border, a title bar, and a System menu, which is the typical style used for modal dialog boxes.

The **BEGIN** and **END** statements mark the beginning and end of the control definitions. The dialog box contains text and a default push button. The push button lets the user send input to the dialog box procedure to terminate the dialog box. The statements, strings, and integers contained between the **BEGIN** and **END** statements describe the contents of the dialog box. (Because you would normally create such a description by using Dialog Editor, this guide does not describe the numbers and statements that make up the description. For a complete description of how to use Dialog Editor, see *Microsoft Windows Programming Tools*.)

The **CTEXT** statement creates a rectangle with the quoted text centered in a rectangle. This statement appears several times, once for each of the various texts that appear in the dialog box.

DEFPUSHBUTTON creates a push button that allows the user to give a default response—in this case, choosing the OK button causes the dialog box to disappear.

The DS_MODALFRAME, WS_CAPTION, WM_SYSMENU, IDOK, and WS_GROUP constants used in the dialog box template are defined in the Windows header file. You should include this file in the resource-definition file by using the **#include** directive at the beginning of the definition file.

The statements in this file were created with a text editor and were based on a dialog box used in another application. You can create many such resources by copying them from other applications and modifying them by using a text editor. You can also create new dialog boxes by using Dialog Editor. (The files created by Dialog Editor contain statements that are somewhat different from the statements shown here, and such files usually are edited only by using Dialog Editor.)

2.4.2 Creating a Header File

It is often useful to create a header file in which to define constants and function prototypes for your application. Most applications consist of at least two source files that share common constants: the C-language source file and the resource-definition file. Since Microsoft Windows Resource Compiler (RC) carries out the same preprocessing as CL, it is useful and convenient to place constant definitions in a single header file and then include that file in both the C-language source file and the resource-definition file.

For example, for the Generic application, you can place the prototypes for **WinMain**, MainWndProc, About, InitApplication, and InitInstance, and the definition of the menu identifier for the About command, in the GENERIC.H header file. The file should look like this:

```
#define IDM_ABOUT 100

int PASCAL          WinMain(HINSTANCE, HINSTANCE, LPSTR, int);
BOOL                InitApplication(HINSTANCE);
BOOL                InitInstance(HINSTANCE, int);
LRESULT FAR PASCAL  MainWndProc(HWND, UINT, WPARAM, LPARAM);
BOOL FAR PASCAL     About(HWND, WORD, WPARAM, LPARAM);
```

Since GENERIC.H refers to Windows data types, you must include it after WINDOWS.H, which defines those data types. The beginning of your source files should look like this:

```
#include <windows.h>    /* required for all Windows applications */
#include "generic.h"    /* specific to this program              */
```

2.4.3 Creating a Dialog Box Procedure

A dialog box is a special kind of window whose window procedure is built into Windows. For every dialog box an application has, the application must have a corresponding dialog box procedure. The Windows built-in window procedure calls a dialog box procedure to handle input messages that can be interpreted only by the application.

The procedure that processes input for Generic's About dialog box is called About. This procedure, like other dialog box procedures, uses the same parameters as a window procedure but processes only messages that are not handled by Windows default processing. (The dialog box procedure returns TRUE if it processes a message and FALSE if it does not.) The dialog box procedure, like the window procedure, requires the **PASCAL** calling convention and the **FAR** keyword in its definition. You must name the dialog box procedure in an **EXPORTS** statement in the application's module-definition file. As with a window procedure, a dialog box procedure must not be called directly from your application.

Unlike a window procedure, a dialog box procedure usually processes only user-input messages, such as WM_COMMAND, and must not send unprocessed messages to the **DefWindowProc** function. Generic's dialog box procedure, About, looks like this:

```
BOOL FAR PASCAL About(hDlg, message, wParam, lParam)
HWND hDlg;          /* handle of dialog box window        */
WORD message;       /* type of message                    */
WPARAM wParam;      /* message-specific information        */
LPARAM lParam;
```

```
{
    switch (message) {
        case WM_INITDIALOG: /* message: initialize dialog box  */
            return TRUE;

        case WM_COMMAND:                      /* received a command */
            if (wParam == IDOK               /* OK box selected?   */
                || wParam == IDCANCEL) {     /* Close command?     */
                EndDialog(hDlg, TRUE);       /* exits dialog box    */
                return TRUE;
            }
            break;
    }
    return FALSE;                            /* did not process a message */
}
```

The About dialog box procedure processes two messages: WM_INITDIALOG
and WM_COMMAND. Windows sends the WM_INITDIALOG message to a
dialog box procedure to let the procedure initialize its controls before displaying
the dialog box. In this case, WM_INITDIALOG returns TRUE so that the focus is
passed to the first control in the dialog box that has the WS_TABSTOP bit set
(this control will be the default push button). If WM_INITDIALOG had returned
FALSE, Windows would not have set the focus to any control.

In contrast to WM_INITDIALOG messages, WM_COMMAND messages are a
result of user input. The About procedure responds to input to the OK button or
the System menu Close command by calling the **EndDialog** function, which
directs Windows to remove the dialog box and continue running the application.
The **EndDialog** function is used to terminate dialog boxes.

2.4.4 Defining a Menu with an About Command

Once you have created an About dialog box for your application, you must provide a way for the user to display the dialog box. In most applications, the About
command would appear as the last command on the application's Help menu. If
the application does not have a Help menu, it usually appears in the first menu,
most often the File menu. In Generic, About is the only command, so it appears as
the only item on the Help menu.

The most common way to create a menu is to define it in a resource-definition file.
Put the following statements in GENERIC.RC:

```
GenericMenu MENU
BEGIN
    POPUP        "&Help"
    BEGIN
        MENUITEM "About Generic...", IDM_ABOUT
    END
END
```

These statements create a menu named GenericMenu with a single item on it, Help. When chosen, the command associated with the item displays a pop-up menu with the single menu item About Generic....

Notice the ampersand (&) in the "&Help" string. This character immediately precedes the command mnemonic a unique character with which the user can access a menu or command. Mnemonics are part of Windows' direct-access method. If a user presses the key for the mnemonic together with the ALT key, Windows selects the menu or chooses the command. In the case of &Help, Windows removes the ampersand and places an underscore under the letter H when displaying the menu.

The user sees the About command when the Help menu is displayed. If the user chooses the About command, Windows sends the window procedure a WM_COMMAND message containing the About command's menu identifier—in this case, IDM_ABOUT.

2.4.5 Processing a WM_COMMAND Message

Now that you have added a menu item to Generic's menu, you will want the application to be able to respond when the user chooses it as a command. To respond, the application must process a WM_COMMAND message. Windows sends this message to the window procedure when the user chooses a command from the window's menu. Windows passes the menu identifier of the command in the *wParam* parameter, so you can check which command was chosen. (In this case, you can use **if** and **else** statements to direct the flow of control, depending on the value of *wParam*. As your application's message processing becomes more complex, you may want to use a **switch** statement instead.) The goal is to have the application display the dialog box if the parameter is equal to IDM_ABOUT, the About command's menu identifier. For any other value, the application must pass the message on to the **DefWindowProc** function. If it does not, all other commands on the menu are effectively disabled.

The WM_COMMAND case should look like this:

```
FARPROC lpProcAbout;          /* pointer to the "About" function */
    .
    .
    .

case WM_COMMAND:               /* message: command from a menu */
    if (wParam == IDM_ABOUT) {
        lpProcAbout = MakeProcInstance((FARPROC) About, hInst);
```

```
            DialogBox(hInst,            /* current instance      */
                "AboutBox",             /* resource to use       */
                hWnd,                   /* parent handle         */
                (DLGPROC) lpProcAbout); /* About instance address */

            FreeProcInstance(lpProcAbout);
            break;
    }

    else                                /* let Windows process it */
        return (DefWindowProc(hWnd, message, wParam, lParam));
```

Before it can display the dialog box, your application must have the procedure-instance address of the dialog box procedure. You create this address by using the **MakeProcInstance** function, which binds the data segment of the current application instance to a pointer. This guarantees that when Windows calls the dialog box procedure, the procedure uses the data in the current instance and not some other instance of the application. **MakeProcInstance** returns the address of the procedure instance. This value should be assigned to a pointer variable that has the **FARPROC** type.

The **DialogBox** function creates and displays the dialog box. It requires the instance handle of the current application and the name of the dialog box template. It uses this information to load the dialog box template from the executable file. **DialogBox** also requires the handle of the parent window (the window to which the dialog box belongs) and the procedure-instance address of the dialog box procedure. **DialogBox** does not return control until the user has closed the dialog box. Typically, the dialog box contains at least a push button to permit the user to close the box.

When the **DialogBox** function returns, the procedure-instance address of the dialog box procedure is no longer needed, so the **FreeProcInstance** function frees the address. This invalidates the content of the pointer variable; an error results if the application attempts to use the value again.

2.5 Creating a Module-Definition File

Every Windows application must have a module-definition file. This file defines the name, code and data segments, memory requirements, and exported functions of the application. For a simple application, like Generic, you need at least the **NAME**, **STACKSIZE**, **HEAPSIZE**, **EXETYPE**, and **EXPORTS** statements. However, most applications include a complete definition of the module, as shown in the following example:

```
;module-definition file for Generic -- used by LINK.EXE

NAME    Generic                 ; application's module name

DESCRIPTION 'Sample Microsoft Windows 3.1 Application'

EXETYPE WINDOWS                 ; required for all Windows apps

STUB    'WINSTUB.EXE'           ; generates error message if app
                                ; is run without Windows

CODE    MOVEABLE DISCARDABLE    ; code can be moved in memory and
                                ; discarded/reloaded

; DATA must be MULTIPLE if program can be invoked more than once.

DATA    MOVEABLE MULTIPLE

HEAPSIZE  1024
STACKSIZE 5120   ; recommended minimum for Windows applications

; All functions that will be called by any Windows function
; MUST be exported.

EXPORTS
    MainWndProc    @1  ; name of window-processing procedure
    About          @2  ; name of About processing procedure
```

The semicolon is the delimiter for comments in the module-definition file.

The **NAME** statement, which is required, defines the name of the application. Windows uses this name (in the example, Generic) to identify the application.

The **DESCRIPTION** statement is optional. In the example, it places the message "Sample Microsoft Windows 3.1 Application" in the application's executable file. This statement is useful for adding version control or copyright information to the file.

The **EXETYPE** statement is used to mark the executable file as a Windows executable file. For a Windows application, the module-definition file must contain the statement **EXETYPE WINDOWS**.

The **STUB** statement specifies another optional file that defines the executable "stub" to be placed at the beginning of the file. When a user tries to run the application without Windows, the stub is run instead. Most Windows applications use the WINSTUB.EXE executable file supplied with the SDK. WINSTUB.EXE displays a warning message and terminates the application if the user attempts to run the application without Windows. You can also supply your own executable stub.

The **CODE** statement defines the memory attributes of the application's code segment. In this example, the code segment contains the executable code that is generated when the GENERIC.C file is compiled. Generic is a small-model application with only one code segment, which is defined as **MOVEABLE DISCARDABLE**. If the application is not running and Windows requires additional space in memory, Windows can move the code segment to make room for other segments and can, if necessary, discard the segment. A discarded code segment is automatically reloaded on demand by Windows.

The **DATA** statement defines the memory requirements of the application's data segment. In this example, the data segment contains storage space for all the static variables declared in the GENERIC.C file. It also contains space for the program stack and local heap. The data segment, like the code segment, is defined as **MOVEABLE**. In addition, the **MULTIPLE** keyword directs Windows to create a new data segment for the application each time the user starts a new instance of the application. Although all instances share the same code segment, each has its own data segment. An application must have the **MULTIPLE** keyword if the user can run more than one copy of it at a time.

The **HEAPSIZE** statement defines the size, in bytes, of the application's local heap. Generic uses its heap to allocate a temporary structure used to register the window class, so it specifies 1024 bytes of storage. Applications that frequently use the local heap should specify larger amounts of memory.

The **STACKSIZE** statement defines the size, in bytes, of the application's stack. The stack is used for temporary storage of function arguments. Any application that calls its own local function must have a stack. Generic specifies 5120 bytes of stack storage, the recommended minimum for a Windows application.

The **EXPORTS** statement defines the names and ordinal values of the functions to be exported by the application. Generic exports its window procedure, MainWnd-Proc, which has an ordinal value of 1 (this is an identifier; it could be any integer, but usually such values are assigned sequentially as the exports are listed). You must export all functions that Windows is to call (except **WinMain**). These functions, referred to as callback functions, include the following:

- All window procedures
- All dialog box procedures
- Special callback functions, such as enumeration functions, that certain Windows API functions require
- Any other function that is to be called from outside your application

For more information about callback functions, see Chapter 14, "C and Assembly Language."

For more information about module-definition statements, see the *Microsoft Windows Programmer's Reference, Volume 4.*

2.6 Creating Generic

Now you are ready to create the sample application Generic.

Follow these steps:

1. Create the C-language source (.C) file.
2. Create the header (.H) file.
3. Create the resource-definition (.RC) file.
4. Create the module-definition (.DEF) file.
5. Create the makefile.
6. Run Microsoft Program Maintenance Utility (NMAKE) on the file to compile and link the application.

2.6.1 Creating the C-Language Source File

The C-language source file contains the **WinMain** function, the MainWndProc window procedure, the About dialog box procedure, and the InitApplication and InitInstance initialization functions. Name the file GENERIC.C.

The contents of the GENERIC.C file look like this:

```
/*****************************************************************
    PROGRAM: GENERIC.C

    PURPOSE: Generic template for Windows applications

    FUNCTIONS:

        WinMain - calls InitApplication, processes message loop
        InitApplication - initializes window data, registers window
        InitInstance - saves instance handle, creates main window
        MainWndProc - processes messages
        About - processes messages for About dialog box

    COMMENTS:

        Windows can have several copies of your application running
        at the same time. The variable hinstCurrent keeps track of
        which instance this application is so that processing will
        be to the correct window.


    *****************************************************************/
```

```
#define STRICT

#include <windows.h> /* required for all Windows applications  */
#include "generic.h" /* specific to this program               */

HINSTANCE hInst;      /* handle current instance               */

/****************************************************************

    FUNCTION: WinMain(HINSTANCE, HINSTANCE, LPSTR, int)

    PURPOSE: Calls initialization function, processes message loop

    COMMENTS:

        Windows recognizes this function by name as the initial
        entry point for the program. This function calls the
        application initialization function, if no other instance
        of the program is running, and always calls the instance
        initialization function. It then executes a message
        retrieval and dispatch loop that is the top-level control
        structure for the remainder of execution. The loop is
        terminated when a WM_QUIT message is received, at which
        time this function exits the application instance by
        returning the value passed by PostQuitMessage.

        If this function must terminate before entering the message
        loop, it returns the conventional value NULL.

****************************************************************/
int PASCAL WinMain(hinstCurrent, hinstPrevious, lpszCmdLine, nCmdShow)
HINSTANCE hinstCurrent;           /* handle of current instance   */
HINSTANCE hinstPrevious;          /* handle of previous instance  */
LPSTR lpszCmdLine;                /* address of command line      */
int nCmdShow;                     /* show-window type (open/icon) */
{
    MSG msg;                      /* message                      */

    if (!hinstPrevious)           /* other instances of app running? */
        if (!InitApplication(hinstCurrent)) /* initialize shared   */
            return FALSE;         /* exits if unable to initialize */

    /* Perform initializations that apply to a specific instance. */

    if (!InitInstance(hinstCurrent, nCmdShow))
        return FALSE;

    /*
     * Acquire and dispatch messages until a WM_QUIT message
     * is received.
     */
```

```
        while (GetMessage(&msg, /* message structure                */
                NULL,          /* handle of window receiving the message */
                NULL,          /* lowest message to examine        */
                NULL))         /* highest message to examine       */
        {
            TranslateMessage(&msg);    /* translates virtual key codes */
            DispatchMessage(&msg);     /* dispatches message to window */

        }
        return (msg.wParam);           /* value from PostQuitMessage   */
}


/****************************************************************

    FUNCTION: InitApplication(HINSTANCE)

    PURPOSE: Initializes window data and registers window class

    COMMENTS:

        This function is called at initialization time only if
        no other instances of the application are running. This
        function performs initialization tasks that can be done
        once for any number of running instances.

        In this case, initialize a window class by filling out a
        structure of type WNDCLASS and calling the RegisterClass
        function. Since all instances of this application use
        the same window class, you need to do this only when the
        first instance is initialized.

****************************************************************/

BOOL InitApplication(hinstCurrent)
HINSTANCE hinstCurrent;  /* handle of current instance            */
{
    WNDCLASS  wc;

    /*
     * Fill in window-class structure with parameters that
     * describe the main window.
     */

    wc.style = NULL;                /* class style(s)              */
    wc.lpfnWndProc = MainWndProc;   /* window procedure            */
                                    /* for windows of this class   */

    wc.cbClsExtra = 0;              /* no per-class extra data     */
    wc.cbWndExtra = 0;              /* no per-window extra data    */
```

```
        wc.hInstance = hinstCurrent;    /* application that owns class */
        wc.hIcon = LoadIcon(NULL, IDI_APPLICATION);
        wc.hCursor = LoadCursor(NULL, IDC_ARROW);
        wc.hbrBackground = GetStockObject(WHITE_BRUSH);
        wc.lpszMenuName =  "GenericMenu";   /* menu name in .RC file  */
        wc.lpszClassName = "GenericWClass"; /* name in CreateWindow    */

        /* Register the window class and return success/failure code. */

        return (RegisterClass(&wc));
}


/*****************************************************************
    FUNCTION:  InitInstance(HINSTANCE, int)

    PURPOSE:  Saves the instance handle and creates a main window

    COMMENTS:

        This function is called at initialization time for every
        instance of this application. This function performs
        initialization tasks that cannot be shared by multiple
        instances.

        In this case, save the instance handle in a static variable
        and create and display the main window.

    *****************************************************************/

BOOL InitInstance(hinstCurrent, nCmdShow)
HINSTANCE hinstCurrent; /* handle of current instance              */
int nCmdShow;           /* param for first ShowWindow call         */
{
    HWND hWnd;          /* handle of main window                   */

    /*
     * Save the instance handle in a static variable, which will be
     * used in subsequent calls from this application to Windows.
     */

    hInst = hinstCurrent;

    /* Create a main window for this application instance.         */
```

```
hWnd = CreateWindow(
    "GenericWClass",                 /* see RegisterClass call */
    "Generic Sample Application",    /* text for title bar     */
    WS_OVERLAPPEDWINDOW,             /* window style           */
    CW_USEDEFAULT,                   /* default horz position  */
    CW_USEDEFAULT,                   /* default vert position  */
    CW_USEDEFAULT,                   /* default width          */
    CW_USEDEFAULT,                   /* default height         */
    NULL,             /* overlapped windows have no parent */
    NULL,             /* use window class menu             */
    hinstCurrent,     /* this instance owns this window    */
    NULL              /* pointer not needed                */
);

/* If the window could not be created, return "failure."      */

if (hWnd == NULL)
    return FALSE;

/*
 * Make the window visible, update its client area, and
 * return "success."
 */

ShowWindow(hWnd, nCmdShow);  /* shows window               */
UpdateWindow(hWnd);          /* sends WM_PAINT message      */
return TRUE;
}


/****************************************************************

    FUNCTION: MainWndProc(HWND, UINT, WPARAM, LPARAM)

    PURPOSE:  Processes messages

    MESSAGES:

        WM_COMMAND    - application menu (About dialog box)
        WM_DESTROY    - destroy window

    COMMENTS:

        To process the IDM_ABOUT message, call MakeProcInstance
        to get the current instance address of the About procedure.
        Then call DialogBox, which will create the dialog box
        according to the information in your GENERIC.RC file and
        turn control over to the About procedure. When it returns,
        free the instance address.


****************************************************************/
```

```
LRESULT FAR PASCAL MainWndProc(hWnd, message, wParam, lParam)
HWND hWnd;        /* window handle                                  */
UINT message;    /* type of message                                */
WPARAM wParam;   /* additional information                         */
LPARAM lParam;   /* additional information                         */
{
    FARPROC lpProcAbout; /* pointer to the "About" function         */
    switch (message) {
        case WM_COMMAND: /* message: command from a menu            */
            if (wParam == IDM_ABOUT) {
                lpProcAbout =
                    MakeProcInstance((FARPROC) About, hInst);

                DialogBox(hInst, /* handle of current instance      */
                    "AboutBox",  /* resource to use                 */
                    hWnd,        /* parent handle                   */
                    (DLGPROC) lpProcAbout); /* instance address     */

                FreeProcInstance(lpProcAbout);
                break;
            }
            else              /* let Windows process it             */
                return (DefWindowProc(hWnd, message, wParam, lParam));

        case WM_DESTROY:       /* message: window being destroyed */
            PostQuitMessage(0);
            break;

        default:          /* passes it on if unprocessed            */
            return (DefWindowProc(hWnd, message, wParam, lParam));
    }
    return NULL;
}


/****************************************************************

    FUNCTION: About(HWND, WORD, WPARAM, LPARAM)

    PURPOSE:  Processes messages for About dialog box

    MESSAGES:

        WM_INITDIALOG - initialize dialog box
        WM_COMMAND    - Input received

    COMMENTS:

        No initialization is needed for this particular dialog
        box, but TRUE must be returned to Windows.

        Wait for user to click OK; then close the dialog box.

    ****************************************************************/
```

```
BOOL FAR PASCAL About(hDlg, message, wParam, lParam)
HWND hDlg;        /* handle of dialog box window              */
WORD message;     /* type of message                          */
WPARAM wParam;    /* message-specific information             */
LPARAM lParam;
{
    switch (message) {
        case WM_INITDIALOG:       /* message: initialize dialog box */
            return TRUE;

        case WM_COMMAND:                        /* received a command */
            if (wParam == IDOK          /* OK box selected?    */
                || wParam == IDCANCEL) {  /* Close command?      */
                EndDialog(hDlg, TRUE);    /* exits dialog box    */
                return TRUE;
            }
            break;
    }
    return FALSE;                       /* did not process a message */
}
```

2.6.2 Creating the Header File

The header file contains definitions and declarations required by the C-language source file that are incorporated into the source code by an **#include** directive. Name the file GENERIC.H. It should look like this:

```
#define IDM_ABOUT 100

int PASCAL          WinMain(HINSTANCE, HINSTANCE, LPSTR, int);
BOOL                InitApplication(HINSTANCE);
BOOL                InitInstance(HINSTANCE, int);
LRESULT FAR PASCAL  MainWndProc(HWND, UINT, WPARAM, LPARAM);
BOOL FAR PASCAL     About(HWND, WORD, WPARAM, LPARAM);
```

2.6.3 Creating the Resource-Definition File

The resource-definition file must contain the Help menu and the dialog box template for the About dialog box. Name the file GENERIC.RC. It should look like this:

```
#include <windows.h>
#include "generic.h"
```

```
GenericMenu MENU
BEGIN
    POPUP          "&Help"
    BEGIN
        MENUITEM "About Generic...", IDM_ABOUT
    END
END

AboutBox DIALOG 22, 17, 144, 75
STYLE DS_MODALFRAME | WS_CAPTION | WS_SYSMENU
CAPTION "About Generic"
BEGIN
    CTEXT "Microsoft Windows"     -1,    0,    5,  144,   8
    CTEXT "Generic Application"   -1,    0,   14,  144,   8
    CTEXT "Version 3.1"           -1,    0,   34,  144,   8
    DEFPUSHBUTTON "OK"            IDOK, 53,   59,   32,  14, WS_GROUP
END
```

2.6.4 Creating the Module-Definition File

The module-definition file must contain the module definitions for Generic. Name the file GENERIC.DEF. It should look like this:

```
;module-definition file for Generic -- used by LINK.EXE

NAME     Generic        ; application's module name

DESCRIPTION 'Sample Microsoft Windows 3.1 Application'

EXETYPE WINDOWS         ; required for all Windows applications

STUB     'WINSTUB.EXE' ; generates error message if application
                       ; is run without Windows

CODE    MOVEABLE DISCARDABLE; code can be moved, discarded/reloaded

;DATA must be MULTIPLE if program can be invoked more than once.

DATA     MOVEABLE MULTIPLE

HEAPSIZE  1024
STACKSIZE 5120  ; recommended minimum for Windows applications

; All functions that will be called by any Windows function
; must be exported.

EXPORTS
    MainWndProc     @1  ; name of window-processing procedure
    About           @2  ; name of About processing procedure
```

2.6.5 Creating the Makefile

Once you have the source files, you can create Generic's makefile and then compile and link the application by using NMAKE. To compile and link Generic, the makefile must carry out these steps:

- Use CL to compile the GENERIC.C file.

- Use Microsoft Segmented Executable Linker (LINK) to link the GENERIC.OBJ object file with the Windows library and the module-definition file, GENERIC.DEF.

- Use RC to create a binary resource file and add it to the executable file of the Windows application.

The following will properly compile and link the files created for Generic:

```
# Standard Windows makefile. NMAKE compares the creation date of
# the file to the left of the colon with the file(s) to the right
# of the colon. If the file(s) on the right are newer than the
# file on the left, NMAKE will execute all of the command lines
# following this line that are indented by at least one tab or
# space. Any valid MS-DOS command line may be used.

# Update the resource if necessary.

generic.res: generic.rc generic.h
    rc /r generic.rc

# Update the object file if necessary.

generic.obj: generic.c generic.h
    cl /c /Gsw /Oas /Zpe generic.c

# Update the executable file if necessary. (If it is necessary,
# add the resource back in.)

generic.exe: generic.obj generic.def
    link /nod generic, , , slibcew libw, generic.def
    rc generic.res

# If the .RES file is new and the .EXE file is not, update the
# resource. Note that the .RC file can be updated without having
# to either compile or link the file.

generic.exe: generic.res
    rc generic.res
```

The first two lines in this makefile direct NMAKE to create a compiled resource file, GENERIC.RES, if either the resource-definition file GENERIC.RC or the new header file GENERIC.H has been updated. The /r option of the rc command creates a compiled resource file without attempting to add it to an executable file, since this must be done as the last step in the process.

The next two lines direct NMAKE to create the GENERIC.OBJ file if GENERIC.C or GENERIC.H has a more recent access date than the current GENERIC.OBJ file. The cl command takes several options that prepare the application for execution under Windows. The minimum required options are /c, /Gw, and /Zp. In this case, CL treats Generic as a small-model application. Generic and all other applications in this guide are small-model applications.

NMAKE then creates the new GENERIC.EXE file if the GENERIC.OBJ or GENERIC.DEF file has a more recent access date than the current GENERIC.EXE file. Small Windows applications, like Generic, must be linked with the Windows SLIBW.LIB library and the Windows version of the C run-time library, SLIBCEW.LIB. The object file GENERIC.OBJ and the module-definition file GENERIC.DEF are used as arguments in the LINK command line.

The last rc command automatically appends the compiled resources in the file GENERIC.RES to the executable file GENERIC.EXE.

2.6.6 Running Microsoft Program Maintenance Utility

Once you have created the makefile, you can compile and link your application by running NMAKE. The following example runs NMAKE using the commands in the file GENERIC:

```
nmake generic
```

2.7 Using Generic as a Template

Generic provides essentials that make it an appropriate starting point for your applications. It contains all the files an application can have: .DEF, .H, .RC, and .C files, and a makefile. The About dialog box, an application standard, is included, as is the About Generic... command on the Help menu.

You can use Generic as a template to build your own applications. To do this, copy and rename the sources of an existing application, such as Generic; then change relevant function names, and insert new code.

The following steps explain how to use Generic as a template and adapt its source files to your application:

1. Choose your application's filename.

2. Copy the following Generic source files, renaming them to match your application's filename: GENERIC.C, GENERIC.H, GENERIC.DEF, GENERIC.RC, and GENERIC.

3. Use a text editor to change each occurrence of Generic in your application's C-language source file to your application's name. This includes changing the following:

   - Class name: GenericWClass
   - Class menu: GenericMenu
   - Window title: Generic Sample Application
   - Header filename: GENERIC.H

4. Use a text editor to change each occurrence of Generic in your application's module-definition file to your application's name. This includes changing the application name Generic.

5. Use a text editor to change each occurrence of Generic in your application's resource-definition file to your application's name. This includes changing the following:

   - Header filename: GENERIC.H
   - Application title: Generic Application
   - Menu name: GenericMenu

6. Use a text editor to change each occurrence of Generic in your application's makefile to your application's name. This includes changing the following:

   - C-language source filename: GENERIC.C
   - Object filename: GENERIC.OBJ
   - Executable filename: GENERIC.EXE
   - Module-definition filename: GENERIC.DEF

As you add new resources and header files to your applications, be sure to use your application's filename to ensure that these names are unique.

2.8 Related Topics

For more information about the elements of a Windows application, see Chapter 1, "Overview of the Windows Environment."

For information about using C run-time functions and assembly language in your Windows applications, see Chapter 14, "C and Assembly Language."

For more information about Windows functions, messages, data types, and structures, see the *Microsoft Windows Programmer's Reference*, *Volumes 2* and *3*.

For more information about using the software development tools mentioned in this chapter, see *Microsoft Windows Programming Tools*.

Programming Windows Applications

Part 2

Output to a Window

In the Microsoft Windows 3.1 operating system, all output to a window is performed by the graphics device interface (GDI).

This chapter covers the following topics:

- How the painting and drawing process works in Windows
- The purpose of the device context and the WM_PAINT message
- Using GDI functions to draw within the client area of a window
- Drawing lines and figures, writing text, and creating pens and brushes

This chapter also explains how to build a sample application, Output, that illustrates some of these concepts.

3.1 Using a Device Context

Some device contexts are especially prepared for output to the client area of a window. This type of device context defines the device, drawing tools, colors, and
other drawing information only for a window's client area, instead of for a
complete device. GDI uses this drawing information to generate output. All GDI
output functions require a device-context handle. No output can be performed
without one.

To draw within a window, you need the window's handle, which you can then use
to retrieve a handle of the device context for the window's client area. The method
you use to retrieve the device-context handle depends on where and when you
want your application to perform output operations. Although an application can
draw and write from anywhere, including from within the **WinMain** function,
most applications do so only within the window procedure. Typically, an application draws and writes in response to a WM_PAINT message. Windows sends this
message to a window procedure when changes to the window may have altered
the content of the client area. Since only the application can determine this context, Windows sends the WM_PAINT message to the window procedure so that
the procedure can restore the client area.

To process the WM_PAINT message, you typically use the **BeginPaint** function.
If you want your application to draw within the client area at any time other than
in response to a WM_PAINT message, you must use the **GetDC** function to retrieve the device-context handle.

Whenever an application retrieves a device context for a window (by retrieving its
handle), that context is only on "temporary loan" from Windows. A device context
is a shared resource: as long as one application has it, no other application can retrieve it. Therefore, your application must release the device context as soon as

possible after using it to draw within the window. If the application retrieves the device-context handle by using the **GetDC** function, it must use the **ReleaseDC** function to release the handle. Similarly, for each **BeginPaint** function, the application must use a corresponding **EndPaint** function.

3.1.1 Using the GetDC Function

Typically, an application uses the **GetDC** function to provide an instant response to some action by the user, such as drawing a line as the user moves the cursor (pointer) through the window. The function returns a device-context handle that the application can use in any GDI output function.

The following example shows how to use the **GetDC** function to retrieve a device-context handle and write the string "Hello Windows!" in the client area:

```
hDC = GetDC(hWnd);
TextOut(hDC, 10, 10, "Hello, Windows!", 15);
ReleaseDC(hWnd, hDC);
```

In this example, the **GetDC** function returns the device-context handle for the window identified by the *hWnd* parameter, and the **TextOut** function writes the string at the coordinates (10,10) in the window's client area. The **ReleaseDC** function releases the device context.

Because Windows sends a WM_ERASEBKGND message to the window procedure while processing a WM_PAINT message, anything your application draws in the client area will be erased the next time the window procedure receives a WM_PAINT message that affects that part of the client area. If the application passes WM_ERASEBKGND on to the **DefWindowProc** function, that function fills the affected area by using the class background brush, erasing any output previously drawn there.

3.1.2 Processing a WM_PAINT Message

Windows posts a WM_PAINT message when the user has changed the window—for example, by closing a window that covered part of another window. Because a window shares the screen with other windows, anything the user does in one window can affect the content and appearance of another window. However, an application can do nothing about the change until it receives the WM_PAINT message.

Windows posts a WM_PAINT message by making it the last message in the application queue. This means any input is processed before the WM_PAINT message. In fact, the **GetMessage** function also retrieves any input generated after the WM_PAINT message is posted. That is, **GetMessage** retrieves the WM_PAINT message from the queue only when there are no other messages. This enables the application to carry out any operations that might affect the appearance of the window. In general, to avoid flicker and other distracting effects, your application should perform output operations as infrequently as possible. Windows helps ensure this by holding the WM_PAINT message until it is the last message in the queue.

The following example shows how to process a WM_PAINT message:

```
PAINTSTRUCT ps;
    .
    .
    .

case WM_PAINT:
    hDC = BeginPaint(hWnd, &ps);

    /* Output operations */

    EndPaint(hWnd, &ps);
    break;
```

The **BeginPaint** and **EndPaint** functions are required. The **BeginPaint** function fills the **PAINTSTRUCT** structure, ps, with information about the paint request, such as the part of the client area that needs redrawing. The function then returns a handle to the device context. Your application can use this handle in any GDI output functions. The **EndPaint** function ends the paint request and releases the device context.

You should not use the **GetDC** and **ReleaseDC** functions in place of the **BeginPaint** and **EndPaint** functions. **BeginPaint** and **EndPaint** perform special tasks, such as validating the client area and sending the WM_ERASEBKGND message, that ensure the paint request is processed properly. If you use **GetDC** and **ReleaseDC**, you must follow the call to **ReleaseDC** with a call to the **ValidateRect** function. If you do not call **ValidateRect**, the WM_PAINT message is not removed from the message queue and your application will receive it again.

3.1.3 Invalidating the Client Area

Windows is not the only source of WM_PAINT messages. The **InvalidateRect** or **InvalidateRgn** function can also generate WM_PAINT messages for your windows. These functions mark all or part of a client area as invalid (in need of redrawing). For example, the following statement invalidates the entire client area of the window identified by the hWnd variable:

```
InvalidateRect(hWnd, NULL, TRUE);
```

In this example, the NULL argument, used in place of a rectangle structure, specifies the entire client area; the TRUE argument causes the background to be erased.

When the client area is marked as invalid, Windows posts a WM_PAINT message. But if other parts of the client area are marked as invalid, Windows does not post another WM_PAINT message. Instead, it adds the invalidated areas to the previous area, so that all areas are processed by the same WM_PAINT message.

If you do not want your application to redraw the client area, use the **ValidateRect** and **ValidateRgn** functions to invalidate only parts of the client area. These functions remove any previous invalidation and will remove the WM_PAINT message if no other invalidated area remains.

If you do not want the application to wait for the WM_PAINT message to be retrieved from the application queue, use the **UpdateWindow** function to force an immediate WM_PAINT message. If there is any invalid part of the client area, **UpdateWindow** pulls the WM_PAINT message for the given window from the queue and sends it directly to the window procedure.

3.1.4 Preparing a Device Context

To prepare a device context, Windows adjusts the device origin so that it aligns with the upper-left corner of the client area instead of with the upper-left corner of the screen. It also sets a rectangular clipping region so that output to a device context is clipped to the client area. This means any output that would otherwise appear outside the client area is not sent to the screen.

3.1.5 Coordinate System

The default coordinate system for a device context is simple. The upper-left corner of the client area is the origin, or the coordinates (0,0). Each pixel to the right represents one unit along the positive x-axis. Each pixel down represents one unit along the positive y-axis.

You can modify this coordinate system by changing the mapping mode and display origins. The mapping mode defines the coordinate-system units. The default mode is MM_TEXT, or one pixel per unit. You can also specify mapping modes that use inches or millimeters as units. The **SetMapMode** function changes the mapping mode for a device. You can move the origin of the coordinate system to any point by calling the **SetViewportOrg** function.

For simplicity, the examples in this chapter and throughout this guide use the default coordinate system.

3.2 Creating, Selecting, and Deleting Drawing Tools

GDI lets you use a variety of drawing tools to draw within a window. GDI provides pens for drawing lines, brushes for filling interiors, and fonts for writing text. To create these tools, use functions such as **CreatePen** and **CreateSolidBrush**. Then select them into the device context by using the **SelectObject** function. When you are done using a drawing tool, delete it by using the **DeleteObject** function.

Use the **CreatePen** function to create a pen for drawing lines and borders. This function returns a handle of a pen that has the specified style, width, and color. (Always check the return value of **CreatePen** to ensure that it is a valid handle.)

The following example creates a dashed, black pen, one pixel wide:

```
HPEN hDashPen;
    .
    .
    .

hDashPen = CreatePen(PS_DASH, 1, RGB(0, 0, 0));
if (hDashPen != NULL)   /* makes sure handle is valid    */
    .
    .
    .
```

The **RGB** macro creates a 32-bit color value representing a mix of red, green, and blue intensities. The three arguments specify the intensity of the colors red, green, and blue, respectively. In this example, all colors have zero intensity, so the specified color is black.

You can create solid brushes for drawing and filling by using the **CreateSolidBrush** function. This function returns a handle of a brush that contains the specified solid color. (Always check the return value of **CreateSolidBrush** to ensure that it is a valid handle.)

The following example creates a red brush:

```
HBRUSH hRedBrush
    .
    .
    .

hRedBrush = CreateSolidBrush(RGB(255, 0, 0));
if (hRedBrush != NULL)    /* makes sure handle is valid */
    .
    .
    .
```

Once you have created a drawing tool, you can select it into a device context by using the **SelectObject** function. The following example selects the red brush for drawing:

```
HBRUSH hOldBrush;
     .
     .
     .

hOldBrush = SelectObject(hDC, hRedBrush);
```

In this example, **SelectObject** returns a handle to the previous brush. In general, you should save the handle of the previous drawing tool so that you can restore it later.

You do not have to create or select a drawing tool before using a device context. Windows provides default drawing tools with each device context; for example, a black pen, a white brush, and the system font.

You can delete drawing objects you no longer need by using the **DeleteObject** function. The following example deletes the brush identified by the handle hRedBrush:

```
DeleteObject(hRedBrush);
```

You must not delete a selected drawing tool. Instead, use the **SelectObject** function to restore a previous drawing tool and remove the tool to be deleted from the selection, as in the following example:

```
SelectObject(hDC, hOldBrush);
DeleteObject(hRedBrush);
```

Although you can create and select fonts for writing text, working with fonts is a fairly complex process and is not described in this chapter. For more information about creating and selecting fonts, see Chapter 18, "Fonts."

3.3 Drawing and Writing

GDI provides a wide variety of output operations, from drawing lines to writing text. Specifically, you can use the **LineTo**, **Rectangle**, **Ellipse**, **Arc**, **Pie**, **Text-Out**, and **DrawText** functions to draw lines, rectangles, circles, arcs, pie wedges, and text, respectively. All these functions use the selected pen and brush to draw borders and fill interiors, and the selected font to write text.

Drawing a Line   You draw a line by using the **LineTo** function, although you usually combine the **MoveTo** and **LineTo** functions to draw a line. The following example draws a line from the coordinates (10,90) to the coordinates (360,90):

```
MoveTo(hDC, 10, 90);
LineTo(hDC, 360, 90);
```

Drawing a Rectangle   You draw a rectangle by using the **Rectangle** function. This function uses the selected pen to draw the border, and the selected brush to fill the interior. The following example draws a rectangle that has its upper-left and lower-right corners at the coordinates (10,30) and (60,80), respectively:

```
Rectangle(hDC, 10, 30, 60, 80);
```

Drawing an Ellipse or Circle   You draw an ellipse or a circle by using the **Ellipse** function. This function uses the selected pen to draw the border, and the selected brush to fill the interior. The following cxample draws an ellipse within the rectangle defined by the coordinates (160,30) and (210,80):

```
Ellipse(hDC, 160, 30, 210, 80);
```

Drawing an Arc   You draw an arc by using the **Arc** function. With this function, you define a bounding rectangle for the circle containing the arc, and then specify the points at which the arc starts and ends. The following example draws an arc within the rectangle defined by the coordinates (10,90) and (360,120); it draws the arc from the coordinates (10,90) to the coordinates (360,90):

```
Arc(hDC, 10, 90, 360, 120, 10, 90, 360, 90);
```

Drawing a Pie Wedge   You draw a pie wedge by using the **Pie** function. A pie wedge consists of an arc and two radii extending from the focus of the arc to its endpoints. The **Pie** function uses the selected pen to draw the border, and the selected brush to fill the interior. The following example draws a pie wedge within the rectangle defined by the coordinates (310,30) and (360,80) and that starts and ends at the coordinates (360,30) and (360,80), respectively:

```
Pie(hDC, 310, 30, 360, 80, 360, 30, 360, 80);
```

Displaying Text   You display text by using the **TextOut** function. This function displays a string starting at the specified point. The following example displays the string "A Sample String" at the coordinates (1,1):

```
TextOut(hDC, 1, 1, "A Sample String", 15);
```

You can also use the **DrawText** function to display text. This function is similar to **TextOut**, except that it lets you write text on multiple lines. The following example displays the string "This long string illustrates the DrawText function" on multiple lines in the specified rectangle:

```
RECT rcTextBox;
LPSTR lpText = "This long string illustrates the DrawText function";
    .
    .
    .

SetRect(&rcTextBox, 1, 10, 160, 40);
DrawText(hDC, lpText, lstrlen(lpText), &rcTextBox, DT_LEFT);
```

This example displays the string pointed to by the lpText variable as one or more left-aligned lines in the rectangle defined by the coordinates (1,10) and (160,40).

Although you can also create and display bitmaps in a window, the process is not described in this chapter. For more information, see Chapter 11, "Bitmaps."

3.4 Sample Application: Output

The sample application Output illustrates how to use the WM_PAINT message to draw within the client area, as well as how to create and use drawing tools. The Output application is a simple extension of the Generic application described in the previous chapter. To create the Output application, make the following modifications to the Generic application:

1. Add new variables.
2. Modify the WM_CREATE case.
3. Add a WM_PAINT case.
4. Modify the WM_DESTROY case.
5. Compile and link the application.

This sample assumes that you have a color display. If you do not, GDI will simulate some of the color output by dithering. Dithering is a method of simulating a color by creating a unique pattern with two or more available colors. For a color screen that cannot display orange, for example, Windows simulates orange by using a pattern of red and yellow pixels. For a monochrome screen, Windows represents colors with black, white, and shades of gray, instead of colors.

3.4.1 Adding New Variables

The Output application requires several new global variables. Add the following variables at the beginning of your C-language source file:

```
HPEN hDashPen;        /* "---" pen handle      */
HPEN hDotPen;         /* "..." pen handle      */
HBRUSH hOldBrush;     /* old brush handle      */
HBRUSH hRedBrush;     /* red brush handle      */
HBRUSH hGreenBrush;   /* green brush handle    */
HBRUSH hBlueBrush;    /* blue brush handle     */
```

Output also requires new local variables in the window procedure. Declare the following variables at the beginning of MainWndProc:

```
HDC hDC;              /* handle of device context */
PAINTSTRUCT ps;       /* paint structure          */
RECT rcTextBox;       /* rectangle around the text */
HPEN hOldPen;         /* old pen handle            */
```

3.4.2 Adding a WM_CREATE Case

To enable Output to draw in its client area, you must create the drawing tools. Since you need only create these tools once, a convenient place to do so is in the WM_CREATE message. Add the following statements to MainWndProc:

```
case WM_CREATE:

    /* Create the brush objects. */

    hRedBrush =   CreateSolidBrush(RGB(255,   0,   0));
    hGreenBrush = CreateSolidBrush(RGB(  0, 255,   0));
    hBlueBrush =  CreateSolidBrush(RGB(  0,   0, 255));

    /* Create the "---" pen. */

    hDashPen = CreatePen(PS_DASH, /* style */
        1,                        /* width */
        RGB(0, 0, 0));            /* color */

    /* Create the "..." pen. */

    hDotPen = CreatePen(2,        /* style */
        1,                        /* width */
        RGB(0, 0, 0));            /* color */
    break;
```

The **CreateSolidBrush** functions create the solid brushes to be used for filling the rectangle, the ellipse, and the circle that Output draws on the screen in response to the WM_PAINT message. The **CreatePen** functions create the dotted and dashed lines used to draw borders.

3.4.3 Adding a WM_PAINT Case

The WM_PAINT message informs your application when it should redraw all or part of its client area. To handle this message, add the following statement to the window procedure:

```
case WM_PAINT:
    {
    TEXTMETRIC tm;
    int nDrawX;
    int nDrawY;
    char szText[300];

    /* Set up a device context to begin painting. */

    hDC = BeginPaint(hWnd, &ps);

    /*
     * Get the size characteristics of the current font.
     * This information will be used for determining the
     * vertical spacing of text on the screen.
     */

    GetTextMetrics(hDC, &tm);

    /*
     * Initialize drawing position to 1/4 inch from the top
     * and from the left of the upper-left corner of the client
     * area of the main windows.
     */

    nDrawX = GetDeviceCaps(hDC, LOGPIXELSX) / 4;    /* 1/4 inch */
    nDrawY = GetDeviceCaps(hDC, LOGPIXELSY) / 4;    /* 1/4 inch */

    /*
     * Send characters to the screen. After displaying each
     * line of text, advance the vertical position for the next
     * line of text. The pixel distance between the top of
     * each line of text is equal to the standard height of the
     * font characters (tmHeight), plus the standard amount of
     * spacing (tmExternalLeading) between adjacent lines.
     */
```

```
lstrcpy(szText, "These characters are being painted using ");
TextOut(hDC, nDrawX, nDrawY, szText, lstrlen(szText));
nDrawY += tm.tmExternalLeading + tm.tmHeight;

lstrcpy(szText, "the TextOut() function, which is fast and ");
TextOut(hDC, nDrawX, nDrawY, szText, lstrlen(szText));
nDrawY += tm.tmExternalLeading + tm.tmHeight;

lstrcpy(szText, "allows programmer control of placement and ");
TextOut(hDC, nDrawX, nDrawY, szText, lstrlen(szText));
nDrawY += tm.tmExternalLeading + tm.tmHeight;

lstrcpy(szText, "formatting details. However, TextOut() ");
TextOut(hDC, nDrawX, nDrawY, szText, lstrlen(szText));
nDrawY += tm.tmExternalLeading + tm.tmHeight;

lstrcpy(szText, "does not provide any automatic formatting.");
TextOut(hDC, nDrawX, nDrawY, szText, lstrlen(szText));
nDrawY += tm.tmExternalLeading + tm.tmHeight;

/*
 * Put text in a 5-inch by 1-inch rectangle and display it.
 * First define the size of the rectangle around the text.
 */

nDrawY += GetDeviceCaps(hDC, LOGPIXELSY) / 4;  /* 1/4 inch */
SetRect(&rcTextBox,
    nDrawX,
    nDrawY,
    nDrawX + (5 * GetDeviceCaps(hDC, LOGPIXELSX)),    /* 5" */
    nDrawY + (1 * GetDeviceCaps(hDC, LOGPIXELSY))     /* 1" */
);

/* Draw the text within the bounds of the above rectangle. */

lstrcpy(szText, "This text is being displayed with a single "
            "call to DrawText(). DrawText() isn't as fast "
            "as TextOut(), and it is somewhat more "
            "constrained, but it provides numerous optional "
            "formatting features, such as the centering and "
            "line breaking used in this example.");
DrawText(hDC,
    szText,
    lstrlen(szText),
    &rcTextBox,
    DT_CENTER | DT_EXTERNALLEADING | DT_NOCLIP
        | DT_NOPREFIX | DT_WORDBREAK);

/*
 * Paint the next object immediately below the bottom
 * of the above rectangle in which the text was drawn.
 */
```

```
nDrawY = rcTextBox.bottom;

/*
 * The (x,y) pixel coordinates of the objects about to
 * be drawn are below, and to the right of, the current
 * coordinate (nDrawX,nDrawY).
 */

/* Draw a red rectangle. */

hOldBrush = SelectObject(hDC, hRedBrush);
Rectangle(hDC,
    nDrawX,
    nDrawY,
    nDrawX + 50,
    nDrawY + 30);

/* Draw a green ellipse. */

SelectObject(hDC, hGreenBrush);
Ellipse(hDC,
    nDrawX + 150,
    nDrawY,
    nDrawX + 150 + 50,
    nDrawY + 30);

/* Draw a blue pie shape. */

SelectObject(hDC, hBlueBrush);
Pie(hDC,
    nDrawX + 300,
    nDrawY,
    nDrawX + 300 + 50,
    nDrawY + 50,
    nDrawX + 300 + 50,
    nDrawY,
    nDrawX + 300 + 50,
    nDrawY + 50);

nDrawY += 50;

/* Restore the old brush. */

SelectObject(hDC, hOldBrush);
```

```
/* Select a "---" pen, and save the old value. */

nDrawY += GetDeviceCaps(hDC, LOGPIXELSY) / 4;   /* 1/4 inch */
hOldPen = SelectObject(hDC, hDashPen);

/* Move to a specified point. */

MoveTo(hDC, nDrawX, nDrawY);
/* Draw a line. */

LineTo(hDC, nDrawX + 350, nDrawY);

/* Select a "..." pen. */

SelectObject(hDC, hDotPen);

/* Draw an arc connecting the line. */

Arc(hDC,
    nDrawX,
    nDrawY - 20,
    nDrawX + 350,
    nDrawY + 20,
    nDrawX,
    nDrawY,
    nDrawX + 350,
    nDrawY);

/* Restore the old pen. */

SelectObject(hDC, hOldPen);

/* Tell Windows you are done painting. */

EndPaint(hWnd,  &ps);
}
break;
```

Note If you "hard-code" strings by using functions such as **lstrcpy**, it may be difficult to translate your application into other languages. If you plan to distribute your application in more than one language, use string tables instead of hard-coded strings. For more information about string tables, see the *Microsoft Windows Programmer's Reference, Volume 4*.

3.4.4 Modifying the WM_DESTROY Case

Before terminating, the Output application should delete the drawing tools created for its window; this frees the memory that each drawing tool uses. To make the application do this, use the **DeleteObject** function to delete the various pens and brushes in the WM_DESTROY case. Modify the WM_DESTROY case so that it looks like this:

```
case WM_DESTROY:

    DeleteObject(hRedBrush);
    DeleteObject(hGreenBrush);
    DeleteObject(hBlueBrush);
    DeleteObject(hDashPen);
    DeleteObject(hDotPen);
    PostQuitMessage(0);
    break;
```

You must call the **DeleteObject** function once for each object you want to delete.

3.4.5 Compiling and Linking

Compile and link the Output application and then start Windows and the application. The application should look like this:

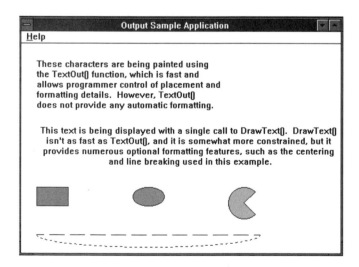

You can use the WM_PAINT case of this application to experiment with a variety of GDI functions. For information about other GDI output functions, see the *Microsoft Windows Programmer's Reference, Volume 2*.

3.5 Related Topics

For more information about working with bitmaps, see Chapter 11, "Bitmaps."

For more information about working with fonts, see Chapter 18, "Fonts."

For more information about window procedures, class and private device contexts, painting functions, messages, data types, and structures, see *Microsoft Windows Programmer's Reference*, *Volumes 2* and *3*.

Keyboard and Mouse Input

Most applications require input from the user—typically, by means of the keyboard or the mouse. With the Microsoft Windows operating system, applications receive keyboard and mouse input in the form of input messages.

This chapter covers the following topics:

- Input messages that Windows sends your application
- Responding to Windows input messages

This chapter also explains how to build a sample Windows 3.1 application, Input, that responds to various types of input messages.

4.1 Windows Input Messages

Whenever the user presses a key, moves the mouse, or clicks a mouse button, Windows responds by sending input messages to the appropriate application. Windows also sends input messages in response to timer input.

Windows provides several types of input messages:

Message type	Description
Keyboard	User input through the keyboard
Character	Keyboard input translated into character codes
Mouse	User input through the mouse
Timer	Input from the system timer
Scroll bar	User input through a window's scroll bars and the mouse
Menu	User input through a window's menus and the mouse

Input messages from the keyboard, mouse, and timer correspond directly to hardware input. Windows passes these messages to your application through the application queue.

Character, menu, and scroll bar messages are created in response to mouse and keyboard actions in the nonclient area of a window, or are the result of translated keyboard messages. Typically, Windows sends these messages directly to the appropriate window procedure.

4.1.1 Message Formats

Input messages come in two formats, depending on how your application receives them:

- Messages that Windows places in the application queue take the form of an **MSG** structure. This structure contains members that identify and contain information about the message. Your application's message loop retrieves this structure from the application queue and dispatches it to the appropriate window procedure.

- Messages that Windows sends directly to a window procedure take the form of four arguments. The arguments correspond to the four window-procedure parameters: *hWnd*, *message*, *wParam*, and *lParam*.

The only difference between these two message forms is that the **MSG** structure contains two additional pieces of information: the current location of the cursor and the current system time. Windows does not pass this information to the window procedure.

4.1.2 Keyboard Input

Much of an application's user input comes from the keyboard. Windows sends keyboard input to an application when the user presses or releases a key. Windows generates keyboard-input messages in response to the following keyboard events:

Message	Event
WM_KEYDOWN	User presses a key.
WM_KEYUP	User releases a key.
WM_SYSKEYDOWN	User presses a system key.
WM_SYSKEYUP	User releases a system key.

The *wParam* parameter of a keyboard-input message specifies the virtual-key code of the key the user pressed. A virtual-key code is a device-independent value for a specific keyboard key. Windows uses virtual-key codes so that it can provide consistent keyboard input no matter what computer your application is running on.

The *lParam* parameter contains the keyboard's scan code for the key, as well as additional information about the keyboard, such as the state of the SHIFT key and whether the current key was previously up or down.

Windows generates two system-key messages, WM_SYSKEYUP and WM_SYSKEYDOWN. System keys are special keys, such as the ALT and F10 keys, that belong to the Windows user interface and cannot be used by an application in any other way.

An application receives keyboard-input messages only when it has the input focus. The input focus is what your application receives when it becomes the active application—that is, when the user has selected the application's window. You can also use the **SetFocus** function to explicitly set the input focus for a given window, and the **GetFocus** function to determine which window has the focus.

4.1.3 Character Input

Applications that read character input from the keyboard must use the **TranslateMessage** function in their message loops. **TranslateMessage** translates a keyboard-input message into a corresponding Windows-character message, WM_CHAR or WM_SYSCHAR. The *wParam* parameter in these messages contains the Windows character codes for the given key. The *lParam* parameter is identical to *lParam* in the keyboard-input message.

4.1.4 Mouse Input

User input can also come from the mouse. Windows sends mouse-input messages to the application when the user moves the cursor into and through a window or presses or releases a mouse button while the cursor is in the window. Windows generates mouse-input messages in response to the following events:

Message	Event
WM_MOUSEMOVE	User moves the cursor into or through the window.
WM_LBUTTONDOWN	User presses the left button.
WM_LBUTTONUP	User releases the left button.
WM_LBUTTONDBLCLK	User presses, releases, and presses again the left button within the system's defined double-click time.
WM_MBUTTONDOWN	User presses the middle button.
WM_MBUTTONUP	User releases the middle button.
WM_MBUTTONDBLCLK	User presses, releases, and presses again the middle button within the system's defined double-click time.
WM_RBUTTONDOWN	User presses the right button.
WM_RBUTTONUP	User releases the right button.
WM_RBUTTONDBLCLK	User presses, releases, and presses again the right button within the system's defined double-click time.

The *wParam* parameter corresponding to each button pressed or released includes a bitmask specifying the current state of the keyboard and mouse buttons, such as whether the mouse buttons, SHIFT key, and CTRL key are down. The *lParam* parameter contains the x- and y-coordinates of the cursor.

Windows sends mouse-input messages to a window only if the cursor is in the window or if your application has captured mouse input by using the **SetCapture** function. This function directs Windows to send all mouse input, regardless of where the cursor is, to the specified window. Applications typically use this function to take control of the mouse when carrying out some critical operation with the mouse, such as selecting something in the client area. Capturing mouse input prevents other applications from taking control of the mouse before the operation is completed.

Since the mouse is a shared resource, it is important for an application to release the captured mouse as soon as it has finished the operation. The application can release the mouse by using the **ReleaseCapture** function; it can also determine which window, if any, has captured the mouse, by using the **GetCapture** function.

Windows sends double-click messages to a window procedure only if the corresponding window class has the CS_DBLCLKS style. Your application must set this style when registering the window class. A double-click message is always the third message in a four-message series. The first two messages are the first button press and release. The second button press is replaced with the double-click message. The last message is the second release. Remember that a double-click message occurs only if the first press and the second press occur within the system's defined double-click time. The application can retrieve the current double-click time by using the **GetDoubleClickTime** function, and it can set it by using the **SetDoubleClickTime** function (this sets the double-click time for all applications, not just your own).

4.1.5 Timer Input

Windows sends timer input to your application when a specified interval elapses for a particular timer. To receive timer input, your application must set a timer by using the **SetTimer** function. The application receives the timer input in two ways:

- Windows places a WM_TIMER message in your application's queue.
- Windows calls a callback function defined in your application. You specify the callback function when you call the **SetTimer** function.

The following example shows how to set a timer so that it generates input at 5-second (5000-millisecond) intervals:

```
idTimer = SetTimer(hWnd, 1, 5000, (TIMERPROC) NULL);
```

The second argument to **SetTimer** is any nonzero value that your application uses to identify the particular timer. The last argument specifies the callback function that will receive timer input. Setting this argument to NULL tells Windows to provide timer input as a WM_TIMER message. Because there is no callback function specified for timer input, Windows sends the timer input through the application queue.

The **SetTimer** function returns a timer identifier—an integer that identifies the timer. You can use this timer identifier to turn the timer off by using it in the **Kill-Timer** function.

4.1.6 Scroll Bar Input

Windows sends a scroll bar message, either WM_HSCROLL or WM_VSCROLL, to a window procedure each time the user clicks when the cursor is in a scroll bar. Applications use the scroll bar messages to direct scrolling within the window. Applications that display text or other data that does not all fit in the client area usually provide some form of scrolling. Scroll bars are an easy way to let the user direct scrolling actions.

To retrieve scroll bar input in your application, add scroll bars to a window. You can do this by specifying the WS_HSCROLL and WS_VSCROLL styles when you create the window. These styles direct the **CreateWindow** function to create horizontal and vertical scroll bars for the window. The following example creates scroll bars for the given window:

```
hWnd = CreateWindow("InputWClass",   /* window class          */
    "Input Sample Application",       /* window name           */
    WS_OVERLAPPEDWINDOW | WS_HSCROLL | WS_VSCROLL,
    CW_USEDEFAULT,                    /* x position            */
    CW_USEDEFAULT,                    /* y position            */
    CW_USEDEFAULT,                    /* width                 */
    CW_USEDEFAULT,                    /* height                */
    NULL,           /* handle of parent window                 */
    NULL,           /* handle of menu or child window          */
    hinst,          /* instance handle                         */
    NULL);          /* additional info                         */
```

Windows displays the scroll bars when it displays the window. It automatically maintains the scroll bars and sends scroll bar messages to the window procedure when the user moves the scroll box in the scroll bar.

When Windows sends a scroll bar message, it sets the *wParam* parameter of the message to indicate the type of scrolling request made. For example, if the user clicks the up arrow of a vertical scroll bar, Windows sets the *wParam* parameter to the value SB_LINEUP. Depending on the event, Windows sets the *wParam* parameter to one of the following values:

Value	Event
SB_LINEUP	User clicks the up arrow or left arrow of a scroll bar.
SB_LINEDOWN	User clicks the down arrow or right arrow of a scroll bar.

Value	Event
SB_PAGEUP	User clicks between the scroll box and the up arrow or left arrow of a scroll bar.
SB_PAGEDOWN	User clicks between the scroll box and the down arrow or right arrow of a scroll bar.
SB_THUMBPOSITION	User releases the mouse button when the cursor is in the scroll box (thumb)—typically, after dragging the box.
SB_THUMBTRACK	User drags the scroll box with the mouse.

4.1.7 Menu Input

Whenever the user chooses a command from a menu, Windows sends a menu-input message to the window procedure for that window. There are two types of menu-input messages:

- WM_SYSCOMMAND, which indicates that the user has chosen a command from the System menu.
- WM_COMMAND, which indicates that the user has chosen a command from the application's menu.

Since menu input is often the primary source of input for an application, its processing can be complex. For more information about menus and menu input, see Chapter 7, "Menus."

4.2 Sample Application: Input

This sample application, Input, illustrates how to process input messages from the keyboard, mouse, timer, and scroll bars. The Input application displays the current or most recent state of each of these input mechanisms. To create the Input application, make the following modifications to the Generic application:

1. Add new variables.
2. Set the window-class style.
3. Modify the **CreateWindow** function.
4. Set the text rectangles.
5. Add a WM_CREATE case.
6. Modify the WM_DESTROY case.

7. Add WM_KEYUP and WM_KEYDOWN cases.

8. Add a WM_CHAR case.

9. Add a WM_MOUSEMOVE case.

10. Add WM_LBUTTONUP and WM_RBUTTONUP cases.

11. Add a WM_LBUTTONDBLCLK case.

12. Add a WM_TIMER case.

13. Add WM_HSCROLL and WM_VSCROLL cases.

14. Add a WM_PAINT case.

15. Compile and link the Input application.

Although Windows does not require a pointing device, this sample is written as if you have a mouse or other pointing device. If you do not have a mouse, the application will not receive mouse-input messages.

4.2.1 How the Input Application Displays Output

The Input application responds to input messages by displaying text that indicates the type of input message. It uses some simple functions to format and display the output.

To create a formatted string, use the **wsprintf** function, the Windows version of the C run-time function **sprintf**. The **wsprintf** function copies a formatted string to a buffer; you can then pass the buffer address as an argument to the **TextOut** function. The following example shows how to create a formatted string:

```
char MouseText[48];
    .
    .
    .

wsprintf(MouseText, "WM_MOUSEMOVE: %x, %d, %d", wParam,
    LOWORD(lParam), HIWORD(lParam));
```

This example copies the formatted string to the MouseText array.

4.2.2 Adding New Variables

Since you will need several new global variables, declare them at the beginning of the C-language source file:

```
char MouseText[48];      /* mouse state          */
char ButtonText[48];     /* mouse-button state   */
char KeyboardText[48];   /* keyboard state       */
char CharacterText[48];  /* latest character     */
char ScrollText[48];     /* scroll status        */
char TimerText[48];      /* timer state          */
RECT rectMouse;
RECT rectButton;
RECT rectKeyboard;
RECT rectCharacter;
RECT rectScroll;
RECT rectTimer;
int idTimer;             /* timer identifier     */
int nTimerCount = 0;     /* current timer count  */
```

The character arrays hold strings that describe the current state of the keyboard, mouse, and timer. The rectangles keep track of where the strings appear on the screen, and make possible the invalidation technique explained in Section 4.2.15, "Adding a WM_PAINT Case."

Since you will also need some local variables for the window procedure, declare them at the beginning of MainWndProc, as follows:

```
HDC hDC;                 /* handle of device context  */
PAINTSTRUCT ps;          /* paint structure           */
char ScrollTypeText[20];
RECT rect;
```

Add the following variables to the InitInstance function:

```
HDC          hDC;
TEXTMETRIC   textmetric;
RECT         rect;
int          nLineHeight;
```

4.2.3 Setting the Window-Class Style

To enable double-click processing, set the window-class style to CS_DBLCLKS. In the initialization function, find this statement:

```
wc.style = NULL;
```

Change it to the following:

```
wc.style = CS_DBLCLKS;
```

This enables double-click processing for windows that belong to this class.

4.2.4 Modifying the CreateWindow Function

To create a window that has vertical and horizontal scroll bars, modify the call to the **CreateWindow** function so that it looks like this:

```
hWnd = CreateWindow("InputWClass",
    "Input Sample Window",
    WS_OVERLAPPEDWINDOW | WS_HSCROLL | WS_VSCROLL,
    CW_USEDEFAULT,
    CW_USEDEFAULT,
    CW_USEDEFAULT,
    CW_USEDEFAULT,
    NULL,
    NULL,
    hinst,
    NULL);
```

4.2.5 Setting the Text Rectangles

To establish the client-area rectangles in which different messages are displayed, add the following statements to the InitInstance function:

```
hDC = GetDC(hWnd);
GetTextMetrics(hDC, &tm);
ReleaseDC(hWnd, hDC);
nLineHeight = tm.tmExternalLeading + tm.tmHeight;

rect.left = GetDeviceCaps(hDC, LOGPIXELSX) / 4;    /* 1/4 inch */
rect.right = GetDeviceCaps(hDC, HORZRES);
rect.top = GetDeviceCaps(hDC, LOGPIXELSY) / 4;    /* 1/4 inch */
rect.bottom = rect.top + nLineHeight;
rectMouse = rect;

rect.top += nLineHeight;
rect.bottom += nLineHeight;
rectButton = rect;

rect.top += nLineHeight;
rect.bottom += nLineHeight;
rectKeyboard = rect;
```

```
rect.top += nLineHeight;
rect.bottom += nLineHeight;
rectCharacter = rect;

rect.top += nLineHeight;
rect.bottom += nLineHeight;
rectScroll = rect;

rect.top += nLineHeight;
rect.bottom += nLineHeight;
rectTimer = rect;
```

4.2.6 Adding a WM_CREATE Case

To set a timer, use the **SetTimer** function. You can do this by adding a
WM_CREATE case to your application, as follows:

```
case WM_CREATE:

    /* Set the timer for five-second intervals. */

    idTimer =  SetTimer(hWnd, NULL, 5000, (TIMERPROC) NULL);
    break;
```

4.2.7 Modifying the WM_DESTROY Case

Your application must also stop the timer before terminating. You can do this by
adding a WM_DESTROY case to the application, as follows:

```
KillTimer(hWnd, idTimer);
```

4.2.8 Adding WM_KEYUP and WM_KEYDOWN Cases

To make your application process key presses, add WM_KEYUP and
WM_KEYDOWN cases to the window procedure, as follows:

```
case WM_KEYDOWN:
    wsprintf(KeyboardText, "WM_KEYDOWN: %x, %x, %x",
        wParam, LOWORD(lParam), HIWORD(lParam));
    InvalidateRect(hWnd, &rectKeyboard, TRUE);
    break;

case WM_KEYUP:
    wsprintf(KeyboardText, "WM_KEYUP: %x, %x, %x",
        wParam, LOWORD(lParam), HIWORD(lParam));
    InvalidateRect(hWnd, &rectKeyboard, TRUE);
    break;
```

4.2.9 Adding a WM_CHAR Case

To make your application process character input, add a WM_CHAR case to the window procedure, as follows:

```
case WM_CHAR:
    wsprintf(CharacterText, "WM_CHAR: %c, %x, %x",
        wParam, LOWORD(lParam), HIWORD(lParam));
    InvalidateRect(hWnd, &rectCharacter, TRUE);
    break;
```

4.2.10 Adding a WM_MOUSEMOVE Case

To make your application process mouse-motion messages, add a WM_MOUSEMOVE case to the window procedure, as follows:

```
case WM_MOUSEMOVE:
    wsprintf(MouseText, "WM_MOUSEMOVE: %x, %d, %d",
        wParam, LOWORD(lParam), HIWORD(lParam));
    InvalidateRect(hWnd, &rectMouse, TRUE);
    break;
```

4.2.11 Adding WM_LBUTTONUP and WM_LBUTTONDOWN Cases

To make your application process mouse-button input messages, add WM_LBUTTONUP and WM_LBUTTONDOWN cases to the window procedure, as follows:

```
case WM_LBUTTONDOWN:
    wsprintf(ButtonText, "WM_LBUTTONDOWN: %x, %d, %d",
        wParam, LOWORD(lParam), HIWORD(lParam));
    InvalidateRect(hWnd, &rectButton, TRUE);
    break;

case WM_LBUTTONUP:
    wsprintf(ButtonText, "WM_LBUTTONUP: %x, %d, %d",
        wParam, LOWORD(lParam), HIWORD(lParam));
    InvalidateRect(hWnd, &rectButton, TRUE);
    break;
```

4.2.12 Adding a WM_LBUTTONDBLCLK Case

To make your application process input messages resulting from double-clicking the left mouse button, add a WM_LBUTTONDBLCLK case to the window procedure, as follows:

```
case WM_LBUTTONDBLCLK:
    wsprintf(ButtonText, "WM_LBUTTONDBLCLK: %x, %d, %d",
        wParam, LOWORD(lParam), HIWORD(lParam));
    InvalidateRect(hWnd, &rectButton, TRUE);
    break;
```

4.2.13 Adding a WM_TIMER Case

To make your application process timer messages, add a WM_TIMER case to the window procedure, as follows:

```
case WM_LBUTTONDBLCLK:
    wsprintf(ButtonText, "WM_LBUTTONDBLCLK: %x, %d, %d",
        wParam, LOWORD(lParam), HIWORD(lParam));
    InvalidateRect(hWnd, &rectButton, TRUE);
    break;
```

4.2.14 Adding WM_HSCROLL and WM_VSCROLL Cases

To make your application process scroll bar messages, add WM_HSCROLL and WM_VSCROLL cases to the window procedure, as follows:

```
case WM_HSCROLL:
case WM_VSCROLL:
    wsprintf(ScrollText, "%s: %s, %x, %x",
        (LPSTR) ((message == WM_HSCROLL) ? "WM_HSCROLL" :
            "WM_VSCROLL"),
        (LPSTR) ((wParam == SB_LINEUP) ? "SB_LINEUP" :
            (wParam == SB_LINEDOWN) ? "SB_LINEDOWN" :
            (wParam == SB_PAGEUP) ? "SB_PAGEUP" :
            (wParam == SB_PAGEDOWN) ? "SB_PAGEDOWN" :
            (wParam == SB_THUMBPOSITION) ? "SB_THUMBPOSITION" :
            (wParam == SB_THUMBTRACK) ? "SB_THUMBTRACK" :
            (wParam == SB_ENDSCROLL) ? "SB_ENDSCROLL" : "unknown"),
        ScrollTypeText,
        LOWORD(lParam),
        HIWORD(lParam));
    InvalidateRect(hWnd, &rectScroll, TRUE);
    break;
```

4.2.15 Adding a WM_PAINT Case

To make your application display the current state of the mouse, keyboard, and timer, use a WM_PAINT message to display the states. Your application repaints only the parts of its client area that require repainting.

Add the following statements to the window procedure:

```
case WM_PAINT:
    hDC = BeginPaint(hWnd, &ps);

    if (IntersectRect(&rect, &rectMouse, &ps.rcPaint))
        TextOut(hDC, rectMouse.left, rectMouse.top,
            MouseText, lstrlen(MouseText));
    if (IntersectRect(&rect, &rectButton, &ps.rcPaint))
        TextOut(hDC, rectButton.left, rectButton.top,
            ButtonText, lstrlen(ButtonText));
    if (IntersectRect(&rect, &rectKeyboard, &ps.rcPaint))
        TextOut(hDC, rectKeyboard.left, rectKeyboard.top,
            KeyboardText, lstrlen(KeyboardText));
    if (IntersectRect(&rect, &rectCharacter, &ps.rcPaint))
        TextOut(hDC, rectCharacter.left, rectCharacter.top,
            CharacterText, lstrlen(CharacterText));
    if (IntersectRect(&rect, &rectTimer, &ps.rcPaint))
        TextOut(hDC, rectTimer.left, rectTimer.top,
            TimerText, lstrlen(TimerText));
    if (IntersectRect(&rect, &rectScroll, &ps.rcPaint))
        TextOut(hDC, rectScroll.left, rectScroll.top,
            ScrollText, lstrlen(ScrollText));

    EndPaint(hWnd, &ps);
    break;
```

4.2.16 Compiling and Linking

Compile and link the Input application. Then start Windows and the Input application. To test the application, press keys on the keyboard, click the mouse button, move the mouse, and use the scroll bars. The application should look like this:

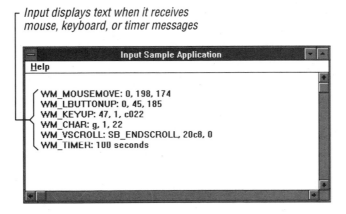

Input displays text when it receives mouse, keyboard, or timer messages

4.3 Related Topics

For more information about the Windows message-based programming model, see Chapter 1, "Overview of the Windows Environment."

For more information about using the cursor for mouse and keyboard input, see Chapter 6, "Cursors."

For more information about menus and menu input, and scroll bar controls, see Chapter 7, "Menus," and Chapter 8, "Controls."

For more information about input functions and messages, see the *Microsoft Windows Programmer's Reference*, *Volumes 2* and *3*.

Icons

A typical application for the Microsoft Windows operating system uses an icon to represent itself when its main window is minimized.

This chapter covers the following topics:

- What an icon is
- Creating and using your own predefined icons
- Specifying an icon for your application's window class
- Changing your application's icon "on the fly"
- Displaying an icon in a dialog box

This chapter also explains how to create a sample Windows 3.1 application, Icon, that illustrates many of these concepts.

5.1 What Is an Icon?

To the user, an icon is a small graphical image that represents an application when that application's main window is minimized. For example, Microsoft Paintbrush uses an icon that looks like a painter's palette to represent its minimized window. Icons are also used in message and dialog boxes.

To the application, an icon is a type of resource. Before resources are compiled, each icon is a separate file that contains a set of bitmap images. The images may be similar in appearance, but each is targeted for a different screen device. When you want the application to use an icon, have the application request the icon resource by name. Windows then determines which of that icon's images is most appropriate for the current screen. Because Windows handles this operation, the application need not check the screen type or determine which icon image is best suited for the current screen. The following figure illustrates what happens when an application requests an icon resource.

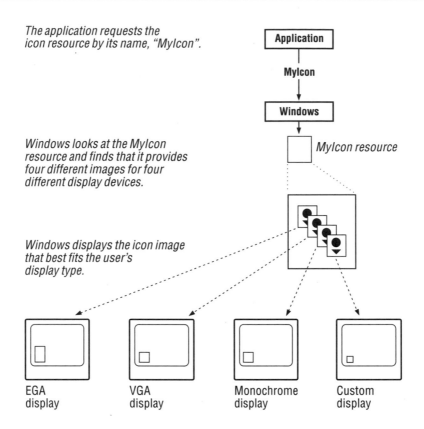

The application requests the icon resource by its name, "MyIcon".

Windows looks at the MyIcon resource and finds that it provides four different images for four different display devices.

Windows displays the icon image that best fits the user's display type.

EGA
display

VGA
display

Monochrome
display

Custom
display

5.2 Using Built-In Icons

Windows provides several built-in icons, which you can use in your applications, and which Windows uses in message boxes to indicate notes, cautions, warnings, and errors.

To use a built-in icon, you must first load it, using the **LoadIcon** function to retrieve the icon handle. The first argument to the function must be NULL, indicating that you are requesting a built-in icon. The second argument identifies the icon you want. For example, the following statement loads the built-in exclamation mark icon:

```
hHandIcon = LoadIcon(NULL, IDI_EXCLAMATION);
```

Once it has loaded a built-in icon, your application can use the icon—for example, by specifying it as the class icon for a particular window class, or by including the icon in a message box. For more information, see Section 5.4, "Specifying a Class Icon," and Section 5.5, "Displaying Your Own Icons."

5.3 Using Your Own Icons

Using an icon requires three steps:

1. Create the icon file by using Microsoft Image Editor (IMAGEDIT.EXE).

2. Define the icon resource by using an **ICON** statement in your application's resource-definition file.

3. Load the icon resource, when it is needed, by using the **LoadIcon** function in your application code.

5.3.1 Creating an Icon File

An icon file contains one or more icon images. You use Image Editor to paint the images and save them in an icon file. The recommended filename extension for an icon file is .ICO. For more information about creating and saving an icon, see *Microsoft Windows Programming Tools*.

5.3.2 Defining an Icon Resource

Once you have an icon file, you must define that icon in your application's resource-definition (.RC) file by adding an **ICON** statement. The **ICON** statement defines a name for the icon and specifies the name of the icon file that contains the icon. For example, the following resource statement adds the icon named MyIcon to your application's resources:

```
MyIcon ICON myicon.ico
```

The filename MYICON.ICO specifies the file that contains the images for the icon named MyIcon. When you compile the resource-definition file, the icon images will be copied from the file MYICON.ICO into your application's resources.

5.3.3 Loading an Icon Resource

Once you have created an icon file and defined the icon resource in the .RC file, your application can load the icon from its resources by using the **LoadIcon** function. This function takes the application's instance handle and the icon's name and returns a handle to the icon. The following example loads MyIcon and stores its handle in the variable hMyIcon.

```
hMyIcon = LoadIcon(hinst, "MyIcon");
```

After loading the icon, the application can display it.

5.4 Specifying a Class Icon

A class icon is an icon that represents a particular window class whenever a window in that class is minimized. You specify a class icon by supplying an icon handle in the **hIcon** field of the window class structure before registering the class. Once the class icon is set, Windows automatically displays that icon when any window you create using that window class is minimized.

The following example shows a definition of the window class wc before the class has been registered. In this definition, the **hIcon** member is set to the handle returned by **LoadIcon**.

```
wc.style = NULL;
wc.lpfnWndProc = MainWndProc;
wc.cbClsExtra = 0;
wc.cbWndExtra = 0;
wc.hInstance = hinst;
wc.hIcon = LoadIcon(NULL, IDI_APPLICATION);
wc.hCursor = LoadCursor(NULL, IDC_ARROW);
wc.hbrBackground = COLOR_WINDOW + 1;
wc.lpszMenuName = NULL;
wc.lpszClassName = "Generic";
```

The **LoadIcon** function returns a handle to the built-in application icon identified by the IDI_APPLICATION constant. If you minimize a window that has this class, you will see a white rectangle with a black border. This is the built-in application icon.

5.5 Displaying Your Own Icons

Windows displays a class icon when the application is minimized and removes it when the application is maximized. All the application does is specify it as the class icon. This meets the requirements of most applications, since most applications typically do not display additional information to the user when the application is minimized.

However, sometimes you may want your application to display its icon itself, instead of letting Windows display a prespecified class icon. This is particularly useful when you want your application's icon to be dynamic, like the icon in the Microsoft Windows Clock application. (The Clock application continues to show the time even when it has been minimized.) Windows lets applications paint within the client area of a minimized window, so that they can paint their own icons.

If you want your application to display its own icon, follow these steps:

1. In the window class structure wc, set the class icon to NULL before registering the window class. Use the following statement:

```
wc.hIcon = NULL;
```

This step is required because it signals Windows to continue sending WM_PAINT messages, as necessary, to the window procedure even though the window has been minimized.

2. Add a WM_PAINT case to your window procedure that draws within the icon's client area if the window is to receive a WM_PAINT message when the window is minimized. Use the following statements:

```
PAINTSTRUCT ps;
HDC hDC;
    .
    .
    .

case WM_PAINT:

    hDC = BeginPaint(hWnd, &ps);
    if (IsIconic(hWnd)) {

        /* Output functions for minimized state     */

    }

    else {

        /* Output functions for nonminimized state */

    }

    EndPaint(hWnd, &ps);
    break;
```

An application must determine whether the window is minimized, since what it paints in the icon may be different from what it paints in the open window. The **IsIconic** function returns a nonzero value if the window is minimized.

The **BeginPaint** function returns a handle of the display context of the icon's client area. **BeginPaint** takes the window handle, hWnd, and a long pointer to the paint structure, ps. **BeginPaint** fills the paint structure with information about the area to be painted. As with any painting operation, each call to **BeginPaint** requires a corresponding call to the **EndPaint** function. **EndPaint** releases any resources that **BeginPaint** retrieved and signals the end of the application's repainting of the client area.

You can retrieve the size of the icon's client area by calling the **GetClientRect** function. For example, to draw an ellipse that fills the icon, you can use the following statement:

```
GetClientRect(hWnd, &rc);
Ellipse(hDC, rc.left, rc.top, rc.right, rc.bottom);
```

You can use any GDI output functions to draw the icon, including the **TextOut** function. The only limitation is the size of the icon, which varies from screen to screen, so make sure that your painting does not depend on a specific icon size.

5.6 Displaying an Icon in a Dialog Box

You can place icons in dialog boxes by using the **ICON** control statement in the **DIALOG** statement. You have already seen an example of a **DIALOG** statement in the About dialog box described with the Generic application. The **DIALOG** statement for that box looks like this:

```
AboutBox DIALOG 22, 17, 144, 75
STYLE DS_MODALFRAME | WS_CAPTION | WS_SYSMENU
CAPTION "About Icon"
BEGIN
    CTEXT "Microsoft Windows"            -1, 37,  5,  68, 8
    CTEXT "Generic Application"          -1,  0, 14, 144, 8
    CTEXT "Version 3.1"                  -1, 38, 34,  64, 8
    DEFPUSHBUTTON "OK"         IDOK, 53, 59, 32, 14, WS_GROUP
END
```

You can add an icon to the dialog box by inserting the following **ICON** statement immediately after the **DEFPUSHBUTTON** statement:

```
ICON "MyIcon", -1, 25, 14, 16, 21
```

When an icon is added to a dialog box, it is treated as is any other control. It must have a control identifier, a position for its upper-left corner, a width, and a height. In this example, 1 is the control identifier, 25 and 14 specify the location of the icon in the dialog box, and 16 and 21 specify the height and width of the icon, respectively. Windows ignores the height and width, however, and sizes the icon automatically.

The name MyIcon identifies the icon you want to use. The icon must be defined in an **ICON** statement elsewhere within the resource-definition file. For example, the following statement defines the icon MyIcon.

```
MyIcon ICON MYICON.ICO
```

5.7 Sample Application: Icon

This sample application shows how to incorporate an icon into your application—in particular, how to do the following:

- Use a custom icon as the class icon.
- Use an icon in the About dialog box.

To create the Icon application, make the following modifications to the Generic application:

1. Add an **ICON** statement to the resource-definition file.
2. Add an **ICON** control statement to the **DIALOG** statement in the resource-definition file.
3. Load the custom icon and use it to set the class icon in the initialization function.
4. Modify the makefile to cause Microsoft Windows Resource Compiler (RC) to add the icon to the application's executable file.
5. Compile and link the application.

This sample assumes that you have created an icon by using Image Editor and have saved the icon in a file named MYICON.ICO.

5.7.1 Adding an ICON Statement

To add an **ICON** statement to your resource-definition file, insert the following line at the beginning of the file, immediately after the **#include** directives:

```
MyIcon ICON myicon.ico
```

5.7.2 Adding an ICON Control Statement

To add an **ICON** control statement to the **DIALOG** statement, insert the following line immediately after the **DEFPUSHBUTTON** statement:

```
ICON "MyIcon", -1, 25, 14, 16, 21
```

5.7.3 Setting the Class Icon

To set the class icon, add the following statement to the initialization function in the C-language source file:

```
wc.hIcon = LoadIcon(hinst, "MyIcon");
```

5.7.4 Adding a MYICON.ICO Line to the Makefile

In the makefile, add the MYICON.ICO file to the list of files on which ICON.RES is dependent. The relevant lines in the makefile should look like this:

```
icon.res: icon.rc icon.h myicon.ico
    rc /r icon.rc
```

This change ensures that, if the MYICON.ICO file changes, ICON.RC will be re-compiled to form a new ICON.RES file.

No other changes are required.

5.7.5 Compiling and Linking

Compile and link the Icon application, and then start Windows and the Icon application. Now, if you choose the About command, Icon displays the About dialog box, which now contains an icon.

5.8 Related Topics

For more information about functions used with icons, see the *Microsoft Windows Programmer's Reference*, *Volume 2*.

For more information about resource-definition statements, see the *Microsoft Windows Programmer's Reference*, *Volume 4*.

For more information about using Image Editor, see *Microsoft Windows Programming Tools*.

Cursors

Chapter **6**

The cursor is a special bitmap that shows the user where actions initiated by the mouse will take place. With most applications for the Microsoft Windows operating system, the user makes selections, chooses commands, and directs other actions by using either the mouse or the keyboard.

This chapter covers the following topics:

- Controlling the shape of the cursor
- Displaying the cursor
- Letting the user select information by using the mouse
- Letting the user move the cursor by using the keyboard

This chapter also explains how to create a sample Windows 3.1 application, Cursor, that illustrates some of these concepts.

6.1 Controlling the Shape of the Cursor

Since no one cursor shape can meet the requirements of all applications, Windows makes it easy for your application to change the shape of the cursor to suit its own requirements. In order to use a particular cursor shape, your application must first retrieve a handle of it by using the **LoadCursor** function. Once the application has loaded the cursor, it can use that cursor shape whenever necessary.

An application can control the shape of the cursor by using either of two methods:

- Using the built-in cursor shapes that Windows provides.
- Using its own customized cursor shapes.

6.1.1 Using Built-In Cursor Shapes

Windows provides several built-in cursor shapes. These include the arrow, hourglass, I-beam, and cross-hair cursors. Most of the built-in cursor shapes have specialized uses. For example, the I-beam cursor is typically used when the user is editing text, and the hourglass cursor is used to indicate that a lengthy operation is in progress, such as reading a disk file.

To use a built-in cursor, use the **LoadCursor** function to retrieve a handle of the built-in cursor. The first argument to **LoadCursor** must be NULL (indicating that a built-in cursor is requested); the second argument must specify the cursor to load. The following example loads the I-beam cursor, IDC_IBEAM, and assigns the resulting cursor handle to the variable hCursor.

```
hCursor = LoadCursor(NULL, IDC_IBEAM);
```

Once an application has loaded a cursor, it can use the cursor; for example, it could display the I-beam cursor when the user is currently editing text. For information about how to display the cursor, see Section 6.2, "Displaying a Cursor."

6.1.2 Using Your Own Cursor Shapes

To create and use your own cursor shapes, follow these steps:

1. Create the cursor shape by using Microsoft Image Editor (IMAGEDIT.EXE).

2. Define the cursor in your resource-definition file by using the **CURSOR** statement.

3. Load the cursor by using the **LoadCursor** function.

6.1.2.1 Creating a Cursor Shape

The first step is to create the cursor shape, by using Image Editor, with which you can see an actual-size version of the cursor shape while you are editing it. Once you have created the cursor, save it in a cursor file. The recommended extension for cursor files is .CUR.

For information about using Image Editor, see the online Help available with Image Editor.

6.1.2.2 Adding a Cursor to Your Application Resources

Next, add a **CURSOR** statement to your resource-definition file. The **CURSOR** statement specifies the file that contains the cursor, and defines a name for the cursor. The application will use this cursor name when loading the cursor. Following is an example of a **CURSOR** statement:

```
Bullseye CURSOR BULLSEYE.CUR
```

In this example, the name of the cursor is Bullseye, and the cursor is in the file BULLSEYE.CUR.

6.1.2.3 Loading a Cursor

In your application code, retrieve a handle to the cursor by using the **LoadCursor** function. For example, the following statement loads the cursor named Bullseye and assigns its handle to the variable hCursor:

```
hCursor = LoadCursor(hinst, "Bullseye");
```

In this example, the **LoadCursor** function loads the cursor from the application's resources. The instance handle hinst identifies the application's resources and is required. The name Bullseye identifies the cursor. It is the same name given in the resource-definition file.

6.2 Displaying a Cursor

Once an application has loaded a cursor shape, it can display the cursor by using one of two methods:

- Specifying it as the class cursor for all windows in a window class
- Explicitly setting the cursor shape when the cursor moves within the client area of a particular window

6.2.1 Specifying a Class Cursor

The class cursor defines the shape the cursor will take when it enters the client area of a window that belongs to that window class. You must specify the class cursor before registering the window class. To do this, load the cursor you want your application to use and assign the cursor's handle to the **hCursor** member of the window-class structure. For example, to use the built-in arrow cursor, IDC_ARROW, in your window, add the following statement to your initialization function:

```
wc.hCursor = LoadCursor(NULL, IDC_ARROW);
```

For each window created using this class, the built-in arrow cursor will appear automatically when the user moves the cursor into the window.

6.2.2 Explicitly Setting a Cursor Shape

Your application does not have to specify a class cursor. Instead, you can set the **hCursor** field to NULL to indicate that the window class has no class cursor. If a window has no class cursor, Windows will not automatically change the shape of the cursor when it moves into the client area of the window. This means that your application will need to display the cursor itself.

To use any cursor, whether built-in or custom, your application must load it first. For example, to load the custom cursor MyCursor (defined in your application's resource-definition file) add the following statements to your initialization function:

```
static HCURSOR hMyCursor; /* static variable */
hMyCursor = LoadCursor(hinst, "MyCursor");
```

Then, to change the cursor shape, use the **SetCursor** function to set the shape each time the cursor moves into the client area. Since Windows sends a WM_MOUSEMOVE message to the window for each cursor movement, you can manage the cursor by adding the following statements to the window procedure:

```
case WM_MOUSEMOVE:
    SetCursor(hMyCursor);
    break;
```

Note If you want your application to display the cursor itself, you must set the class-cursor member to NULL. Otherwise, Windows will attempt to set the cursor shape for each WM_MOUSEMOVE message, even though your application is also setting the cursor shape. This will result in a noticeable flicker as the cursor is moved through the window.

6.2.3 Example: Displaying the Hourglass During a Lengthy Operation

Whenever your application begins a lengthy operation, such as reading or writing a large block of data to a disk file, it should change the shape of the cursor to an hourglass. This lets users know that a lengthy operation is in progress and that they should wait before attempting to continue their work. After the operation is complete, your application should restore the cursor to its previous shape.

To change the cursor to an hourglass, use the following statements:

```
HCURSOR hSaveCursor;
HCURSOR hHourGlass;
    .
    .
    .

hHourGlass = LoadCursor(NULL, IDC_WAIT);
    .
    .
    .

SetCapture(hWnd);
hSaveCursor = SetCursor(hHourGlass);

/* Lengthy operation */

SetCursor(hSaveCursor);
ReleaseCapture();
    .
    .
    .
```

In this example, the application defines the variables that will be used to store the cursor handles. Both variables are type **HCURSOR**. After defining variables, the application first captures the mouse input, using the **SetCapture** function. This keeps the user from attempting to use the mouse to carry out work in another application while the lengthy operation is in progress. Once the application has captured the mouse input, Windows directs all mouse input messages to the specified window, regardless of whether the mouse is in that window. The application can then process the messages as appropriate.

After capturing the mouse input, the application then changes the cursor shape by using the **SetCursor** function. **SetCursor** returns a handle to the previous cursor shape, so that the shape can be restored later. The application saves this handle in the variable hSaveCursor. After the lengthy operation is complete, the application restores the previous cursor shape.

Finally, the **ReleaseCapture** function releases the mouse input.

6.3 Using the Cursor with the Mouse

With a typical Windows application, the user performs many types of tasks by using a mouse—for example, choosing commands from a menu, selecting text or graphics, or directing scrolling operations. For most of these tasks, Windows automatically handles the mouse input; for example, when the user chooses a menu command, Windows automatically sends the application a message that contains the command identifier.

The application, however, handles one common task itself: the user's selecting information within the client area. So that the user can select this information (by using the mouse), the application must perform the following tasks:

- Start processing the selection.

  When the user presses the mouse button to start selecting information, the application must note the location of the cursor and temporarily capture all mouse input to ensure that other applications do not interfere with the selection process.

- Provide visual feedback during the selection.

  As the user drags the mouse across the screen, the application should show the user what information is currently being selected. For example, some applications highlight selected information; others draw a dotted rectangle around it.

- Complete the selection.

  When the user releases the mouse button, the application must note the final location of the cursor and signal the end of the selection process.

When the selection process is complete, the user can then choose an action to perform on the selected information. For example, when using a word-processing application, the user might select several words, then choose a command that changes the selected text to a different font. The following sections discuss each step in more detail and explain how to let the user select graphics in a window's client area.

Note The mouse is just one of many possible pointing devices. Other pointing devices such as graphics tablets, joysticks, and light pens may operate differently but still provide input identical to that of a mouse. The following examples can also be used with these devices. Remember that when a pointing device is present, Windows automatically controls the position and shape of the cursor as the user moves the pointing device.

6.3.1 Starting a Graphics Selection

Because graphics can be virtually any shape, they are potentially more difficult to select than simple text. The simplest approach to selecting graphics is to let the user "stretch" a selection rectangle so that it encloses the desired information.

This section explains how to use the "rubber rectangle" method of selecting graphics. You can use the WM_LBUTTONDOWN, WM_LBUTTONUP, and WM_MOUSEMOVE messages to create the rectangle. This lets the user create the selection by choosing a point, pressing the left mouse button, and dragging to another point before releasing. As the user drags the mouse, your application can provide instant feedback by inverting the border of the rectangle described by the starting and current points.

For this method, the application starts the selection upon receiving the WM_LBUTTONDOWN message. The application must then do three things: capture the mouse input, save the starting (original) point, and save the current point, as follows:

```
BOOL fTrack = FALSE;    /* global variables */
int OrgX = 0, OrgY = 0;
int PrevX = 0, PrevY = 0;
    .
    .
    .

case WM_LBUTTONDOWN:
    fTrack = TRUE;
    PrevX = LOWORD(lParam);
    PrevY = HIWORD(lParam);
    OrgX = LOWORD(lParam);
    OrgY = HIWORD(lParam);
    InvalidateRect(hWnd, NULL, TRUE);
    UpdateWindow(hWnd);

    /* Capture all input even if mouse goes outside window. */

    SetCapture(hWnd);
    break;
```

When the application receives the WM_LBUTTONDOWN message, the fTrack variable is set to TRUE to indicate that a selection is in progress. As with any mouse message, the *lParam* parameter contains the current x- and y-coordinates of the mouse in the low and high-order words, respectively. These are saved as the origin x and y values, OrgX and OrgY, as well as the previous values, PrevX and PrevY. The PrevX and PrevY variables will be updated immediately when the next WM_MOUSEMOVE message is received. The OrgX and OrgY variables remain unchanged and will be used to determine a corner of the bitmap to be copied. (The variables fTrack, OrgX, OrgY, PrevX, and PrevY must be global variables.)

To provide immediate visual feedback in response to the WM_LBUTTONDOWN message, the application invalidates the screen and notifies the window procedure that it must repaint the screen. The application does this by calling the functions **InvalidateRect** and **UpdateWindow**.

The **SetCapture** function directs all subsequent mouse input to the window even if the cursor moves outside of the window. This ensures that the selection process will continue uninterrupted.

Your application should respond to the WM_PAINT message by redrawing the invalidated portions of the screen, as in the following example:

```
case WM_PAINT:
    {
        PAINTSTRUCT      ps;
        HDC              hDC;

        hDC = BeginPaint(hWnd, &ps);
        if (OrgX != PrevX || OrgY != PrevY) {
            MoveTo(hDC, OrgX, OrgY);
            LineTo(hDC, OrgX, PrevY);
            LineTo(hDC, PrevX, PrevY);
            LineTo(hDC, PrevX, OrgY);
            LineTo(hDC, OrgX, OrgY);
        }
        EndPaint(hWnd, &ps);
    }
    break;
```

6.3.2 Extending a Graphics Selection

You may want some of your applications to be able to extend an existing selection. One way to do this is to have the user hold the SHIFT key when making a selection. Since the *wParam* parameter contains a flag that specifies whether the SHIFT key is being pressed, it is easy to check for this and to extend the selection, as necessary. In this case, extending a selection means preserving its previous OrgX and OrgY values when you start it. To do this, change the WM_LBUTTONDOWN case so it looks like this:

```
case WM_LBUTTONDOWN:
    fTrack = TRUE;
    PrevX = LOWORD(lParam);
    PrevY = HIWORD(lParam);

    if (!(wParam & MK_SHIFT)) { /* If shift key   */
        OrgX = LOWORD(lParam);  /* is not pressed */
        OrgY = HIWORD(lParam);
    }

    InvalidateRect(hwnd, NULL, TRUE);
    UpdateWindow(hwnd);

    /*
     * Capture all input even if the mouse goes outside
     * the window.
     */

    SetCapture(hwnd);
    break;
```

6.3.3 Showing a Graphics Selection

As the user makes the selection, your application must provide feedback about his
or her progress. For the application to do this, you can draw a border around the
selection rectangle by using the **LineTo** function upon receiving each new
WM_MOUSEMOVE message. To prevent the application from losing information already on the screen, draw a line that inverts the screen rather than drawing
over it. You can do this by using the **SetROP2** function to set the binary raster
mode to R2_NOT, as in the following example:

```
case WM_MOUSEMOVE:
    {
        RECT rectClient;
        int  NextX;
        int  NextY;

        if (fTrack) {
            NextX = LOWORD(lParam);
            NextY = HIWORD(lParam);

            /* Do not draw outside the window's client area. */

            GetClientRect(hwnd, &rectClient);

            if (NextX < rectClient.left)
                NextX = rectClient.left;
            else
                if (NextX >= rectClient.right)
                    NextX = rectClient.right - 1;
```

```
        if (NextY < rectClient.top)
            NextY = rectClient.top;
        else
            if (NextY >= rectClient.bottom)
                NextY = rectClient.bottom - 1;

        /*
         * If the mouse position has changed, then clear the
         * previous rectangle and draw the new one.
         */

        if (NextX != PrevX || NextY != PrevY) {
            hdc = GetDC(hwnd);
            SetROP2(hdc, R2_NOT); /* erases previous box */
            MoveTo(hdc, OrgX, OrgY);
            LineTo(hdc, OrgX, PrevY);
            LineTo(hdc, PrevX, PrevY);
            LineTo(hdc, PrevX, OrgY);
            LineTo(hdc, OrgX, OrgY);

            /* Get the current mouse position. */

            PrevX = NextX;
            PrevY = NextY;
            MoveTo(hdc, OrgX, OrgY); /* draws new box */
            LineTo(hdc, OrgX, PrevY);
            LineTo(hdc, PrevX, PrevY);
            LineTo(hdc, PrevX, OrgY);
            LineTo(hdc, OrgX, OrgY);
            ReleaseDC(hwnd, hdc);
        }
    }
}
break;
```

The application processes the WM_MOUSEMOVE message only if the fTrack variable is TRUE (that is, if a selection is in progress). The purpose of the WM_MOUSEMOVE processing is to remove the border around the previous rectangle and draw a new border around the rectangle described by the current and original positions. Since the border is the inverse of what was originally on the screen, inverting again restores it completely. The first four **LineTo** functions remove the previous border; the next four draw a new border. Before drawing the new border, the application updates the PrevX and PrevY values by assigning them the current values contained in the *lParam* parameter.

6.3.4 Ending a Graphics Selection

Finally, when the user releases the left button, your application should save the final point and signal the end of the selection process. The following statements complete the selection:

```
case WM_LBUTTONUP:
    fTrack = FALSE;   /* no longer carrying out selection */
    ReleaseCapture(); /* releases hold on mouse input    */

    X = LOWORD(lParam); /* saves current value           */
    Y = HIWORD(lParam);
    break;
```

When the application receives a WM_LBUTTONUP message, it immediately sets fTrack to FALSE to indicate that selection processing has been completed. It also releases the mouse capture by using the **ReleaseCapture** function. It then saves the current mouse position in the variables X and Y. This, together with the selection-origin information saved on receiving the WM_LBUTTONDOWN message, records the selection the user has made. The application can now manipulate the selection and can redraw the selection rectangle, as necessary.

For some of your applications, you might want to check the final cursor position to ensure that it represents a point to the lower right of the original point. This is the way most rectangles are described—by their upper-left and lower-right corners.

Note that the **ReleaseCapture** function is required, since a corresponding **Set-Capture** function was called. In general, the application should release the mouse immediately after the mouse capture is no longer needed.

6.4 Using the Cursor with the Keyboard

Because Windows does not require a pointing device, applications should provide the user with a way to duplicate mouse actions with the keyboard. To allow the user to move the cursor by using the keyboard, use the **SetCursorPos**, **SetCursor**, **GetCursorPos**, **ClipCursor**, and **ShowCursor** functions to display and move the cursor.

6.4.1 Moving the Cursor

To move the cursor directly from your application, use the **SetCursorPos** function. This function is useful for letting the user move the cursor by using the keyboard.

To move the cursor, use the WM_KEYDOWN message and filter for the virtual-key values of the arrow keys: VK_LEFT, VK_RIGHT, VK_UP, and VK_DOWN. For each keystroke, the application should update the position of the cursor. The following example shows how to retrieve the cursor position and convert the coordinates to client coordinates:

```
case WM_KEYDOWN:
    if (wParam != VK_LEFT && wParam != VK_RIGHT
        && wParam != VK_UP && wParam != VK_DOWN)
        break;

GetCursorPos(&ptCursor);

/* Convert screen coordinates to client coordinates. */

ScreenToClient(hwnd, &ptCursor);

switch (wParam) {

    /*
     * Adjust the cursor position according to which key
     * was pressed. Accelerate the movement by adding the
     * repeat variable to the cursor position.
     */

    case VK_LEFT:
        ptCursor.x -= repeat;
        break;

    case VK_RIGHT:
        ptCursor.x += repeat;
        break;

    case VK_UP:
        ptCursor.y -= repeat;
        break;

    case VK_DOWN:
        ptCursor.y += repeat;
        break;

    default:
        return NULL;
}

repeat++;        /* increases repeat rate */

/* Ensure that the cursor doesn't go outside client area. */

GetClientRect(hwnd, &Rect);

if (ptCursor.x >= Rect.right)
    ptCursor.x = Rect.right - 1;
else
    if (ptCursor.x < Rect.left)
        ptCursor.x = Rect.left;

if (ptCursor.y >= Rect.bottom)
    ptCursor.y = Rect.bottom - 1;
```

```
    else
        if (ptCursor.y < Rect.top)
            ptCursor.y = Rect.top;

    /* Convert the coordinates to screen coordinates. */

    ClientToScreen(hwnd, &ptCursor);
    SetCursorPos(ptCursor.x, ptCursor.y);
    break;

case WM_KEYUP:
    repeat = 1; /* clears repeat count */
    break;
```

In this example, the first **if** statement filters for the virtual-key values of the arrow keys: VK_LEFT, VK_RIGHT, VK_UP, and VK_DOWN. After this filtering operation, the **GetCursorPos** function retrieves the current cursor position. If the mouse is available, the user could potentially move the cursor with the mouse at any time; therefore, there is no guarantee that the position values saved on the previous keystroke are correct.

After retrieving the current cursor position, the application calls the **ScreenTo-Client** function to convert the cursor position to client coordinates. The application does this for two reasons: Mouse messages give the mouse position in client coordinates, and client coordinates do not need to be updated if the window moves. In other words, it is convenient to use client coordinates, because the system uses them and because it usually means less work for the application.

In the example, the repeat variable provides accelerated cursor motion. Advancing the cursor one unit for each keystroke can be frustrating for users if they need to move to the other side of the screen. You can accelerate the cursor motion by increasing the number of units the cursor advances when the user holds down a key. When the user holds down a key, Windows sends multiple WM_KEYDOWN messages without matching WM_KEYUP messages. To accelerate the cursor, you simply increase the number of units to advance each time a WM_KEYDOWN message is received.

After accelerating cursor motion, the application calls the **GetClientRect** function to retrieve the current size of the client area and store it in the Rect structure. This information is useful for ensuring that the cursor motion remains within the client area.

Following the call to **GetClientRect**, the **if** statements check the current cursor position to ensure that it is within the client area. The application then adjusts the cursor position, if necessary.

In preparation for the **SetCursorPos** function, the **ClientToScreen** function converts the values in the ptCursor structure from client coordinates to screen coordinates. Because **SetCursorPos** requires screen coordinates rather than client coordinates, you must convert the coordinates before calling **SetCursorPos**.

The **SetCursorPos** function moves the cursor to the desired location.

Within the WM_KEYUP case, the application restores the initial value of the repeat variable when the user releases the key.

6.4.2 Using the Cursor When No Mouse Is Available

When no mouse is available, the application must display and move the cursor in response to keyboard actions. To determine whether a mouse is present, use the **GetSystemMetrics** function and specify the SM_MOUSEPRESENT constant, as follows:

```
GetSystemMetrics(SM_MOUSEPRESENT);
```

This function returns a nonzero value if the mouse is present.

You will need to display the cursor and update its position when the application is activated; when the application is deactivated, you will need to hide the cursor. The following statements carry out both activation functions:

```
case WM_ACTIVATE:
    if (!GetSystemMetrics(SM_MOUSEPRESENT)) {
        if (!HIWORD(lParam)) {
            if (wParam) {
                SetCursor(hMyCursor);
                ClientToScreen(hWnd, &ptCursor);
                SetCursorPos(ptCursor.x, ptCursor.y);
            }
            ShowCursor(wParam);
        }
    }
    break;
```

In this example, the cursor functions are called only if no mouse is available; that is, if the **GetSystemMetrics** function returns FALSE. Since Windows positions and updates the cursor automatically if a mouse is present, the cursor functions, if carried out, would disrupt this processing.

The next step is to determine whether the window is minimized (an icon). The cursor must not be displayed or updated if the window is an icon. In a WM_ACTIVATE message, the high-order word is nonzero if the window is minimized, so the cursor functions are called only if this value is zero.

The final step is to check the *wParam* parameter to determine whether the window is being activated or deactivated. This parameter is nonzero if the window is being activated. When a window is activated, the **SetCursor** function sets the cursor shape and the **SetCursorPos** function positions the cursor. The **ClientToScreen** function converts the cursor position to screen coordinates, as required by **Set-CursorPos**. Finally, the **ShowCursor** function shows or hides the cursor, depending on the value of *wParam*.

When the system has no mouse installed, applications must be careful when using the cursor. In general, applications must hide the cursor when the window is closed, destroyed, or relinquishes control. If an application fails to hide the cursor, it prevents subsequent windows from using the cursor. For example, if an application sets the cursor to the hourglass, displays the cursor, then relinquishes control to a dialog box, the cursor remains on the screen (possibly in a new shape) but cannot be used by the dialog box.

6.5 Sample Application: Cursor

This sample application, Cursor, illustrates how to incorporate cursors and how to use the mouse and keyboard in your applications. It illustrates the following:

- Using a custom cursor as the class cursor
- Showing the hourglass cursor during a lengthy operation
- Using the mouse to select a portion of the client area
- Using the keyboard to move the cursor

To create the Cursor application, make the following modifications to the Generic application:

1. Add a **CURSOR** statement to your resource-definition file.
2. Add new variables.
3. Load the custom cursor and use it to set the class cursor in the initialization function.
4. Prepare the hourglass cursor.
5. Add a lengthy operation to the window procedure (for simplicity, use the ENTER key to "trigger" the operation).
6. Add WM_LBUTTONDOWN, WM_MOUSEMOVE, and WM_LBUTTONUP cases to the window procedure to support selection.
7. Add a WM_KEYDOWN case to the window procedure to support keyboard-controlled cursor movement.
8. Add a WM_PAINT case to the window procedure to redraw the client area after it has been invalidated.
9. Add a BULLSEYE.CUR line to the makefile.
10. Compile and link the application.

This sample assumes that your system has a mouse; if your system does not have a mouse, the application might not operate as described. However, it is fairly easy to adjust the sample to work with both the mouse and the keyboard or with only the keyboard.

6.5.1 Adding a CURSOR Statement

To use a custom cursor, you must first create a cursor file by using Image Editor. Then specify the name of the file in a **CURSOR** statement in the resource-definition file, as follows.

```
Bullseye CURSOR BULLSEYE.CUR
```

Make sure that the file BULLSEYE.CUR contains a cursor.

6.5.2 Adding New Variables

Since your application will require several new variables, add the following statements to the beginning of your C-language source file:

```
char szStr[255];          /* general-purpose string buffer */

HCURSOR hSaveCursor;      /* handle of current cursor       */
HCURSOR hHourGlass;       /* handle of hourglass cursor     */

BOOL fTrack = FALSE;      /* TRUE if left button clicked    */
int OrgX = 0, OrgY = 0;   /* original cursor position       */
int PrevX = 0, PrevY = 0; /* current cursor position        */
int X = 0, Y = 0;         /* last cursor position           */
RECT Rect;                /* selection rectangle            */

POINT ptCursor;           /* x and y coordinates of cursor  */
int repeat = 1;           /* repeat count of keystroke      */
```

In this example, the hSaveCursor and hHourGlass variables hold the cursor handles to be used for the lengthy operation. The fTrack variable holds a Boolean flag indicating whether a selection is in progress. The variables OrgX, OrgY, PrevX, and PrevY hold the original and current cursor positions as a selection is being made. OrgX and OrgY, along with the variables X and Y, hold the original and final coordinates of the selection when the selection is complete. The ptCursor structure holds the current position of the cursor in the client area. (This position is updated when the user presses an arrow key.) The Rect structure holds the current dimensions of the client area and is used to ensure that the cursor stays within the client area. The repeat variable holds the current repeat count for each keyboard motion.

6.5.3 Setting the Class Cursor

To set the class cursor, modify a statement in the initialization function. Specifically, assign the cursor handle to the **hCursor** member of the window-class structure. Make the following change in the C-language source file. Find this line:

```
wc.hCursor = LoadCursor(NULL, IDC_ARROW);
```

Change it to the following:

```
wc.hCursor = LoadCursor(hinst, "Bullseye");
```

6.5.4 Preparing the Hourglass Cursor

Since you will be using the hourglass cursor during a lengthy operation, you need to load it. The most convenient place to load it is from within the initialization tasks handled by the InitInstance function. Add the following statement to Init-Instance:

```
hHourGlass = LoadCursor(NULL, IDC_WAIT);
```

This makes the hourglass cursor available whenever it is needed.

6.5.5 Adding a Lengthy Operation

A lengthy operation can take many forms. This sample is a function named sieve that computes several hundred prime numbers. The operation begins when the user presses the ENTER key. Add the following statements to the window procedure:

```
case WM_CHAR:
    if (wParam == VK_RETURN) {
        SetCapture(hwnd);

        /* Set the cursor to an hourglass. */

        hSaveCursor = SetCursor(hHourGlass);

        lstrcpy(szStr, "Calculating prime numbers...");
        InvalidateRect(hwnd, NULL, TRUE);
        UpdateWindow(hwnd);
        sprintf(szStr, "Calculated %d primes. ", sieve());
        InvalidateRect(hwnd, NULL, TRUE);
        UpdateWindow(hwnd);
```

```
                SetCursor(hSaveCursor);    /* restores previous cursor */
                ReleaseCapture();
        }
        break;
```

When the user presses ENTER, Windows generates a WM_CHAR message whose *wParam* parameter contains a value representing a carriage return. Upon receiving the WM_CHAR message, the window procedure checks for this value and carries out the sample lengthy operation, sieve. This function, called Eratosthenes Sieve Prime-Number Program, is from *Byte*, January 1983. It is defined as follows:

```
#define NITER      20                          /* number of iterations */
#define BUFF_SIZE      8190

BYTE abFlags[BUFF_SIZE + 1] = { 0 };

int PASCAL sieve(void)
{
    int i, k;
    int iter, count;

    for (iter = 1; iter <= NITER; iter++) { /* sieve NITER times  */
        count = 0;
        for (i = 0; i <= BUFF_SIZE; i++)  /* sets all flags TRUE  */
            abFlags[i] = TRUE;

        for (i = 2; i <= BUFF_SIZE; i++)
            if (abFlags[i]) {                 /* found a prime?       */
                for (k = i + i; k <= BUFF_SIZE; k += i)
                    abFlags[k] = FALSE;  /* cancels its multiples */
                count++;
            }
    }
    return count;
}
```

6.5.6 Adding WM_LBUTTONDOWN, WM_MOUSEMOVE, and WM_LBUTTONUP Cases

To carry out a selection, use the statements described in Section 6.3, "Using the Cursor with the Mouse." Add the following statements to your window procedure:

```
case WM_LBUTTONDOWN:
    fTrack = TRUE;
    szStr[0] = '\0';
    PrevX = LOWORD(lParam);
    PrevY = HIWORD(lParam);
```

```
                 if (!(wParam & MK_SHIFT)) { /* If shift key   */
                     OrgX = LOWORD(lParam);  /* is not pressed */
                     OrgY = HIWORD(lParam);
                 }

                 InvalidateRect(hwnd, NULL, TRUE);
                 UpdateWindow(hwnd);

                 /*
                  * Capture all input even if the mouse goes outside
                  * the window.
                  */

                 SetCapture(hwnd);
                 break;
             case WM_MOUSEMOVE:
                 {
                     RECT rectClient;
                     int  NextX;
                     int  NextY;

                     if (fTrack) {
                         NextX = LOWORD(lParam);
                         NextY = HIWORD(lParam);

                         /* Do not draw outside the window's client area. */

                         GetClientRect(hwnd, &rectClient);

                         if (NextX < rectClient.left)
                             NextX = rectClient.left;
                         else
                             if (NextX >= rectClient.right)
                                 NextX = rectClient.right - 1;

                         if (NextY < rectClient.top)
                             NextY = rectClient.top;
                         else
                             if (NextY >= rectClient.bottom)
                                 NextY = rectClient.bottom - 1;

                         /*
                          * If the mouse position has changed, then clear the
                          * previous rectangle and draw the new one.
                          */

                         if (NextX != PrevX || NextY != PrevY) {
                             hdc = GetDC(hwnd);
                             SetROP2(hdc, R2_NOT); /* erases previous box */
```

```
                    MoveTo(hdc, OrgX, OrgY);
                    LineTo(hdc, OrgX, PrevY);
                    LineTo(hdc, PrevX, PrevY);
                    LineTo(hdc, PrevX, OrgY);
                    LineTo(hdc, OrgX, OrgY);

                    /* Get the current mouse position. */

                    PrevX = NextX;
                    PrevY = NextY;
                    MoveTo(hdc, OrgX, OrgY); /* draws new box */
                    LineTo(hdc, OrgX, PrevY);
                    LineTo(hdc, PrevX, PrevY);
                    LineTo(hdc, PrevX, OrgY);
                    LineTo(hdc, OrgX, OrgY);
                    ReleaseDC(hwnd, hdc);
                }
            }
        }
        break;

    case WM_LBUTTONUP:
        fTrack = FALSE;   /* no longer carrying out selection */
        ReleaseCapture(); /* releases hold on mouse input     */

        X = LOWORD(lParam); /* saves current value            */
        Y = HIWORD(lParam);
        break;
```

6.5.7 Adding WM_KEYDOWN and WM_KEYUP Cases

To let the user control the cursor by using the keyboard, add WM_KEYDOWN and WM_KEYUP cases to your application's window procedure. The statements in the WM_KEYDOWN case retrieve the current position of the cursor and update the position when an arrow key is pressed. Add the following statements to the window procedure:

```
POINT ptCursor;     /* x and y coordinates of cursor */
int repeat = 1;     /* repeat count of keystroke     */
RECT Rect;          /* selection rectangle           */
    .
    .
    .

case WM_KEYDOWN:
    if (wParam != VK_LEFT && wParam != VK_RIGHT
        && wParam != VK_UP && wParam != VK_DOWN)
        break;
```

```
GetCursorPos(&ptCursor);

/* Convert screen coordinates to client coordinates. */

ScreenToClient(hwnd, &ptCursor);

switch (wParam) {

    /*
     * Adjust the cursor position according to which key
     * was pressed. Accelerate the movement by adding the
     * repeat variable to the cursor position.
     */

    case VK_LEFT:
        ptCursor.x -= repeat;
        break;

    case VK_RIGHT:
        ptCursor.x += repeat;
        break;

    case VK_UP:
        ptCursor.y -= repeat;
        break;

    case VK_DOWN:
        ptCursor.y += repeat;
        break;

    default:
        return NULL;
}

repeat++;        /* increases repeat rate */

/* Ensure that the cursor doesn't go outside client area. */

GetClientRect(hwnd, &Rect);

if (ptCursor.x >= Rect.right)
    ptCursor.x = Rect.right - 1;
else
    if (ptCursor.x < Rect.left)
        ptCursor.x = Rect.left;

if (ptCursor.y >= Rect.bottom)
    ptCursor.y = Rect.bottom - 1;
else
    if (ptCursor.y < Rect.top)
        ptCursor.y = Rect.top;
```

```
/* Convert the coordinates to screen coordinates. */

ClientToScreen(hwnd, &ptCursor);
SetCursorPos(ptCursor.x, ptCursor.y);
break;
```

In this example, the **GetCursorPos** function retrieves the cursor position in screen coordinates. To check the position of the cursor within the client area, the coordinates are converted to client coordinates by using the **ScreenToClient** function. The **switch** statement then checks for the arrow keys; each time it encounters an arrow key, the statement adds the current contents of the repeat variable to the appropriate coordinate of the cursor location.

The example then checks the new position to make sure it is still in the client area (adjusting it if necessary), using the **GetClientRect** function to retrieve the dimensions of the client area. Finally, the **ClientToScreen** function converts the position back to screen coordinates, and the **SetCursorPos** function sets the new position.

The WM_KEYUP case restores the initial value of the repeat variable when the user releases the key, as follows:

```
case WM_KEYUP:
    repeat = 1; /* clears repeat count */
    break;
```

6.5.8 Adding a WM_PAINT Case

To ensure that the text string and selection rectangle are redrawn when necessary (for example, when another window has temporarily covered the client area), add the following case to the window procedure:

```
case WM_PAINT:
    {
        PAINTSTRUCT ps;

        hdc = BeginPaint(hwnd, &ps);
        TextOut(hdc, 1, 1, szStr, lstrlen(szStr));
        if (OrgX != PrevX || OrgY != PrevY) {
            MoveTo(hdc, OrgX, OrgY);
            LineTo(hdc, OrgX, PrevY);
            LineTo(hdc, PrevX, PrevY);
            LineTo(hdc, PrevX, OrgY);
            LineTo(hdc, OrgX, OrgY);
        }
        EndPaint(hwnd, &ps);
    }
    break;
```

6.5.9 Adding a BULLSEYE.CUR Line to the Makefile

In the makefile, add the file BULLSEYE.CUR to the list of files on which CURSOR.RES is dependent. The relevant lines in the makefile should look like this:

```
cursor.res: cursor.rc cursor.h bullseye.cur
    rc /r cursor.rc
```

This change ensures that, if the file BULLSEYE.CUR changes, CURSOR.RC will be recompiled to form a new CURSOR.RES file.

6.5.10 Compiling and Linking

Compile and link the Cursor application. Then start Windows and the Cursor application. Now, when you move the cursor into the client area, it changes to the bull's-eye shape.

Press and hold down the left mouse button, drag the mouse to a new position, and release the mouse button. You should see a selection that looks like this:

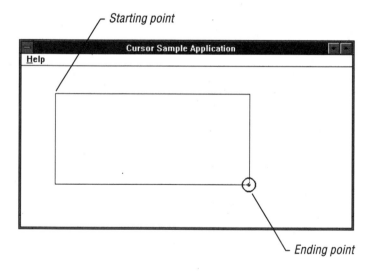

Press the arrow keys to move the cursor. Then press ENTER to see the application display the hourglass cursor, indicating that a lengthy operation is in progress.

6.6 Related Topics

For more information about keyboard and mouse input, see Chapter 4, "Keyboard and Mouse Input."

For more information about cursor functions, window-management messages, and input messages, see the *Microsoft Windows Programmer's Reference*, *Volumes 2 and 3*.

For more information about resource-definition statements, see the *Microsoft Windows Programmer's Reference*, *Volume 4*.

For more information about Image Editor, see *Microsoft Windows Programming Tools*.

Menus

Most applications for the Microsoft Windows operating system use menus so that the user can select and carry out commands or actions.

This chapter covers the following topics:

- What a menu is
- Defining a menu
- Including a menu in your application
- Processing input from a menu
- Modifying an existing menu
- Working with special menu features

This chapter also explains how to create a sample Windows 3.1 application, Edit-Menu, that uses and processes input from menus.

7.1 Menus and Menu Items

A menu is a list of items that, to a user, are your application's commands. Each menu item can be displayed as text or as a bitmap. By choosing a menu item (with the mouse or the keyboard), the user tells the application to perform the command associated with that item. Windows responds to this action by sending the application a message that identifies which command the user chose.

To use a menu in your application, follow these general steps:

1. Define the menu in your resource-definition file.
2. Specify the menu in your application code. There are two common ways to do this:
   - When registering the window class, specify a menu (called the class menu) for that entire window class.
   - When creating a window, specify a menu for that window.
3. Initialize the menu, if necessary.

When you have defined and initialized a menu for your application, the user can choose commands from the menu, and you can have your application add, change, or replace items, or even the entire menu, as necessary.

7.2 Defining a Menu

The first step in using a menu is to define it in your application's resource-definition (.RC) file by using a **MENU** statement. A **MENU** statement consists of the menu name, the **MENU** keyword, and a pair of **BEGIN** and **END** keywords that enclose one or more of the following menu-definition statements:

- The **MENUITEM** statement defines a menu item by name, appearance (text or bitmap), and identifier.

- The **POPUP** statement defines a pop-up menu, which defines further menu items by name, appearance, and identifier.

For example, the following **MENU** statement defines a menu named SampleMenu:

```
SampleMenu MENU
    BEGIN
        MENUITEM "Exit!", IDM_EXIT
        MENUITEM "Recalculate!", IDM_RECALC
        POPUP "Options"
        BEGIN
            MENUITEM "Scylla", IDM_SCYLLA
            MENUITEM "Charybdis", IDM_CHARYBDIS
        END
    END
```

In this example, the first line indicates the beginning of a menu definition and names the menu SampleMenu.

The first **MENUITEM** statement defines the first item on the menu. The text Exit! will appear as the leftmost item on the menu bar. When the user chooses the Exit! command, Windows sends the application a WM_COMMAND message whose *wParam* parameter specifies the menu identifier IDM_EXIT. The second **MENUITEM** statement similarly defines the Recalculate! item.

The **POPUP** statement defines a pop-up menu named Options that will appear on the menu bar. When the user selects Options from the menu bar, a menu appears in which the user can choose between the Scylla and Charybdis commands.

Within the **POPUP** statement are two definitions for the Scylla and Charybdis menu items, each with its own text and menu identifier.

When the user chooses the Exit!, Recalculate!, Scylla, or Charybdis command, Windows notifies the application of the user's choice by passing it that item's menu identifier. Note that Windows does not notify the application when the user selects the Options pop-up menu; instead, Windows simply displays that menu.

For more information about the **MENU**, **POPUP**, and **MENUITEM** resource statements, see the *Microsoft Windows Programmer's Reference*, *Volume 4*.

7.2.1 Menu Identifiers

Each menu item is identified by a unique constant, usually called a menu identifier, which Windows passes to the application when the user chooses the command associated with the item. You define each menu identifier by using the **#define** directive in the resource-definition file or the header file, as in the following example:

```
#define IDM_EXIT        111
#define IDM_RECALC      112
#define IDM_SCYLLA      113
#define IDM_CHARYBDIS   114
```

You use menu identifiers to direct the flow of control, depending on which command the user chooses. For more information about handling menu input, see Section 7.4, "Processing Input from a Menu."

7.3 Including a Menu in Your Application

Once you have defined a menu in the resource-definition file, you can include it in your application code. You do this by associating it with a window. Any overlapped or pop-up window can have a menu; a child window cannot (although child windows can have System menus).

This section explains two common ways to include a menu in your application:

- Specify the menu as the class menu when registering a window class. All windows of that class will then include that menu.

- Specify the menu when creating a window. The window will then include the menu.

7.3.1 Specifying the Menu for a Window Class

When you register a window class, you are setting the default attributes (including the default menu) for all windows in that class. The default menu for a window class is known as the class menu. You can override this default menu by explicitly supplying a menu handle when you create a window of that class. To specify the class menu when you register the window class, assign the name of the menu, as given in the resource-definition file, to the **lpszMenuName** member of the window-class structure, as follows:

```
wc.lpszMenuName = "SampleMenu";
```

In this example, **lpszMenuName** is part of a **WNDCLASS** structure named wc. The menu name SampleMenu is the name given to the menu in the application's resource-definition file.

7.3.2 Specifying a Menu for a Specific Window

A window need not use the class menu, since the class menu is simply a default, not a requirement. To use a menu other than the class menu, load the menu you want from your application resources by using the **LoadMenu** function. This function returns a menu handle. Then, when you call the **CreateWindow** function to create the window, pass the menu handle as the function's *hMenu* parameter.

The following example loads and specifies a menu by using the **LoadMenu** and **CreateWindow** functions:

```
HWND hWnd;                /* handle of current window */
HMENU hSampleMenu;        /* menu handle              */
    .
    .
    .
hSampleMenu = LoadMenu(hinst, "SampleMenu");
hWnd = CreateWindow("SampleWindow",
    "SampleWindow",
    WS_OVERLAPPEDWINDOW,
    CW_USEDEFAULT,
    CW_USEDEFAULT,
    CW_USEDEFAULT,
    CW_USEDEFAULT,
    (HWND) NULL,
    hSampleMenu,
    hinst,
    (LPSTR) NULL);
```

In this example, the **LoadMenu** function loads the menu named SampleMenu. The hinst variable specifies that the resource is to be loaded from the application's resources. **LoadMenu** then returns a menu handle, which is stored in the hSample-Menu variable.

The application calls the **CreateWindow** function to create a new window named SampleWindow. Finally, the application passes hSampleMenu, the menu handle that **LoadMenu** returned, to **CreateWindow**. This tells Windows to use Sample-Menu for the window, instead of using the class menu (if any).

7.4 Processing Input from a Menu

When a user chooses a command from a menu, Windows sends the corresponding window procedure a WM_COMMAND message whose *wParam* parameter contains the menu identifier of the item. The window procedure must carry out any tasks associated with the chosen command. For example, if the user chooses the Open command, the window procedure prompts for the filename, opens the file, and displays it in the window's client area.

The most common way to process menu input is with a **switch** statement in the window procedure. Usually, the **switch** statement directs processing according to the value of the *wParam* parameter in the WM_COMMAND message. Each case processes a different menu identifier, as in the following example:

```
case WM_COMMAND:
    switch (wParam)
        {
        case IDM_NEW:
            /* operations for creating a new file     */
            break;

        case IDM_OPEN:
            /* operations for opening a file           */
            break;

        case IDM_SAVE:
            /* operations for saving this file         */
            break;

        case IDM_SAVEAS:
            /* operations for saving this file         */
            break;

        case IDM_EXIT:
            /* operations for exiting the application  */
            break;
        }
    break;
```

In this example, the *wParam* parameter contains the menu identifier of the item associated with the command the user chose. For each command the user chooses, the application performs the appropriate operations.

7.5 Working with Menus from Your Application

Windows provides functions you can use to change existing menus and create new menus, while your application runs. This section explains the following:

- Enabling and disabling menu items
- Checking and clearing (removing a check mark from) menu items
- Adding, changing, and deleting menu items
- Using bitmaps as menu items
- Replacing menus
- Creating and initializing menus from your application

When you create a window, it receives a private copy of the class menu. The application can alter that window's copy of the menu without affecting other windows' menus.

Note Whenever you make changes to menus on the menu bar, you must call the **DrawMenuBar** function to display the changes.

7.5.1 Enabling and Disabling Menu Items

Usually, a menu item is enabled; its text appears normal, and the user can choose it as a command. A disabled item appears normal but does not respond to mouse clicks or keyboard selection. An unavailable item has grayed (sometimes called "dimmed") text and does not respond to mouse clicks or keyboard selection. Typically, you disable a menu item, or make it unavailable, when the action it represents is not appropriate. For example, you might make the Print command in the File menu unavailable when the system does not have a printer installed.

7.5.1.1 Setting the Initial State of a Menu Item

In the resource-definition file, you can specify whether a menu item is initially disabled or grayed. To do so, use the **INACTIVE** or **GRAYED** options with the **MENUITEM** statement. For example, the following statement specifies that the Print menu item is initially grayed:

```
MENUITEM "Print", IDM_PRINT, GRAYED
```

The information in the resource-definition file applies only to the initial state of the menu. You can change the command's state later, using the **EnableMenuItem** function in your C-language source file. **EnableMenuItem** enables or disables a menu item or makes it unavailable.

7.5.1.2 Disabling a Menu Item

A disabled menu item appears normal but does not respond to mouse clicks or keyboard selection. A disabled item is commonly used as a title for related menu options. The following example disables a menu item:

```
EnableMenuItem(hMenu, IDM_SAVE, MF_DISABLED);
```

This example disables a menu item on the menu represented by the menu handle hMenu. The menu identifier of the item is IDM_SAVE. By specifying the value MF_DISABLED, you direct Windows to disable the specified item.

7.5.1.3 Disabling a Menu Item and Making It Unavailable

So that the user can tell that a command is not currently available, you may want your application to make it unavailable rather than simply disabling it. Making a menu item unavailable disables it and redisplays its text in grayed letters. To disable a menu item and make it unavailable, specify the value MF_GRAYED when you call **EnableMenuItem**, as in the following example:

```
EnableMenuItem(hMenu, IDM_PRINT, MF_GRAYED);
```

This example disables an item on the menu represented by the menu handle hMenu. The menu identifier of the item is IDM_PRINT. By specifying the value MF_GRAYED, you tell Windows to disable the specified item and redisplay its text in grayed letters.

7.5.1.4 Enabling a Menu Item

You can enable a disabled menu item by calling **EnableMenuItem** and specifying the MF_ENABLED value. The following example enables the item identified by ID_EXIT:

```
EnableMenuItem(hMenu, ID_EXIT, MF_ENABLED);
```

7.5.2 Checking and Clearing Menu Items

You can display a check mark next to a menu item to indicate that the user has chosen it. Typically, you check an item when it is part of a group of items that are mutually exclusive. The check mark indicates the user's latest choice. For example, if a group consists of the commands Left, Right, and Center, your application might check the Left command to indicate that the user chose that command most recently.

7.5.2.1 Setting an Initial Check Mark

In the resource-definition file, you can specify whether a menu item is initially checked. To do so, use the **CHECKED** option in the **MENUITEM** statement. For example, the following **MENUITEM** statement specifies that the Left menu item is initially checked:

```
MENUITEM "Left", IDM_LEFT, CHECKED
```

7.5.2.2 Checking a Menu Item

The information in the resource-definition file applies only to the initial state of the menu. You can check or clear a menu item later, using the **CheckMenuItem** function in your C-language source file. **CheckMenuItem** checks or clears a specified menu item.

The following example places a check mark next to the item whose menu identifier is IDM_LEFT:

```
CheckMenuItem(hMenu, IDM_LEFT, MF_CHECKED);
```

7.5.2.3 Clearing a Menu Item

To clear (or "uncheck") a menu item, you call the **CheckMenuItem** function and specify the value MF_UNCHECKED. The following example clears the check mark (if any) from the item whose menu identifier is IDM_RIGHT:

```
CheckMenuItem(hMenu, IDM_RIGHT, MF_UNCHECKED);
```

If you change the menus in the menu bar, you must call the **DrawMenuBar** function to display the changes.

7.5.3 Adding Menu Items

You can add new items to the end of existing menus, or insert new items after particular items.

7.5.3.1 Appending an Item to an Existing Menu

To append an item to the end of an existing menu, you use the **AppendMenu** function. With this function, you can add a new item to the end of the specified menu and specify whether the new item is checked, enabled, grayed, and so on.

The following example appends the menu item Raspberries to the end of the Fruit menu. The example disables the new item and makes it unavailable if raspberries are not currently in season.

```
AppendMenu(hFruitMenu,
    RaspberriesInSeason ? MF_ENABLED : MF_GRAYED,
    IDM_RASPBERRIES,
    "Raspberries");
```

7.5.3.2 Inserting an Item in an Existing Menu

To insert an item in an existing menu, you use the **InsertMenu** function. This function inserts the specified menu item at the specified position and moves subsequent items down to accommodate the new item. Like the **AppendMenu** function, **InsertMenu** lets you specify the state of the new menu item when you insert it.

The following example inserts the menu item Kumquats before the existing item Melons. The example disables the new item and makes it unavailable.

```
InsertMenu(hFruitMenu,
    IDM_MELONS,
    MF_BYCOMMAND | MF_GRAYED,
    IDM_KUMQUATS,
    "Kumquats");
```

You can also insert menu items by numerical position rather than before a specific item. The following example inserts the item Bananas, making it the third item in the Fruit menu. (The first item has position 0, the second item 1, and so on.)

```
InsertMenu(hFruitMenu,
    2,
    MF_BYPOSITION | MF_GRAYED,
    IDM_BANANAS,
    "Bananas");
```

7.5.4 Changing Existing Menus

You can change existing menus and menu items by using the **ModifyMenu** function. For example, you might need to change the text of a menu item. With **ModifyMenu**, you can enable or disable the item, check or clear it, or make it unavailable.

In the following example, the **ModifyMenu** function changes the text of the Water item to Wine. The example also changes the item's menu identifier.

```
ModifyMenu(hMenu,
    IDM_WATER,
    MF_BYCOMMAND,
    IDM_WINE,
    "Wine");
```

When you use **ModifyMenu**, you are essentially telling Windows to replace an existing menu item with a new one. The third, fourth, and fifth **ModifyMenu** parameters specify the attributes of the new item.

For example, the following statement changes the item text from Wine to Cabernet. Although only the item's text is changing, the statement still specifies all the attributes of the item (in this case, just the menu identifier).

```
ModifyMenu(hMenu,
    IDM_WINE,
    MF_BYCOMMAND,
    IDM_WINE,
    "Cabernet");
```

7.5.4.1 Performing Several Changes at Once

When you use **ModifyMenu** to change a menu item, you can also check or clear the item, enable or disable it, or make it unavailable.

The following example not only changes the Water command to Wine, it enables the command (if it is not enabled already), checks it, and changes its menu identifier:

```
ModifyMenu(hMenu,
    IDM_WATER,
    MF_BYCOMMAND | MF_ENABLED | MF_CHECKED,
    IDM_WINE,
    "Wine");
```

7.5.5 Deleting Menu Items

You can remove menu items and any pop-up menus associated with those items by using the **DeleteMenu** function. **DeleteMenu** permanently removes the specified item from the specified menu and moves subsequent items up to fill the gap.

```
DeleteMenu(hFruitMenu,  /* menu handle                     */
    1,                   /* deletes second item            */
    MF_BYPOSITION);      /* specifies item by menu position */
```

This example deletes the Fruit menu's second item. Windows moves any subsequent items up to fill the gap.

The following example deletes the same item, but specifies it by its menu identifier rather than by its position on the menu:

```
DeleteMenu(hFruitMenu,  /* menu handle                       */
    IDM_ORANGES,         /* deletes Oranges item             */
    MF_BYCOMMAND);       /* specifies item by menu identifier */
```

7.5.6 Using Bitmaps as Menu Items

You can also use bitmaps as menu items. There are two ways to do this:

- When you insert or append a new item, specify that you want to use a bitmap instead of text for that item.

- Use the **ModifyMenu** function to change an existing item so that it appears as a bitmap instead of text.

You cannot specify a bitmap as a menu item in the .RC file.

The following example loads a bitmap named Apples and then uses the **Modify-Menu** function to replace the text of the Apples menu item with this bitmap image of an apple.

```
HMENU hMenu;
HBITMAP hBitmap;
    .
    .
    .

hBitmap = LoadBitmap(hinst, "Apples");

hMenu = GetMenu(hWnd);
ModifyMenu(hMenu,
    IDM_APPLES,                  /* item to replace           */
    MF_BYCOMMAND | MF_BITMAP,
    IDM_APPLES,                  /* menu identifier of new item */
    (LPSTR) MAKELONG(hBitmap, 0))
```

In this example, the **LoadBitmap** function first loads the bitmap from the file and returns a handle of the bitmap, saved in the hBitmap variable.

The **GetMenu** function then retrieves the handle of the current window's menu and places it in the variable hMenu. This variable is passed as the first parameter of the **ModifyMenu** function, which specifies the menu to change. The second parameter of the **ModifyMenu** function—in this case, IDM_APPLES—specifies the item to be modified.

The third parameter specifies how to make the changes. MF_BYCOMMAND indicates to Windows that you are specifying the item to be changed by its menu identifier rather than by its position. MF_BITMAP indicates that the new item will be a bitmap rather than text.

The fourth parameter, set to IDM_APPLES, specifies the new menu identifier for the item being modified. In this example, the menu identifier does not change.

The new bitmap handle must be passed as the low-order word of the fifth parameter of **ModifyMenu**. The **MAKELONG** macro combines the 16-bit handle with a 16-bit constant to make the 32-bit argument. Casting the parameter to an **LPSTR** data type prevents the compiler from issuing a warning, since the compiler "expects" this parameter to be a string.

7.5.7 Replacing Menus

You can replace menus by using the **SetMenu** function. Typically, you replace a menu when the application changes modes and requires a completely new set of commands. For example, an application might replace a spreadsheet menu with a charting menu when the user changes from a spreadsheet to a charting mode.

In the following example, the **GetMenu** function retrieves the menu handle of the spreadsheet menu and saves it in order for it to be restored later. The **SetMenu** function replaces the spreadsheet menu with a charting menu loaded from the application's resources.

```
HMENU hMenu, hOldMenu;
HMENU hSpreadsheetMenu;
    .
    .
    .

hOldMenu = GetMenu(hWnd);
hMenu = LoadMenu(hinst, "ChartMenu");
SetMenu(hWnd, hMenu);
    .
    .
    .
```

You can also load menus from resources other than those belonging to the application (by using the module handle of a library).

7.5.8 Creating New Menus

You can create new menus while your application runs, using the **CreateMenu** function. **CreateMenu** creates a new, empty menu; you can then add items to it by using the **AppendMenu** or **InsertMenu** function. The following example creates an empty pop-up menu and appends it to the window's menu. It then appends three items to the new pop-up menu.

```
HMENU hWinMenu;
HMENU hVeggieMenu;
    .
    .
    .

hVeggieMenu = CreateMenu();

AppendMenu(hWinMenu,
    MF_POPUP | MF_ENABLED,
    hVeggieMenu,
    "Veggies");

AppendMenu(hVeggieMenu,
    MF_ENABLED,
    IDM_CELERY,
    "Celery");
```

```
AppendMenu(hVeggieMenu,
    MF_ENABLED,
    IDM_LETTUCE,
    "Lettuce");

AppendMenu(hVeggieMenu,
    MF_ENABLED,
    IDM_PEAS,
    "Peas");
```

7.5.9 Initializing Menus

Your application can, if necessary, initialize a menu before Windows displays the menu. Although you can specify a menu item's initial state (disabled, grayed, or checked) in the resource-definition file, this method does not work if the initialization differs from time to time. For example, to disable the Print command only if the user's system has no printer installed, you could disable the Print item when you initialize its menu. (Disabling the Print item in the .RC file would not work, since the application cannot determine whether a printer is available until the application is running.)

Just before Windows displays a menu, it sends a WM_INITMENU message to the window procedure for the window that owns that menu. This enables the window procedure to check the state of the menu items and, if necessary, modify them before Windows displays the menu. In the following example, the window function processes the WM_INITMENU message and sets the state of a menu item, based on the value of the wChecked variable:

```
WORD wChecked = IDM_LEFT;
    .
    .
    .

case WM_INITMENU:
    if (GetMenu(hWnd) != wParam)
        break;
    CheckMenuItem(wParam, IDM_LEFT,
        IDM_LEFT == wChecked ? MF_CHECKED : MF_UNCHECKED);
    CheckMenuItem(wParam, IDM_CENTER,
        IDM_CENTER == wChecked ? MF_CHECKED : MF_UNCHECKED);
    CheckMenuItem(wParam, IDM_RIGHT,
        IDM_RIGHT == wChecked ? MF_CHECKED : MF_UNCHECKED);
    break;
```

In this example, the WM_INITMENU message passes the given menu handle in the *wParam* message parameter.

To ensure that Windows is about to display the correct menu, the **GetMenu** function retrieves a handle of the current window's menu and compares that handle with the value of *wParam*. If these are not equal, the window's menu should not be initialized. Otherwise, the menu is correct and you can use the **CheckMenu-Item** function to initialize the items in the menu.

7.6 Using Special Menu Features

So far, this chapter has discussed "standard" menus, which drop down from a menu bar that contains items the user selects by using the mouse, the arrow keys, or mnemonics. In addition to these menu features, Windows provides the following special features:

- Accelerator keys, which provide a keyboard shortcut for selecting menu items
- Cascading menus, which you can use to create several levels of pop-up menus
- Floating pop-up menus, which are normal pop-up menus except that they can appear anywhere on the screen (usually at the current mouse position)
- Customized check marks, for which you use your own bitmaps instead of using the standard Windows check mark.

7.6.1 Providing Accelerator Keys for Menus and Menu Items

Accelerator keys are shortcut keys with which the user can choose a command from a menu by using a single keystroke. For example, a user could select the Delete command simply by pressing the DEL key. Accelerator keys are part of the resource-definition file and are tied into the application through the C-language source code.

To provide accelerator keys to menus and menu items in your application, follow these steps:

1. In the resource-definition file, mark the accelerator key for each item in the **MENUITEM** statements.
2. In the resource-definition file, create an accelerator table. An accelerator table lists the accelerator keys and corresponding menu identifiers. You create it using the **ACCELERATORS** resource statement.
3. In the C-language source file, load the accelerator table by using the **LoadAccelerators** function.
4. Change the message loop so that it processes accelerator-key messages.

7.6.1.1 Adding Accelerator Text to a Menu Item

The menu text should indicate each item's accelerator key so that the user can tell
which key to use for the command. Add the key assignments to the **MENUITEM**
definitions in the .RC file. For example, suppose your application has the following pop-up menu defined in its resource-definition file:

```
GroceryMenu MENU
    POPUP         "&Meats"
    BEGIN
        MENUITEM      "&Beef\tF9",          IDM_BEEF
        MENUITEM      "&Chicken\tShift+F9",  IDM_CHICKEN
        MENUITEM      "&Lamb\tCtrl+F9",      IDM_LAMB
        MENUITEM      "&Pork\tAlt+F9",       IDM_PORK
    END
END
```

The pop-up menu Meats has the four items Beef, Chicken, Lamb, and Pork. Each
item has a mnemonic, indicated by the ampersand (&), and an accelerator key separated from the name with a tab (\t). Whenever a menu item has a corresponding
accelerator key, it should be displayed in this way. The accelerator keys in this
sample are F9, SHIFT+F9, CTRL+F9, and ALT+F9.

7.6.1.2 Creating an Accelerator Table

To use accelerator keys, add an accelerator table to the resource-definition file
by using the **ACCELERATORS** statement. This statement lists the accelerator
keys and the corresponding menu identifiers of the associated items. In the
ACCELERATORS statement, as with other resource statements, **BEGIN** starts
the entry and **END** marks its end. Following is a typical accelerator table:

```
GroceryMenu ACCELERATORS
BEGIN
    VK_F9,    IDM_BEEF,      VIRTKEY
    VK_F9,    IDM_CHICKEN,   VIRTKEY, SHIFT
    VK_F9,    IDM_LAMB,      VIRTKEY, CONTROL
    VK_F9,    IDM_PORK,      VIRTKEY, ALT
END
```

This example defines four accelerator keys, one for each menu item. The first accelerator key is simply the F9 key; the other three are key combinations using the
ALT, SHIFT, or CTRL key in combination with the F9 key.

The accelerator keys are defined by using the Windows virtual-key code, as indicated by the **VIRTKEY** option. Virtual keys are device-independent key values
that Windows translates for each computer. These keys offer a way to guarantee
that the same key is used on all computers without your needing to know what the
actual value of the key is on any computer. You may also use ASCII key codes for
accelerators, in which case, you would use the ASCII option.

The **ACCELERATORS** statement associates each accelerator key with a menu identifier. In the preceding example, the IDM_BEEF, IDM_CHICKEN, IDM_LAMB, and IDM_PORK constants are the menu identifiers of the items on the Grocery menu. When the user presses an accelerator key, these are the values that are passed to the window procedure.

7.6.1.3 Loading an Accelerator Table

The accelerator table, like any other resource, must be loaded before your application can use it. To load the accelerator table, use the **LoadAccelerators** function. This function takes a handle of the current instance of the application and the name of the accelerator table (as defined in the .RC file); it returns a handle of the accelerator table for the associated menu. Typically, you load a menu's accelerator table when that menu's window has just been created—that is, within the WM_CREATE case of the window procedure. The following example shows how to load an accelerator table:

```
HINSTANCE hinst;      /* handle of current instance  */
HACCEL hAccTable;     /* handle of accelerator table */
    .
    .
    .

case WM_CREATE:

hAccTable = LoadAccelerators(hinst, "GroceryMenu");
    break;
```

In this example, the **LoadAccelerators** function loads the accelerator table for GroceryMenu into memory. The function then assigns the handle identifying the table to the hAccTable variable. The hinst variable identifies the application's resource-definition file; GroceryMenu is the name of the accelerator table.

Once the table is loaded, the application can use the **TranslateAccelerator** function to translate accelerator keys for that menu.

7.6.1.4 Changing the Message Loop to Process Accelerator Keys

To use the accelerator table, you must add the **TranslateAccelerator** function to the message loop. When the message loop receives a keyboard-input message containing an accelerator key, **TranslateAccelerator** converts the message to a WM_COMMAND message containing the appropriate menu identifier for that accelerator key, and sends the resulting WM_COMMAND message to the window procedure.

The message loop should test each message to determine whether it is an accelerator-key message; if it is, the loop should translate and dispatch the message by using **TranslateAccelerator**. If the message is not an accelerator-key message, the loop should process it as usual.

Note   TranslateAccelerator also translates accelerator keys for commands the user chooses from the System menu. In such cases, the function translates the keyboard-input message into a WM_SYSCOMMAND message.

After you add the **TranslateAccelerator** function, the message loop should look like this:

```
while (GetMessage(&msg, NULL, NULL, NULL)) {

    if (!TranslateAccelerator(hWnd, hAccTable, &msg)) {
        TranslateMessage(&msg);
        DispatchMessage(&msg);
    }
}
```

In this example, the **TranslateAccelerator** function checks each message to determine whether it is an accelerator-key message. If the message is an accelerator-key message, the window handle hWnd identifies the window whose messages are to be translated (if any are found). The window handle must identify the window that contains the menu with the accelerator keys. The accelerator handle hAccTable specifies the accelerator table to use when translating the accelerator keys. If the message was generated by means of an accelerator key, the **Translate-Accelerator** function converts the keystroke to a WM_COMMAND message containing the appropriate menu identifier, and sends that WM_COMMAND message to the window procedure.

If the message is not an accelerator-key message, the application processes it as usual, by using the **TranslateMessage** and **DispatchMessage** functions.

7.6.2 Using Cascading Menus

You can provide more than one level of pop-up menus in your applications. Such multilevel pop-up menus are called cascading menus. A multilevel menu structure can help minimize the number of items on a single pop-up menu, without requiring a dialog box in which the user refines his or her choice. The following figure shows an example of cascading menus:

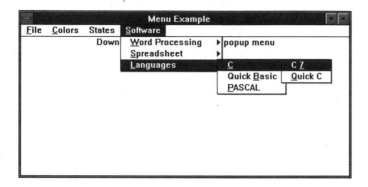

In this example, the user selected the Software menu and then chose the Languages command from the Software menu. At this point, the Languages pop-up menu appeared to the right of the cursor. The user then moved the cursor over the Languages pop-up menu and chose "C." The C pop-up menu then appeared, from which the user chose either C version 7.0 or QuickC (Microsoft QuickC®).

Cascading menus are simply nested pop-up menus. The menu definition for the preceding example in figure looks like this:

```
MenuMenu MENU
BEGIN
    .
    .
    .

    POPUP "&Software"
       BEGIN

       POPUP "&Word Processing"
            BEGIN
            MENUITEM  "&Word 5.0", IDM_WORD
            MENUITEM  "W&rite", IDM_WRITE
            END

       POPUP "&Spreadsheet"
            BEGIN
            MENUITEM "&Microsoft Excel", IDM_EXCEL
            MENUITEM "&1+2=4", IDM_124
            END
```

```
        POPUP "&Languages"
            BEGIN
            POPUP "&C"
                BEGIN
                MENUITEM "C &7.0", IDM_C60
                MENUITEM "&Quick C", IDM_QUICKC
                END
            MENUITEM  "Quick &Basic", IDM_QUICKBASIC
            MENUITEM  "&PASCAL", IDM_PASCAL
            END
    END
        .
        .
        .

END
```

Note A cascading pop-up menu has its own menu handle. To control items on a cascading pop-up menu, you must first retrieve a handle of the menu by calling the **GetSubMenu** function.

7.6.3 Using Floating Pop-up Menus

Usually, pop-up menus are attached to another menu—that is, they appear when the user chooses a command on that menu. With Windows, however, you can also provide pop-up menus that float, which means they appear at the current cursor position when the user presses a certain key or clicks a mouse button.

To create a floating pop-up menu, you use the **CreatePopupMenu** and **Track-PopupMenu** functions. If you want the floating pop-up menu to appear when the user presses a certain key or mouse button, create the floating pop-up menu within the **case** statement that handles the input message from that key or button.

The following example displays a floating pop-up menu when the user presses the left mouse button:

```
    case WM_LBUTTONDOWN:
        GetClientRect(hWnd, (LPRECT)&rc);
        if (PtInRect((LPRECT)&rc, MAKEPOINT(lParam)))
            HandlePopupMenu(hWnd, MAKEPOINT(lParam));
        break;
        .
        .
        .
```

```
void FAR PASCAL HandlePopupMenu(hwnd, point)
HWND    hwnd;
POINT   point;

{
    HMENU hMenu;
    HMENU hMenuTrackPopup;

    /* Get the menu for the pop-up menu from the resource file. */

    hMenu = LoadMenu(hInst, "PopupMenu");
    if (!hMenu)
        return;

    /*
     * Get the first menu in the pop-up menu to use in the call
     * to TrackPopupMenu. This could also have been created by
     * using CreatePopupMenu and then added by using InsertMenu
     * or AppendMenu.
     */

    hMenuTrackPopup = GetSubMenu(hMenu, 0);

    /*
     * Convert the mouse point to screen coordinates, because that
     * is what TrackPopup expects.
     */

    ClientToScreen(hwnd, (LPPOINT)&point);

    /* Draw and track the "floating" pop-up menu. */

    TrackPopupMenu(hMenuTrackPopup, 0, point.x, point.y, 0, hwnd, NULL);

    DestroyMenu(hMenu);
}
```

In this example, the *lParam* parameter of the WM_LBUTTONDOWN message contains the current position of the mouse. The **MAKEPOINT** macro converts this long value to a point, which is then stored in the currentpoint structure.

Once the menu is complete, the application displays it at the current cursor position by calling **TrackPopupMenu**. (The x and y members of the currentpoint structure specify the current position of the cursor.)

After the user has chosen a command from the menu, the application destroys the menu, freeing the memory the menu used. The application re-creates the menu each time the user presses the right mouse button.

7.6.4 Designing Your Own Check Marks

Usually when you check a menu item, Windows displays the standard Windows check mark next to the item's text. An item that is not checked has no special mark next to it at all. Instead of using the standard Windows check mark, however, you can specify a bitmap that Windows will display when a menu item is checked. You can also specify a bitmap to display when an item is not checked (cleared).

Custom check marks can be particularly useful for helping the user distinguish between commands that perform an action and commands that can be checked but are not. Some Windows applications use the following menu-item conventions based on certain types of commands:

Type of command	Convention
Commands that perform an action (for example, display another menu or a dialog box)	Do not display a check mark for such an item.
Commands that are currently checked	Display either a normal Windows check mark or a custom check mark. When the user chooses a checked item again, the check mark is cleared.
Commands that can be checked but are not	Display a custom check mark. When the user chooses a cleared item, either a standard Windows check mark or a different custom check mark is displayed.

To provide your own check-mark bitmaps, follow these steps:

1. Use Microsoft Image Editor (IMAGEDIT.EXE) to create the bitmaps you want to use as check marks.

   Windows requires that your check-mark bitmaps be the same size as the standard check marks. Although you can, during run time, stretch or shrink your check-mark bitmaps to the right size, try to start with a bitmap that is close to the right size. (The size of the standard check marks depends on the current screen. To determine the current size of the standard check marks, use the **Get-MenuCheckMarkDimensions** function.)

   You can also create a bitmap by hand—by coding the individual bits. For more information, see Chapter 11, "Bitmaps."

2. In your application's resource-definition file, define each bitmap's name and source file by using the **BITMAP** statement, as in the following example:

```
BitmapChecked BITMAP check.bmp
BitmapNotChecked BITMAP nocheck.bmp
```

3. In your application source code, use the **LoadBitmap** function to load each bitmap from your application resources.

4. Use the **GetMenuCheckMarkDimensions** function to determine the size of the standard check marks on the current screen.

5. If necessary, use the **StretchBlt** function to stretch or shrink each bitmap to the right size.

6. Use the **SetMenuItemBitmaps** function to specify the check-mark bitmaps for each menu item.

7. Before your application terminates, it should destroy the bitmaps to free memory.

The following example shows how to specify check-mark bitmaps for a menu item:

```
SetMenuItemBitmaps(hMenu,        /* menu handle            */
    0,                           /* position of menu item  */
    MF_BYPOSITION,
    hbmCheckOff,                 /* bitmap for cleared item */
    hbmCheckOn);                 /* bitmap for checked item */
```

7.6.5 Using Owner-Drawn Menu Items

Your application can take complete control over the appearance of menu items by using owner-drawn items. An owner-drawn item is one for which your application has total responsibility for drawing in its normal, selected (highlighted), checked, and cleared states.

For example, suppose your application provides a menu from which the user can choose a font. Your application could draw each item by using the font that the item represents; the item for roman would be drawn with a roman font, the item for italic would be drawn in italic, and so on.

You cannot define an owner-drawn item in your application's resource-definition (.RC) file. Instead, you must create a new item or modify an existing one by using the MF_OWNERDRAW menu flag. You can use any of the following functions to specify an owner-drawn menu item:

- **AppendMenu**
- **InsertMenu**
- **ModifyMenu**

When you call any of these functions, you can pass a 32-bit value as the *lpNewItem* parameter. This 32-bit value can represent any information that is meaningful to your application, and will be available to your application when the item is to be displayed. For example, the value could contain a pointer to a structure; the structure, in turn, might contain a string and the handle of a logical font that your application will use to draw the string.

Before Windows displays an owner-drawn item for the first time, it sends the WM_MEASUREITEM message to the window that owns the item's menu. This message's *lParam* parameter points to a **MEASUREITEMSTRUCT** structure that identifies the item and contains the optional 32-bit value for the item. When your application receives the WM_MEASUREITEM message, it must fill in the **itemWidth** and **itemHeight** members of the structure before returning from processing the message. Windows uses the information in these members when creating the bounding rectangle in which your application draws the menu item; it also uses the information to detect the user's interaction with the command associated with the item.

When the item must be drawn (for example, when it is first displayed or when the user chooses it as a command), Windows sends the WM_DRAWITEM message to the window that owns the menu. The *lParam* parameter of the WM_DRAWITEM message points to a **DRAWITEMSTRUCT** structure. Like the **MEASUREITEMSTRUCT** structure, **DRAWITEMSTRUCT** contains information about the item and its optional 32-bit data. In addition, **DRAWITEM-STRUCT** contains flags that indicate the state of the item (such as grayed or checked) as well as a bounding rectangle and a device context with which your application will draw the item.

In response to the WM_DRAWITEM message, your application must perform the following actions before returning from processing the message:

1. Determine the type of drawing that is necessary. To do so, check the **item-Action** member of the **DRAWITEMSTRUCT** structure.

2. Draw the menu item appropriately, using the bounding rectangle and device context obtained from the **DRAWITEMSTRUCT** structure. Your application must draw only within the bounding rectangle. For performance reasons, Windows does not clip portions of the image that are drawn outside the rectangle.

3. Restore all GDI objects selected for the menu item's device context.

For example, if the menu item is selected, Windows sets the **itemAction** member of the **DRAWITEMSTRUCT** structure to ODA_SELECT, and sets the ODS_SELECTED bit in the **itemState** member. This is your application's cue to redraw the menu item so that the item indicates that it has been selected.

7.7 Sample Application: EditMenu

The EditMenu sample application illustrates the two most common menus, the Edit menu and the File menu, and shows how to use accelerator keys in an application.

Note The accelerator keys shown in this sample are reserved and should be used only as accelerator keys for the Edit menu.

To create the EditMenu application, make the following modifications to the Generic application:

1. Add the Edit and File menus to the resource-definition file.
2. Add definitions to the header file.
3. Add an accelerator table to the resource-definition file.
4. Add a new variable.
5. Load the accelerator table.
6. Modify the message loop in the **WinMain** function.
7. Modify the WM_COMMAND case.
8. Compile and link the application.

EditMenu does not show how to use the clipboard. This task is described in Chapter 13, "Clipboard."

7.7.1 Adding New Menus to the Resource-Definition File

You must add an Edit and a File menu to the **MENU** statement in the resource-definition file. The **MENU** statement should now look like this:

```
EditMenuMenu MENU
BEGIN
    POPUP       "&File"
    BEGIN
        MENUITEM    "&New",                 IDM_NEW
        MENUITEM    "&Open...",             IDM_OPEN
        MENUITEM    "&Save",                IDM_SAVE
        MENUITEM    "Save &As...",          IDM_SAVEAS
        MENUITEM    "&Print",               IDM_PRINT
        MENUITEM    SEPARATOR
        MENUITEM    "E&xit",                IDM_EXIT
        MENUITEM    SEPARATOR
        MENUITEM    "&About EditMenu...",        IDM_ABOUT
    END
```

```
POPUP  "&Edit"
    BEGIN
        MENUITEM    "&Undo\tAlt+BkSp",      IDM_UNDO    ,GRAYED
        MENUITEM    SEPARATOR
        MENUITEM    "Cu&t\tShift+Del",      IDM_CUT
        MENUITEM    "&Copy\tCtrl+Ins",      IDM_COPY
        MENUITEM    "&Paste\tShift+Ins",    IDM_PASTE   ,GRAYED
        MENUITEM    "C&lear\tDel",          IDM_CLEAR   ,GRAYED
    END

END
```

The File menu contains seven items and two separators. Each item has a mnemonic, indicated by the ampersand (&).

The Edit menu contains five items and a separator. Each item has a mnemonic and an accelerator key, which is separated from the name by a tab (\t). Whenever an item has a corresponding accelerator key, it should be displayed in this way. In the Edit menu, the five accelerator keys are ALT+BKSP, DEL, CTRL+INS, SHIFT+INS, and SHIFT+DEL. The separator between the Undo and Cut items places a horizontal bar between these items in the menu. A separator is recommended between menu items that otherwise have nothing in common. For example, the Undo command, when chosen, affects only the application, whereas the remaining commands affect the clipboard.

7.7.2 Adding Definitions to the Header File

You must declare each menu identifier in your application's header file. These constants are used both in the C-language source file and in the resource-definition file.

A menu identifier can be any integer value. The only restriction is that it must be unique within a menu, because no two items in a menu can have the same identifier.

Add the following lines to the header file:

```
#define IDM_ABOUT 100

/* File-menu items */

#define    IDM_NEW        101
#define    IDM_OPEN       102
#define    IDM_SAVE       103
#define    IDM_SAVEAS     104
#define    IDM_PRINT      105
#define    IDM_EXIT       106
```

```
/* Edit-menu items */

#define    IDM_UNDO    200
#define    IDM_CUT     201
#define    IDM_COPY    202
#define    IDM_PASTE   203
#define    IDM_CLEAR   204
```

7.7.3 Adding an Accelerator Table to the Resource-Definition File

Add the following **ACCELERATORS** statement to the resource-definition file:

```
EditMenu ACCELERATORS
BEGIN
    VK_BACK,   IDM_UNDO,  VIRTKEY, ALT
    VK_DEL, IDM_CUT,    VIRTKEY, SHIFT
    VK_INS, IDM_COPY,   VIRTKEY, CONTROL
    VK_INS, IDM_PASTE,  VIRTKEY, SHIFT
    VK_DEL, IDM_CLEAR,  VIRTKEY
END
```

This statement defines five accelerator keys, one for each menu item. Four accelerators are key combinations using the ALT, SHIFT, or CTRL key.

The **ACCELERATORS** statement associates each accelerator key with a menu identifier. The IDM_UNDO, IDM_CUT, IDM_COPY, IDM_PASTE, and IDM_CLEAR constants identify the Edit-menu items. When the user presses an accelerator key, these are the values that are passed to the window procedure.

7.7.4 Adding a New Variable

Add the following statement to the beginning of the source file:

```
HACCEL hAccTable;        /* handle of accelerator table */
```

The hAccTable variable is a handle of the accelerator table. It receives the return value of the **LoadAccelerators** function and is used in the **TranslateAccelerator** function to identify the accelerator table.

7.7.5 Loading the Accelerator Table

Before using the accelerator table, you must load it from the application's resources. Add the following statements to the application's InitInstance function:

```
hAccTable = LoadAccelerators(hinst, "EditMenu");
```

This statement loads the accelerator table into memory and assigns the handle identifying the table to the hAccTable variable. The hinst variable identifies the application's resource-definition file, and EditMenu is the name of the accelerator table. After you have loaded the table, you can use it in the **TranslateAccelerator** function.

7.7.6 Modifying the Message Loop

To use the accelerator table, you must add the **TranslateAccelerator** function to the message loop. After you add the function, the message loop should look like this:

```
while (GetMessage(&msg, NULL, NULL, NULL)) {

    if (!TranslateAccelerator(hWnd, hAccTable, &msg)) {
        TranslateMessage(&msg);
        DispatchMessage(&msg);
    }
}
```

7.7.7 Modifying the WM_COMMAND Case

Your application must be able to process menu commands. In this application, instead of performing tasks, all menu commands activate a "Command not implemented" message box. Replace the WM_COMMAND case with the following statements:

```
case WM_COMMAND:
    switch (wParam) {
        case IDM_ABOUT:
            lpProcAbout =
                MakeProcInstance((FARPROC) About, hInst);
            DialogBox(hInst, "AboutBox", hWnd,
                (DLGPROC) lpProcAbout);
            FreeProcInstance(lpProcAbout);
            break;

        /* File-menu commands */

        case IDM_NEW:
        case IDM_OPEN:
        case IDM_SAVE:
        case IDM_SAVEAS:
        case IDM_PRINT:
```

```
                    MessageBox(
                        GetFocus(),
                        "Command not implemented",
                        "EditMenu Sample Application",
                        MB_ICONASTERISK | MB_OK);
                    break;

                case IDM_EXIT:
                    DestroyWindow(hWnd);
                    break;

                /* Edit-menu commands */

                case IDM_UNDO:
                case IDM_CUT:
                case IDM_COPY:
                case IDM_PASTE:
                case IDM_CLEAR:
                    MessageBox(
                        GetFocus(),
                        "Command not implemented",
                        "EditMenu Sample Application",
                        MB_ICONASTERISK | MB_OK);
                    break;
            }
            break;
```

7.7.8 Compiling and Linking

Compile and link the EditMenu application. Start Windows and the EditMenu application, and, without opening the pop-up menus, press any of the five accelerator keys. You will notice that the "Command not implemented" message appears when you choose a command.

7.8 Related Topics

For more information about how to process input messages, see Chapter 4, "Keyboard and Mouse Input."

For more information about bitmaps, see Chapter 11, "Bitmaps."

For more information about menu functions and resource-definition statements, see the *Microsoft Windows Programmer's Reference, Volumes 2* and *4.*

Controls

Controls are special windows you can use applications for the Microsoft Windows operating system to make them easier to use.

This chapter covers the following topics:

- What a control is
- Creating a control
- Using controls in application windows

This chapter also explains how to create a sample Windows 3.1 application, EditCntl, that illustrates those concepts.

8.1   What Is a Control?

A control is a predefined child window that carries out a specific kind of input or output. For example, to make your application retrieve a filename from the user, you can create and display an edit control in which the user types the filename. An edit control is a window that receives and displays keyboard input.

A control, like any other window, belongs to a window class. The window class defines both the control's window procedure and its default attributes. The window procedure is important because it determines the appearance of the control and how it will respond to user input. Window procedures for controls are predefined in Windows, so no extra coding is required in your application when you use a control.

8.2   Creating a Control

In Windows, you can create a control either from within a dialog box or from within the client area of any other type of window.

This chapter discusses using controls in a standard window. For information about how to create controls within a dialog box, see Chapter 9, "Dialog Boxes."

To create a control in a window other than a dialog box, use the **CreateWindow** function. When creating the control, specify its window class, style, parent window, and identifier. If **CreateWindow** is successful, it returns a control handle that you can use in subsequent functions to move, size, paint, or destroy a window, or to direct a window to carry out tasks.

The following example shows how to create a push button control:

```
hButtonWnd = CreateWindow(
    "BUTTON",                              /* control class     */
    "OK",                                  /* button label      */
    BS_PUSHBUTTON | WS_CHILD | WS_VISIBLE, /* control styles    */
    20,                                    /* x-coordinate      */
    40,                                    /* y-coordinate      */
    30,                                    /* width in pixels   */
    12,                                    /* height in pixels  */
    hWnd,                                  /* parent window     */
    IDOK,                                  /* control identifier */
    hinst,                                 /* instance handle   */
    NULL);
```

This example creates a push button that belongs to the BUTTON window class and has the BS_PUSHBUTTON style. The push button is a child window and will be visible when first created. The WS_CHILD style is required, but you need not specify the WS_VISIBLE style if you plan to use the **ShowWindow** function to show the push button. **CreateWindow** places the button at the coordinates (20,40) in the parent window's client area. The width and height are 30 and 12 pixels, respectively. The parent window is identified by the hWnd handle. The constant IDOK identifies the push button.

8.2.1 Specifying a Control Class

The control's window class, or control class, defines the control's window procedure and default attributes. You specify a control class when creating the control, by including the class name (for example, BUTTON) in the *lpClassName* parameter of the **CreateWindow** function.

Windows provides the following built-in control classes:

Class	Description
BUTTON	Produces a small, labeled window that the user can choose in order to generate yes or no, on or off types of input.
EDIT	Produces a window in which the user can type and edit text (called an edit control).
LISTBOX	Produces a window that contains a list of names from which the user can select one or more names.
COMBOBOX	Produces a combination control consisting of an edit control linked with a list box. The user can select items from the list box or type in the edit control or do both.
SCROLLBAR	Produces a window that looks and functions like a scroll bar in a window.
STATIC	Produces a small window that contains text or simple graphics. Static controls are often used to label other controls or to separate a group of controls.

8.2.2 Choosing a Control Style

The control styles, which depend on the control class, determine the control's appearance and function. You specify a control style when creating the control, by including the style (for example, BS_PUSHBUTTON) in the *dwStyle* parameter of the **CreateWindow** function.

Windows provides many predefined control styles. Following are some of the most common:

Style	Description
BS_PUSHBUTTON	Specifies a push button, a small window containing a label that the user can choose in order to notify the parent window.
BS_DEFPUSHBUTTON	Specifies a default push button, which is identical to a push button except that it has a special border.
BS_CHECKBOX	Specifies a check box, which the user can select to turn the control on or off. When the control is on, the box contains an X.
BS_RADIOBUTTON	Specifies a radio button (a circle). The user can select the circle to turn the control on or off. When the control is on, the circle contains a solid bullet.
ES_LEFT	Specifies a single-line, left-aligned edit control.
ES_MULTILINE	Specifies a multiline edit control.
SS_LEFT	Specifies a left-aligned, static edit control.
SS_RIGHT	Specifies a right-aligned, static edit control.
LBS_STANDARD	Specifies a standard list box. A standard list box includes a scroll bar and notifies its parent window when the user makes a selection.
CBS_DROPDOWN	Specifies a combo box consisting of an edit control and a list box that is displayed when the user selects a box next to the selection field. If the user selects an item in the list box, the edit control displays the selected item.

For a complete list of control styles, see the *Microsoft Windows Programmer's Reference, Volume 4.*

8.2.3 Setting the Parent Window

Because every control is a child window, it requires a parent window. You specify the parent window when creating the control, by including the handle of the parent window in the *hWndParent* parameter of the **CreateWindow** function.

As with any child window, a control is affected by changes to its parent window. For example, if Windows disables the parent window, it also disables the control.

If Windows paints, moves, or destroys the parent window, it also paints, moves, or destroys the control.

Although a control can be any size and can be moved to any position, it is restricted to the client area of the parent window. Windows clips the control if you move it outside the parent window's client area or make it larger than the client area.

8.2.4 Choosing a Control Identifier

When you create a control, you give it a unique identifier. You do this by including it in the *hMenu* parameter of the **CreateWindow** function. The control supplies its identifier in any notification message it sends to the window procedure of the parent window. The control identifier is especially useful if you have several controls in a window. It is the quickest, easiest way to distinguish one control from another.

8.3 Using Controls

Once you have created a control, you have several options:

- Receiving user input through the control
- Performing specialized tasks, such as returning a string of text
- Enabling or disabling input to the control
- Moving or sizing the control
- Destroying the control

8.3.1 Receiving User Input

As the user interacts with the control, the control sends information about the interaction, in the form of a notification message, to the parent window. A notification message is a WM_COMMAND message in which the *wParam* parameter contains the control identifier and the *lParam* parameter contains the notification code and the control handle.

For example, when the user clicks a button, the button sends a WM_COMMAND message to the window procedure of the parent window. The WM_COMMAND message's *wParam* parameter contains the button's control identifier; the high-order word of the message's *lParam* parameter contains the notification code BN_CLICKED, which indicates that the user has clicked the button.

Since a notification message has the same basic form as menu input, you process notification messages much as you would menu input. If you have carefully selected control identifiers so that they do not conflict with menu identifiers, you can process notification messages in the same **switch** statement you use to process menu input.

8.3.2 Sending Control Messages

Most controls accept and process a variety of control messages, which are special messages that direct the control to carry out some task that is unique to the control. For example, the WM_GETTEXTLENGTH message directs an edit control to return the length of a selected line of text.

To send a control message to a control, use the **SendMessage** function. Supply the message number and any required *wParam* and *lParam* parameter values. For example, the following statement sends the WM_GETTEXTLENGTH message to the edit control identified by the handle hEditWnd; it then returns the length of the selected line in the edit control:

```
nLength = SendMessage(hEditWnd, WM_GETTEXTLENGTH, 0, 0L);
```

Many controls also process standard window messages, such as WM_HSCROLL and WM_VSCROLL. To send such messages to controls, use the same method you use to send control messages.

8.3.3 Disabling and Enabling Input to a Control

To disable or enable input to a control, use the **EnableWindow** function.

When you disable a control, it does not respond to user input. So that the user can tell that the control is disabled, it appears dimmed. To disable a control, use **EnableWindow**, specifying the value FALSE for the *fEnable* parameter, as follows:

```
EnableWindow(hButton, FALSE);
```

To restore input to the disabled control, enable it by using the **EnableWindow** function with *fEnable* set to TRUE, as follows:

```
EnableWindow(hButton, TRUE);
```

8.3.4 Moving and Sizing a Control

To move or size a control, use the **MoveWindow** function. This function moves the control to the specified coordinates in the parent window's client area and sets the control to the given width and height. The following example shows how to use **MoveWindow** to move and size a control:

```
MoveWindow(hButtonWnd, 10, 10, 30, 12, TRUE);
```

This example moves a control to the coordinates (10,10) in the client area and sets the width and height to 30 and 12 pixels, respectively. The value TRUE specifies that the control should be repainted after being moved.

Windows automatically moves a control when moving the parent window. A control's position is always relative to the upper-left corner of the parent's client area, so when the parent window moves, the control remains fixed in the client area but moves relative to the screen. Although Windows does not size a control when it sizes the parent window, it sends a WM_SIZE message to the parent window to indicate the new size of the parent window. You can use this message to specify a new size for the control.

8.3.5 Destroying a Control

To destroy a control, use the **DestroyWindow** function. This function deletes any internal record of the control and removes it from the parent window's client area. The following example shows how to destroy a control:

```
DestroyWindow(hEditWnd);
```

Windows automatically destroys a control when destroying the parent window. In general, you will need to destroy a control only if you no longer need it in the parent window.

8.4 Creating and Using Some Common Controls

The rest of this chapter explains more about the following common controls:

- Buttons
- Static controls
- List boxes
- Combo boxes
- Edit controls
- Scroll bars

8.4.1 Buttons

A button is a small window used for simple yes or no, on or off types of input. Following are some of the most common types of buttons:

- Push buttons
- Default push buttons
- Check boxes
- Radio buttons
- Owner-drawn buttons
- Group boxes

8.4.1.1 Push Buttons

A push button is a button that the user can select to carry out a specific action. The button contains text that indicates what that button does. When the user clicks a push button, the application usually carries out the associated action immediately. For example, if the user clicks the Cancel button in a dialog box, the application immediately removes the dialog box and cancels the user's changes to the dialog box (if any).

To create a button, specify BUTTON as its window class and specify the button style(s) in the *dwStyle* parameter. For example, the following call to the **CreateWindow** function creates a push button that has the label Cancel:

```
HWND hCancelButton;
      .
      .
      .
hCancelButton = CreateWindow(
    "BUTTON", "Cancel",
    BS_PUSHBUTTON | WS_CHILD | WS_VISIBLE,
    20,40, 80,20, hWnd, IDCANCEL, hinst, NULL);
```

Because this example specifies the WS_VISIBLE style, Windows displays the push button after creating it. The control identifier of the push button is IDCANCEL. This constant is defined in the WINDOWS.H header file and is intended to be used with Cancel push buttons.

8.4.1.2 Default Push Buttons

A default push button typically allows the user to signal the completion of some activity, such as filling in an edit control with a filename. A default push button, as with other buttons, responds to both mouse and keyboard input. If the user clicks the button, the button sends a BN_CLICKED notification message to the parent window. The button need not have the input focus in order to respond to mouse input. It does require the focus, however, to respond to keyboard input. So that the user can call the keyboard, call the **SetFocus** function to give the input focus to the button. The user can then press ENTER or the SPACEBAR to direct the button to send a BN_CLICKED notification message to the parent window.

Creating a default push button is similar to creating a push button. Specify BUTTON as the window class of the button, and specify the button style(s) in the *dwStyle* parameter. For example, the following call to the **CreateWindow** function creates a default push button that has the label OK:

```
HWND hDefButton;
    .
    .
    .

hDefButton = CreateWindow(
    "BUTTON", "OK",
    BS_DEFPUSHBUTTON | WS_CHILD | WS_VISIBLE,
    20,40, 80,20, hWnd, IDOK, hinst, NULL);
```

Since this example specifies the WS_VISIBLE style, Windows displays the default push button after creating it. The control identifier is IDOK. This constant is defined in the WINDOWS.H header file and is intended to be used with default push buttons, such as this OK button.

8.4.1.3 Check Boxes

A check box typically allows the user to select an option to use in the current task. By convention, within a group of check boxes, the user can select more than one option. (To present options that are mutually exclusive, use radio buttons instead of check boxes.)

For example, you might present a group of check boxes from which the user selects font properties for the next output operation. The user could select both bold and italic by checking both the Bold and the Italic check boxes.

To create a check box, use the BS_CHECKBOX style, as in the following example:

```
#define IDC_ITALIC    201
HWND hCheckBox;
    .
    .
    .

hCheckBox = CreateWindow("BUTTON", "Italic",
    BS_CHECKBOX | WS_CHILD | WS_VISIBLE,
    20,40, 80,20, hWnd, IDC_ITALIC, hinst, NULL);
```

In this example, the check box label is Italic and the control identifier is IDC_ITALIC.

A check box responds to mouse and keyboard input much as a push button would. That is, it sends a notification message to the parent window when the user clicks the check box or presses the SPACEBAR. However, a check box can display a check (an X) in its box to show that it is currently selected.

To display a check in a check box, send the control the BM_SETCHECK message. You can also determine whether the check box is already checked by sending the BM_GETCHECK message. For example, to place a check in the check box, use the following function:

```
SendMessage(hCheckBox, BM_SETCHECK, 1, 0L);
```

This means you can select or clear a check box whenever you want; for example, when the parent window procedure receives a BN_CLICKED notification message. Windows also provides a BS_AUTOCHECKBOX style that automatically changes its state (selects or clears it) each time the user clicks it.

8.4.1.4 Radio Buttons

Although radio buttons work in much the same way as check boxes, they are usually used in groups and represent mutually exclusive options. For example, you might use a group of radio buttons to allow the user to specify text alignment (right-aligned, left-aligned, or centered). The user could then select only one type of alignment at a time.

Create a radio button as you would any button. Specify BUTTON as the window class of the radio button, and specify the button style(s) in the *dwStyle* parameter. For example, the following call to the **CreateWindow** function creates a radio button that has the label Right:

```
HWND HRightJustifyButton
#define IDC_RIGHTJUST
    .
    .
    .

hRightJustifyButton = CreateWindow("BUTTON", "Right",
    BS_RADIOBUTTON | WS_CHILD | WS_VISIBLE,
    20, 40, 80, 20, hWnd, IDC_RIGHTJUST, hinst, NULL);
```

As you do with a check box, you must send a BM_SETCHECK message to the radio button to display a check (actually, a solid circle) in the radio button when the user selects that button. Also, since radio buttons represent mutually exclusive choices, you should also send the BM_SETCHECK message to the previously selected radio button (if any) to clear it. You can determine which radio button in a group is selected by sending the BM_GETCHECK message to each button.

You can create radio buttons in a dialog box by using the BS_AUTORADIOBUTTON style. When all the radio buttons in a group box have this style, Windows automatically clears the previously selected button when the user selects a different radio button.

You can also use the **CheckRadioButton** function to select a radio button and clear other buttons in a dialog box. When you call **CheckRadioButton**, you specify the identifiers of the first and last buttons in a range of radio buttons and the identifier of the button (within that range) that is to be selected. Windows clears all the buttons in the specified range and then selects the appropriate radio button. For example, in a group of radio buttons representing types of text alignment, you might call **CheckRadioButton** to select the Right button, as in the following example:

```
CheckRadioButton(hDlg, ID_RIGHTLEFTJUST, ID_LEFTJUST,
    ID_RIGHTJUST)
```

In this example, **CheckRadioButton** would select the radio button identified by ID_RIGHTJUST and clear all the other buttons whose identifiers fall within the range specified by ID_RIGHTLEFTJUST and ID_LEFTJUST, regardless of whether they are radio buttons.

8.4.1.5 Owner-Drawn Buttons

An owner-drawn button is similar to other buttons, except that the application is responsible for maintaining the button's appearance, including whether the button has the input focus, is disabled, or is selected. Windows notifies your application when the button has been clicked.

To create an owner-drawn button, use the BS_OWNERDRAW style, as in the following example:

```
hMyOwnButton = CreateWindow("BUTTON", NULL,
    BS_OWNERDRAW | WS_CHILD | WS_VISIBLE,
    20, 40, 30, 12, hWnd, ID_MYBUTTON,
    hinst, NULL);
```

Whenever the button must be drawn, Windows sends the WM_DRAWITEM message to the window that owns the button. The *lParam* parameter of the WM_DRAWITEM message contains a pointer to a **DRAWITEMSTRUCT** structure. This structure contains, among other information, the control identifier, a value specifying the type of drawing action required, a value indicating the state of the button, a bounding rectangle for the button, and a device-context handle for the button.

In response to the WM_DRAWITEM message, your application must perform the following actions before returning from processing the message:

1. Determine the type of drawing that is required. To do so, the application examines the **itemAction** member of the **DRAWITEMSTRUCT** structure.

2. Draw the button appropriately, using the bounding rectangle and device context obtained from **DRAWITEMSTRUCT**.

3. Restore all graphics device interface (GDI) objects selected for the button's device context.

For example, if the button has lost the input focus, Windows sets the **itemAction** member of **DRAWITEMSTRUCT** to ODA_FOCUS but does not set the ODS_FOCUS bit in the **itemState** member. This is your application's cue to redraw the button so that it no longer appears to have the focus.

8.4.1.6 Group Boxes

Group boxes are rectangles that enclose two or more related buttons or other controls. You can send the WM_SETTEXT message to the group box to place a label in the upper-left corner of the box. Group boxes do not respond to user input; that is, they do not generate notification messages.

8.4.2 Static Controls

A static control is a small window that contains text or graphics. You typically use a static control to label some other control or to create boxes and lines that separate one group of controls from another.

The most commonly used static control is the SS_LEFT style—a left-aligned line of text. That is, the control writes the line's text starting at the left end of the control, displaying as much of the label as will fit in the control and clipping the rest. The control uses the system font for the text, so you can calculate an appropriate size for the control by retrieving the font metrics for this font. For more information about fonts and font metrics, see Chapter 18, "Fonts."

Like group boxes, static controls do not respond to user input; that is, they do not generate notification messages. However, you can change the appearance and location of a static control at any time. For example, you can change the text associated with a static control by using the **SetWindowText** function or the WM_SETTEXT message.

8.4.3 List Boxes

A list box is a box that contains a list of selectable items, such as filenames. You typically use a list box to display a list of items from which the user can select one or more. There are several styles associated with a list box. Following are the most common styles:

List box style	Description
LBS_BORDER	Specifies a surrounding border.
LBS_NOTIFY	Sends notification messages to the parent window when the user selects an item.
LBS_SORT	Sorts its items alphabetically.
WS_VSCROLL	Specifies a vertical scroll bar.

These four styles are included in the LBS_STANDARD style. The following example creates a standard list box:

```
HWND hListBox
#define IDC_LISTBOX 203
    .
    .
    .

hListBox = CreateWindow("Listbox", NULL,
    LBS_STANDARD | WS_CHILD | WS_VISIBLE,
    20, 40, 120, 56, hWnd, IDC_LISTBOX,
    hinst, NULL);
```

8.4.3.1 Adding a String to a List Box

Use the LB_ADDSTRING message to add a string to a list box. This message copies the given string to the list box, which displays it in the list. If the list box has the LBS_SORT style, the string is sorted alphabetically. Otherwise, Windows simply places the string at the end of the list. The following example shows how to add a string:

```
int nIndex;
    .
    .
    .

nIndex = SendMessage(hListBox,
    LB_ADDSTRING, NULL,
    (LONG)(LPSTR) "Horseradish");
```

The LB_ADDSTRING message returns an integer that represents the index of the string in the list. You can use this index in subsequent list box messages to identify the string, but only as long as you do not add, delete, or insert any other string. Doing so may change the string's index.

You can also add a string to a list box by sending the LB_INSERTSTRING message to the list box. Unlike the LB_ADDSTRING message, LB_INSERTSTRING lets you specify where Windows should place the new string in the list box. When it receives the LB_INSERTSTRING message, the list box does not sort the list, even if the list box was created by using the LBS_SORT style.

8.4.3.2 Deleting a String from a List Box

You can delete a string from the list box by supplying the index of the string in the LB_DELETESTRING message, as in the following example:

```
SendMessage(hListBox, LB_DELETESTRING, nIndex, (LPSTR) NULL);
```

8.4.3.3 Adding Filenames to a List Box

As noted previously, a common use for a list box is to display a list of filenames, directories, or disk drives, or a combination of these. The LB_DIR message instructs the list box to fill itself with such a list. The message's *wParam* parameter contains a value specifying the MS-DOS attributes of the files, and the *lParam* parameter points to a string containing a valid filename template, which can include the question mark (?) or asterisk (*) wildcards.

For example, to fill a list box with the names of all files in the current directory that have the .TXT extension, plus a list of directories and disk drives, you would send the LB_DIR message, as in the following example:

```
#define FILE_LIST 4010;
    .
    .
    .

int nFiles;
    .
    .
    .

nFiles = SendMessage(hListBox, LB_DIR, FILE_LIST,
    (LPSTR) "*.TXT");
```

The return value of the LB_DIR message indicates how many items the list box contains.

Note If the list box is in a dialog box, you can call the **DlgDirList** function to perform the same task.

A list box responds to both mouse and keyboard input. If the user clicks a string or presses the SPACEBAR in the list box, the list box selects the string and indicates the selection by inverting the string text and canceling the selection from the last item that was selected, if any. The user can also press a character key to select an item in the list box; the next item in the list box that begins with the character is selected. If the list box has the LBS_NOTIFY style, the list box also sends an LBN_SELCHANGE notification message to the parent window. If the user double-clicks a string and LBS_NOTIFY is specified, the list box sends the LBN_SELCHANGE and LBN_DBLCLK messages to the parent window.

You can always retrieve the index of the selected string by using the LB_GETCURSEL and LB_GETTEXT messages. LB_GETCURSEL retrieves the selection's index in the list box, and LB_GETTEXT retrieves the selection from the list box, copying it to a buffer that you supply.

8.4.3.4 Using a Multiple-Selection List Box

A user can select only one list box item at a time, by default. To allow the user to select more than one item, create the list box by using either of the following styles:

Style	Description
LBS_MULTIPLESEL	A list box created with the LBS_MULTIPLESEL style is the same as a standard list box, except that the user can select more than one item in the list box.
	Pressing the SPACEBAR or clicking on an item in this style of list box changes the selection state of the item. If the user presses a character key while the list box has the focus, the selection moves to the next item that begins with that character; the item is not chosen unless the user presses the SPACEBAR.
LBS_EXTENDEDSEL	A list box created with the LBS_EXTENDEDSEL style provides an easy method for selecting several contiguous items in the list box, as well as for selecting separate items.

8.4.3.5 Using a Multicolumn List Box

Usually, a list box displays its items in a single column. If you anticipate that a list box will contain a large number of items, you may want to create the list box by using the LBS_MULTICOLUMN style. This style specifies a list box that can display its items in several columns, "snaking" the items from the bottom of one column to the next. Because of this, the list box need not be scrolled vertically. However, if the list box may contain more items than it can display at one time, you should create it by using the WM_HSCROLL style to allow the user to scroll the list box horizontally.

The directory window that Windows File Manager displays is an example of a window that contains a multicolumn list box. The following example shows how to create a multicolumn list box that occupies the entire client area of the parent window:

```
#define IDC_MULTILISTBOX
RECT Rect;
HWND hMultiListBox

    .

    .

    .

GetClientRect(hWnd, (LPRECT) &Rect);

hMultiListBox = CreateWindow("Listbox",
    NULL,
    WS_CHILD | WS_VISIBLE | LBS_SORT |
    LBS_MULTICOLUMN | WS_HSCROLL | LBS_NOTIFY,
    Rect.left,
    Rect.top,
    Rect.right,
    Rect.bottom,
    hWnd,
    IDC_MULTILISTBOX,
    hinst,
    NULL);
```

In this example, the **GetClientRect** function retrieves the coordinates of the client area of the parent window, which are then passed to the **CreateWindow** function to set the location and size of the list box.

To set the width of the columns in a multicolumn list box, send the list box a LB_SETCOLUMNWIDTH message.

8.4.3.6 Using an Owner-Drawn List Box

Like a button, a list box can be created as an owner-drawn control. In the case of list boxes, however, your application is required to draw only the items in the list box.

Creating an Owner-Drawn List Box   To create an owner-drawn list box, use the LBS_OWNERDRAWFIXED or LBS_OWNERDRAWVARIABLE style. The LBS_OWNERDRAWFIXED style specifies an owner-drawn list box whose items are the same height; the style LBS_OWNERDRAWVARIABLE specifies a list box whose items can vary in height.

Adding an Item to an Owner-Drawn List Box   To add an item to the list box, send the list box the LB_ADDSTRING or LB_INSERTSTRING message. The message's *lParam* parameter can contain any 32-bit value that you want to associate with the item. If *lParam* contains a pointer to a string, the LBS_HASSTRINGS list box style allows the list box to maintain the memory and pointers for the string. This allows the application to use the LB_GETTEXT message to retrieve the text for the particular item. Also, if you created the list box by using the LBS_HASSTRINGS and the LBS_SORT styles, Windows automatically sorts the items in the list box.

If you create the list box by using the LBS_SORT style (and not the LBS_HASSTRINGS style), Windows cannot determine the order of the items within the list box. In this case, when you add an item to the list box (using the LB_ADDSTRING message), Windows will send one or more WM_COMPAREITEM messages to the owner of the list box. This message's *lParam* parameter points to a **COMPAREITEMSTRUCT** structure that contains identifying information for two items in the list box. When your application returns from processing the message, the return value specifies which of the items should appear above the other. Windows sends this message repeatedly until all the items in the list box are sorted.

Measuring an Item in an Owner-Drawn List Box

When you add or insert an item in a list box, Windows determines the size of the item by sending the WM_MEASUREITEM message to the owner of the list box. Windows requires this information so it can detect the user's interaction with items in the list box. If you created the list box with the LBS_OWNERDRAWFIXED style, Windows sends the message only once, because all the items in the list box will be the same size. For a list box that was created by using the LBS_OWNERDRAWVARIABLE style, Windows sends a WM_MEASUREITEM message for each item when that item is added to the list box.

The *lParam* parameter of WM_MEASUREITEM contains a pointer to a **MEASUREITEMSTRUCT** structure. In addition to the control type and identifier, this structure also contains the number of the list box item to be measured (if the list box is of the LBS_OWNERDRAWVARIABLE style) and optional 32-bit data associated with the item. Each time the owner window receives the WM_MEASUREITEM message, it must fill in the **itemHeight** member of **MEASUREITEMSTRUCT** with the height of the item before returning from processing the message.

Displaying or Updating an Item in an Owner-Drawn List Box

When Windows displays the list box, or whenever the appearance of an item in the list box should change, Windows sends the WM_DRAWITEM message to the window that owns the list box. The *lParam* parameter of the WM_DRAWITEM message contains a pointer to a **DRAWITEMSTRUCT** structure. This structure contains information identifying the list box item and the type of drawing required. As with an owner-drawn button, your application uses this information to determine how to draw the item.

Deleting an Item from an Owner-Drawn List Box   To delete an item from an owner-drawn list box, send the list box a LB_DELETESTRING message. Upon receiving this message, Windows sends a WM_DELETEITEM message to the owner window. (Windows also sends this message for each item when the list box is destroyed.) The *lParam* parameter of this message points to a **DELETEITEM-STRUCT** structure; this structure identifies the list box, the list box item that is being deleted, and the 32-bit optional data associated with the item. Your application should use this information to clean up any memory that was used for the item.

8.4.4 Combo Boxes

A combo box is a single control that consists of a list box combined with a static control or edit control. Depending on the style you use to create the list box, the list box can be displayed at all times, or it can be hidden until the user displays it. Except where noted, the mouse and keyboard interface for the edit control and list box of a combo box is identical to that of a standard edit control or list box.

The CBS_SIMPLE style creates a combo box with an edit control and a list box that is always displayed below the edit control. When the combo box has the focus, the user can type in the edit control. If an item in the list box matches what the user has typed, the matching item moves to the top of the list box. The user can also select items from the list box by using the mouse or the DOWN ARROW and UP ARROW keys.

The CBS_DROPDOWN style is similar to CBS_SIMPLE except that the list box is displayed only if the user selects the arrow next to the edit control or presses the ALT+DOWN ARROW or ALT+UP ARROW key combination. Even when the list box is hidden, the user can select items from the list box by using the UP ARROW and DOWN ARROW keys.

A combo box created with the CBS_DROPDOWNLIST appears identical to a CBS_DROPDOWN combo box, except that the edit control is replaced by a static text field. Instead of typing in the edit control, the user can select items from the list box by typing the first letter of the item. The user can also use the mouse or the UP ARROW and DOWN ARROW keys to select items in the combo box.

You add and delete items to the list box portion of a combo box in much the same way you would with a standard list box, but by using the messages CB_ADDSTRING, CB_INSERTSTRING, CB_DELETESTRING, and CB_DIR. Windows also provides additional combo box messages for retrieving the contents of the edit control, matching text with a list box item, and handling the contents of the edit control.

In many respects, a combo box is similar to a list box in the way it reports the user's interaction with the control. All of the list box notification codes have parallel combo box notification codes. In addition to these, Windows sends notification codes to indicate the following:

- The list box of the combo box is being dropped down (CBN_DROPDOWN).
- The list box of the combo box is being hidden (CBN_CLOSEUP).
- The user has changed the text in the edit control, and Windows has updated the screen (CBN_EDITCHANGE).
- The user has changed the text in the edit control, but Windows has not yet updated the screen (CBN_EDITUPDATE).
- The combo box has lost the input focus (CBN_KILLFOCUS). In the case of CBS_DROPDOWN and CBS_DROPDOWNLIST combo boxes, this causes Windows to remove the list box from the screen.
- The combo box has gained the focus (CBN_SETFOCUS).

Like a list box, a combo box can be created with a fixed- or variable-height owner-drawn style. In the case of combo boxes, however, the owner window is responsible for drawing items in the list box and in the edit control. For example, if the user selects an item in the list box, the owner of the combo box receives a WM_DRAWITEM message for the list box item (to draw it as selected) and another WM_DRAWITEM message for the edit control.

You can also specify the CBS_SORT style for a combo box; Windows sorts owner-drawn combo boxes in the same manner as it sorts owner-drawn list boxes.

There is no multicolumn style for combo boxes.

8.4.5 Edit Controls

An edit control is a rectangular child window in which the user can type and edit text. Edit controls have a variety of features, such as multiline editing and scrolling. You specify the features you want by specifying a control style.

Edit control styles define how the control will appear and operate. For example, the ES_MULTILINE style creates an edit control in which you can type more than one line of text. The styles ES_AUTOHSCROLL and ES_AUTOVSCROLL direct the control to scroll horizontally or vertically if the user types more text than can fit in the control's client area. If these styles are not specified and the user types more text than can fit on one line, the text wraps to the next line if the control is a multiline edit control. You can also use the WS_HSCROLL and (for a multiline edit control) WS_VSCROLL styles to allow the user to scroll the text in the control.

Your application can use an edit control in which a user can type a password or other private text without displaying what is typed. The ES_PASSWORD style creates an edit control that does not display text as the user types it; instead, the control displays an arbitrary character for each character that the user types. By default, this character is an asterisk (*). To change the character displayed by the control, send the EM_SETPASSWORDCHAR message to the control.

You can set tab stops in a multiline edit control by sending the EM_SETTABSTOPS message to the control. This message specifies the number of tab stops the control should contain and the distances between the tab stops.

An edit control sends notification messages to its parent window. For example, it sends an EN_CHANGE message when the user makes a change to the text. An edit control can also receive messages, such as EM_GETLINE and EM_LINELENGTH. The control carries out the specified action when it receives a message.

A powerful feature of edit controls is the ability to "undo" a change to its contents. To determine whether an edit control can undo an action, send it the EM_CANUNDO message; the control will return a nonzero value if it can undo the last change. If the control can undo the change, your application can send the EM_UNDO message to the control to reverse the last change made to it.

8.4.6 Scroll Bars

Scroll bars are predefined controls that can be positioned anywhere in a window. They allow a user to select a value from a continuous range of values. The scroll bar sends a notification message to its parent window whenever the user clicks the control by using the mouse or moves the scroll box (or "thumb") by using the keyboard; this allows the parent window to process the messages so that it can determine the value selected by the user and position the scroll box appropriately.

To create a child-window scroll bar, use the SBS_HORZ or SBS_VERT style. You can create a scroll bar with any desired size. If you want the width (of a vertical scroll bar) or height (of a horizontal scroll bar) to match the size of a window scroll bar, you can use the appropriate system metrics, as shown in the following example:

```
hScrollBar = CreateWindow("Scrollbar", NULL,
    WS_CHILD | WS_VISIBLE | SBS_VERT,
    20, 20,
    GetSystemMetrics(SM_CXVSCROLL), 50,
    hWnd, IDSCROLLBAR, hinst, NULL);
```

The **GetSystemMetrics** function returns the current value for SM_CXVSCROLL, which is the width of a standard window scroll bar.

Scroll bars do not have a special set of notification messages. Instead, they send the same messages (WM_HSCROLL and WM_VSCROLL) sent by window scroll bars. The *wParam* parameter of these messages contains a value that indicates what kind of scrolling is being performed. Your application uses this information to determine how to position the scroll box and what that position means to your application.

Windows is capable of properly positioning the scroll box associated with a list box or edit control, based on the contents of the control. However, a scroll bar that is a child window represents a range of values known only to your application. As a result, your application must set the scrolling range for the scroll bar and must position the scroll box each time the user moves it.

The **SetScrollRange** function establishes the range of values that the scroll bar represents. For example, if your application has a scroll bar with which the user can select a day in a given month, you would call **SetScrollRange** to set the scroll bar range to the number of days in a particular month. The following example shows how your application could set the range for the month of January:

```
SetScrollRange(hScrollBar, SB_CTL, 1, 31, TRUE);
```

In this example, SB_CTL means the scroll bar is a separate control, not a control associated with a window. The third and fourth parameters specify the scroll bar range, and the fourth parameter is set to TRUE to direct Windows to redraw the scroll bar to reflect the new range.

Even if you have established the range of values that the scroll bar represents, Windows still cannot position the scroll box properly when the user moves it; your application must do this. Each time your application receives a WM_HSCROLL or WM_VSCROLL message for the scroll bar, it must check the *wParam* parameter of the message to determine how far the user moved the scroll box. Your application can then call the **SetScrollPos** function to position the scroll box. Also, if you allow the user (through your application) to change the value represented by the scroll box position without using the scroll bar (such as by typing in an edit control), your application must reposition the scroll box based on the new value.

8.5 Sample Application: EditCntl

This sample application illustrates how you can use an edit control in an application's main window to provide multiline text entry and editing. The EditCntl application fills the client area of its main window with a multiline edit control and monitors the size of the client area to ensure that the control always just fits. When completed, the EditCntl application looks like this:

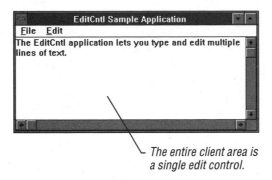

The entire client area is
a single edit control.

To create the application, make the following modifications to the EditMenu application created in Chapter 7, "Menus":

1. Add a new constant to the header file.

2. Add new variables.

3. Add a **CreateWindow** function.

4. Modify the WM_COMMAND case.

5. Add a WM_SETFOCUS case.

6. Add a WM_SIZE case.

7. Compile and link the application.

8.5.1 Adding a Constant to the Header File

The edit control requires a control identifier. Use the following statement to add a constant to the header file:

```
#define IDC_EDIT 300
```

8.5.2 Adding New Variables

To hold the window handle of the edit control, create a global variable. To do this, add the following statement to the beginning of the C-language source file:

```
HWND hEditWnd /* handle of edit window */
```

You must also create a local variable in the **WinMain** function to hold the coordinates of the client area rectangle. These coordinates are used to determine the size of the control. To do this, add the following statement to the beginning of the **WinMain** function:

```
RECT Rect;
```

8.5.3 Adding a CreateWindow Function

Before you can create the edit control, you must retrieve the dimensions of the client area to determine the size of the control. After creating the main window, add the following statements to the **WinMain** function:

```
GetClientRect(hWnd, (RECT FAR*) &Rect);

hEditWnd = CreateWindow("EDIT",
    NULL,
    WS_CHILD | WS_VISIBLE |
    ES_MULTILINE |
    WS_VSCROLL | WS_HSCROLL |
    ES_AUTOHSCROLL | ES_AUTOVSCROLL,
    0,
    0,
    Rect.right - Rect.left,
    Rect.bottom - Rect.top,
    hWnd,
    IDC_EDIT,
    hinst,
    NULL);

if (!hEditWnd) {
    DestroyWindow(hWnd);
    return NULL;
}
```

The **GetClientRect** function retrieves the dimensions of the main window's client area and places that information in the Rect structure. The **CreateWindow** function creates the edit control, using the width and height computed by the Rect structure.

The **CreateWindow** function creates the edit control, using the predefined EDIT control class and specifying the WS_CHILD window style. You can use the predefined controls as child windows only, not as main or pop-up windows. Since a child window requires a parent window, you must specify the handle of the main window, hWnd, when calling the function.

For this edit control, a number of control styles are also specified. These control styles, like window styles, define how the edit control will look and operate. This one is a multiline control, meaning the user will be able to type more than one line of text in it. Also, the control will automatically scroll horizontally or vertically if the user types more text than can fit in it.

The upper-left corner of the control is placed at the upper-left corner of the parent window's client area. A child window's coordinates are always relative to the parent window's client area. The next two arguments, Rect.right – Rect.left and Rect.bottom – Rect.top, define the height and width of the control, ensuring that it fills the client area when first displayed.

Since an edit control sends notification messages to its parent window, the control must have an identifier. Child windows cannot have menus, so use the menu argument in the **CreateWindow** function to specify the control identifier instead. For this control, the identifier is IDC_EDIT. Any notification messages sent to the parent window by the control will contain this identifier.

If the **CreateWindow** function cannot create the edit control, the function returns NULL. In such a case, your application cannot continue, so you should use the **DestroyWindow** function to destroy the main window before terminating the application.

8.5.4 Modifying the WM_COMMAND Case

Child window controls notify the parent window of events by using a WM_COMMAND message. The *wParam* parameter of this message identifies the control that generated the message.

To recognize an out-of-memory notification from the edit control, add the following code to the WM_COMMAND case:

```
case IDC_EDIT:
    if (HIWORD(lParam) == EN_ERRSPACE) {
        MessageBox(
            GetFocus(),
            "Out of memory.",
            "EditCntl Sample Application",
            MB_ICONHAND | MB_OK);
    }
    break;
```

8.5.5 Adding a WM_SETFOCUS Case

To set the input focus to the edit control whenever the parent window is activated, add the following statements to the window procedure:

```
case WM_SETFOCUS:
        SetFocus(hEditWnd);
        break;
```

8.5.6 Adding a WM_SIZE Case

Because Windows sends a WM_SIZE message to the window procedure whenever the width or height of a window changes, you must add a WM_SIZE case to the window procedure. Changing the main window size does not automatically change the size of the edit control. The WM_SIZE case is necessary to change the size of the control.

Add the following statements to the window procedure:

```
case WM_SIZE:
    MoveWindow(hEditWnd, 0, 0, LOWORD(lParam),
        HIWORD(lParam), TRUE);
    break;
```

8.5.7 Compiling and Linking

Compile and link the EditCntl application, and then start Windows and run the application. Now, you can insert and delete text, and you can use the mouse instead of the keyboard to select text. And since you specified ES_MULTILINE, ES_AUTOVSCROLL, and ES_AUTOHSCROLL when creating the edit control, the control can edit a full screen of text, then scroll and edit more.

The EditCntl application illustrates the first step required to create a simple text editor. To create a complete editor, you can add a File menu to the main window to open and save text files and to copy or retrieve text from the edit control, and add an Edit menu to the main window to copy, cut, and paste text through the clipboard. Later chapters illustrate some simple ways to incorporate these features into your application.

8.6 Related Topics

For more information about processing input messages and about using controls in dialog boxes, see Chapter 4, "Keyboard and Mouse Input," and Chapter 9, "Dialog Boxes."

For more information about control functions and resource-definition statements, see the *Microsoft Windows Programmer's Reference*, *Volumes 2* and *4*.

Dialog Boxes

Dialog boxes are pop-up windows that users interact with when using your Microsoft Windows application. Typically, dialog boxes contain one or more controls.

This chapter covers the following topics:

- What a dialog box is
- Creating and using both modal and modeless dialog boxes
- Creating a dialog box procedure
- Using controls in dialog boxes

This chapter does not contain a discussion of a sample application that uses dialog boxes. How you can use dialog boxes has changed for Windows version 3.1, which now provides common dialog boxes. For more information about using common dialog boxes in your applications, see the *Microsoft Windows Programmer's Reference, Volume 1*.

9.1 What Is a Dialog Box?

A dialog box is a pop-up window that an application uses to display or prompt for information—typically, information needed to complete a command. A dialog box contains one or more controls with which the user can type text, choose options, and direct the action of a particular command.

You have seen a dialog box already in the Generic application: the About dialog box. This dialog box contains static text controls that provide information about the application, and a push button control that the user can use to close the dialog box and return to the main window. To process a dialog box, you need to supply a dialog box template, a dialog box procedure, and some means to call the dialog box.

A dialog box template is text that describes the dialog box and the controls it contains. You can use either a text editor or Windows Dialog Editor (DLGEDIT.EXE) to create the template. Once you have created the template, you add it to your resource-definition file.

A dialog box procedure is a callback function; Windows calls the dialog box procedure and passes it messages for the dialog box. Although a dialog box procedure is similar to a window procedure, Windows carries out special processing for dialog boxes. Therefore, the dialog box procedure does not have the same responsibilities as a window procedure.

The most common way to display a dialog box is in response to menu input. For example, the Open command on the File menu requires additional information to complete its task; it displays a dialog box to prompt for the additional information.

There are two types of dialog box: modal and modeless.

9.1.1 Modal Dialog Boxes

You have already seen a modal dialog box (About) in the Generic application. A modal dialog box temporarily disables the parent window and requires the user to complete the requested action before returning control to the parent window. Modal dialog boxes are useful for gathering information your application requires in order to proceed. For example, Microsoft Windows Notepad displays a modal dialog box when the user chooses the Open command from the File menu. Notepad cannot carry out the Open command until the user specifies a file.

Although you can specify almost any window style for a modal dialog box, the recommended styles are DS_MODALFRAME, WS_CAPTION, and WS_SYSMENU. The DS_MODALFRAME style gives the dialog box its characteristic thick border.

A modal dialog box starts its own message loop to process messages from the application queue without returning to the **WinMain** function. To prevent input from going to the parent window, the dialog box disables the parent window before processing input. For this reason, you must not create a modal dialog box by using the WS_CHILD style, since disabling the parent window also disables all child windows belonging to the parent window.

To display a modal dialog box, use the **DialogBox** or **DialogBoxIndirect** function. To terminate a modal dialog box, use the **EndDialog** function.

9.1.2 Modeless Dialog Boxes

A modeless dialog box, unlike a modal dialog box, does not disable the parent window. This means that the user can continue to work in the parent window while the modeless dialog box is displayed. For example, Microsoft Windows Write uses a modeless dialog box for its Find command. This allows the user to continue editing the document without having to close the Find dialog box.

Most modeless dialog boxes have the WS_POPUP, WS_CAPTION, WS_BORDER, and WS_SYSMENU styles. The typical modeless dialog box has a System menu, a title bar, and a thin black border.

Although Windows automatically disables some of the System-menu commands for the dialog box, the menu still contains a Close command. The user can use this command instead of a push button to close the dialog box. You can also include controls in the dialog box, such as edit controls and check boxes.

A modeless dialog box receives its input through the message loop in the **Win-Main** function. If the dialog box has controls, and you want to let the user move to and select those controls by using the keyboard, call the **IsDialogMessage** function in the main message loop. This function determines whether a keyboard input message is for the dialog box and, if necessary, processes it. The **WinMain** function's message loop for an application that has a modeless dialog box will look like this:

```
while (GetMessage(&msg, NULL, NULL, NULL) {
    if (hDlg == NULL || !IsDialogMessage(hDlg, &msg)) {
        TranslateMessage(&msg);
        DispatchMessage(&msg);
    }
}
```

Since a modeless dialog box may not be present at all times, your application must check the hDlg variable that holds the handle in order to determine whether it is valid. If the variable is valid, **IsDialogMessage** determines whether the message is for the dialog box. If so, the message is processed and must not be further processed by the **TranslateMessage** and **DispatchMessage** functions.

To terminate a modeless dialog box, use the **DestroyWindow** function.

9.2 Using a Dialog Box

To create and use a dialog box, follow these steps:

1. Create a dialog box template and add it to the resource-definition file.

2. Create a dialog box procedure to support the box.

3. Export the dialog box procedure.

4. Display the dialog box by calling the **DialogBox** or **DialogBoxIndirect** function (for a modal dialog box) or the **CreateDialog** or **CreateDialogIndirect** function (for a modeless dialog box).

5. Close the dialog box by calling either the **EndDialog** function (for modal dialog boxes) or the **DestroyWindow** function (for modeless dialog boxes).

9.2.1 Creating a Dialog Box Procedure

A dialog box procedure has the following form:

```
BOOL FAR PASCAL DlgProc(hDlg, message, wParam, lParam)
HWND hDlg;
UINT message;
WPARAM wParam;
LPARAM lParam;
{
    switch (message) {

        /* Place message cases here. */

        default:
            return FALSE;
    }
}
```

This is basically a window procedure, except that the **DefWindowProc** function is not called. The dialog box procedure should not call **DefWindowProc**, because default processing of dialog box messages is handled internally when the dialog box procedure returns FALSE. If the procedure returns TRUE, no further processing takes place. (The WM_INITDIALOG message is an exception to this rule about how TRUE and FALSE affect the processing in a dialog box procedure.)

The dialog box procedure must be defined as a **FAR PASCAL** function and must have the specified parameters. **BOOL** is the required type for the return value.

Just as it does with window procedures, Windows sends messages to a dialog box procedure when it has information to give the procedure or requires the procedure to carry out some action. Unlike a window procedure, a dialog box procedure responds to a message by returning a Boolean value. If the procedure processes the message, it returns TRUE. Otherwise, it returns FALSE.

In this dialog box procedure, the hDlg variable receives the handle of the dialog box. The other parameters serve the same purpose as in a window procedure. The **switch** statement is used as a filter for different messages. Most dialog box procedures process the WM_INITDIALOG and WM_COMMAND messages, but little else.

The dialog box procedure can, if necessary, give the input focus to any control in the dialog box by processing the WM_INITDIALOG message. After setting the focus to the desired control, the procedure should return FALSE; otherwise, Windows sets the input focus to the control of its choosing.

The WM_COMMAND message is sent to the dialog box procedure by the controls in the dialog box. If there are controls in the dialog box, they send notification messages when the user carries out some action within them. For example, a dialog box procedure with a push button can check WM_COMMAND messages for the control identifier of the push button. When it finds this identifier (which is in the message's *wParam* parameter), the procedure can carry out the corresponding task.

If you specify the WS_SYSMENU style when creating the dialog box, you should include a WM_COMMAND **switch** statement for the IDCANCEL control identifier, which is sent when the user chooses the Close command in the dialog box's System menu. The statement should include a call to the **EndDialog** function.

9.2.2 Using Controls in Dialog Boxes

You use controls in dialog boxes much as you use them in regular windows. When a control is in a dialog box, however, you can use several special functions to access the control and send messages to it. For example, the **SendDlgItem-Message** function sends a message to a control in the dialog box, and the **Set-DlgItemText** function sets the text of a control. You need not supply the control handle in these functions. Instead, you supply the dialog box handle and the control identifier. If you want the control handle, you use the **GetDlgItem** function.

9.3 Related Topics

For more information about input messages and controls, see Chapter 4, "Keyboard and Mouse Input," and Chapter 8, "Controls."

For more information about functions used with controls and dialog boxes, see the *Microsoft Windows Programmer's Reference, Volume 2*.

File Input and Output

The Microsoft Windows 3.1 operating system provides common dialog boxes for many standard operations. (A common dialog box is a dialog box that a Windows-based application displays by calling a single function rather than by creating a dialog box procedure and a resource file containing a dialog box template.) An application can create a common dialog box for opening a file by calling the **GetOpenFileName** function and one for closing a file by calling the **GetSaveFileName** function. Common dialog boxes simplify the development of applications for Windows and assist users by providing a standard set of controls. Common dialog boxes can even be customized to meet the special requirements of an application. For more information about common dialog boxes, see the *Microsoft Windows Programmer's Reference, Volume 1*.

The information in this chapter is provided for developers who choose not to use the common dialog boxes for file input and output.

10.1 Overview

File input and output in Windows-based applications are similar to file input and output in standard C run-time applications. However, there are enough differences between the two systems to make a review of file input and output important. For example, although you can use C run-time stream input and output (I/O) functions in Windows, it is preferable to use the low-level, C run-time input and output functions. Also, since Windows is a multitasking operating system, you must manage open files carefully.

In Windows, applications that do not use the common dialog boxes should use the **OpenFile** function to work with files. **OpenFile** opens and manages files, returning a file handle that you can use with the low-level C run-time functions to read and write data.

This chapter covers the following topics:

- Handling files in the Windows operating system
- Using the **OpenFile** function to create, open, close, reopen, prompt for, and check the status of disk files
- Using the low-level, C run-time input and output functions to read from and write to disk files

This chapter also explains how to create a sample application, EditFile, that illustrates some of these concepts.

10.2 Rules for Handling Files in Windows

In Windows, multitasking imposes some special restrictions on file access that you do not encounter in the standard C environment. Since there may be several applications working with files at the same time, you must follow some simple rules to avoid conflicts and potential overwriting of files.

- **Keep a file open only while you have execution control.**

  You should close the file before calling the **GetMessage** function, or any other function that may yield execution control. Closing the file prevents it from being affected by changes in the disk environment that may be caused by other applications. For example, suppose your application is writing to a floppy disk and temporarily relinquishes control to another application, and the other application tells the user to remove the floppy disk and replace it with another. When your application gets control back and attempts to write to the disk as before, without having closed and reopened the file, it could destroy data on the new disk.

  Another reason to keep files closed is the MS-DOS open-file limit. MS-DOS sets a limit on the number of open files that can exist at one time. If many applications attempt to open and use files, they can quickly exhaust the available files.

  To prevent open-file problems, the **OpenFile** function provides an OF_REOPEN option that you can use to close and reopen files. Whenever you open or create a file, **OpenFile** automatically copies the relevant facts about the file, including the path and filename and the current position of the file pointer, in an **OFSTRUCT** structure. This means you can close the file, then reopen it by supplying nothing more than the structure.

  If the user changes disks while working in another application, when your application calls the **OpenFile** function, the function will fail to reopen your file. If your application specifies the OF_PROMPT option when reopening a file, **OpenFile** automatically displays a message box asking the user to insert the correct disk.

- **Follow MS-DOS conventions when carrying out file operations.**

  Ultimately, Windows depends on the MS-DOS file-handling functions to carry out all file input and output. This means that you must follow MS-DOS conventions when carrying out file operations. For example, in MS-DOS, a filename can have from one to eight characters and a filename extension can have from zero to three characters. The name must not contain spaces. Furthermore, filenames must be specified in the OEM character set, not the Windows character set.

The **OpenFile** function translates filenames from the Windows character set to the OEM set, using the **AnsiToOem** function. If a filename contains lowercase extended characters, however, an application should call the **AnsiUpper** function before calling **OpenFile**; otherwise, the extended characters are converted incorrectly. (All filenames that contain lowercase extended characters must be converted by calling **AnsiUpper** and then **AnsiToOem**.)

Note All edit controls and list boxes use the Windows character set by default, so if you plan to display MS-DOS filenames or allow users to enter filenames, they may see unexpected characters wherever an OEM character is not identical to a Windows character. If your application processes international filenames, it must be prepared to handle filenames that do not contain conventional single-byte character values. For such filenames, use the **AnsiNext** and **AnsiPrev** functions to move forward and backward in a string. These functions correctly handle strings that contain characters that are not one byte in length, such as strings in computers that are using Japanese characters.

- **Use unique filenames for each instance of your application.**

  Since more than one instance of an application can run at a time, one instance can end up overwriting the temporary file of another instance. You can prevent this by using unique filenames for each instance of your application.

  To create unique filenames, use the **GetTempFileName** function. This function creates a unique name by combining a unique integer with a prefix and filename extension that you supply. **GetTempFileName** creates names that follow MS-DOS filename requirements.

  Note The **GetTempFileName** function uses the TEMP environment variable to create the path and filename of the temporary file. If the user has not set the variable, the temporary file will be placed in the root directory of the current drive. If the variable does not specify a valid directory, you will not be able to create the temporary file.

- **Close files before displaying a message box, or use system-modal error message boxes.**

  As mentioned previously, your application should not relinquish control while it has open files on floppy disks. If your application uses a message box that is not system-modal, the user can move to another application while the message box is on display. If your application still has open files, switching applications like this can cause file I/O problems.

  To avoid such problems, whenever your application displays an alert or error message by using the **MessageBox** function, it should either close any open files before displaying the message box, or if closing files is not feasible, make the message box system-modal.

10.3 Creating a File

To create a new file, use the **OpenFile** function. When you call **OpenFile**, you specify the following:

- A null-terminated filename for the file
- A buffer with the type **OFSTRUCT**
- The OF_CREATE option

The following example creates the FILE.TXT file and returns a handle of the file. The application can then use this file handle with low-level, C run-time I/O functions.

```
int hFile;
OFSTRUCT OfStruct;
          .
          .
          .

hFile = OpenFile("FILE.TXT", &OfStruct, OF_CREATE);
```

The **OpenFile** function creates the file, if necessary, and opens it for writing. If the file already exists, the function truncates it to zero length and opens it for writing.

If you want to avoid overwriting an existing file, you can check whether the file exists, before creating a new file, by calling **OpenFile** as follows:

```
hFile = OpenFile("FILE.TXT", &OfStruct, OF_EXIST);
if (hFile >= 0) {
    wAction = MessageBox(hWnd,
        (LPSTR) "File exists. Overwrite?",
        (LPSTR) "File",
        MB_OKCANCEL);
    if (wAction == IDCANCEL)

/* End this processing. */

    }
}

/* Open the file. */
```

10.4 Opening an Existing File

You can open an existing file by using the OF_READ, OF_WRITE, or OF_READWRITE option in the **OpenFile** function. These options direct **Open-File** to open existing files for reading, writing, or reading and writing. The following example opens the FILE.TXT file for reading:

```
hFile = OpenFile("FILE.TXT", &OfStruct, OF_READ);
```

If the file fails to open, you can display a dialog box to indicate that the file was not found. You can also use **OpenFile** to prompt for the file, as described in Section 10.7, "Prompting for a File."

10.5 Reading From and Writing To a File

Once you have opened a file, you can read from it or write to it by using low-level, C run-time functions. The following example opens the FILE.TXT file for reading and then reads 512 bytes from it:

```
char buffer[512];
int count;
        .
        .
        .
hFile = OpenFile("FILE.TXT", &OfStruct, OF_READ);
if (hFile >= 0) {
    count = _lread(hFile, buffer, 512);
    _lclose(hFile);
}
```

In this example, the file handle is checked before bytes are read from the file. **OpenFile** returns 1 if the file could not be found or opened. The **_lclose** function closes the file immediately after it has been read.

The following example opens the FILE.TMP file for writing and then writes bytes from the character-array buffer:

```
hFile = OpenFile("FILE.TMP", &OfStruct, OF_WRITE);
if (hFile >= 0) {
    _lwrite(hFile, buffer, count);
    _lclose(hFile);
}
```

You should always close floppy disk files after reading or writing. This is to prevent problems if you remove the current disk while working with another application. You can always reopen a disk file by using the OF_REOPEN option.

10.6 Reopening a File

If you open a file on a floppy disk, you should close it before your application re-linquishes control to another application. The most convenient time to close the file is immediately after reading or writing. The file can always be reopened by using **OpenFile** with the OF_REOPEN option:

```
hFile = OpenFile((LPSTR) NULL, &OfStruct, OF_REOPEN | OF_READ);
```

In this example, **OpenFile** uses the filename specified in the OfStruct structure to open the file.

10.7 Prompting for a File

By using the OF_PROMPT option in the **OpenFile** function, you can automatically prompt the user to insert the correct disk before reopening a file. **OpenFile** uses the filename to create a prompt string. If you are reopening a file, you must use the OF_REOPEN and OF_PROMPT options in addition to specifying how you want to open the file:

```
hFile = OpenFile((LPSTR) NULL, &OfStruct, OF_PROMPT | OF_REOPEN
    | OF_READ);
```

If you reopen a file as read-only, Windows will check whether the date and time match the date and time the file was first opened.

10.8 Checking the Status of an Open File

You can retrieve the current status of an open file by using the low-level, C run-time function **fstat**. This function fills a structure with information about a file, such as its length, in bytes (specified in the **size** field), and the date and time it was created. The following example fills the FileStatus structure with information about the FILE.TXT file:

```
stat FileStatus;
    .
    .
    .

fstat(hFile, &FileStatus);
```

10.9 Sample Application: EditFile

The EditFile application is a simple application for Windows that uses the **Open-File** and C run-time functions to open and save small text files. When this application is completed, you will be able to view text files in an edit control. By using the Open command in the application's File menu, you can specify the file to be opened. You will also be able to make changes to a file or enter new text, and save the text by using the Save or Save As command in the dialog box.

10.9.1 Adding a Definition to the Header File

To support the SaveAs dialog box, you must add the following constant definition to the header file:

```
#define MAXFILESIZE 0x7FFF
```

10.9.2 Adding a SaveAs Dialog Box

The EditFile application requires a dialog box to support the Save As command. The SaveAs dialog box prompts for a filename and enables the user to type the name in an edit control. Add the following **DIALOG** statement to the resource file:

```
SaveAs DIALOG 10, 10, 180, 53
STYLE DS_MODALFRAME | WS_CAPTION | WS_SYSMENU
CAPTION "Save As"
BEGIN
    LTEXT "Save As File &Name:", IDC_FILENAME, 4,  4,  72, 10
    LTEXT "",                     IDC_PATH,    84,  4,  92, 10
    EDITTEXT                      IDC_EDIT,     4, 16, 100, 12
    DEFPUSHBUTTON  "Save",        IDOK,       120, 16,  50, 14
    PUSHBUTTON     "Cancel",      IDCANCEL,   120, 36,  50, 14
END
```

10.9.3 Adding Include Statements

You must include additional C run-time header files to support file input and output operations. Add the following statements to the beginning of the C-language source file:

```
#include <sys\types.h>
#include <sys\stat.h>
```

10.9.4 Adding New Variables

You must declare the following global variables at the beginning of the file:

```
HANDLE hEditBuffer;          /* handle of editing buffer    */
HANDLE hOldBuffer;           /* handle of old buffer        */
HCURSOR hHourGlass;          /* handle of hourglass cursor  */
HCURSOR hSaveCursor;         /* handle of current cursor    */
int hFile;                   /* handle of file              */
int count;                   /* number of chars read or written */
PSTR pBuffer;                /* address of read/write buffer */
OFSTRUCT OfStruct;           /* information from OpenFile()  */
struct stat FileStatus;      /* information from fstat()     */
PSTR pEditBuffer;            /* address of edit buffer       */
BOOL fChanges = FALSE;       /* TRUE if file is changed      */
BOOL fSaveEnabled = FALSE;   /* TRUE if text is in edit buffer */

char Untitled[] =            /* default window title         */
    "Edit File - (untitled)";
```

The hEditBuffer variable holds the handle of the current editing buffer. This buffer, located in the application's heap, contains the current file text. To load a file, you allocate the buffer, load the file, and then pass the buffer handle to the edit control. The hOldBuffer variable is used to replace an old buffer with a new one. The hHourGlass and hSaveCursor handles hold cursor handles for lengthy operations.

The hFile variable holds the file handle returned by the **OpenFile** function. The count variable holds a count of the number of characters to be read or written. The pBuffer variable is a pointer and holds the address of the character that contains the characters to be read or written. The OfStruct structure holds information about the file.

The FileStatus structure also holds information about the file. The fChanges variable is TRUE if the user has changed the contents of the file. The fSaveEnabled variable is TRUE if the user has given a valid name for the file to be saved. The Untitled variable holds the main window's title, which changes whenever a new file is loaded.

10.9.5 Replacing the WM_COMMAND Case

Replace the WM_COMMAND case so that it processes all File-menu commands except Print. The New command should clear the current filename and empty the edit control if there is any text in it. The Open command should retrieve the selected filename, open the file, and fill the edit control. The Save command should write the contents of the edit control back to the current file. Finally, the Save As command should prompt the user for a filename and write the contents of the edit control.

10.9.5.1 Handling the New Command

If the user chooses the New command and there is text in the current file that has been modified, your application should prompt the user with a message box to determine whether the changes should be saved. Add the following statements to the WM_COMMAND case:

```
case IDM_NEW:

    if (!QuerySaveFile(hWnd))
        return NULL;

    fChanges = FALSE;
    FileName[0] = 0;
    SetNewBuffer(hWnd, NULL, Untitled);
    break;
```

The locally defined function QuerySaveFile checks the file for changes and prompts the user to save the changes. If the changes are saved, the filename is cleared and the editing buffer is emptied by the locally defined function SetNewBuffer.

10.9.5.2 Handling the Open Command

If the user chooses the Open command and there is text in the current file that has been modified, your application should prompt the user to determine whether the changes should be saved before opening the new file. Add the following statements to the WM_COMMAND case:

```
case IDM_OPEN:
    if (!QuerySaveFile(hWnd))
        return NULL;

    lpOpenDlg = MakeProcInstance((FARPROC) OpenDlg, hinst);
    hFile = DialogBox(hinst, "Open", hWnd, (DLGPROC) lpOpenDlg);
    FreeProcInstance(lpOpenDlg);

    if (hFile == -1)
        return NULL;

    hEditBuffer =
        LocalAlloc(LMEM_MOVEABLE | LMEM_ZEROINIT,
            FileStatus.st_size+1);

    if (!hEditBuffer) {
        _lclose(hFile);
        MessageBox(hWnd, "Not enough memory.",
            NULL, MB_OK | MB_ICONHAND);
        return NULL;
    }
```

```
hSaveCursor = SetCursor(hHourGlass);
pEditBuffer = LocalLock(hEditBuffer);
IOStatus = read(hFile, pEditBuffer, FileStatus.st_size);
_lclose(hFile);

if (IOStatus != FileStatus.st_size) {
    sprintf(str, "Error reading %s.", FileName);
    SetCursor(hSaveCursor);             /* removes hourglass */
    MessageBox(hWnd, str, NULL,
        MB_OK | MB_ICONEXCLAMATION);
}

LocalUnlock(hEditBuffer);
sprintf(str, "EditFile - %s", FileName);
SetNewBuffer(hWnd, hEditBuffer, str);
SetCursor(hSaveCursor);                 /* restores cursor   */
break;
```

When the IDM_OPEN case is processed, the QuerySaveFile function checks the existing file for changes before displaying the Open dialog box. The **DialogBox** function returns a file handle of the open file. This handle is created in the OpenDlg dialog box procedure. If the file cannot be opened, the function returns NULL and processing ends. Otherwise, the **LocalAlloc** function allocates the space necessary to load the file into memory. The amount of space allocated is determined by the FileStatus structure, which is filled with information about the open file by the OpenDlg dialog box procedure. If there is no available memory, a message box is displayed and processing ends. Otherwise, the **SetCursor** function displays the hourglass cursor, the **LocalLock** function locks the new buffer, and the C run-time **read** function copies the contents of the file into memory. If the file was not read completely, a message box is displayed. **SetCursor** restores the cursor before the **MessageBox** function is called. The **LocalUnlock** function unlocks the editing buffer, and after a new window title is created, SetNewBuffer changes the editing buffer and title.

10.9.5.3 Handling the Save Command

If the user chooses the Save command and there is no current filename, the application should carry out the same action as the Save As command. Add the following statements to the WM_COMMAND case:

```
case IDM_SAVE:
    if (!FileName[0])
        goto saveas;

    if (fChanges)
        SaveFile(hWnd);

    break;
```

The IDM_SAVE case checks for a filename and, if none exists, skips to the IDM_SAVEAS case. If a filename does exist, the locally defined SaveFile function saves the file only if changes have been made to it.

10.9.5.4 Handling the Save As Command

The Save As command should always prompt for a filename. You should save the file only if the user gives a valid filename. Add the following statements to the WM_COMMAND case:

```
case IDM_SAVEAS:
saveas:
    lpSaveAsDlg = MakeProcInstance((FARPROC) SaveAsDlg, hinst);
    Success = DialogBox(hinst, "SaveAs", hWnd, (DLGPROC) lpSaveAsDlg);
    FreeProcInstance(lpSaveAsDlg);

    if (Success == IDOK) {
        sprintf(str, "EditFile - %s", FileName);
        SetWindowText(hWnd, str);
        SaveFile(hWnd);
    }
    break;                              /* user canceled */
```

The **DialogBox** function displays the SaveAs dialog box. The **MakeProcInstance** and **FreeProcInstance** functions create and free the procedure-instance address for the SaveAsDlg dialog box procedure. The **DialogBox** function returns IDOK from SaveAsDlg if the user enters a valid filename. The **SetWindowText** function then changes the window title, and the SaveFile function saves the contents of the editing buffer to the file.

10.9.5.5 Handling the Exit Command

The Exit command should now prompt the user to determine whether the current file should be saved. Also, to keep track of the changes to the file, your application should process notification messages from the edit control window. Modify the IDM_EXIT case and add the IDC_EDIT case to the WM_COMMAND case, as follows:

```
case IDM_EXIT:
    QuerySaveFile(hWnd);
    DestroyWindow(hWnd);
    break;

case IDC_EDIT:
    if (HIWORD(lParam) == EN_CHANGE)
        fChanges = TRUE;
    return NULL;
```

10.9.6 Adding WM_QUERYENDSESSION and WM_CLOSE Cases

You must process the WM_QUERYENDSESSION and WM_CLOSE messages to prevent the contents of your files from being lost when the user closes a file or ends a session. Add the following statements to the window procedure:

```
case WM_QUERYENDSESSION:        /* message: to end the session? */
    return (QuerySaveFile(hWnd));

case WM_CLOSE:                  /* message: close the window    */
    if (QuerySaveFile(hWnd))
        DestroyWindow(hWnd);
    break;
```

Windows sends a WM_QUERYENDSESSION message to the window procedure when the user has chosen to exit Windows. The session ends only if TRUE is returned. The QuerySaveFile function checks for changes to the file, saves them if the user requests they be saved, and returns TRUE or FALSE depending on whether the user canceled or confirmed the operation.

Windows sends the WM_CLOSE message to the window procedure when the user chooses the Close command in the main window's System menu. QuerySaveFile carries out the same task as in WM_QUERYENDSESSION, but to complete the WM_CLOSE case, the application must also destroy the main window by using the **DestroyWindow** function.

10.9.7 Modifying the OpenDlg Dialog Box Procedure

You must modify the IDOK case in the OpenDlg dialog box procedure in order to open and check the size of the file that is selected by the user. Add the following statements immediately after the call to the AddExt function in the IDOK case of the OpenDlg dialog box procedure:

```
if ((hFile = OpenFile(OpenName, &OfStruct, OF_READ)) < 0) {
    sprintf(str, "Error %d opening %s.",
        OfStruct.nErrCode, OpenName);
    MessageBox(hDlg, str, NULL, MB_OK | MB_ICONHAND);
}

else {
    fstat(hFile, &FileStatus);
    if (FileStatus.st_size > MAXFILESIZE) {
        sprintf(str,
            "Not enough memory to load %s.\n%s exceeds %ld bytes.",
            OpenName, OpenName, MAXFILESIZE);
        MessageBox(hDlg, str, NULL,
            MB_OK | MB_ICONHAND);
        return TRUE;
    }
```

```
    lstrcpy(FileName, OpenName);
    EndDialog(hDlg, hFile);
    return TRUE;
    }
```

The **OpenFile** function opens the specified file for reading and, if successful, returns a file handle. If the file cannot be opened, the case displays a message box containing the error number generated by MS-DOS. If the file is opened, the C runtime **fstat** function copies information about the file into the FileStatus structure. The file size is checked to make sure the file does not exceed the maximum size given by the MAXFILESIZE constant. The case displays an error message if the size is too big. Otherwise, the **strcpy** function copies the new name to the FileName variable and the **EndDialog** function terminates the dialog box and returns the file handle, hFile, to the **DialogBox** function.

10.9.8 Adding a SaveAsDlg Dialog Box Procedure

You must supply a dialog box procedure for the SaveAs dialog box. This procedure retrieves a filename from the edit control and copies the name to the global variable FileName. The dialog box procedure should look like this:

```
int FAR PASCAL SaveAsDlg(hDlg, message, wParam, lParam)
HWND hDlg;
UINT message;
WPARAM wParam;
LPARAM lParam;
{
    char TempName[128];

    switch (message) {
        case WM_INITDIALOG:
            if (!FileName[0])
                fSaveEnabled = FALSE;

            else {
                fSaveEnabled = TRUE;
                DlgDirList(hDlg, DefPath, NULL, IDC_PATH, 0x4010);
                SetDlgItemText(hDlg, IDC_EDIT, FileName);
                SendDlgItemMessage(hDlg, IDC_EDIT, EM_SETSEL, 0,
                    MAKELONG(0, 0x7fff));
            }

            EnableWindow(GetDlgItem(hDlg, IDOK), fSaveEnabled);
            SetFocus(GetDlgItem(hDlg, IDC_EDIT));
            return FALSE;        /* FALSE since focus changed */
```

```
        case WM_COMMAND:
            switch (wParam) {
                case IDC_EDIT:
                    if (HIWORD(lParam) == EN_CHANGE && !fSaveEnabled)
                        EnableWindow(GetDlgItem(hDlg, IDOK),
                            fSaveEnabled = TRUE);
                    return TRUE;

                case IDOK:
                    GetDlgItemText(hDlg, IDC_EDIT, TempName, 128);
                    if (CheckFileName(hDlg, FileName, TempName)) {
                        SeparateFile(hDlg, (LPSTR) str,
                            (LPSTR) DefSpec, (LPSTR) FileName);
                        if (str[0]) lstrcpy(DefPath, str);
                        EndDialog(hDlg, IDOK);
                    }
                    return TRUE;

                case IDCANCEL:
                    EndDialog(hDlg, IDCANCEL);
                    return TRUE;
            }
            break;
    }
    return FALSE;
}
```

The WM_INITDIALOG case enables or disables the Save button. The button should be disabled if there is no current filename. The **EnableWindow** function, along with the fSaveEnabled variable, enables or disables the button. If there is a current filename, it should be the proposed name. The **SetDlgItemText** function copies the filename to the edit control, and the **SendDlgItemMessage** function selects the entire name for editing. The **DlgDirList** function sets the IDC_PATH control to the current directory. Since there is no list box to fill, no list box identifier is given.

The WM_COMMAND case processes notification messages from the controls in the dialog box. When the function receives the EN_CHANGE notification from the edit control IDC_EDIT, it uses the **EnableWindow** function to enable the Save button, if it is not already enabled.

When the function receives a notification from the Save button, it uses the **GetDlgItemText** function to retrieve the filename in the edit control, then checks the validity of the filename by using the locally defined function CheckFileName. This function ensures that the filename contains no path separators or wildcards. It then determines whether the file already exists; if the file does exist, CheckFileName uses the **MessageBox** function to ask the user whether the file should be overwritten. Finally, the dialog box procedure uses the SeparateFile function to copy the filename to the DefSpec and DefPath variables.

10.9.9 Adding Helper Functions

To support the EditFile application, you must add several functions to your
C-language source file:

Function	Description
CheckFileName	Checks a filename for wildcards, adds the default filename extension if one is needed, and checks for the existence of the file.
SaveFile	Saves the contents of the editing buffer in a file.
QuerySaveFile	Prompts the user to save changes if the file has changed without having been saved.
SetNewBuffer	Frees the existing editing buffer and replaces it with a new one.

The CheckFileName function verifies that a filename is not empty and that it contains no wildcards. It also checks to see whether the file already exists by using the
OpenFile function and the OF_EXIST option. If the file exists, CheckFileName
prompts the user to see whether the file should be overwritten. To create this function, add the following statements:

```
BOOL CheckFileName(hWnd, pDest, pSrc)
HWND hWnd;
PSTR pDest, pSrc;
{
    PSTR pTmp;

    if (!pSrc[0])
        return FALSE;  /* indicates no filename specified */

    pTmp = pSrc;
    while (*pTmp) {        /* searches string for wildcards   */
        switch (*pTmp++) {
            case '*':
            case '?':
                MessageBox(hWnd, "Wildcards not allowed.",
                    NULL, MB_OK | MB_ICONEXCLAMATION);
                return FALSE;
        }
    }

    AddExt(pSrc, DefExt);  /* adds default extension if needed */

    if (OpenFile(pSrc, &OfStruct, OF_EXIST) >= 0) {
        sprintf(str, "Replace existing %s?", pSrc);
        if (MessageBox(hWnd, str, "EditFile",
            MB_OKCANCEL | MB_ICONHAND) == IDCANCEL);
            return FALSE;
    }
    lstrcpy(pDest, pSrc);
    return TRUE;
}
```

To open a file for writing, the SaveFile function uses the OF_CREATE option of the **OpenFile** function. The OF_CREATE option directs **OpenFile** to delete the existing contents of the file. The SaveFile function then retrieves a file-buffer handle from the edit control, locks the buffer, and copies the contents to the file. To create this function, add the following statements:

```
BOOL SaveFile(hWnd)
HWND hWnd;
{
    int IOStatus;           /* result of file write */

    if ((hFile = OpenFile(FileName, &OfStruct,
            OF_PROMPT | OF_CANCEL | OF_CREATE)) < 0) {
        sprintf(str, "Cannot write to %s.", FileName);
        MessageBox(hWnd, str, NULL, MB_OK | MB_ICONEXCLAMATION);
        return FALSE;
    }

    hEditBuffer = SendMessage(hEditWnd, EM_GETHANDLE, 0, 0L);
    pEditBuffer = LocalLock(hEditBuffer);
    hSaveCursor = SetCursor(hHourGlass);
    IOStatus = _lwrite(hFile, pEditBuffer, strlen(pEditBuffer));
    _lclose(hFile);
    SetCursor(hSaveCursor);

    if (IOStatus != strlen(pEditBuffer)) {
        sprintf(str, "Error writing to %s.", FileName);
        MessageBox(hWnd, str, NULL, MB_OK | MB_ICONHAND);
        fSuccess = FALSE;
    }

    else {
        fSuccess = TRUE;    /* indicates file was saved          */
        fChanges = FALSE;   /* indicates changes have been saved */
    }

    LocalUnlock(hEditBuffer);
    return fSuccess;
}
```

The EM_GETHANDLE message, sent by using the **SendMessage** function, directs the edit control to return the handle of its editing buffer. This buffer is located in local memory, so it is locked by using the **LocalLock** function. Once this buffer is locked, its contents are written to the file by using the **_lwrite** function. The **SetCursor** function displays the hourglass cursor to indicate a lengthy operation. If **_lwrite** fails to write all bytes, the SaveFile function displays a message box. The **LocalUnlock** function unlocks the editing buffer before the SaveFile function returns.

The QuerySaveFile function checks for changes to the file and prompts the user to save or delete the changes, or cancel the operation. If the user wants to save the changes, the function prompts the user for a filename by using the SaveAs dialog box. To create this function, add the following statements:

```
BOOL QuerySaveFile(hWnd)
HWND hWnd;
{
    int Response;
    FARPROC lpSaveAsDlg;

    if (fChanges) {
        sprintf(str, "Save current changes: %s", FileName);
        Response = MessageBox(hWnd, str,
            "EditFile",  MB_YESNOCANCEL | MB_ICONEXCLAMATION);
        if (Response == IDYES) {

check_name:
            if (!FileName[0]) {
                lpSaveAsDlg = MakeProcInstance((FARPROC) SaveAsDlg,
                    hinst);
                Response = DialogBox(hinst, "SaveAs",
                    hWnd, (DLGPROC) lpSaveAsDlg);
                FreeProcInstance(lpSaveAsDlg);

                if (Response == IDOK)
                    goto check_name;

                else
                    return FALSE;
            }
            SaveFile(hWnd);
        }
        else if (Response == IDCANCEL)
            return FALSE;
    }
    else
        return TRUE;
}
```

The SetNewBuffer function retrieves and frees the editing buffer before allocating and setting a new editing buffer. It then updates the edit control window. To create this function, add the following statements:

```
void SetNewBuffer(hWnd, hNewBuffer, Title)
HWND hWnd;
HANDLE hNewBuffer;
PSTR Title;
{
    HANDLE hOldBuffer;
```

```
                hOldBuffer = SendMessage(hEditWnd, EM_GETHANDLE, 0, 0L);
                LocalFree((HLOCAL) hOldBuffer);
                if (!hNewBuffer)        /* allocates buffer if none exists */
                    hNewBuffer = LocalAlloc(LMEM_MOVEABLE | LMEM_ZEROINIT, 1);

                SendMessage(hEditWnd, EM_SETHANDLE, hNewBuffer, 0L);
                InvalidateRect(hEditWnd, NULL, TRUE);    /* updates buffer */
                UpdateWindow(hEditWnd);
                SetWindowText(hWnd, Title);
                SetFocus(hEditWnd);
                fChanges = FALSE;
            }
```

The new text will not be displayed until the edit control repaints its client area.
The **InvalidateRect** function invalidates part of the edit control's client area. The
NULL argument means that the entire control needs repainting, and TRUE specifies that the background should be erased before repainting. All of this prepares
the control for painting. The **UpdateWindow** function causes Windows to send
the edit control a WM_PAINT message immediately.

10.9.10 Exporting the SaveAsDlg Dialog Box Procedure

You must export the SaveAsDlg dialog box procedure. Add the following line to
the **EXPORTS** statement in your module-definition file:

```
SaveAsDlg @4
```

10.9.11 Adding Space to the Heap

You must add extra space to the local heap. This space is required to support the
edit control, which uses memory from the local heap to store its current text. Make
the following change to the module-definition file:

```
HEAPSIZE 0x4000
```

This statement allocates an initial heap size of 16K, which is more than enough for
most edit-control operations. If the edit-control buffer needs to become larger, the
local heap will increase up to 64K minus the **STACKSIZE** setting. Because locally declared variables are also stored on the heap, files cannot be opened that are
larger than 64K minus the **STACKSIZE** setting minus the storage for locally declared variables.

10.9.12 Compiling and Linking

Compile and link the application, and then start Windows and the EditFile application. Choose the Open command, select a file, and EditFile will read and display the file. If the file is larger than can fit in the window, you can use the arrow keys to scroll left and right or up and down.

10.10 Related Topics

For a comparison of the Windows operating system to the standard C environment, see Chapter 1, "Overview of the Windows Environment."

For more information about using C and assembly language in a Windows-based application, see Chapter 14, "C and Assembly Language."

For more information about the **OpenFile** function, see the *Microsoft Windows Programmer's Reference, Volume 2*.

Bitmaps

Your application for the Microsoft Windows operating system can use bitmaps to display images that are otherwise too cumbersome to draw by using graphics device interface (GDI) output functions. This chapter shows how to create and display bitmaps for monochrome and color screens.

This chapter covers the following topics:

- What a bitmap is
- Creating and displaying bitmaps
- Adding color to monochrome bitmaps
- Deleting bitmaps

This chapter also explains how to create a sample Windows 3.1 application, Bitmap, which illustrates many of these concepts.

11.1 What Is a Bitmap?

In general, the term bitmap refers to an image formed by a pattern of bits, rather than by a pattern of lines. In Windows, there are two kinds of bitmaps:

- A device-dependent bitmap is a pattern of bits, in memory, that can be displayed on an output device. Because there is a close correlation between the bits in memory and the pixels on the screen, a memory bitmap is said to be device dependent. For such bitmaps, the way the bits are arranged in memory depends on the intended output device.

- A device-independent bitmap (DIB) describes the appearance of an image, rather than the way that image is represented internally by a particular display device. Because this external definition can be applied to any display device, it is referred to as device independent.

11.2 Creating a Bitmap

You create a bitmap by supplying GDI with the dimensions and color format of the bitmap, and, optionally, the initial value of the bitmap bits. GDI then returns a handle to the bitmap. You can use this handle in subsequent GDI functions to select and display the bitmap.

You can create bitmaps in the following ways:

- Use Microsoft Image Editor (IMAGEDIT.EXE) to draw the bitmap image and save it in a file. Then add the bitmap file to your application's resources. Your application loads the bitmap by using the **LoadBitmap** function.

- Your application can first create a blank bitmap and then use GDI output functions to draw the bitmap bits.
- To hard-code a bitmap, your application can create a blank bitmap and initialize its bits by using an array of bits.
- Your application can create a bitmap and initialize its bits by using the image in an existing device-independent bitmap (DIB).

11.2.1 Creating and Loading a Bitmap File

You can create a bitmap by using Image Editor. Using this application, you specify the dimensions of the bitmap, and then fill it in by painting in the blank area with such tools as a brush, spray can, and even text. Any of these tools can produce images using colors from a palette of up to 28 colors, which you can define.

To create and load a bitmap using this method, follow these steps:

1. Start Image Editor and create the bitmap by following the directions given in *Microsoft Windows Programming Tools*.

2. After creating the bitmap image, save it in a file that has the filename extension .BMP.

3. In your application's resource-definition (.RC) file, add a **BITMAP** statement that defines that bitmap as an application resource. For example, the following statement specifies that a bitmap resource is in the file DOG.BMP:

```
IDDOGBMP BITMAP dog.bmp
```

The name IDDOGBMP is a resource identifier; the filename DOG.BMP specifies the file that contains the bitmap.

4. In your application's source file, load the bitmap by using the **LoadBitmap** function. This function takes the bitmap's resource name, loads the bitmap into memory, and returns a handle of the bitmap. For example, the following statement loads the bitmap resource named Dog and stores the resulting bitmap handle in the variable hDogBitmap:

```
hDogBitmap = LoadBitmap(hinst, MAKEINTRESOURCE(IDDOGBMP));
```

5. Select the bitmap into a device context by using the **SelectObject** function. For example, the following statement loads the bitmap specified by hDogBitmap into the device context specified by hdcMemory:

```
SelectObject(hdcMemory, hDogBitmap);
```

6. Display the bitmap by using the **BitBlt** function. For example, the following statement displays a copy of the bitmap in the memory device context hdcMemory on the device identified by hDC:

```
BitBlt(hDC, 10, 10, 100, 150, hdcMemory, 0, 0, SRCCOPY)
```

This example displays the bitmap beginning at the coordinates (10,10) of the destination device context. The bitmap is 100 units wide and 150 units high. The bitmap is taken from the memory device context beginning at the coordinates (0,0). The SRCCOPY value specifies that Windows should copy the source bitmap to the destination.

11.2.2 Creating and Filling a Blank Bitmap

You can create a bitmap "on the fly" by creating a blank bitmap and then filling it in by using GDI output functions. Using this method, your application is not limited to external bitmap files, preloaded bitmap resources, or bitmaps that are hard-coded in your application source code.

Follow these general steps:

1. Create a blank bitmap by using the **CreateCompatibleBitmap** or **Create-Bitmap** function.

2. Select the bitmap into a memory device context by using the **SelectObject** function.

3. Draw the bitmap image by using GDI output functions.

The following example creates a star-shaped bitmap by first making a bitmap that is compatible with the display and then filling the compatible bitmap by using the **Polygon** function:

```
HDC hDC;
HDC hMemoryDC;
HBITMAP hBitmap;
HBITMAP hOldBitmap;
POINT Points[5] = { 32, 0, 16, 63, 63, 16, 0, 16, 48, 63 };

hDC = GetDC(hWnd);
hMemoryDC = CreateCompatibleDC(hDC);
hBitmap = CreateCompatibleBitmap(hDC, 64, 64);
hOldBitmap = SelectObject(hMemoryDC, hBitmap);
PatBlt(hMemoryDC, 0, 0, 64, 64, WHITENESS);
Polygon(hMemoryDC, Points, 5);
BitBlt(hDC, 0, 0, 64, 64, hMemoryDC, 0, 0, SRCCOPY);
SelectObject(hMemoryDC, hOldBitmap);
DeleteDC(hMemoryDC);
ReleaseDC(hWnd, hDC);
```

In this example, the **GetDC** function retrieves a handle to the device context. The bitmap will be compatible with the screen. (If you want a bitmap to be compatible with some other device, you should use the **CreateDC** function to retrieve a handle of that device.)

The **CreateCompatibleDC** function creates the memory device context in which the image of the bitmap will be drawn. Following this, the **CreateCompatible-Bitmap** function creates the blank bitmap, setting the size of the bitmap to 64 by 64 pixels. The number of bits in the bitmap depends on the color format of the screen. If the screen is a color screen, the bitmap will be a color bitmap and might have many bits for each pixel.

After the bitmap has been created, the **SelectObject** function selects the bitmap into the memory device context and prepares it for drawing. The handle of the previously selected bitmap is saved in the variable hOldBitmap. The **PatBlt** function then clears the bitmap and sets all pixels to white. **PatBlt**, or a similar function, is required because the image in a blank bitmap is initially undefined. You cannot depend on having a clean bitmap to draw in.

The **Polygon** function draws the star by using the endpoints specified in the array of **POINT** structures, Points. The **BitBlt** function then copies the bitmap from the memory device context to the screen.

The **SelectObject** and **DeleteDC** functions restore the previous bitmap and delete the memory device context. Once the bitmap has been drawn, the memory device context is no longer needed. You cannot delete a device context when any bitmap other than the context's original bitmap is selected.

Finally, the **ReleaseDC** function releases the device context. The bitmap handle hBitmap may now be used in subsequent GDI functions.

11.2.3 Creating a Bitmap with Hard-Coded Bits

You can create a bitmap and set its initial image to an array of bitmap bits by using the **CreateDIBitmap** function. This function creates a memory bitmap of a given size with a device-dependent color format; it initializes the bitmap image by translating a device-independent bitmap definition into the device-dependent format required by the display device and copying this device-dependent information to the memory bitmap. Typically, this method is useful for creating small bitmaps for use with pattern brushes, but you may also find it useful for creating larger bitmaps.

Note Unless the bitmap is monochrome (that is, having a single color plane and one bit per pixel), the memory bitmap created by **CreateBitmap** is device-specific and therefore might not be suitable for display on some devices.

The following example creates a 64-by-32-pixel monochrome bitmap; the example initializes the bitmap by using the bits in the array Square.

```
HBITMAP         hBitmap;
HANDLE          hDibInfo;
PBITMAPINFO     pDibInfo;

BYTE Square[] = {
0x00,0x00,0x00,0x00,0x00,0x00,0x00,0x00,
0x00,0x00,0x00,0x00,0x00,0x00,0x00,0x00,
0x00,0x00,0x00,0x00,0x00,0x00,0x00,0x00,
0x00,0x00,0x00,0x00,0x00,0x00,0x00,0x00,
0x00,0x00,0x00,0x00,0x00,0x00,0x00,0x00,
0x00,0x00,0x00,0x00,0x00,0x00,0x00,0x00,
0x00,0x00,0x00,0x00,0x00,0x00,0x00,0x00,
0x00,0x00,0x00,0x00,0x00,0x00,0x00,0x00,
0x00,0x00,0x00,0x00,0x00,0x00,0x00,0x00,
0x00,0x00,0x00,0x00,0x00,0x00,0x00,0x00,
0x00,0x00,0x00,0x00,0x00,0x00,0x00,0x00,
0x00,0x00,0xFF,0xFF,0xFF,0xFF,0x00,0x00,
0x00,0x00,0xFF,0xFF,0xFF,0xFF,0x00,0x00,
0x00,0x00,0xFF,0xFF,0xFF,0xFF,0x00,0x00,
0x00,0x00,0xFF,0xFF,0xFF,0xFF,0x00,0x00,
0x00,0x00,0xFF,0xFF,0xFF,0xFF,0x00,0x00,
0x00,0x00,0xFF,0xFF,0xFF,0xFF,0x00,0x00,
0x00,0x00,0xFF,0xFF,0xFF,0xFF,0x00,0x00,
0x00,0x00,0xFF,0xFF,0xFF,0xFF,0x00,0x00,
0x00,0x00,0xFF,0xFF,0xFF,0xFF,0x00,0x00,
0x00,0x00,0xFF,0xFF,0xFF,0xFF,0x00,0x00,
0x00,0x00,0x00,0x00,0x00,0x00,0x00,0x00,
0x00,0x00,0x00,0x00,0x00,0x00,0x00,0x00,
0x00,0x00,0x00,0x00,0x00,0x00,0x00,0x00,
0x00,0x00,0x00,0x00,0x00,0x00,0x00,0x00,
0x00,0x00,0x00,0x00,0x00,0x00,0x00,0x00,
0x00,0x00,0x00,0x00,0x00,0x00,0x00,0x00,
0x00,0x00,0x00,0x00,0x00,0x00,0x00,0x00,
0x00,0x00,0x00,0x00,0x00,0x00,0x00,0x00,
0x00,0x00,0x00,0x00,0x00,0x00,0x00,0x00,
0x00,0x00,0x00,0x00,0x00,0x00,0x00,0x00,
0x00,0x00,0x00,0x00,0x00,0x00,0x00,0x00 };

if (pDibInfo = (PBITMAPINFO) LocalAlloc(LMEM_FIXED,
      sizeof(BITMAPINFOHEADER) + 2 * sizeof(RGBQUAD))) {
   HBRUSH hOldBrush, hBrush;
   pDibInfo->bmiHeader.biSize = (LONG) sizeof(BITMAPINFOHEADER);
   pDibInfo->bmiHeader.biWidth = 64L;
   pDibInfo->bmiHeader.biHeight = 32;
   pDibInfo->bmiHeader.biPlanes = 1;
   pDibInfo->bmiHeader.biBitCount = 1;
   pDibInfo->bmiHeader.biCompression = 0L;
   pDibInfo->bmiHeader.biSizeImage = 0L;
   pDibInfo->bmiHeader.biXPelsPerMeter = 0L;
```

```
pDibInfo->bmiHeader.biYPelsPerMeter = 0L;
pDibInfo->bmiHeader.biClrUsed = 0L;
pDibInfo->bmiHeader.biClrImportant = 0L;
pDibInfo->bmiColors[0].rgbRed = 0;
pDibInfo->bmiColors[0].rgbGreen = 0;
pDibInfo->bmiColors[0].rgbBlue = 0;
pDibInfo->bmiColors[1].rgbRed = 0xFF;
pDibInfo->bmiColors[1].rgbGreen = 0xFF;
pDibInfo->bmiColors[1].rgbBlue = 0xFF;
hDC = GetDC(hWnd);
hBitmap = CreateDIBitmap(hDC,
    LPBITMAPINFOHEADER & pDibInfo->bmiHeader, CBM_INIT,
    (LPSTR) Square, (LPBITMAPINFO) pDibInfo, DIB_RGB_COLORS);
    .
    . /* Use the bitmap. */
    .

ReleaseDC(hWnd, hDC);
DeleteObject(hBitmap);
LocalFree((HANDLE) pDibInfo);
}
```

The **CreateDIBitmap** function creates and initializes the bitmap before returning the bitmap handle. The width and height of the bitmap are 64 and 32 pixels, respectively. The bitmap has one bit for each pixel, making it a monochrome bitmap.

The Square array contains the bits used to initialize the bitmap. The **BITMAP-INFO** structure determines how the bits in the array are interpreted. It defines the width and height of the bitmap, how many bits (1, 4, 8, or 24) are used in the array to represent each pixel, and a table of colors for the pixels. Since the Square array defines a monochrome bitmap, the bit count per pixel is 1 and the color table contains only two entries, one for black and one for white. If a given bit in the array is 0, GDI draws a black pixel for that bit; if the given bit is 1, GDI draws a white pixel.

Since the Square array defines a monochrome bitmap, you could also use the **CreateBitmap** function to create the bitmap:

```
hBitmap = CreateBitmap(64, 32, 1, 1, Square);
```

This is possible because all monochrome memory bitmaps are device independent. For color bitmaps, however, **CreateBitmap** cannot use the same bitmap-bit specification as can **CreateDIBitmap**.

Once you have created and initialized the bitmap, you can use its handle in subsequent GDI functions. If you want to change the bitmap, you can draw in it by selecting it into a memory device context as described in Section 11.2.2, "Creating and Filling a Blank Bitmap." If you want to replace the bitmap image with another or want to change a portion of it, you can use the **SetDIBits** function to copy another array of bits into the bitmap. The following example replaces the current bitmap image with the bits in the array Circle:

```
BYTE Circle[] = {
    .
    .
    .

};

SetDIBits(hDC, hBitmap, 0, 32, Circle,
    (BITMAPINFO FAR*) &myDIBInfo, DIB_RGB_COLORS);
```

The **SetDIBits** function copies the bits in the Circle array into the bitmap specified by the hBitmap variable. The array contains 32 scan lines, representing the image of a 64-by-32-pixel monochrome bitmap. If you want to retrieve the current bits in a bitmap before replacing them, you can use the **GetDIBits** function. This function copies a specified number of scan lines from the bitmap into a device-independent bitmap specification. You can also use **GetBitmapBits** to retrieve bits from a monochrome bitmap.

Again, since the Circle array defines a monochrome bitmap, you could call **SetBitmapBits** instead to change the bitmap:

```
SetBitmapBits(hBitmap, 256, Circle);
```

The preceding examples show how to create and modify a small bitmap. Typically, you will not want to hard-code larger bitmaps in your application source code. Instead, you can store a larger bitmap in a device-independent bitmap file created by Image Editor or other tools. A device-independent bitmap file consists of a **BITMAPFILEHEADER** structure followed by a **BITMAPINFO** structure and an array of bytes that together define the bitmap.

For more information about Windows color palettes, see Chapter 19, "Color Palettes."

11.2.4 Drawing a Color Bitmap

Since hard-coding a color bitmap may require considerable effort, it is usually simpler to create a compatible bitmap and draw in it. For example, to create a color bitmap that has a red, green, and blue plaid pattern, you simply create a blank bitmap and use the **PatBlt** function, with the red, green, and blue brushes, to draw the pattern. This method has the advantage of generating a reasonable bitmap even if the screen does not support color. This is because GDI provides dithered brushes for monochrome screens when a color brush is requested. A dithered brush is a unique pattern of pixels that represents a color when that color is not available for the device.

The following statements create the color bitmap by drawing it:

```
#define PATORDEST        0x00FA0089L

HDC hdc;
HDC hdcMemory;
HBITMAP hBitmap;
HBITMAP hOldBitmap;
HBRUSH hRedBrush;
HBRUSH hGreenBrush;
HBRUSH hBlueBrush;
HBRUSH hOldBrush;
    .
    .
    .

hdc = GetDC(hwnd);
if ((hdcMemory = CreateCompatibleDC(hdc)) == NULL)
    return NULL;
if ((hBitmap = CreateCompatibleBitmap(hdc, 64, 32)) == NULL)
    return NULL;
hOldBitmap = SelectObject(hdcMemory, hBitmap);
hRedBrush = CreateSolidBrush(RGB(255, 0, 0));
hGreenBrush = CreateSolidBrush(RGB(0, 255, 0));
hBlueBrush = CreateSolidBrush(RGB(0, 0, 255));

PatBlt(hdcMemory, 0, 0, 64, 32, BLACKNESS);
hOldBrush = SelectObject(hdcMemory, hRedBrush);
PatBlt(hdcMemory, 0, 0, 24, 11, PATORDEST);
PatBlt(hdcMemory, 40, 10, 24, 12, PATORDEST);
PatBlt(hdcMemory, 20, 21, 24, 11, PATORDEST);
SelectObject(hdcMemory, hGreenBrush);
PatBlt(hdcMemory, 20, 0, 24, 11, PATORDEST);
PatBlt(hdcMemory, 0, 10, 24, 12, PATORDEST);
PatBlt(hdcMemory, 40, 21, 24, 11, PATORDEST);
SelectObject(hdcMemory, hBlueBrush);
PatBlt(hdcMemory, 40, 0, 24, 11, PATORDEST);
PatBlt(hdcMemory, 20, 10, 24, 12, PATORDEST);
PatBlt(hdcMemory, 0, 21, 24, 11, PATORDEST);

BitBlt(hdc, 0, 0, 64, 32, hdcMemory, 0, 0, SRCCOPY)

SelectObject(hdcMemory, hOldBrush);
DeleteObject(hRedBrush);
DeleteObject(hGreenBrush);
DeleteObject(hBlueBrush);
SelectObject(hdcMemory, hOldBitmap);
ReleaseDC(hwnd, hdc);
DeleteDC(hdcMemory);
```

In this example, the **CreateSolidBrush** function creates the red, green, and blue brushes needed to make the plaid pattern. The **SelectObject** function selects each brush into the memory device context as that brush is needed, and the **PatBlt** function paints the colors into the bitmap. Each color is painted three times, each time into a small rectangle. In this example, the application instructs **PatBlt** to overlap the different color rectangles slightly. Since the PATORDEST raster-operation code is specified, **PatBlt** uses a Boolean OR operator to combine the brush color with the color already in the bitmap. The result is a different color border around each rectangle. After the bitmap is complete, **BitBlt** copies it from the memory device context to the screen.

11.3 Displaying a Bitmap

Windows provides several ways to display a bitmap:

- Display a memory bitmap by using the **BitBlt** function to copy the bitmap from the memory device context to a screen.
- Use the **StretchBlt** function to copy a stretched or compressed bitmap from a memory device context to a screen.
- Use the **CreatePatternBrush** function to create a brush that incorporates the bitmap. Any subsequent GDI functions that use the brush, such as **PatBlt**, will display that bitmap.
- Use the **SetDIBitsToDevice** function to display a device-independent bitmap directly on the output device.
- Display the bitmap as a menu item in a menu by replacing the original menu-item text, defined in the .RC file, with the bitmap. The user can then choose the command associated with the menu item to carry out an action. For information about replacing a menu item with a bitmap, see Chapter 7, "Menus."

11.3.1 Using the BitBlt Function to Display a Memory Bitmap

You can display any bitmap by using the **BitBlt** function. This function copies a bitmap from a source to a destination device context. To display a bitmap with **BitBlt**, you must first create a memory device context and select the bitmap into it. The following example displays a bitmap by using **BitBlt**:

```
HDC hDC, hdcMemory;
       .
       .
       .

hDC = GetDC(hWnd);
if((hdcMemory = CreateCompatibleDC(hDC)) == NULL)
    return FALSE;
```

```
ReleaseDC(hWnd, hDC);
hOldBitmap = SelectObject(hdcMemory, hBitmap);

if (hOldbitmap) {
    BitBlt(hDC, 100, 30, 64, 32, hdcMemory, 0, 0, SRCCOPY);
    SelectObject(hdcMemory, hOldBitmap);
}

DeleteDC(hdcMemory);
```

In the example, the **GetDC** function specifies the device context for the client area of the window identified by the hWnd variable. The **CreateCompatibleDC** function creates a memory device context that is compatible with the device context. The **SelectObject** function selects the bitmap, identified by the hBitmap variable, into the memory device context and returns the previously selected bitmap. If **SelectObject** cannot select the bitmap, it returns zero.

The **BitBlt** function copies the bitmap from the memory device context into the screen device context. The function places the upper-left corner of the bitmap at the coordinates (100,30), copying the entire bitmap, 64 bits wide by 32 bits high. The hDC and hdcMemory variables identify the destination and source contexts, respectively. The raster-operation code SRCCOPY directs **BitBlt** to copy the source bitmap without combining it with patterns or colors already at the destination.

The **SelectObject**, **DeleteDC**, and **ReleaseDC** functions clean up after the bitmap has been displayed. In general, when your application has finished using memory and device contexts, it should release them as soon as possible. Windows maintains a cache of five device contexts that are retrieved by the **GetDC**, **GetWindowDC**, and **BeginPaint** functions. If an application does not release one of these device contexts after using it, other applications might not be able to retrieve a context when one is needed. If you retrieve a device context by using **GetDC**, **GetWindowDC**, or **BeginPaint**, you must later release it by using **ReleaseDC**; if you create the device context by using any other function, you must later delete it by using **DeleteDC**. Before deleting a device context, you must call **SelectObject**, since you must not delete a device context while any bitmap other than the context's original bitmap is selected.

In the previous example, the width and height of the bitmap were given as 64 and 32 pixels, respectively. Another way to specify the width and height of the bitmap to be displayed is to retrieve these dimensions from the bitmap itself. You can do this by using the **GetObject** function, which fills a specified structure with the dimensions of the given object. For example, to retrieve the width and height of a bitmap, you would use the following statements:

```
BITMAP Bitmap;
    .
    .
    .
GetObject((HGDIOBJ) hBitmap, sizeof(BITMAP), &Bitmap);
```

The next example copies the width and height of the bitmap to the **bmWidth** and **bmHeight** members of the structure Bitmap. You can use these values in **BitBlt** as follows:

```
BitBlt(hDC, 100, 30, Bitmap.bmWidth, Bitmap.bmHeight,
    hdcMemory, 0, 0, SRCCOPY);
```

The **BitBlt** function can display both monochrome and color bitmaps. No special steps are required to display bitmaps of different formats. Be aware, however, that **BitBlt** may convert the bitmap if its color format is not the same as that of the destination device. For example, when displaying a color bitmap on a monochrome screen, **BitBlt** converts the pixels having the current background color to white and all other pixels to black.

11.3.2 Stretching a Bitmap

Your bitmaps are not limited to their original size. You can stretch or compress them by using the **StretchBlt** function in place of **BitBlt**. For example, you can quadruple the size of a 64-by-32-pixel bitmap by using the following statement:

```
StretchBlt(hDC, 100, 30, 128, 64, hdcMemory,
    0, 0, 64, 32, SRCCOPY);
```

The **StretchBlt** function has two additional parameters that **BitBlt** does not. In particular, **StretchBlt** specifies the width and height of the source bitmap. The first width and height, given as 128 and 64 pixels in the preceding example, apply only to the final size of the bitmap in the destination device context.

To compress a bitmap, **StretchBlt** removes pixels from the copied bitmap. This means that some of the information in the bitmap is lost when it is displayed. To minimize the loss, you can set the current stretching mode, which **StretchBlt** uses to combine some of the information with the pixels that will be displayed. The stretching mode can be one of the following:

Mode	Purpose
WHITEONBLACK	Preserves white pixels at the expense of black pixels; for example, a white outline on a black background.
BLACKONWHITE	Preserves black pixels at the expense of white pixels; for example, a black outline on a white background.

Mode	Purpose
COLORONCOLOR	Displays color bitmaps. Attempting to combine colors in a bit-map can lead to undesirable effects.

The **SetStretchBltMode** function sets the stretching mode. In the following example, **SetStretchBltMode** sets the stretching mode to WHITEONBLACK:

```
SetStretchBltMode(hDC, WHITEONBLACK);
```

11.3.3 Using a Bitmap in a Pattern Brush

You can use a bitmap in a brush by creating a pattern brush. After creating the pattern brush, you can select the brush into a device context and use the **PatBlt** function to copy it to the screen; or the **Rectangle**, **Ellipse**, and other drawing functions can use the brush to fill interiors. When Windows draws with a pattern brush, it fills the specified area by repeatedly copying the bitmap horizontally and vertically as necessary. It does not adjust the size of the bitmap to fit in the area as does the **StretchBlt** function.

If you use a bitmap in a pattern brush, the bitmap should be at least 8 pixels wide by 8 pixels high—the default pattern size used by most display drivers. (You can use large bitmaps, but only the upper-left, 8-by-8 corner will be used.) You may hard-code the bitmap, create and draw it, or load it as a resource. In any case, once you have the bitmap handle, you can create the pattern brush by using the **CreatePatternBrush** function. The following example loads a bitmap and uses it to create a pattern brush:

```
hBitmap = LoadBitmap(hinst, "checks");
hBrush = CreatePatternBrush(hBitmap);
```

You can then select the brush into a device context by using the **SelectObject** function:

```
hOldBrush = SelectObject(hDC, hBrush);
```

Since the bitmap is part of the brush, this call to the **SelectObject** function does not affect the device context's selected bitmap.

After selecting the brush, you can use the **PatBlt** function to fill a specified area with the bitmap. For example, the following statement fills the upper-left corner of a window with the bitmap:

```
PatBlt(hDC, 0, 0, 100, 100, PATCOPY);
```

The PATCOPY raster operation directs **PatBlt** to completely replace the destination image with the pattern brush.

You can also use a pattern brush as a window's background brush. To do this, simply assign the brush handle to the **hbrBackground** member of the window-class structure, as in the following example:

```
pWndClass->hbrBackground = CreatePatternBrush(hBitmap);
```

Once you have assigned the brush handle to **hbrBackground**, Windows uses the pattern brush whenever it erases the window's background. You can also change the current background brush for a window class by using the **SetClassWord** function. For example, if you want to use a new pattern brush after a window has been created, you can use the following statement:

```
SetClassWord(hWnd, GCW_HBRBACKGROUND, hBrush);
```

Note that this statement changes the background brush for all windows of this class. If you want to change only the background for one window, you must explicitly process the WM_ERASEBKGND messages that the window receives. The following example shows how to process this message:

```
case WM_ERASEBKGND:

    UnrealizeObject(hBrush);
    hOldBrush = SelectObject((HDC) wParam, (HGDIOBJ) hBrush);
    GetClientRect(hwnd, &Rect);
    PatBlt((HDC) wParam, Rect.left, Rect.top,
        Rect.right - Rect.left, Rect.bottom - Rect.top, PATCOPY);
    SelectObject((HDC) wParam, (HGDIOBJ) hOldBrush);
    return TRUE;
```

The WM_ERASEBKGND message passes a handle of a device context in the *wParam* parameter. The **SelectObject** function selects the desired background brush into the device context. The **GetClientRect** function retrieves the area that needs to be erased. The **PatBlt** function copies the pattern, overwriting anything already in the update rectangle. The final **SelectObject** function restores the previous brush to the device context.

Whenever your application or the user moves a window in which a pattern brush has been or will be used, your application must align the pattern brushes to the new position by using the **UnrealizeObject** function. This function resets a brush's drawing origin so that any patterns displayed after the move match the patterns displayed before the move.

You can use the **DeleteObject** function to delete a pattern brush that is no longer needed. This function does not, however, delete the bitmap along with the brush. To delete the bitmap, call **DeleteObject** again and specify the bitmap handle.

11.3.4 Displaying a Device-Independent Bitmap

One of the advantages of device-independent bitmaps is that you can display them directly without having to create an intermediate memory bitmap. The **SetDIBits-ToDevice** function sets all or part of a device-independent bitmap directly to an output device, significantly reducing the memory required to display the bitmap. When you call **SetDIBitsToDevice** to display a bitmap, you must supply the following information:

- The device context of the target output device

- The location in the device context where the bitmap will appear

- The size of the bitmap on the output device

- The number of scan lines in the source-bitmap buffer from which you are copying the bitmap

- The location of the first pixel in the source bitmap to copy to the output device

- The device-independent bitmap-information structure and a buffer containing the bitmap to be displayed

- Whether the color table of the DIB specification contains literal red, green, blue (RGB) color values or logical-palette color indices

Note The origin for device-independent bitmaps is the lower-left corner of the bitmap, not the upper-left corner as for other graphics operations.

Following is an example of how an application calls **SetDIBitsToDevice**:

```
SetDIBitsToDevice(hDC, 0, 0, lpbi->bmciHeader.bcWidth,
    lpbi->bmciHeader.bcHeight, 0, 0, 0,
    lpbi->bmciHeader.bcHeight,
    pBuf, (BITMAPINFO FAR*) lpbi,
    DIB_RGB_COLORS);
```

In this example, hDC identifies the device context of the target output device; **SetDIBitsToDevice** uses this information to identify the screen and determine the correct color format for the device bitmap.

The next two parameters specify the point on the display surface where **SetDIBits-ToDevice** will begin drawing the bitmap; in this case, it is the origin of the device context itself. The next two parameters supply the width and height of the bitmap.

The sixth and seventh parameters, both of which are set to zero in this example, specify the first pixel in the source bitmap to be set on the display device; again, since both are zero, **SetDIBitsToDevice** begins with the first pixel in the bitmap buffer.

The next two parameters are used for banding purposes. The first of these two parameters is set to zero, indicating that the beginning scan line should be the first in the buffer; the second parameter is set to the height of the bitmap. As a result, the entire source bitmap will be set on the display surface in a single band.

The actual bitmap bits are contained in the pBuf buffer, and the *lpbi* parameter supplies the **BITMAPINFO** data structure that describes the color format of the source bitmap.

The last parameter is a usage flag that indicates whether the bitmap color table contains actual RGB color values or indices into the currently realized logical palette. DIB_RGB_COLORS specifies that the color table contains explicit color values.

11.4 Adding Color to a Monochrome Bitmap

If your computer has a color screen, you can add color to a monochrome bitmap by setting the foreground and background colors of the display context. The foreground and background colors specify which colors the white and black bits of the bitmap will have when displayed. You set the foreground and background colors by using the **SetTextColor** and **SetBkColor** functions. The following example sets the foreground color to red and the background color to green:

```
SetTextColor(hDC, RGB(255, 0, 0));
SetBkColor(hDC, RGB(0, 255, 0));
```

In this example, the hDC variable contains the handle of the device context. The **SetTextColor** function sets the foreground color to red, and the **SetBkColor** function sets the background color to green. The **RGB** function creates an RGB color value by using the three specified values. Each value represents an intensity for each of the primary display colors—red, green, and blue—with the value 255 representing the highest intensity, and zero, the lowest. You can produce colors other than red, green, and blue by combining the color intensities. For example, the following statement creates a yellow RGB value:

```
RGB(255, 255, 0)
```

Once you have set the foreground and background colors, no further action is required. You can display a bitmap (as described earlier), and Windows will automatically add the foreground and background colors. The foreground color is applied to the white bits (the bits set to 1) and the background color to the black bits (the bits set to zero). Note that the background mode, as specified by the **SetBkMode** function, does not apply to bitmaps. Also, the foreground and background colors do not apply to color bitmaps.

When displayed in color, the bitmap named Dog will be red and the background will be green.

11.5 Deleting a Bitmap

A bitmap, like any resource, occupies memory while in use. After you have finished using a bitmap or before your application terminates, it is important that you delete the bitmaps you have created, in order to make that memory available to other applications. To delete a bitmap, first remove it from any device context in which it is currently selected. Then, delete it by using the **DeleteObject** function.

The following example deletes the bitmap identified by the hBitmap variable, after removing it as the currently selected bitmap in the memory device context identified by the hdcMemory variable:

```
SelectObject(hdcMemory, hOldBitmap);
DeleteObject(hBitmap);
```

The **SelectObject** function removes the bitmap from selection by replacing it with a previous bitmap identified by the hOldBitmap variable. The **DeleteObject** function deletes the bitmap. Thereafter, the bitmap handle in hBitmap is no longer valid and must not be used.

11.6 Sample Application: Bitmap

This sample shows how to incorporate a variety of bitmap operations in an application. In particular, it shows how to do the following:

- Load and display a monochrome bitmap
- Create and display a color bitmap
- Stretch and compress a bitmap by using the mouse
- Set the stretching mode
- Create and use a pattern brush
- Use a pattern brush for the window background

In this application, the user specifies (by using the mouse) where and how the bitmap will be displayed. If the user drags the mouse while holding down the left button, and then releases that button, the application uses the **StretchBlt** function to fill the selected rectangle with the current bitmap. If the user clicks the right button, the application uses the **BitBlt** function to display the bitmap.

To create the Bitmap application, make the following modifications to the Generic application:

1. Add constant definitions and a function declaration to the header file.

2. Add two monochrome bitmaps, created by using Image Editor, to the resource-definition file.

3. Add Bitmap, Pattern, and Mode menus to the resource-definition file.

4. Add global and local variables.

5. Add a WM_CREATE case to the window procedure to create bitmaps and add bitmaps to the menus.

6. Modify the WM_DESTROY case in the window procedure to delete bitmaps.

7. Add WM_LBUTTONUP, WM_MOUSEMOVE, and WM_LBUTTONDOWN cases to the window procedure to create a selection rectangle and display bitmaps.

8. Add a WM_RBUTTONUP case to the window procedure to display bitmaps.

9. Add a WM_ERASEBKGND case to the window procedure to erase the client area.

10. Modify the WM_COMMAND case to support the menus.

11. Modify the **link** command line in the makefile to include the SELECT.LIB library file.

12. Compile and link the application.

11.6.1 Modifying the Header File

Add the following function declarations and constant definitions to the header file:

```
#define IDM_BITMAP1             200
#define IDM_BITMAP2             201
#define IDM_BITMAP3             202

#define IDM_PATTERN1            300
#define IDM_PATTERN2            301
#define IDM_PATTERN3            302
#define IDM_PATTERN4            303

#define IDM_BLACKONWHITE        400
#define IDM_WHITEONBLACK        401
#define IDM_COLORONCOLOR        402

#define PATORDEST       0x00FA0089L

HBITMAP MakeColorBitmap(HWND);
```

11.6.2 Adding Bitmap Resources

To add the bitmaps Dog and Cat to your application resources, add the following
statements to your resource-definition file:

```
Dog BITMAP dog.bmp
Cat BITMAP cat.bmp
```

The Dog bitmap is the white outline of a dog on a black background. The Cat bitmap is the black outline of a cat on a white background.

11.6.3 Adding Bitmap, Pattern, and Mode Menus

You must create a **MENU** statement that defines the Bitmap, Pattern, and Mode
menus used to choose the various bitmaps and modes that are part of the application. Add the following **MENU** statement to your resource-definition file:

```
BitmapMenu MENU
BEGIN
    POPUP "&Bitmap"
    BEGIN
        MENUITEM "", IDM_BITMAP1
    END

    POPUP "&Pattern"
    BEGIN
        MENUITEM "", IDM_PATTERN1
    END

    POPUP "&Mode"
    BEGIN
        MENUITEM "&WhiteOnBlack", IDM_WHITEONBLACK, CHECKED
        MENUITEM "&BlackOnWhite", IDM_BLACKONWHITE
        MENUITEM "&ColorOnColor", IDM_COLORONCOLOR
    END
END
```

The Bitmap and Pattern menus each contain a single **MENUITEM** statement.
This statement defines a menu item that serves as a placeholder only. The application will add the actual items to use in the menu by using the **AppendMenu**
function.

11.6.4 Adding Global and Local Variables

You must declare the pattern arrays, the bitmap and context handles, and other global variables used to create and display the bitmaps. To define these global variables, add the following statements to the beginning of your source file:

```
short White[]     = { 0xFF, 0xFF, 0xFF, 0xFF, 0xFF, 0xFF, 0xFF, 0xFF };
short Black[]     = { 0x00, 0x00, 0x00, 0x00, 0x00, 0x00, 0x00, 0x00 };
short Zigzag[]    = { 0xFF, 0xF7, 0xEB, 0xDD, 0xBE, 0x7F, 0xFF, 0xFF };
short CrossHatch[] = { 0xEF, 0xEF, 0xEF, 0xEF, 0x00, 0xEF, 0xEF, 0xEF };

HBITMAP hbmpWhite;
HBITMAP hbmpBlack;
HBITMAP hbmpZigZag;
HBITMAP hbmpCrossHatch;
HBITMAP hbmpDog;
HBITMAP hbmpCat;
HBITMAP hbmpClrPattern;
HBITMAP hmenuBitmap1;
HBITMAP hmenuBitmap2;
HBITMAP hmenuBitmap3;
HBITMAP hBitmap;
HBITMAP hOldBitmap;

HBRUSH hBrush;        /* brush handle                        */
WORD fwStretchMode;   /* type of stretch mode to use         */

HDC hdc;              /* handle of device context            */
HDC hdcMemory;        /* handle of memory device context     */
BITMAP Bitmap;        /* bitmap structure                    */

BOOL fTrack = FALSE;  /* TRUE if user is selecting a region   */
RECT Rect;

WORD fwPrevBitmap  = IDM_BITMAP1;
WORD fwPrevPattern = IDM_PATTERN1;
WORD fwPrevMode    = IDM_WHITEONBLACK;
WORD fwPrevItem;

WORD fwShape = SL_BLOCK;  /* shape to use for selection rectangle */
```

In this example, the pattern arrays White, Black, Zigzag, and CrossHatch contain the bits defining the 8-by-8-pixel bitmap images. The variables hbmpWhite, hbmpBlack, hbmpZigZag, and hbmpCrossHatch contain the bitmap handles of the brush patterns; hbmpDog, hbmpCat, and hbmpClrPattern contain the bitmap handles of the bitmaps to be displayed; hmenuBitmap1, hmenuBitmap2, and hmenuBitmap3 contain the bitmap handles of bitmaps to be displayed in the Bitmaps menu; hBrush, hBitmap, and fwStretchMode contain the current background brush, bitmap, and stretching mode; and hdc, hdcMemory, and hOldBitmap contain handles used with the memory device context. The Bitmap structure specifies the dimensions of the current bitmap. The fTrack variable indicates a selection in progress. The Rect structure defines the current selection rectangle. The variables fwPrevBitmap, fwPrevPattern, fwPrevMode, and fwPrevItem identify the previously chosen bitmap, pattern, and stretching mode. These identifiers are used to place and remove check marks in the menus.

Add the following local variables to the MainWndProc function:

```
HMENU    hMenu;
HBRUSH   hOldBrush;
HBITMAP  hOurBitmap;
```

11.6.5 Adding a WM_CREATE Case

The Bitmap application must have a WM_CREATE case and supporting variable and function declarations to create or load the bitmaps and to set the menus. The WM_CREATE case creates four 8-by-8-pixel monochrome bitmaps to be used as patterns in a pattern brush for the window background. It also creates or loads three 64-by-32-pixel bitmaps to be displayed in the window. So that the user can choose a bitmap or pattern for viewing, the WM_CREATE case adds the bitmap or pattern to the Bitmap or Pattern menu by using the **AppendMenu** function. Finally, the case sets the initial values of the brush, bitmap, and stretching modes and creates the memory device context from which the bitmaps are copied.

The WM_CREATE case creates the four patterns by using the **CreateBitmap** function. It loads two bitmaps, Dog and Cat, and creates a third by using the Make-ColorBitmap function defined within the application. After creating the patterns and bitmaps, the WM_CREATE case creates pop-up menus, appends the patterns and bitmaps to the appropriate menus, and replaces the existing Bitmap and Pattern menus with the new pop-up menus. Next, it sets the hBrush, hBitmap, and fwStretchMode variables to the initial values for the background brush, bitmap, and stretching modes. Finally, the case creates the memory device context from which the bitmaps will be copied to the screen. To create this case, add the following statements to your window procedure:

```
case WM_CREATE:

    hbmpWhite = CreateBitmap(8, 8, 1, 1, (LPSTR) White);
    hbmpBlack = CreateBitmap(8, 8, 1, 1, (LPSTR) Black);
    hbmpZigZag = CreateBitmap(8, 8, 1, 1, (LPSTR) Zigzag);
    hbmpCrossHatch = CreateBitmap(8, 8, 1, 1, (LPSTR) CrossHatch);

    hbmpDog = LoadBitmap(hinst, "dog");
    hbmpCat = LoadBitmap(hinst, "cat");
    if ((hbmpClrPattern = MakeColorBitmap(hwnd)) == NULL)
        return -1;

    hmenuBitmap1 = LoadBitmap(hinst, "dog");
    hmenuBitmap2 = LoadBitmap(hinst, "cat");
```

```
    if ((hmenuBitmap3 = MakeColorBitmap(hwnd)) == NULL)
        return -1;

hmenu = CreateMenu();
AppendMenu(hmenu, MF_STRING | MF_CHECKED, IDM_PATTERN1,
    "&White");
AppendMenu(hmenu, MF_STRING | MF_CHECKED, IDM_PATTERN2,
    "&Black");
AppendMenu(hmenu, MF_BITMAP, IDM_PATTERN3,
    (LPSTR) hbmpZigZag);
AppendMenu(hmenu, MF_BITMAP, IDM_PATTERN4,
    (LPSTR) hbmpCrossHatch);

ModifyMenu(GetMenu(hwnd), 1, MF_POPUP | MF_BYPOSITION,
    (UINT) hmenu, "&Pattern");

hmenu = CreateMenu();

/* Use bitmaps for menu items. */

AppendMenu(hmenu, MF_BITMAP, IDM_BITMAP1,
    (LPSTR) hmenuBitmap1);
AppendMenu(hmenu, MF_BITMAP, IDM_BITMAP2,
    (LPSTR) hmenuBitmap2);
AppendMenu(hmenu, MF_BITMAP, IDM_BITMAP3,
    (LPSTR) hmenuBitmap3);

ModifyMenu(GetMenu(hwnd), 0, MF_BYPOSITION | MF_POPUP,
    (UINT) hmenu, "&Bitmap");

hBrush = CreatePatternBrush(hbmpWhite);
fwStretchMode = IDM_BLACKONWHITE;

/* Select the first bitmap */

hdc = GetDC(hwnd);
hdcMemory = CreateCompatibleDC(hdc);
ReleaseDC(hwnd, hdc);
hOldBitmap = SelectObject(hdcMemory, hbmpDog);
GetObject(hbmpDog, 16, (LPSTR) &Bitmap);

break;
```

The **CreateBitmap** and **LoadBitmap** functions work as described in earlier sections in this chapter. The MakeColorBitmap function is created for this application. It creates and draws a color bitmap, using the same method described in Section 11.2.2, "Creating and Filling a Blank Bitmap." The statements of this function are specified later in this section. Note that each bitmap is loaded or created twice. This is required, since no single bitmap handle may be selected into two device contexts at the same time. To display a bitmap in a menu requires a selection, as does displaying the bitmap in the client area.

The **CreateMenu** function creates an empty menu and returns a handle to the menu. The **ChangeMenu** functions that specify the pattern handles add the patterns as menu items to the new menu. The MF_BITMAP option specifies that a bitmap will be added. The **CheckMenuItem** function places a check mark next to the current menu item, and the last **ChangeMenu** function replaces the existing Pattern menu. The same steps are then repeated for the Bitmap menu.

The **CreateCompatibleDC** function creates a memory device context that is compatible with the display. The **SelectObject** function selects the current bitmap into the memory device context so that it is ready to be copied to the display. The **Get-Object** function copies the dimensions of the bitmap into the Bitmap structure. The structure can then be used in subsequent **BitBlt** and **StretchBlt** functions to specify the width and height of the bitmap.

The following MakeColorBitmap function creates a color bitmap by creating a bitmap that is compatible with the display; then it paints a plaid color pattern by using red, green, and blue brushes and the **PatBlt** function. To use this function, add the following definition to the end of your source file:

```
HBITMAP MakeColorBitmap(HWND hwnd)
{
    HDC hdc;
    HDC hdcMemory;
    HBITMAP hBitmap;
    HBITMAP hOldBitmap;
    HBRUSH hRedBrush;
    HBRUSH hGreenBrush;
    HBRUSH hBlueBrush;
    HBRUSH hOldBrush;

        .
        .
        .

    hdc = GetDC(hwnd);
    if ((hdcMemory = CreateCompatibleDC(hdc)) == NULL)
        return NULL;
    if ((hBitmap = CreateCompatibleBitmap(hdc, 64, 32)) == NULL)
        return NULL;
    hOldBitmap = SelectObject(hdcMemory, hBitmap);
    hRedBrush = CreateSolidBrush(RGB(255, 0, 0));
    hGreenBrush = CreateSolidBrush(RGB(0, 255, 0));
    hBlueBrush = CreateSolidBrush(RGB(0, 0, 255));

    PatBlt(hdcMemory, 0, 0, 64, 32, BLACKNESS);
    hOldBrush = SelectObject(hdcMemory, hRedBrush);
    PatBlt(hdcMemory, 0, 0, 24, 11, PATORDEST);
    PatBlt(hdcMemory, 40, 10, 24, 12, PATORDEST);
    PatBlt(hdcMemory, 20, 21, 24, 11, PATORDEST);
    SelectObject(hdcMemory, hGreenBrush);
    PatBlt(hdcMemory, 20, 0, 24, 11, PATORDEST);
    PatBlt(hdcMemory, 0, 10, 24, 12, PATORDEST);
    PatBlt(hdcMemory, 40, 21, 24, 11, PATORDEST);
```

```
        SelectObject(hdcMemory, hBlueBrush);
        PatBlt(hdcMemory, 40, 0, 24, 11, PATORDEST);
        PatBlt(hdcMemory, 20, 10, 24, 12, PATORDEST);
        PatBlt(hdcMemory, 0, 21, 24, 11, PATORDEST);

        BitBlt(hdc, 0, 0, 64, 32, hdcMemory, 0, 0, SRCCOPY)

        SelectObject(hdcMemory, hOldBrush);
        DeleteObject(hRedBrush);
        DeleteObject(hGreenBrush);
        DeleteObject(hBlueBrush);
        SelectObject(hdcMemory, hOldBitmap);
        ReleaseDC(hwnd, hdc);
        DeleteDC(hdcMemory);
        return hBitmap;
}
```

This function carries out the same steps described at the end of Section 11.2.3, "Creating a Bitmap with Hard-Coded Bits."

11.6.6 Modifying the WM_DESTROY Case

Before your application terminates, it must delete any bitmaps, patterns, brushes, and memory device contexts it has created. You delete bitmaps, patterns, and brushes by using the **DeleteObject** function. You delete the memory device context by using the **DeleteDC** function. Modify the WM_DESTROY case so that it looks like this:

```
case WM_DESTROY:
    SelectObject(hdcMemory, hOldBitmap);
    DeleteDC(hdcMemory);
    DeleteObject(hBrush);
    DeleteObject(hbmpWhite);
    DeleteObject(hbmpBlack);
    DeleteObject(hbmpZigZag);
    DeleteObject(hbmpCrossHatch);
    DeleteObject(hbmpDog);
    DeleteObject(hbmpCat);
    DeleteObject(hbmpClrPattern);
    DeleteObject(hmenuBitmap1);
    DeleteObject(hmenuBitmap2);
    DeleteObject(hmenuBitmap3);

    PostQuitMessage(0);
    break;
```

11.6.7 Adding WM_LBUTTONUP, WM_MOUSEMOVE, and WM_LBUTTONDOWN Cases

So that the user can select a rectangle in which to copy the current bitmap, you must add WM_LBUTTONUP, WM_MOUSEMOVE, and WM_LBUTTONDOWN cases to your application's window procedure. These cases use the selection functions (described in Chapter 20, "Dynamic-Link Libraries") to create a selection rectangle and supply feedback to the user. The WM_LBUTTONUP case then uses the **StretchBlt** function to fill the rectangle. To create these cases, add the following statements to your window procedure:

```
case WM_LBUTTONDOWN:

    fTrack = TRUE;
    SetRectEmpty(&Rect);
    StartSelection(hwnd, MAKEPOINT(lParam), &Rect,
        (wParam & MK_SHIFT) ? (SL_EXTEND | fwShape) : fwShape);
    break;

case WM_MOUSEMOVE:

    if (fTrack)
        UpdateSelection(hwnd, MAKEPOINT(lParam), &Rect,
            fwShape);
    break;

case WM_LBUTTONUP:

    fTrack = FALSE;
    EndSelection(MAKEPOINT(lParam), &Rect);
    ClearSelection(hwnd, &Rect, fwShape);

    hdc = GetDC(hwnd);
    SetStretchBltMode(hdc, fwStretchMode);
    StretchBlt(hdc, Rect.left, Rect.top,
        Rect.right - Rect.left, Rect.bottom - Rect.top,
        hdcMemory, 0, 0,
        Bitmap.bmWidth, Bitmap.bmHeight,
        SRCCOPY);
    ReleaseDC(hwnd, hdc);
    break;
```

To use these functions, you also must include the SELECT.H file (defined in Chapter 20, "Dynamic-Link Libraries"), by adding the following statement to the beginning of your source file:

```
#include "select.h"
```

11.6.8 Adding a WM_RBUTTONUP Case

You will need to use the **BitBlt** function to display the current bitmap. To do this, include the function in a WM_RBUTTONUP case in your window procedure, as follows:

```
case WM_RBUTTONUP:

    hdc = GetDC(hwnd);
    BitBlt(hdc, LOWORD(lParam), HIWORD(lParam),
        Bitmap.bmWidth, Bitmap.bmHeight,
        hdcMemory, 0, 0, SRCCOPY);
    ReleaseDC(hwnd, hdc);
    break;
```

11.6.9 Adding a WM_ERASEBKGND Case

To ensure that the selected background brush is used, you must create a WM_ERASEBKGND case, by adding the following statements to your window procedure:

```
case WM_ERASEBKGND:

    UnrealizeObject(hBrush);
    hOldBrush = SelectObject((HDC) wParam, (HGDIOBJ) hBrush);
    GetClientRect(hwnd, &Rect);
    PatBlt((HDC) wParam, Rect.left, Rect.top,
        Rect.right - Rect.left, Rect.bottom - Rect.top, PATCOPY);
    SelectObject((HDC) wParam, (HGDIOBJ) hOldBrush);
    return TRUE;
```

The hOldBrush variable is declared as a local variable. The **UnrealizeObject** function sets the pattern alignment if the window has moved. The **SelectObject** function sets the background brush, and the **GetClientRect** function determines which part of the client area must be erased. The **PatBlt** function copies the pattern to the update rectangle. The final **SelectObject** function restores the previous brush.

11.6.10 Modifying the WM_COMMAND Case

To support the Bitmap, Pattern, and Mode menus, you must change the WM_COMMAND case. In your window procedure, replace the current WM_COMMAND case with the following statements:

```
case WM_COMMAND:
    switch (wParam) {
        case IDM_ABOUT:
            lpProcAbout =
                MakeProcInstance((FARPROC) About, hinst);
```

```
                DialogBox(hinst,
                    "AboutBox",
                    hwnd,
                    (DLGPROC) lpProcAbout);
                FreeProcInstance(lpProcAbout);
                break;

            case IDM_BITMAP1:

                fwPrevItem = fwPrevBitmap;
                fwPrevBitmap = wParam;
                GetObject(hbmpDog, 16, (LPSTR) &Bitmap);
                SelectObject(hdcMemory, hbmpDog);
                break;

            case IDM_BITMAP2:

                fwPrevItem = fwPrevBitmap;
                fwPrevBitmap = wParam;
                GetObject(hbmpCat, 16, (LPSTR) &Bitmap);
                SelectObject(hdcMemory, hbmpCat);
                break;

            case IDM_BITMAP3:

                fwPrevItem = fwPrevBitmap;
                fwPrevBitmap = wParam;
                GetObject(hbmpClrPattern, 16, (LPSTR) &Bitmap);
                hOurBitmap = SelectObject(hdcMemory, hbmpClrPattern);
                break;

            case IDM_PATTERN1:

                fwPrevItem = fwPrevPattern;
                fwPrevPattern = wParam;
                DeleteObject(hBrush);
                hBrush = CreatePatternBrush(hbmpWhite);
                InvalidateRect(hwnd, (LPRECT) NULL, TRUE);
                UpdateWindow(hwnd);
                break;

            case IDM_PATTERN2:

                fwPrevItem = fwPrevPattern;
                fwPrevPattern = wParam;
                DeleteObject(hBrush);
                hBrush = CreatePatternBrush(hbmpBlack);
                InvalidateRect(hwnd, (LPRECT) NULL, TRUE);
                UpdateWindow(hwnd);
                break;
```

```
                    case IDM_PATTERN3:

                        fwPrevItem = fwPrevPattern;
                        fwPrevPattern = wParam;
                        DeleteObject(hBrush);
                        hBrush = CreatePatternBrush(hbmpZigZag);
                        InvalidateRect(hwnd, (LPRECT) NULL, TRUE);
                        UpdateWindow(hwnd);
                        break;

                    case IDM_PATTERN4:

                        fwPrevItem = fwPrevPattern;
                        fwPrevPattern = wParam;
                        DeleteObject(hBrush);
                        hBrush = CreatePatternBrush(hbmpCrossHatch);
                        InvalidateRect(hwnd, (LPRECT) NULL, TRUE);
                        UpdateWindow(hwnd);
                        break;

                    case IDM_BLACKONWHITE:

                        fwPrevItem = fwPrevMode;
                        fwPrevMode = wParam;
                        fwStretchMode = BLACKONWHITE;
                        break;

                    case IDM_WHITEONBLACK:

                        fwPrevItem = fwPrevMode;
                        fwPrevMode = wParam;
                        fwStretchMode = WHITEONBLACK;
                        break;

                    case IDM_COLORONCOLOR:

                        fwPrevItem = fwPrevMode;
                        fwPrevMode = wParam;
                        fwStretchMode = COLORONCOLOR;
                        break;
                }

                CheckMenuItem(GetMenu(hwnd), fwPrevItem, MF_UNCHECKED);
                CheckMenuItem(GetMenu(hwnd), wParam, MF_CHECKED);
                break;
```

Note that this new WM_COMMAND case handles the IDM_ABOUT case by using a **switch** statement instead of an **if** statement.

11.6.11 Modifying the Makefile

The resource file BITMAP.RES is dependent on the bitmap files DOG.BMP and CAT.BMP. To ensure that Microsoft Windows Resource Compiler (RC) updates BITMAP.RES whenever DOG.BMP or CAT.BMP changes, add the following to the makefile:

```
bitmap.res: bitmap.rc bitmap.h dog.bmp cat.bmp
    rc /r bitmap.rc
```

You must also modify the **link** command line in the makefile to include the SELECT.LIB library file. This file contains the import declarations for the selection routines that are used with the WM_LBUTTONUP, WM_MOUSEMOVE, and WM_LBUTTONDOWN cases. For more information about creating the library, see Chapter 20, "Dynamic-Link Libraries."

To include the SELECT.LIB library file, modify the **link** command line so that it looks like this:

```
link /nod bitmap, , , slibcew libw select.lib, bitmap.def
```

11.6.12 Compiling and Linking

After making the necessary changes, compile and link the Bitmap application. Start Windows and then the Bitmap application.

To display the Dog or Cat bitmaps, press the left mouse button, drag the mouse to form a rectangle, and release the button. Use the menus to change the background and the stretching mode. Note the effect of the stretching mode on the Dog and Cat bitmaps.

11.7 Related Topics

For more information about functions used for selection, see Chapter 6, "Cursors," and Chapter 20, "Dynamic-Link Libraries."

For more information about using bitmaps in menus, see Chapter 7, "Menus."

For more information about functions used with bitmaps, see the *Microsoft Windows Programmer's Reference, Volume 2*.

For more information about Image Editor, see *Microsoft Windows Programming Tools*.

Printing

Most applications provide a way for users to get printed copies of their program data. With most operating systems, your application must deal with the varied capabilities and requirements of many different printers. With the Microsoft Windows operating system, your application need not provide any printer-specific code; it can simply print on the current printer. Windows, and the Windows printer drivers, translate your application's print request to information any printer can use.

This chapter covers the following topics:

- Printing with Windows
- Getting information about the printer
- Printing a line of text
- Printing a bitmap
- Processing printing errors
- Canceling print operations
- Using banding to print graphics images

This chapter also explains how to create a sample Windows 3.1 application, PrntFile, that illustrates many of the concepts explained in the chapter.

12.1 Printing with Windows

With Windows, your application does not print by interacting directly with the printer. Instead, it prints by sending output to a printer device context. This means that, when writing your application, you need not worry about each printer's specific capabilities or requirements.

Printing in Windows is handled by the graphics device interface (GDI). In general, the procedure for printing information is similar to that for displaying information; you retrieve a handle to a device context, then send output to that device context. Typically, an application follows these steps in order to print to the current printer:

1. The application first retrieves information about the current printer, such as its model name, device driver, and printer port, from the WIN.INI initialization file. This information is necessary for the application to create a device context for the current printer.

2. When your application sends output to a printer device context, Windows activates the print spooler to manage the print request.

3. Your application uses six printer functions to control the print job. If necessary, your application can use printer escapes to communicate with the printer's device driver.

12.1.1 Functions and Printer Escapes

Six functions provide most of the functionality required for an application that implements printing for Windows version 3.1:

Function	Description
AbortDoc	Terminates a print job. Supersedes the ABORTDOC printer escape.
EndDoc	Ends a print job. Supersedes the ENDDOC printer escape.
EndPage	Ends a page. Supersedes the NEWFRAME printer escape.
SetAbortProc	Sets the abort function for a print job. Supersedes the SETABORTPROC printer escape.
StartDoc	Starts a print job. Supersedes the STARTDOC printer escape.
StartPage	Prepares the printer driver to receive data. Supersedes the NEWFRAME and BANDINFO printer escapes.

The functions in the preceding list are new for Windows 3.1. Another function, **ResetDC**, is also new for Windows 3.1. **ResetDC** updates a device context, allowing an application to change the paper orientation or paper bin within a single print job. This ability was not supported by a printer escape in previous versions of Windows.

The **PrintDlg** function displays a Print dialog box or a Print Setup dialog box. These dialog boxes are two of the common dialog boxes that are new for Windows 3.1. The Print dialog box makes it possible for the user to specify the properties of a particular print job. The Print Setup dialog box makes it possible for the user to select additional job properties and configure the printer.

With previous versions of Windows, applications used printer escapes to communicate with the device driver associated with the printer. Most applications no longer need to use printer escapes. Support for escapes is still provided, however, for backward compatibility with previous versions of Windows and because in some cases (for example, complex graphics data on PostScript printers) printer escapes offer functionality that the functions do not. Applications should use the new printer functions whenever possible, to maximize their compatibility with future Windows versions.

For information about printer escapes, see the *Microsoft Windows Programmer's Reference, Volume 3*.

12.2 Retrieving Information About the Current Printer

To create a printer device context for your application, you need information about the printer, such as its type and the computer port to which it is connected. Windows Control Panel adds information about the current printer to the device=

setting in the [windows] section of the WIN.INI file. Any application can retrieve this information by using the **GetProfileString** function. You can then use the information with the **CreateDC** function to create a printer device context for a particular printer on a particular computer port.

Printer information from the WIN.INI file consists of three settings, separated by commas:

- The name of the current printer device driver (for example, EPSON9)
- The name of the current printer model (for example, Epson FX-80)
- The current printer port (for example, LPT1:)

The following example retrieves printer information for the currently selected default printer and divides the fields into separate strings:

```
char  pPrintInfo[80];
LPSTR lpTemp;
LPSTR lpPrintDevice;
LPSTR lpPrintDriver;
LPSTR lpPrintPort;

GetProfileString("windows",
    "device",
    "",
    (LPSTR) pPrintInfo, 80);
lpTemp = lpPrintDevice = (LPSTR) pPrintInfo;
lpPrintDriver = lpPrintPort = (LPSTR) NULL;

while (*lpTemp) {
    if (*lpTemp == ',') {
        *lpTemp++ = 0;
        while (*lpTemp == ' ')
            lpTemp++;
        if (!lpPrintDriver)
            lpPrintDriver = lpTemp;
        else {
            lpPrintPort = lpTemp;
            break;
        }
    }

    else
        lpTemp = AnsiNext(lpTemp);
}
```

In this example, the **GetProfileString** function retrieves information about the currently selected default printer from the device= field in the [windows] section of the WIN.INI file. The function then copies the line to the pPrintInfo array.

A **while** statement divides the line into three separate fields: the printer driver name, the name of the printer model, and the printer port.

Because the fields are separated by commas, an **if** statement checks for a comma and, if necessary, replaces the comma with a zero in order to end the field with a terminating null character.

Another **while** statement skips any leading spaces in the next field. Each pointer—lpPrintDrvName, lpPrintModel, and lpPrintPort—receives the address of the beginning of its respective field.

These pointers are then used in a call to the **CreateDC** function to create a printer device context for the current printer.

12.3 Printing a Line of Text

Printing a single line of text requires the following steps:

1. Create the device context for the printer.
2. Start the print request (also called a print job).
3. Start a page.
4. Print the line.
5. End the page.
6. End the print request.
7. Delete the device context.

The following example prints a single line of text on the currently selected default printer:

```
LPSTR lpPrintDevice;
LPSTR lpPrintDriver;
LPSTR lpPrintPort;

HDC       hdcPrint;
DOCINFO   DocInfo;              /* used in StartDoc function    */

hdcPrint = CreateDC(lpPrintDriver,
    lpPrintDevice,
    lpPrintPort,
    (LPSTR) NULL);
```

```
if (hdcPrint != NULL) {
    DocInfo.cbSize = sizeof(DOCINFO);
    DocInfo.lpszDocName = "Test";
    DocInfo.lpszOutput = (LPSTR) NULL;
    StartDoc(hdcPrint, &DocInfo);
    StartPage(hdcPrint);
    TextOut(hdcPrint, 10, 10, "A single line of text.", 22);
    EndPage(hdcPrint);
    EndDoc(hdcPrint);
    DeleteDC(hdcPrint);
}
```

In this example, the **CreateDC** function creates the device context for the printer and returns a handle of the printer device context. This example stores the handle in the variable hdcPrint. When calling **CreateDC**, an application must supply the first three parameters; the fourth parameter can be set to NULL. In this example, it is assumed that the **GetProfileString** function has been used to supply the parameters to the **CreateDC** function. The last parameter to **CreateDC** specifies how to initialize the printer. NULL specifies the default print settings. For more information about specifying print settings that differ from the default settings, see Chapter 17, "Print Settings."

After the device context has been created, the **StartDoc** function starts the print request by sending Windows the handle of the device context and a far pointer to a **DOCINFO** structure. The **DOCINFO** structure has three members, which describe the size of the structure, the name of the document being sent to the printer (that is, the name that is displayed by Print Manager), and the name of the output file (if the application sends output to a file). If the name of the output file is NULL, the output is sent to the device specified by the device context. (In this example, the output goes to the port specified by the lpPrintPort parameter in the call to the **CreateDC** function).

The **StartPage** function instructs the printer driver to begin a new page frame. The **TextOut** function copies the line of text to the printer. The line will be placed starting at the coordinates (10,10) on the printer paper. The default units are printer pixels. The default printer coordinates are relative to the upper-left corner of the printable area. (An application can change either of these by changing the mapping mode associated with the device context.)

Note Do not expect the line of text to be printed immediately. The spooler collects all output for a print request before sending it to the printer, so any printing does not begin until after the call to the **EndDoc** function.

The **EndPage** function completes the page. The **EndDoc** function signals the end of the print request. Finally, the **DeleteDC** function deletes the printer device context.

12.4 Printing a Bitmap

Printing a bitmap is similar to printing a line of text. To print a bitmap, follow these steps:

1. Create a memory device context that is compatible with the bitmap.
2. Load the bitmap, and select it into the memory device context.
3. Start the print request.
4. Indicate the beginning of a new page frame.
5. Use the **BitBlt** function to copy the bitmap from the memory device context to the printer.
6. Indicate the ending of the current page frame.
7. End the print request.
8. Remove the bitmap from the memory device context and delete the device context.

The following example prints a bitmap named Dog that has been added to the resource-definition file.

```
char    pPrintInfo[80];
LPSTR  lpTemp;
LPSTR  lpPrintDevice;
LPSTR  lpPrintDriver;
LPSTR  lpPrintPort;

HDC        hdcPrint, hdcMemory;
HBITMAP    hBitmap, hOldBitmap;
BITMAP     Bitmap;
DOCINFO    DocInfo;            /* used in StartDoc function    */

    /*
     * Use GetProfileString to retrieve strings declared above and
     * parse them as shown in the earlier example.
     */

hdcPrint = CreateDC(lpPrintDriver,
    lpPrintDevice,
    lpPrintPort,
    (LPSTR) NULL);

if (hdcPrint != NULL) {
    hdcMemory = CreateCompatibleDC(hdcPrint);
    hBitmap = LoadBitmap(hAppInstance, "Dog");
    GetObject(hBitmap, sizeof(BITMAP), &Bitmap);
    hOldBitmap = SelectObject(hdcMemory, hBitmap);

    DocInfo.cbSize = sizeof(DOCINFO);
```

```
        DocInfo.lpszDocName = "Test";
        DocInfo.lpszOutput = (LPSTR) NULL;
        StartDoc(hdcPrint, &DocInfo);
        StartPage(hdcPrint);
        BitBlt(hdcPrint, 10, 30,
            Bitmap.bmWidth,
            Bitmap.bmHeight,
            hdcMemory, 0, 0, SRCCOPY);
        EndPage(hdcPrint);
        EndDoc(hdcPrint);
        DeleteDC(hdcPrint);
        SelectObject(hdcMemory, hOldBitmap);
        DeleteDC(hdcMemory);
        DeleteObject(hBitmap);
}
```

In this example, the application retrieves the printer device context. The **CreateCompatibleDC** function then creates a memory device context that is compatible with the printer's device context.

The **LoadBitmap** function loads the bitmap Dog from the application's resources, and the **GetObject** function retrieves information about the bitmap, such as its height and width. These values are used later in the **BitBlt** function.

The **SelectObject** function selects the bitmap into the memory device context.

The statements for creating the printer device context and starting the print request are identical to those used in the example that printed a line of text.

To send the bitmap image to the printer, the application uses the **BitBlt** function. **BitBlt** copies the bitmap from the memory device context to the printer, placing the bitmap at the coordinates (10,30). (The **BitBlt** function takes the place of the **TextOut** function, used in the previous example to print a line of text.)

The statements that end the current page frame and end the document are identical to those used in the previous example.

After the print request is complete, the **SelectObject** and **DeleteDC** functions remove the bitmap from selection and delete the memory device context. Since the bitmap is no longer needed, the **DeleteObject** function removes it from memory.

12.5 Processing Errors During Printing

Although GDI and the spooler attempt to report all printing errors to the user, your application must be prepared to report and handle out-of-disk-space and out-of-memory conditions. When there is an error in processing the **EndPage** function, it returns a value less than zero. In this case, the return value includes an SP_NOTREPORTED bit. If the bit is zero, GDI has already notified the user.

If the bit is set, the application must notify the user. The bit is typically set for general-failure, out-of-disk-space, and out-of-memory errors.

The following example processes unreported errors during printing:

```
int status;
    .
    .
    .

status = EndPage(hdcPrint);

if (status < 0) {  /* Any unreported errors? */
    if (status & SP_NOTREPORTED) {  /* Yes */
        switch (status) {

            case SP_OUTOFDISK:

                /* Inform user; perform any required processing. */

                break;

            case SP_OUTOFMEMORY:

                /* Inform user; perform any required processing. */

                break;

            default:

                /* Inform user; perform any required processing. */

                break;
        }
    }

    else   /* Reported, but may need further action */
        switch (status | SP_NOTREPORTED) {

            case SP_OUTOFDISK:

                /* Perform any required processing. */

                break;

            case SP_OUTOFMEMORY:

                /* Perform any required processing. */

                break;
        }
}
```

In this example, the first **if** statement determines whether the value that the **End-Page** function returns, status, is less than zero and the SP_NOTREPORTED bit is set. (When Windows sets the SP_NOTREPORTED bit, it indicates that this error has not been reported to the user.) If these two conditions are met, then the application must process the unreported error.

The application then uses a **switch** statement to provide special responses to the SP_OUTOFDISK and SP_OUTOFMEMORY errors. For all other unreported errors, the application simply provides a general-failure alert.

If the status variable is less than zero but SP_NOTREPORTED is not set, Windows has already reported the error to the user. However, the application can still process these reported errors.

In most cases, the correct response to an unreported error is to display a message box explaining the error and to terminate the print request. If the error has already been reported, you can terminate the request and then restart it after additional disk space or memory has been made available.

12.6 Canceling a Print Operation

Your application should always give the user a chance to cancel a lengthy printing operation. A common way to do this is to display a dialog box when the printing operation begins. During printing, the user can click the dialog box's Cancel button to cancel the print operation.

To provide a dialog box from which the user can cancel a printing operation, follow these steps:

1. In your application's resource-definition (.RC) file, define a modeless dialog box from which the user can cancel a print operation.

2. In your application source code, provide a dialog box procedure that drives the dialog box.

3. In your application source code, provide a print-canceling function that processes messages for the dialog box.

4. Modify your application's printing procedure so that it displays the dialog box and correctly processes messages.

5. Export the dialog box procedure and print-canceling function in the module-definition (.DEF) file.

12.6.1 Defining a Dialog Box That Cancels a Print Operation

In your application's resource-definition file, provide a dialog box template for the dialog box that the user can use to cancel the print operation. Add the following statements:

```
AbortDlg DIALOG 20, 20, 90, 64
STYLE DS_MODALFRAME | WS_CAPTION | WS_SYSMENU
CAPTION "PrntFile"
BEGIN
    DEFPUSHBUTTON "Cancel", IDCANCEL,   29, 44, 32, 14, WS_GROUP
    CTEXT     "Sending",         -1,           0,  8, 90, 8
    CTEXT     "text",            IDC_FILENAME, 0, 18, 90, 8
    CTEXT     "to print spooler.", -1,         0, 28, 90, 8
END
```

12.6.2 Defining a Dialog Box Procedure for the Abort Dialog Box

In your application source code, you must provide a dialog box procedure for the Abort dialog box. The procedure should process the messages WM_INITDIALOG and WM_COMMAND. So that the user can choose the Cancel button by using the keyboard, the procedure takes control of the input focus when the dialog box is initialized. The dialog box procedure then ignores all messages until a WM_COMMAND message appears. Command input causes the function to destroy the window and set the fAbort flag to TRUE. The following example shows the required statements for the dialog box procedure:

```
int FAR PASCAL AbortDlg(hWnd, msg, wParam, lParam)
HWND hWnd;
UINT msg;
WPARAM wParam;
LPARAM lParam;
{
    if (msg == WM_COMMAND) {
        if (wParam == IDCANCEL) {

            /* The user has canceled the print operation. */

            fAbort = TRUE; /* global flag                */

            EndDialog(hWnd, wParam);
            return TRUE;
        }
    }
```

```
    else if (msg == WM_INITDIALOG) {

        /* Set the input focus for user input. */

        SetFocus(hWnd);
        return TRUE;
    }

    return FALSE;
}
```

12.6.3 Defining a Function That Cancels a Print Operation

In your application code, you must provide a print-canceling function to process messages for the Abort dialog box. A print-canceling function retrieves messages from the application queue and dispatches them if they are intended for the Abort dialog box. The function continues to loop until it encounters the WM_DESTROY message or until the print operation is complete.

Applications that make lengthy print requests must pass a print-canceling function to GDI to handle special situations during printing operations. The most common situation occurs when a printing operation fills the available disk space before the spooler can copy the data to the printer. Since the spooler can continue to print even though disk space is full, GDI calls the print-canceling function to determine whether it is necessary for the application to cancel the print operation or whether it can simply wait until disk space is free.

To specify the print-canceling function, first retrieve the procedure-instance address for the function:

```
lpAbortProc = MakeProcInstance((FARPROC) AbortProc, hinst);
```

Then call the **SetAbortProc** function, specifying the Abort function's address:

```
SetAbortProc(hDC, (ABORTPROC) lpAbortProc);
```

GDI will then call the print-canceling function during spooling. The function must have the following form:

```
int CALLBACK AbortProc(hdcPrint, Code)
HDC hdcPrint;
int Code;
```

- The *hdcPrint* parameter identifies the printer device context.
- The *Code* parameter specifies the nature of the call. It can take one of two values:

Value	Meaning
SP_OUTOFDISK	Spooler has run out of disk space while spooling the data file. The printing operation will continue if the application waits for disk space to become free.
0	Spooler operation is continuing without error.

Once GDI has called the print-canceling function, the function can return TRUE to continue the spooler operation immediately, or FALSE to cancel the printing operation. Most print-canceling functions call the **PeekMessage** function to temporarily yield control; they then return TRUE to continue the print operation. Yielding control typically gives the spooler enough time to free some disk space.

If the print-canceling function returns FALSE, the printing operation is canceled and the SP_APPABORT error value is returned by the application's next call to the **EndPage** or **EndDoc** function.

Important If your application encounters a printing error or a canceled print operation, it must not attempt to terminate the operation by using the **EndDoc** or **AbortDoc** functions. GDI automatically terminates the operation before returning the error value.

The following example shows the statements required for the print-canceling function:

```
int CALLBACK AbortProc(hdcPrinter, Code)
HDC hdcPrinter;   /* for multiple printer display contexts */
int Code;         /* for printing status                  */
{
    MSG msg;

/* Process the messages intended for the Abort dialog box. */

    while (PeekMessage((LPMSG) &msg,
            NULL, NULL, NULL, PM_REMOVE))
        if (!IsDialogMessage(hAbortDlgWnd,
                (LPMSG) &msg)) {
            TranslateMessage((LPMSG) &msg);
            DispatchMessage((LPMSG) &msg);
        }

/*
 * The fAbort argument is TRUE (return is FALSE)
 * if the user has canceled the print operation.
 */

    return (!fAbort);
}
```

12.6.4 Performing a Cancelable Print Operation

Before beginning a print operation, your application should do the following to ensure that the user can cancel the operation:

1. Define a print-canceling function, as described in the preceding section.

2. Use the **MakeProcInstance** function to retrieve the procedure-instance address for the print-canceling function.

When your application begins a print operation, it should do the following:

1. Use the **SetAbortProc** function to specify the print-canceling function the application will use during the print operation. When calling **SetAbortProc**, specify the procedure-instance address of the application's print-canceling function.

2. Use the **CreateDialog**, **ShowWindow**, and **UpdateWindow** functions to create and display the Abort dialog box.

3. Use the **EnableWindow** function to disable your parent window.

4. Start the normal print operation, but check the return value from the **EndPage** function (or the NEXTBAND escape) after each call. If the return value is less than zero, the user has canceled the operation or an error has occurred.

5. Use the **DestroyWindow** function to destroy the Abort dialog box, if necessary. (Windows destroys the box automatically if the user cancels the print operation.)

6. Use the **EnableWindow** function to reenable the parent window.

12.6.5 Canceling a Print Operation with the AbortDoc Function

You can use the **AbortDoc** function to cancel a print operation, even if you do not have a print-canceling function or an Abort dialog box. Applications can use **AbortDoc** to cancel the operation at any time.

12.7 Using Banding to Print Images

Banding is a technique used to implement the full functionality of the Windows graphics device interface (GDI) in printer drivers that can print graphics only by using bitmaps. An application that exploits the banding process can enhance its printing performance.

Most dot-matrix printers and many laser printers can print only bitmaps and text. When an application that uses such GDI graphic objects as polygons and lines prints to a device that does not support these objects, the printer driver does not send output directly to the printer. Rather, the printer driver generates a bitmap in memory. When all graphics have been rendered into the bitmap, the bitmap itself is printed.

For most printers, this bitmap can be very large. For example, a 300-dots-per-inch (dpi) laser printer requires nearly a megabyte to render a single letter-size page. If memory is limited, the image is broken into a sequence of smaller rectangles, called bands, which cover the page. Each of these individual rectangles is rendered and sent to the printer separately.

There are two ways that the graphics calls can be duplicated on each band. If the application does not exploit the banding process, GDI will capture all graphics calls for a page into a metafile. When the application calls the **EndPage** function or the NEWFRAME (next page) escape, GDI plays the entire metafile into each band. Alternatively, the application may request a band from the printer driver and produce the output itself. This optimizes printing significantly, because in this case GDI does not create, write, and reread a disk-based metafile.

Whether GDI or the application requests the band from the driver, the process is very similar. Banding printer drivers implement the NEXTBAND escape. This escape causes the printer driver to send the previous band to the printer (if any) and to initialize itself to render the new band. It also returns a rectangle defining the bounds of the band bitmap relative to the whole page. Output calls made to the driver's device context after using the NEXTBAND escape go directly to the printer driver.

GDI (or the banding application) calls the NEXTBAND escape to retrieve the coordinates of the first band. Then it calls NEXTBAND again after each band is rendered so that the printer driver can send the current band to the print manager and retrieve the coordinates of the next band. When all bands have been printed, NEXTBAND causes the printer driver to eject the page and return an empty rectangle to the application, indicating the end of a page.

Note An application that uses banding should determine the end of a page by waiting for NEXTBAND to return an empty rectangle. A banding application should not use the NEXTFRAME escape.

To use banding to print an image, follow these steps:

1. Use the **CreateDC** function to retrieve a device context for the printer.

2. Use the **Escape** function and the NEXTBAND escape to retrieve the coordinates of a band:

```
Escape(hdcPrinter, NEXTBAND, 0, (LPSTR) NULL, &rcRect);
```

The function sets the rcRect structure to the coordinates of the current band. The coordinates are in device units, and all subsequent GDI calls are clipped to this rectangle.

3. Determine whether the rcRect structure specifies an empty rectangle. (An empty rectangle marks the end of a page.) If the rectangle is empty, terminate the banding operation.

4. Use the **DPtoLP** function to translate the rcRect coordinates from device units to logical units.

```
DPtoLP(hdcPrinter, (POINT FAR*) &rcRect, 2);
```

5. Use GDI output functions and other functions to draw within the band. To save time, the application should carry out only those GDI functions that affect the current band. If an application does not need to save time, GDI will clip all output that does not appear in the band, so no special action is required.

6. Repeat steps 2 through 5.

Once the banding operation is complete, use the **DeleteDC** function to remove the printer device context.

The following example shows how to print using banding:

```
DOCINFO  DocInfo;

hdcPrint = CreateDC(lpPrintDriver, /* values from GetProfileString */
    lpPrintDevice,
    lpPrintPort,
    (LPSTR) NULL);

if (hdcPrinter != NULL) {
    DocInfo.cbSize = sizeof(DOCINFO);
    DocInfo.lpszDocName = "Test";
    DocInfo.lpszOutput = (LPSTR) NULL;
    StartDoc(hdcPrinter, &DocInfo);

    for (;;) {
        Escape(hdcPrinter, NEXTBAND, 0, (LPSTR) NULL, &rcRect);
        if (IsRectEmpty(&rcRect)
            break;

        DPtoLP(hdcPrinter, (POINT FAR*) &rcRect, 2);

        /*
         * Place output function here. To save time, use rcRect to
         * filter output functions that do not fall in this band.
         */

    }
    EndDoc(hdcPrinter);
    DeleteDC(hdcPrinter);
}
```

12.8 Sample Application: PrntFile

This section explains how to add printing capability to the EditFile application, described in Chapter 10, "File Input and Output," by copying the current text from the edit control and printing it by using the methods described in this chapter. To add printing capability, modify the EditFile application as follows:

1. Add an AbortDlg dialog box template to the resource-definition file.
2. Add new variables for printing.
3. Add an IDM_PRINT case to the WM_COMMAND case.
4. Create the AbortDlg dialog box procedure and the AbortProc function.
5. Add a GetPrinterDC function.
6. Export the AbortDlg dialog box procedure and AbortProc function.
7. Compile and link the application.

This example shows how to print the contents of the edit control, including the statements required to support the print-canceling function and the dialog box procedure for the Abort dialog box.

12.8.1 Adding an AbortDlg Dialog Box

To support printing, most applications use a new dialog box, AbortDlg. With this dialog box, the user can cancel a print operation by clicking the Cancel button. To create this dialog box, add the following **DIALOG** statement to the resource-definition file:

```
AbortDlg DIALOG 20, 20, 90, 64
STYLE DS_MODALFRAME | WS_CAPTION | WS_SYSMENU
CAPTION "PrntFile"
BEGIN
    DefPushButton "Cancel", IDCANCEL,   29, 44, 32, 14, WS_GROUP
    Ctext     "Sending",            -1,        0,  8, 90,  8
    Ctext     "text",               IDC_FILENAME, 0, 18, 90,  8
    Ctext     "to print spooler.",  -1,        0, 28, 90,  8
END
```

12.8.2 Adding Variables for Printing

Your application must also declare new variables to support printing. Add the following declarations to the beginning of your source file:

```
HDC hdcPrinter;              /* handle of printer device context */
int LineSpace;               /* spacing between lines            */
int LinesPerPage;            /* lines per page                   */
int CurrentLine;             /* current line                     */
int LineLength;              /* line length                      */
WORD wLines;                 /* number of lines to print         */
WORD wIndex;                 /* index into lines to print        */
char szLine[128];        /* buffer to store lines before printing */
TEXTMETRIC TextMetric;   /* information about character size     */
BOOL bAbort;             /* FALSE if user cancels printing       */
HWND hAbortDlgWnd;
FARPROC lpAbortDlg, lpAbortProc;
```

The hdcPrint variable is the handle of the printer device context. It receives the return value from the **CreateDC** function. The variables LineSpace and LinesPerPage hold the amount of spacing between lines and the number of lines that can be printed per page, respectively. The CurrentLine variable is a counter that keeps track of the current line on the current page. Lines of text are printed one line at a time. The dwLines variable contains the number of lines in the edit control. The TextMetric structure receives information about the font to be used to print the lines; this example uses only the members TextMetric.tmHeight and Text-Metric.tmExternalLeading. The PhysPageSize structure receives the physical width and height of the printer paper. The height is used to determine how many lines per page can be printed.

12.8.3 Adding an IDM_PRINT Case

For your application to carry out the printing operation, you must add an IDM_PRINT case to the WM_COMMAND case of the main window procedure. To do this, add the following statements:

```
case IDM_PRINT:

    hdcPrinter = GetPrinterDC();

    if (!hdcPrinter) {
        sprintf(str, "Cannot print %s", Filename);
        MessageBox(hWnd, str, NULL, MB_OK | MB_ICONHAND);
        break;
    }
```

```
lpAbortDlg =  MakeProcInstance((FARPROC) AbortDlg, hinst);
lpAbortProc = MakeProcInstance((FARPROC) AbortProc, hinst);

SetAbortProc(hdcPrinter, (ABORTPROC) lpAbortProc);

DocInfo.cbSize = sizeof(DOCINFO);
DocInfo.lpszDocName = "PrntFile text";
DocInfo.lpszOutput = (LPSTR) NULL;

if (StartDoc(hdcPrinter, &DocInfo) < 0) {
    MessageBox(hWnd, "Unable to start print job",
        NULL, MB_OK | MB_ICONHAND);
    FreeProcInstance(AbortDlg);
    FreeProcInstance(AbortProc);
    DeleteDC(hdcPrinter);
    break;
}

StartPage(hdcPrinter);

fAbort = FALSE;              /* clears abort flag */
hAbortDlgWnd = CreateDialog(hinst, "AbortDlg", hWnd,
    (DLGPROC) lpAbortDlg);

ShowWindow(hAbortDlgWnd, SW_NORMAL);
UpdateWindow(hAbortDlgWnd);
EnableWindow(hWnd, FALSE);
GetTextMetrics(hdcPrinter, &TextMetric);

LineSpace = TextMetric.tmHeight + TextMetric.tmExternalLeading;
LinesPerPage = GetDeviceCaps (hdcPrinter, VERTRES) / LineSpace;
dwLines = SendMessage(hEditWnd, EM_GETLINECOUNT, 0, 0L);
CurrentLine = 1;

for (dwIndex = IOStatus = 0; dwIndex < dwLines; dwIndex++) {
    pLine[0] = 128;                     /* maximum buffer size */
    pLine[1] = 0;
    LineLength = SendMessage(hEditWnd, EM_GETLINE,
        (WORD) dwIndex, (LONG) ((LPSTR) pLine));
    TextOut(hdcPrinter, 0, CurrentLine*LineSpace, (LPSTR) pLine,
        LineLength);

    if (++CurrentLine > LinesPerPage ) {
        EndPage(hdcPrinter);
        CurrentLine = 1;
        IOStatus = EndPage(hdcPrinter);
        if (IOStatus < 0 || fAbort)
            break;
        StartPage(hdcPrinter);
    }
}
```

```
if (IOStatus >= 0 && !fAbort) {
    EndPage(hdcPrinter);
    EndDoc(hdcPrinter);
}

EnableWindow(hWnd, TRUE);
DestroyWindow(hAbortDlgWnd);
FreeProcInstance(AbortDlg);
FreeProcInstance(AbortProc);
DeleteDC(hdcPrinter);
break;
```

The locally defined GetPrinterDC function checks the WIN.INI file for the current printer and creates a device context for that printer. If there is not a current printer or the device context cannot be created, the function returns NULL and processing ends with a warning. Otherwise, the **MakeProcInstance** function creates procedure-instance addresses for the AbortDlg dialog box procedure and the AbortProc function. The **SetAbortProc** function sets the abort function. The **Start-Doc** function starts the printing job and sets the printing title (shown in the Print Manager application). If **StartDoc** fails, the **FreeProcInstance** function frees the AbortDlg and AbortProc procedure instances and the **DeleteDC** function deletes the device context before processing ends.

The **CreateDialog** function creates the AbortDlg dialog box, and the **Enable-Window** function disables the main window. This prevents users from attempting to work in the main window while printing. Users can, however, continue to work in some other application.

Because the edit control may contain more than one line, you should provide adequate spacing between lines. This keeps one line from overwriting or touching another. The **GetTextMetrics** function retrieves current font information, such as height and external leading, which can be used to compute adequate line spacing. The height is the maximum height of characters in the font. The external leading is the recommended amount of space, in addition to the height, that should be used to separate lines of text in this font. The line spacing, which is assigned to the LineSpace variable, is the sum of the height and external leading members, Text-Metric.tmHeight and TextMetric.tmExternalLeading.

Because the edit control might contain more lines than can fit on a single page, you should determine how many lines can fit on a page and advance to the next page whenever this line limit is reached. An application can use the **GetText-Metrics** and **GetDeviceCaps** functions (as shown in the preceding example) to determine how many lines fit on a page.

The **TextOut** function can print only one line at a time, so a **for** statement provides the loop required to print more than one line of text. The EM_GETLINECOUNT message, sent to the edit control by using the **Send-Message** function, retrieves the number of lines to be printed and determines the number of times to loop. On each execution of the loop, the EM_GETLINE message copies the contents of a line from the edit control to the line buffer pLine. The loop counter dwIndex is used with the EM_GETLINE message to specify which line to retrieve from the edit control. The EM_GETLINE message also causes **SendMessage** to return the length of the line. The length is assigned to the LineLength variable.

After a line has been copied from the edit control, it is printed by using the **Text-Out** function. The product of the variables CurrentLine and LineSpacing determines the y-coordinate of the line on the page. The x-coordinate is set to zero. After a line is printed, the value of the CurrentLine variable is increased by one. If CurrentLine is greater than LinesPerPage, it is time to advance to the next page. Because any text printed beyond the physical bottom of a page is clipped and because there is no automatic page advance, you should keep track of the number of lines printed on a page and call the **EndPage** function to advance to the next page when necessary. If there are any errors during printing, the **EndPage** function returns an error value and processing ends.

After all lines in the edit control have been printed, the **EndPage** function advances the final page and the **EndDoc** function terminates the print request. The **DeleteDC** function deletes the printer device context, since it is no longer needed, and the **DestroyWindow** function destroys the AbortDlg dialog box.

12.8.4 Creating the AbortDlg Dialog Box Procedure and AbortProc Function

The AbortDlg dialog box procedure provides support for the AbortDlg dialog box that appears while the printing is in progress. The AbortProc function processes messages intended for the AbortDlg dialog box and cancels the printing operation if the user has requested it.

The AbortDlg dialog box procedure sets the input focus and sets the name of the file being printed. It also sets the fAbort variable to TRUE if the user clicks the Cancel button. To create this dialog box procedure, add the following statements to the C-language source file:

```
int FAR PASCAL AbortDlg(hDlg, msg, wParam, lParam)
HWND hDlg;
UINT msg;
WPARAM wParam;
LPARAM lParam;
{
    switch (msg) {
        case WM_COMMAND:

            return (fAbort = TRUE);
```

```
        case WM_INITDIALOG:

            SetFocus(GetDlgItem(hDlg, IDCANCEL));
            SetDlgItemText(hDlg, IDC_FILENAME, Filename);
            return (TRUE);
        }

    return (FALSE);
}
```

The AbortProc function checks for messages in the application queue and dispatches them to the AbortDlg dialog box procedure or to other windows in the application. If one of these messages causes the AbortDlg dialog box procedure to set the fAbort variable to TRUE, the AbortProc function returns this value, directing Windows to stop the printing operation. To create this function, add the following statements to the C-language source file:

```
int FAR PASCAL AbortProc(hdcPrinter, Code)
HDC hdcPrinter;     /* for multiple printer display contexts */
int Code;           /* printing status                       */
{
    MSG msg;

    while (!fAbort && PeekMessage(&msg, NULL, NULL, NULL, TRUE))
        if (!IsDialogMessage(hAbortDlgWnd, &msg)) {
            TranslateMessage(&msg);
            DispatchMessage(&msg);
        }

    return (!fAbort);
}
```

12.8.5 Adding a GetPrinterDC Function

To create a printer device context for your application, you must add a function to your C-language source file. The GetPrinterDC function uses the **PrintDlg** function to use the Print common dialog box and then creates a printer device context by using the driver name, device name, and printer port given in the **PRINTDLG** structure. To create this function, add the following statements to the C-language source file:

```
HDC GetPrinterDC()
{
    HDC         hDC;
    LPDEVMODE   lpDevMode = NULL;
    LPDEVNAMES  lpDevNames;
    LPSTR       lpszDriverName;
    LPSTR       lpszDeviceName;
    LPSTR       lpszPortName;
```

```
if (!PrintDlg((LPPRINTDLG) &pd))
    return (NULL);

if (pd.hDC) {
    hDC = pd.hDC;
}

else {
    if (!pd.hDevNames)
        return (NULL);

    lpDevNames = (LPDEVNAMES) GlobalLock(pd.hDevNames);
    lpszDriverName =
        (LPSTR) lpDevNames + lpDevNames->wDriverOffset;
    lpszDeviceName =
        (LPSTR) lpDevNames + lpDevNames->wDeviceOffset;
    lpszPortName    =
        (LPSTR) lpDevNames + lpDevNames->wOutputOffset;
    GlobalUnlock(pd.hDevNames);

    if (pd.hDevMode)
        lpDevMode = (LPDEVMODE) GlobalLock(pd.hDevMode);

    hDC = CreateDC(lpszDriverName, lpszDeviceName,
        lpszPortName, (LPSTR) lpDevMode);

    if (pd.hDevMode && lpDevMode)
        GlobalUnlock(pd.hDevMode);
}
if (pd.hDevNames)
    GlobalFree(pd.hDevNames);
if (pd.hDevMode)
    GlobalFree(pd.hDevMode);
return(hDC);
}
```

12.8.6 Exporting the AbortDlg Dialog Box Procedure and AbortProc Function

You must export the AbortDlg dialog box procedure and the AbortProc function.
Add the following lines to your module-definition file under the **EXPORTS** statement:

```
AbortDlg    @5  ; Called so user can cancel the print function
AbortProc   @6  ; Processes messages intended for Abort dialog box
```

12.8.7 Compiling and Linking

Compile and link the PrntFile application, and then start Windows and activate PrntFile; you will see that the Print command has been added to the File menu. You can print by opening a file or by typing text from the keyboard and then choosing the Print command.

12.9 Related Topics

For more information about device contexts, see Chapter 3, "Output to a Window."

For more information about controlling printer settings, see Chapter 17, "Print Settings."

For more information about using fonts, see Chapter 18, "Fonts."

For more information about functions used with device contexts, see *Microsoft Windows Programmer's Reference*, *Volume 2*.

Clipboard

The clipboard is the main data-exchange feature of the Microsoft Windows operating system. It is a common area for storing data handles through which applications can exchange formatted data. The clipboard holds any number of different data formats and corresponding data handles, all representing the same data, but in as many different formats as an application is able to supply. For example, a pie chart might be held in the clipboard as both a metafile picture and a bitmap. An application pasting the pie chart would have to choose which representation matched its requirements. In general, the format that provides the most information is the most desirable, as long as the application understands that format.

This chapter covers the following topics:

- Copying text to the clipboard
- Pasting text from the clipboard
- Pasting a bitmap from the clipboard
- Using special clipboard features such as private data formats

This chapter also explains how to build a sample Windows 3.1 application, ClipText, that illustrates many of the concepts explained in the chapter.

13.1 Using the Clipboard

To copy data to the clipboard, you format the data by using either a predefined or private format. For most formats, you allocate global memory and copy the data into it. You then use the **SetClipboardData** function to copy the memory handle to the clipboard.

In Windows applications, copying and pasting are carried out through Edit-menu commands. To add Edit menu to an application, follow the steps described in Chapter 7, "Menus."

Windows provides several predefined data formats for use in data interchange. The following list describes the clipboard formats:

Value	Meaning
CF_BITMAP	The data is a bitmap.
CF_DIB	The data is a memory object containing a **BITMAPINFO** structure followed by the bitmap data.
CF_DIF	The data is in Data Interchange Format (DIF).
CF_DSPBITMAP	The data is a bitmap representation of a private format. This data is displayed in bitmap format in lieu of the privately formatted data.

Value	Meaning
CF_DSPMETAFILEPICT	The data is a metafile representation of a private data format. This data is displayed in metafile-picture format in lieu of the privately formatted data.
CF_DSPTEXT	The data is a textual representation of a private data format. This data is displayed in text format in lieu of the privately formatted data.
CF_METAFILEPICT	The data is a metafile (see the description of the **META-FILEPICT** structure in the *Microsoft Windows Programmer's Reference*, *Volume 3*).
CF_OEMTEXT	The data is an array of text characters in the OEM character set. Each line ends with a carriage return–linefeed (CR-LF) combination. A null character signals the end of the data.
CF_OWNERDISPLAY	The data is in a private format that the clipboard owner must display.
CF_PALETTE	The data is a color palette.
CF_PENDATA	The data is for the pen extensions to the Windows operating system.
CF_RIFF	The data is in Resource Interchange File Format (RIFF).
CF_SYLK	The data is in Microsoft Symbolic Link (SYLK) format.
CF_TEXT	The data is an array of text characters. Each line ends with a carriage return–linefeed (CR-LF) combination. A null character signals the end of the data.
CF_TIFF	The data is in Tag Image File Format (TIFF).
CF_WAVE	The data describes a sound wave. This is a subset of the CF_RIFF data format; it can be used only for RIFF WAVE files.

When you paste data from the clipboard by using the **GetClipboardData** function, you specify the format you expect. The clipboard supplies the data only if it has been copied in that format.

Windows supports two formats for text, CF_TEXT and CF_OEMTEXT. CF_TEXT is the default Windows text clipboard format. Windows uses the CF_OEMTEXT format for text in non-Windows applications. If you call **GetClipboardData** to retrieve data in one text format and discover that the other text format is the only one available, Windows automatically converts the text to the requested format before supplying it to your application.

Note Clipboard data objects can be any size. Your application must be able to work with clipboard data objects larger than 64K. For more information about working with large data objects, see Chapter 16, "More Memory Management."

13.1.1 Copying Text to the Clipboard

To copy a short string of text to the clipboard, your application should follow these steps:

1. Copy the string to global memory.
2. Open the clipboard.
3. Clear the clipboard.
4. Give the global memory handle to the clipboard.
5. Close the clipboard.

The application should copy text to the clipboard when the user chooses the Copy command from the Edit menu. To process the menu input and copy the text string to the clipboard, your application should have a WM_COMMAND case in its window procedure. To implement the Cut and Copy commands, add the following statements:

```
case IDM_CUT:
case IDM_COPY:

    if (hText != NULL) {

        /* Allocate memory and copy the string to it. */

        hData = GlobalAlloc(GMEM_MOVEABLE, GlobalSize (hText));

        if (hData == NULL  ||
                (lpData = GlobalLock(hData)) == NULL ||
                (lpszText = GlobalLock(hText)) == NULL) {
            OutOfMemory();
            return TRUE;
        }

        lstrcpy(lpData, lpszText);
        GlobalUnlock(hData);
        GlobalUnlock(hText);

        /*
         * Clear the current contents of the clipboard,
         * and set the data handle to the new string.
         */

        if (OpenClipboard(hwnd)) {
            EmptyClipboard();
            SetClipboardData(CF_TEXT, hData);
            CloseClipboard();
        }

        hData = NULL;
```

```
            if (wParam == IDM_CUT) {
                GlobalFree(hText);
                hText = NULL;
                EnableMenuItem(GetMenu (hwnd), IDM_CUT, MF_GRAYED);
                EnableMenuItem(GetMenu(hwnd), IDM_COPY, MF_GRAYED);
                InvalidateRect(hwnd, NULL, TRUE);
                UpdateWindow(hwnd);
            }
        }

        return TRUE;
```

The **GlobalAlloc** function allocates enough memory to hold the string. The GMEM_MOVEABLE flag specifies movable memory. The clipboard can take either fixed or movable memory but should not be given discardable memory. Movable memory is the most efficient.

Note Always check the return value when allocating or locking memory; a NULL return value indicates an out-of-memory condition.

You must lock movable memory in order to retrieve the memory address. Use the Windows **lstrcpy** function instead of the C run-time **strcpy** function, since **strcpy** cannot handle mixed pointers (string is a short pointer, and lpData is a long pointer). The clipboard requires the string to have a terminating null character. Finally, the memory must be unlocked before it can be copied to the clipboard.

Each time your application copies the string to the clipboard, this code allocates another global memory object. The reason is that once the application passes a data handle to the clipboard, the clipboard takes ownership of it. This means that the application can no longer use the handle other than to view contents, and that it must not attempt to free the handle or change its contents.

The **OpenClipboard** function opens the clipboard for the specified window. **OpenClipboard** will fail if another window already has the clipboard open.

The **EmptyClipboard** function clears all existing handles in the clipboard and assigns ownership of the clipboard to the window that has it open. An application must empty the clipboard before copying data to it.

The **SetClipboardData** function copies the memory handle to the clipboard and identifies the data format, CF_TEXT. The clipboard is then closed by the **Close-Clipboard** function.

Since the clipboard now owns the global memory identified by the hData variable, it is convenient to set this handle to zero to prevent attempts to free or change the memory.

13.1.2 Pasting Text from the Clipboard

An application can paste text from the clipboard into its client area. That is, it can retrieve a text handle from the clipboard and display it in the client area by using the **TextOut** function. To do this, the application must do the following:

1. Open the clipboard.
2. Retrieve the data handle associated with CF_TEXT or CF_OEMTEXT.
3. Close the clipboard.

The user should be able to paste only if there is text in the clipboard. To prevent attempts to paste when no text is present, your application should check the clipboard before Windows displays the Edit menu by processing the WM_INITMENU message. If the clipboard is empty, the application should disable the Paste command; if text is present, the application should enable it. Add the following statements to the window procedure:

```
case WM_INITMENU:

    if (wParam == (WPARAM) GetMenu(hwnd)) {
        if (OpenClipboard(hwnd)) {
            if (IsClipboardFormatAvailable(CF_TEXT)
                    || IsClipboardFormatAvailable(CF_OEMTEXT))
                EnableMenuItem((HMENU) wParam, IDM_PASTE, MF_ENABLED);

            else
                EnableMenuItem((HMENU) wParam, IDM PASTE, MF_GRAYED);

            CloseClipboard();
            return TRUE;
        }

        else    /*  Clipboard is not available            */
            return FALSE;
    }

    return TRUE;
```

In this example, the first **if** statement checks the WM_INITMENU's *wParam* parameter against the menu handle returned by the **GetMenu** function. Since many applications have at least two menus, including a System menu, it is important to ensure that the message applies to the Edit menu.

The two calls to the **IsClipboardFormatAvailable** function check for the CF_TEXT or CF_OEMTEXT format. Based on whether the CF_TEXT or CF_OEMTEXT format is found, the **EnableMenuItem** function enables or disables the Paste command.

Your application must be able to paste from the clipboard when the user chooses the Paste command from the Edit menu. To make your application process the menu input and retrieve the text from the clipboard, add an IDM_PASTE case to the WM_COMMAND case in the window procedure. Add the following statements immediately after the IDM_COPY case:

```
case IDM_PASTE:

    if (OpenClipboard(hwnd)) {
        if ((hClipData = GetClipboardData(CF_TEXT)) == NULL) {
            CloseClipboard();
            break;
        }

        if (hText != NULL)
            GlobalFree(hText);

        hText = GlobalAlloc(GMEM_MOVEABLE, GlobalSize(hClipData));

        if (hText == NULL ||
                (lpClipData = GlobalLock(hClipData)) == NULL ||
                (lpszText = GlobalLock(hText)) == NULL) {
            OutOfMemory();
            CloseClipboard();
            break;
        }

        lstrcpy(lpszText, lpClipData);
        GlobalUnlock(hClipData);
        CloseClipboard();
        GlobalUnlock(hText);
        EnableMenuItem(GetMenu(hwnd), IDM_CUT, MF_ENABLED);
        EnableMenuItem(GetMenu(hwnd), IDM_COPY, MF_ENABLED);

        /* Copy text to the application window. */

        InvalidateRect(hwnd, NULL, TRUE);
        UpdateWindow(hwnd);
        return TRUE;
    }

    else
        return FALSE;
}

break;
```

In this example, the **OpenClipboard** function opens the clipboard for the specified window if it is not already open. The **GetClipboardData** function then retrieves the data handle for the text (if there is no such data, the function retrieves zero). You should check this handle before using it, because it is a global-memory handle. The clipboard format is CF_TEXT, so the global memory is assumed to contain a null-terminated string consisting of characters in the Windows character set. This means the global memory can be locked by using the **GlobalLock** function, and the contents can be displayed in the client area by using the **TextOut** function.

Your application must not modify or delete the data it retrieves from the clipboard. The application can examine it or make a copy of it, but it must not change the data. To examine the data, the application might need to lock the handle, as in this example, but must never leave a data handle locked. The application should unlock the handle immediately after using it.

Data handles returned by the **GetClipboardData** function are for temporary use only. Handles belong to the clipboard, not to the application requesting data. Do not rely on a handle remaining valid indefinitely. In general, the application should copy the data associated with the handle, and then release it without changes.

The **CloseClipboard** function closes the clipboard; your application should always close the clipboard immediately after it has been used so that other applications can use it. Before closing the clipboard, be sure you unlock the data retrieved by **GetClipboardData**.

13.1.3 Pasting Bitmaps from the Clipboard

In addition to retrieving text, your Windows application can retrieve a bitmap from the clipboard and display it in the client area. To make the application retrieve and display a bitmap, you use the same technique as for pasting text, but you make a few changes to accommodate bitmaps.

First, modify the WM_INITMENU case in the window procedure so that it recognizes the CF_BITMAP format. After you change it, the WM_INITMENU case should look like this:

```
case WM_INITMENU:

    if (wParam == (WPARAM) GetMenu(hwnd)) {
        if (OpenClipboard(hwnd)) {
            if (IsClipboardFormatAvailable(CF_BITMAP))
                EnableMenuItem((HMENU) wParam, IDM_PASTE, MF_ENABLED);

            else
                EnableMenuItem((HMENU) wParam, IDM_PASTE, MF_GRAYED);

            CloseClipboard();
            return TRUE;
        }
    }
```

```
            else   /* Clipboard not available        */
                return FALSE;
        }

        return TRUE;
```

Although retrieving a bitmap from the clipboard is as easy as retrieving text, displaying a bitmap requires more work than does displaying text. In general, you must do the following:

1. Retrieve the bitmap data handle from the clipboard. Bitmap data handles from the clipboard are graphics device interface (GDI) bitmap handles (created by using functions such as **CreateBitmap**).

2. Create a compatible display context, and select the data handle into it.

3. Use the **BitBlt** function to copy the bitmap to the client area.

4. Release the bitmap handle from the current selection.

For more information about displaying a bitmap, see Chapter 11, "Bitmaps."

13.1.4 Windows Clipboard Application

The user can view the contents of the clipboard by using the Windows application Clipboard (CLIPBRD.EXE); for this reason, Clipboard is also known as the clipboard viewer. It lists the names of all the formats for which handles (NULL or otherwise) exist in the clipboard, and displays the contents of the clipboard in one of these formats.

The clipboard viewer can display all the standard data formats. If there are handles for more than one standard data format, the clipboard viewer displays only one format, choosing from the following list, in decreasing order of priority: CF_TEXT, CF_OEMTEXT, CF_METAFILEPICT, CF_BITMAP, CF_SYLK, and CF_DIF.

For more information about clipboard formats, see the *Microsoft Windows Programmer's Reference*, *Volume 4*.

13.2 Using Special Clipboard Features

The clipboard provides several features that an application can use to improve the usability of the clipboard and save itself some work. These features are as follows:

- Applications can delay the formatting of data passed to the clipboard; for example, if the data format is complex and no other application is likely to use that format, an application can save time by not formatting that data until necessary.

- Applications can draw within the Clipboard application's client area. By using this feature, an application can display data formats that Clipboard cannot.

13.2.1 Rendering Data on Request

If an application uses many data formats, it can save formatting time by passing NULL data handles to the **SetClipboardData** function, instead of generating all the data handles when the user chooses a Cut or Copy command. The application need not generate a data handle until another application requests a handle by calling the **GetClipboardData** function.

When the application calls the **GetClipboardData** function with a request for a format for which a NULL data handle has been set, Windows sends a WM_RENDERFORMAT message to the clipboard owner. When an application receives this message, it can do the following:

1. Format the data last copied to the clipboard (the *wParam* parameter of WM_RENDERFORMAT specifies the format being requested).

2. Allocate a global memory object and copy the formatted data to it.

3. Pass the global memory handle and the format number to the clipboard by using the **SetClipboardData** function.

To accomplish these steps, the application must maintain a record of the last data copied to the clipboard. The application may discard this data when it receives the WM_DESTROYCLIPBOARD message, which is sent to the clipboard owner whenever the clipboard is emptied by a call to the **EmptyClipboard** function.

13.2.2 Rendering Formats Before Termination

When an application is destroyed, it is no longer capable of rendering data it has copied to the clipboard. Accordingly, when the application that owns the clipboard is being destroyed, Windows sends that application a special message, WM_RENDERALLFORMATS. Upon receiving a WM_RENDERALLFORMATS message, an application should follow the steps described in Section 13.2.1, "Rendering Data on Request," for all formats that the application is capable of generating.

13.2.3 Registering a Private Format

In addition, an application can create and use private formats, or even new public ones. To create and use a new data-interchange format, an application must do the following:

1. Call the **RegisterClipboardFormat** function to register the name of the new format.
2. Use the value returned by **RegisterClipboardFormat** as the code for the new format when calling the **SetClipboardData** function.

Registering the format name ensures that the application is using a unique format number. In addition, it allows Clipboard to display the correct name of the data being held in the clipboard. For more information about displaying private data types in Clipboard, see Section 13.2.4, "Controlling Data Display in the Clipboard."

If two or more applications register formats that have the same name, the applications will all receive the same format code. This allows applications to create their own public data types. If two or more applications register a format called WORKSHEET, for example, they will all have the same format number when calling the **SetClipboardData** and **GetClipboardData** functions, and will have a common basis for transferring WORKSHEET data between them.

13.2.4 Controlling Data Display in the Clipboard

There are two reasons why you might want your application to control the display of information in Clipboard:

- The application may have a private data type that is difficult or impossible to display in a meaningful way.
- The application may have a private data type that requires special information to display.

13.2.4.1 Using a Display Format for Private Data

You can use a display format to represent a private data format that would otherwise be difficult or impossible to display. The data associated with display formats are text, bitmaps, or metafile pictures that the clipboard viewer can display as substitutes for the corresponding private data. To use a display format, you copy both the private data and the display data to the clipboard. When the clipboard viewer chooses a format to display, it chooses the display format instead of the private data.

There are three display formats: CF_DSPTEXT, CF_DSPBITMAP, and CF_DSPMETAFILEPICT. The data associated with these formats is identical to the text, bitmap, and metafile-picture formats, respectively. Since text, bitmaps, and metafile pictures are also standard formats, the clipboard viewer can display them without help from the application.

The following description assumes that the application has already followed the steps described in Section 13.1.1, "Copying Text to the Clipboard," to take ownership of the clipboard and set data handles.

To force the display of a private data type in a standard data format, the application must take the following steps:

1. Open the clipboard for alteration by calling the **OpenClipboard** function.
2. Create a global handle that contains text, a bitmap, or a metafile picture, specifying the information that should be displayed in the clipboard viewer.
3. Set the handle to the clipboard by calling the **SetClipboardData** function. The format code passed should be CF_DSPTEXT if the handle is for text, CF_DSPBITMAP if the handle is for a bitmap, and CF_DSPMETAFILEPICT if it is for a metafile picture.
4. Signal that the application has finished altering the clipboard by calling the **CloseClipboard** function.

13.2.4.2 Taking Full Control of the Clipboard-Viewer Display

An application can take complete control of the display and scrolling of information in the clipboard viewer. This control is useful when the application has a sophisticated private data type that only it can display. Microsoft Write uses this facility for displaying formatted text.

For the following description, assume that the application has already followed the steps described in Section 13.1.1, "Copying Text to the Clipboard," to take ownership of the clipboard and set data handles.

To take full control of the clipboard-viewer display, follow these steps:

1. Open the clipboard for alteration by calling the **OpenClipboard** function.
2. Call the **SetClipboardData** function, using CF_OWNERDISPLAY as the data format, with a NULL handle.
3. Signal that the application has finished altering the clipboard by calling the **CloseClipboard** function.

The clipboard owner will then receive special messages associated with the display of information in the clipboard viewer:

Message	Action
WM_PAINTCLIPBOARD	Paints the specified portion of the window.
WM_SIZECLIPBOARD	Notes the window size change.
WM_VSCROLLCLIPBOARD	Scrolls the window vertically.
WM_HSCROLLCLIPBOARD	Scrolls the window horizontally.

Message	Action
WM_ASKCBFORMATNAME	Supplies the name of the displayed format.

For full descriptions of these messages, see the *Microsoft Window's Programmer's Reference, Volume 3*.

13.2.4.3 Using the Clipboard-Viewer Chain

Chaining together clipboard-viewer windows provides a way for applications to be notified whenever a change is made to the clipboard. The notification, in the form of a WM_DRAWCLIPBOARD message, is passed down the viewer chain whenever the **CloseClipboard** function is called. The recipient of the WM_DRAWCLIPBOARD message must determine the nature of the change (Empty, Set, and so on) by calling **EnumClipboardFormats**, **GetClipboard-Data**, and other functions, as necessary.

Any window that has made itself a link in the viewer chain must be prepared to do the following:

1. Remove itself from the chain before it is destroyed.
2. Pass along WM_DRAWCLIPBOARD messages to the next link in the chain.

The code for this action looks like this:

```
case WM_DESTROY:

    ChangeClipboardChain(hwnd, my_save_next);

    /* rest of processing for WM_DESTROY */

    break;

case WM_DRAWCLIPBOARD:

    if (my_save_next != NULL)
        SendMessage(my_save_next, WM_DRAWCLIPBOARD, wParam, lParam);

     /* rest of processing for WM_DRAWCLIPBOARD */

    break;
```

The my_save_next variable is the value returned from the **SetClipboardViewer** function. These clipboard-viewer chain actions should be the first steps taken by the **switch** statement branches that process the WM_DESTROY and WM_DRAWCLIPBOARD messages.

13.3 Sample Application: ClipText

This sample application illustrates how to copy to and paste from the clipboard. To create the ClipText application, make the following modifications to the Edit-Menu application created in Chapter 7, "Menus":

1. Add new variables.

2. Modify the instance initialization code.

3. Add a WM_INITMENU case.

4. Modify the WM_COMMAND case to process the IDM_CUT, IDM_COPY, and IDM_PASTE cases.

5. Add a WM_PAINT case.

6. Add an OutOfMemory function.

7. Compile and link the application.

This sample uses global memory to store the text to be copied. For a full explanation of global memory, see Chapter 15, "Memory Management."

13.3.1 Adding New Variables

To contain the handle of the client area text string and its initial data, you must add the following new global variables to the beginning of your C-language source file:

```
HANDLE hText = NULL; /* handle of current client-area text */
char szInitialClientAreaText[] =
    "This program demonstrates the use of ... ";
HANDLE hData, hClipData;        /* handles of clip data   */
LPSTR lpData, lpClipData;       /* addresses of clip data */
```

You must also add variables for painting and clipboard data manipulation. Add these variables to the beginning of your MainWndProc main window procedure:

```
HDC hdc;
HMENU hMenu;
PAINTSTRUCT ps;
RECT rcClient;
LPSTR lpszText;
```

13.3.2 Modifying the Instance Initialization Code

When an instance of ClipText is started, it must allocate a global memory object and fill it with an initial client-area text string. To do this, add the following statements to the instance initialization code:

```
hText = GlobalAlloc(GMEM_MOVEABLE,
    (DWORD) sizeof(szInitialClientAreaText));

if (hText == NULL || (lpszText = GlobalLock(hText)) == NULL) {
    OutOfMemory();
    return FALSE;
}

lstrcpy(lpszText, szInitialClientAreaText);
GlobalUnlock(hText);
```

13.3.3 Adding a WM_INITMENU Case

To prepare the Edit menu for pasting, you must add a WM_INITMENU case to
your window procedure. In general, the Paste command should not be available in
this menu unless there is selected text in the clipboard to paste. Add the following
statements to the window procedure:

```
case WM_INITMENU:

    if (wParam == (WPARAM) GetMenu(hwnd)) {
        if (OpenClipboard(hwnd)) {
            if (IsClipboardFormatAvailable(CF_TEXT)
                    || IsClipboardFormatAvailable(CF_OEMTEXT))
                EnableMenuItem((HMENU) wParam, IDM_PASTE, MF_ENABLED);

            else
                EnableMenuItem((HMENU) wParam, IDM_PASTE, MF_GRAYED);

            CloseClipboard();
            return TRUE;
        }

        else     /* Clipboard is not available          */
            return FALSE;
    }

    return TRUE;
```

These statements process the WM_INITMENU message only if the specified
menu is found on the menu bar. The **IsClipboardFormatAvailable** function determines whether text data is present in the clipboard. If data is present, the **Enable-
MenuItem** function enables the Paste command. Otherwise, the Paste command is
disabled.

13.3.4 Modifying the WM_COMMAND Case

To process the Edit menu commands, you must modify the IDM_CUT, IDM_COPY, and IDM_PASTE cases in the WM_COMMAND case. The IDM_CUT and IDM_COPY cases must create a global memory object, fill it with text, and copy the handle of the object to the clipboard; the IDM_CUT case must also discard the current client-area text. The IDM_PASTE case must retrieve a handle from the clipboard, use its contents to replace the current client-area text, and request that the client area be repainted.

Replace the existing IDM_CUT and IDM_COPY cases with the following statements:

```
case IDM_CUT:
case IDM_COPY:

    if (hText != NULL) {

        /* Allocate memory and copy the string to it. */

        hData = GlobalAlloc(GMEM_MOVEABLE, GlobalSize (hText));

        if (hData == NULL  ||
                (lpData = GlobalLock(hData)) == NULL ||
                (lpszText = GlobalLock(hText)) == NULL) {
            OutOfMemory();
            return TRUE;
        }

        lstrcpy(lpData, lpszText);
        GlobalUnlock(hData);
        GlobalUnlock(hText);

        /*
         * Clear the current contents of the clipboard,
         * and set the data handle to the new string.
         */

        if (OpenClipboard(hwnd)) {
            EmptyClipboard();
            SetClipboardData(CF_TEXT, hData);
            CloseClipboard();
        }

        hData = NULL;
```

```
        if (wParam == IDM_CUT) {
            GlobalFree(hText);
            hText = NULL;
            EnableMenuItem(GetMenu (hwnd), IDM_CUT, MF_GRAYED);
            EnableMenuItem(GetMenu(hwnd), IDM_COPY, MF_GRAYED);
            InvalidateRect(hwnd, NULL, TRUE);
            UpdateWindow(hwnd);
        }
    }

    return TRUE;
```

The **GlobalAlloc** function allocates the global memory object used to pass text data to the clipboard. The **lstrcpy** function copies the client-area text into the object after the handle has been locked by the **GlobalLock** function. The handle must be unlocked before it can be copied to the clipboard. The **EmptyClipboard** function is used to remove any existing data from the clipboard.

Replace the IDM_PASTE case with the following statements:

```
case IDM_PASTE:

    if (OpenClipboard(hwnd)) {
        if ((hClipData = GetClipboardData(CF_TEXT)) == NULL) {
            CloseClipboard();
            break;
        }

        if (hText != NULL)
            GlobalFree(hText);

        hText = GlobalAlloc(GMEM_MOVEABLE, GlobalSize(hClipData));

        if (hText == NULL ||
                (lpClipData = GlobalLock(hClipData)) == NULL ||
                (lpszText = GlobalLock(hText)) == NULL) {
            OutOfMemory();
            CloseClipboard();
            break;
        }

        lstrcpy(lpszText, lpClipData);
        GlobalUnlock(hClipData);
        CloseClipboard();
        GlobalUnlock(hText);
        EnableMenuItem(GetMenu(hwnd), IDM_CUT, MF_ENABLED);
        EnableMenuItem(GetMenu(hwnd), IDM_COPY, MF_ENABLED);
```

```
                          /* Copy text to the application window. */

                          InvalidateRect(hwnd, NULL, TRUE);
                          UpdateWindow(hwnd);
                          return TRUE;
                  }

              else
                  return FALSE;
      }

  break;
```

The **GetClipboardData** function returns a handle of a global memory object. The **GlobalLock** function locks this handle, returning the object address that is used to make a copy of the new client-area text.

13.3.5 Adding a WM_PAINT Case

A WM_PAINT case is necessary to draw the current client-area text on the screen when the window has been minimized, resized, or overlaid. To create this case, add the following statements to the window procedure:

```
case WM_PAINT:

    hdc = BeginPaint(hwnd, &ps);
    if (hText != NULL) {
        if ((lpszText = GlobalLock (hText)) == NULL) {
            OutOfMemory();
        }

        else {
            GetClientRect(hwnd, &rectClient);
            DrawText(hdc, lpszText, -1, &rectClient,
                DT_EXTERNALLEADING | DT_NOPREFIX | DT_WORDBREAK);
            GlobalUnlock (hText);
        }
    }

    EndPaint(hwnd, &ps);
    break;
```

13.3.6 Adding an OutOfMemory Function

You must add a function that displays a message box when your application is out of memory. To do this, add the following statements to the application source file:

```
void OutOfMemory(void)
{
    MessageBox(NULL, "Out of Memory", NULL,
        MB_ICONHAND | MB_SYSTEMMODAL);
    return;
}
```

In the application's header file, add a forward reference to the OutOfMemory function:

```
void OutOfMemory(void);
```

13.3.7 Compiling and Linking

After compiling and linking the ClipText application, start Windows, Clipboard, and ClipText. Then, choose the Copy command in the Edit menu. You should see something that looks similar to this:

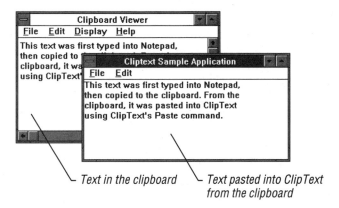

Text in the clipboard   Text pasted into ClipText
                               from the clipboard

13.4 Related Topics

For more information about display contexts, see Chapter 3, "Output to a Window."

For more information about bitmaps, see Chapter 11, "Bitmaps."

For more information about handling memory, see Chapter 15, "Memory Management," and Chapter 16, "More Memory Management."

For more information about using Windows dynamic data exchange (DDE) instead of the clipboard, see Chapter 22, "Dynamic Data Exchange."

For more information about clipboard-management functions, clipboard data formats, and clipboard file formats, see the *Microsoft Windows Programmer's Reference*, *Volumes 2* and *4*.

Advanced Programming Topics

Part **3**

C and Assembly Language

Parts 1 and 2 of the *Microsoft Windows Guide to Programming* introduced the functions you use in the context of a C- or assembly-language application to create an application for the Microsoft Windows 3.1 operating system. The focus in these parts was on the Windows-specific elements of a Windows application.

A complete Windows application might not use only these Windows-specific functions, however. Instead, your application will probably use standard C run-time library functions and your own functions, which will be called back by Windows or by other modules in your application. You should know how to incorporate these functions properly in your applications.

This chapter covers the following topics:

- Choosing a memory model
- Using the NULL constant
- Using command-line arguments and the MS-DOS environment
- Writing exported functions
- Using C run-time functions
- Writing assembly-language code

14.1 Choosing a Memory Model

Like any MS-DOS application, a Windows application can contain one or more code segments and one or more data segments, depending on the memory model you select when compiling the source-code modules of your application. For information about the memory-model options that are available to you, see Chapter 16, "More Memory Management."

The memory model you choose will affect how efficiently your application will run with the Windows operating system. In most cases, the best model is the mixed model. When using the mixed model, you compile your modules to have default small- or medium-model settings and to name the data segments. You then override these default settings by using explicit **FAR** calls (in coded segments with the small-model settings) to call functions in other segments, or by using explicit **NEAR** calls (in segments with the medium-model settings) to call functions in the same segment. The mixed model has the following advantages:

- Near calls reduce the amount of code generated by the compiler and make the functions execute more quickly.
- Compiling the modules by using named code segments partitions the code segments into smaller segments, which are easier for Windows to manage as it moves the code segments in memory.

To create an application by using the mixed model (with the small-model default settings), follow these steps:

1. Provide prototypes for all functions in your source code that are called from outside the code segment that defines them. For the sake of convenience, you can place these prototypes in a header (.H) file. You must provide prototypes for all function calls made by one code segment to another as far calls using the **FAR** keyword. Following is an example of a function prototype for a far call:

```
int FAR MyCalculation(int, int);
```

2. Compile your C modules by using the **/AS** option to create the application that will use the small memory model.

3. Compile your C modules by using the **/NT** option to name the code segments of your application.

For more information about these and other compiler options, see *Microsoft Windows Programming Tools*.

Creating an application by using the mixed model with medium-model default settings is similar to this procedure, except for two differences: You would explicitly declare as **NEAR** those functions that are called only within the data segment that defines them, and you should compile the modules by using the **/AM** option to produce the medium-model default settings.

14.2 Using the NULL Constant

The symbolic constant NULL has different definitions for Windows and the Microsoft C Optimizing Compiler (CL). The WINDOWS.H header file defines NULL as follows:

```
#define NULL 0
```

On the other hand, the CL library header files (such as STDDEF.H) define NULL as follows:

```
#ifndef NULL
#define NULL ((void *) 0)
#endif
```

To avoid compiler warnings, you should use NULL only for pointers and handles. You should not use NULL for such data types as **int** and **WORD**.

You can avoid such compiler warnings by making sure that your application includes WINDOWS.H before any header file from the C run-time library that defines NULL, as shown in the following example:

```
#include <windows.h>
#include <stddef.h>
```

Because the header files in the C run-time library do not define NULL if it has already been defined, the preprocessor does not override the initial definition in WINDOWS.H.

14.3 Using Command-Line Arguments and the MS-DOS Environment

Your application can retrieve the command-line arguments specified when the user started the application; it can also retrieve the current MS-DOS environment.

When a Windows application runs, the Windows startup function copies the command-line arguments to the **__argc** and **__argv** variables. Like their counterparts in a standard C application, these variables represent the number of arguments and an array of strings containing the arguments. In addition, the **environ** variable receives a pointer to an array of strings that contain the current MS-DOS environment at the time the application was started.

To use these variables, you must declare them as external to your application, as follows:

```
extern int     __argc;
extern char ** __argv;
extern char *  environ[];
```

You can also retrieve the command-line parameters by parsing the *lpszCmdLine* parameter, which Windows passes to your application's **WinMain** function.

If your application does not require access to the command-line arguments or the MS-DOS environment, you can reduce the size of your heap and code by eliminating C run-time initialization code. For information about how to do this, see Section 14.5.10, "Eliminating C Run-Time Startup Code."

A dynamic-link library (DLL) cannot access the **__argc**, **__argv**, and **environ** variables. Instead, to retrieve the command-line arguments, the library must parse the *lpszCmdLine* parameter, which Windows passes to the LibEntry function. For more information about LibEntry, see Chapter 20, "Dynamic-Link Libraries."

Since a dynamic-link library does not have access to the **environ** variable, it must call the **GetDOSEnvironment** function to retrieve the environment string.

14.4 Writing Exported Functions

Typically, the functions you define in your application do not require any special treatment. There are two exceptions to this rule:

- Functions in a dynamic-link library that are called outside of the library
- Callback functions (also called callback procedures)

For information about writing functions in a dynamic-link library, see Chapter 20, "Dynamic-Link Libraries."

Callback functions are functions in your application that are called by Windows, not by your application. Following are the common types of callback functions:

- **WinMain**. This is the entry point for your application.
- Application window procedures. These procedures process messages sent to the window.
- Application dialog box procedures. These procedures process messages sent to the dialog box.
- Enumeration callback functions. These functions handle the results of Windows enumeration functions.
- Memory-notification functions. These functions are called by Windows to notify your application that a memory object is about to be discarded.
- Window-hook functions (filters). These functions process messages sent to the windows of other applications. Most window-hook functions must be in a library.

14.4.1 Creating a Callback Function

For all callback functions, you must follow these steps:

1. Define the callback function by using the **PASCAL** keyword. This causes the function parameters to be pushed onto the stack from right to left, just like standard Windows functions.

2. Define the callback function by using the **FAR** keyword. This allows the function to be called outside the code segment that contains the function. This rule does not apply to the **WinMain** function.

3. Compile the module that contains the callback function by using the **/Gw** option (not the **GW** option). This adds the proper Windows prolog and epilog code to the function, ensuring that the current data segment is used by the function when it runs.

4. List the callback function in the **EXPORTS** statement of the application's module-definition (.DEF) file. This defines the ordinal value and attributes of the callback function.

With the exception of the **WinMain** function, your application passes the procedure-instance address of the callback function to a Windows function to tell Windows when it should execute the callback function. For example, when you create a dialog box, one of the parameters of the function that creates the dialog box is the procedure-instance address of the function that will handle the messages sent to the dialog box.

To create a procedure-instance address of a function, call the **MakeProcInstance** function. This function returns a procedure-instance address that points to prolog code that is executed before the function is executed. The prolog code binds the data segment of the instance of your application to the callback function. Thus, when the function is executed, it has access to variables and data in the data segment of the application instance. You need not create a procedure-instance address for the **WinMain** function or any window procedure that your application registers by using the **RegisterClass** function.

When your application no longer needs the callback function (that is, when you are certain Windows will no longer call it), you should call **FreeProcInstance** to free the function from the data segment.

14.4.2 Creating the WinMain Function

Every Windows application must have a **WinMain** function; like the main function of a standard C-language application, the **WinMain** function in effect serves as the entry point for your application. It contains statements and Windows functions that create windows and read and dispatch input intended for the application. The function definition has the following form:

```
int PASCAL WinMain(hinstCurrent, hinstPrevious, lpszCmdLine, nCmdShow)
HINSTANCE hinstCurrent;
HINSTANCE hinstPrevious;
LPSTR lpszCmdLine;
int nCmdShow;
{
        .
        .
        .
}
```

Like all Windows functions, **WinMain** is declared with the **PASCAL** keyword. As a result, your definition of **WinMain** must contain all four parameters, even if your application does not use them all.

Even though Windows calls it directly, **WinMain** must not be declared with the **FAR** keyword or exported in the definition file, because it is called from startup code added by the linker to the same data segment. **WinMain** is implicitly declared **NEAR** or **FAR**, depending on the memory model that you use to compile the module that defines **WinMain**. This memory model must be consistent with the memory model of the C run-time link library containing the startup code that calls **WinMain**.

14.5 Using C Run-Time Functions

The Microsoft Windows 3.1 Software Development Kit (SDK) contains special versions of the C-language run-time libraries that differ from the equivalent libraries supplied with CL. The following sections describe other ways in which the Windows C run-time libraries differ from those supplied with CL.

14.5.1 Using Windows C Libraries

You can use the Windows C run-time libraries with CL version 5.1 and later. The Windows-specific versions of the C run-time libraries are adapted for the Windows environment. The Windows prolog and epilog code have been added to all C run-time functions that require them. This prevents problems associated with code-segment movement in low-memory situations. Many C run-time functions have been rewritten to avoid the assumption that the contents of the DS register equal the contents of the SS register, which is not true for Windows dynamic-link libraries. For information about calling C run-time library functions from a dynamic-link library (with DS equal to SS), see Chapter 20, "Dynamic-Link Libraries."

The SDK contains two sets of run-time libraries. One set is linked with Windows applications, and the other set is linked with Windows dynamic-link libraries. These libraries contain application- or DLL-startup code in addition to C run-time functions, including memory-model-dependent replacement functions. As a result, the SDK requires only one import library, LIBW.LIB. This import library is memory-model independent.

The **install** command in version 3.1 of the SDK always names the Windows versions of the C run-time libraries according to the following naming convention:

{S|M|C|L}{LIB|DLL}C[E]W.LIB

S, M, C, and L represent small, medium, compact, or large memory model libraries, respectively. LIB and DLL indicate libraries intended to be linked with application and DLL modules, respectively. E indicates the emulated math library. Because of this naming convention, you must explicitly name the Windows version of the C run-time library when linking your application. The following shows an example of using the **link** command to link an application module to a Windows C run-time library:

```
link generic, , , /nod slibcew libw, generic.def
```

The **/nod** (no default directory search) option is recommended to prevent **link** from searching for a C run-time function in an MS-DOS version of the C run-time library if it does not find the function in the Windows version of the library. When you use this option, your application will not compile if you inadvertently called a C run-time function that is not supported by the Windows C run-time libraries.

The SDK also contains Windows-specific versions of the C run-time header files. These files help you detect during compilation whether you have inadvertently called a C run-time function that is not supported in the Windows environment. To perform this check, add the following directive to your module header file prior to any **#include** directives for the C run-time header files:

```
#define _WINDOWS
```

The set of C run-time functions that support calling from Windows applications includes a subset of functions that support calling from Windows dynamic-link libraries. The Windows-specific header files identify this subset. If you are creating a dynamic-link library, you should include both of these directives before any **#include** directives for the C run-time header files, as shown in the following example:

```
#define _WINDOWS
#define _WINDLL
```

14.5.2 Allocating Memory

Although the Windows versions of the C run-time libraries supply replacements for such memory-allocation functions as **malloc** and **free**, you should instead use Windows-specific memory-allocation functions. For example, although **malloc** allocates a fixed memory object in the local heap, the Windows **LocalAlloc** function allows you to define the object as movable in the local heap.

14.5.3 Handling Strings

You can use the C run-time string functions to handle strings. However, in the small and medium memory models, these functions do not handle strings declared as far pointers or arrays, such as a dynamically allocated global memory object created by the **GlobalAlloc** function. The C run-time buffer-manipulation functions (such as **memcpy** and **memset**) are subject to the same restrictions in the small and medium models.

Windows provides the following functions for handling far strings:

- **lstrcat**
- **lstrcmp**
- **lstrcmpi**
- **lstrcpy**
- **lstrlen**

To compare or test characters in the Windows character set, use the following functions instead of the equivalent C run-time functions:

- **AnsiLower**
- **AnsiLowerBuff**
- **AnsiNext**
- **AnsiPrev**
- **AnsiUpperBuff**
- **IsCharAlpha**
- **IsCharAlphaNumeric**
- **IsCharLower**
- **IsCharUpper**

Windows uses a different collating sequence than do the C run-time functions.

Windows also provides the **wsprintf** and **wvsprintf** functions as replacements for the C run-time **sprintf** and **vsprintf** functions. The Windows versions have the following advantages:

- They use far buffers rather than near buffers.
- They are much smaller.
- They allow you to eliminate the C startup code if your application does not require other C run-time functions. For more information, see Section 14.5.10, "Eliminating C Run-Time Startup Code."

Note that the Windows versions support only a subset of the string format specifications. In particular, they do not support floating-point formats, pointer format, and octal base.

Important If you replace a **sprintf** or **vsprintf** function with its equivalent Windows function, be sure to cast any string passed as a **%s** argument to a far pointer:

```
char buffer[100];
char *str1; /* near pointer in small or medium model */
    .
    .
    .

sprintf(buffer,"Str1=%s",str1);            /*  Valid  */
wsprintf(buffer,"Str1=%s",(LPSTR)str1); /*  Valid  */
wsprint(buffer,"Str1=%s",str1);            /* INVALID */
```

14.5.4 Using File Input and Output

Use the Windows **OpenFile** function to create, open, reopen, or delete a file. **OpenFile** returns an MS-DOS file handle that you can use with such C run-time functions as **read**, **write**, **lseek**, and **close**. If you compile your C module by using the small or medium memory model, the *buffer* parameter of **read** and **write** is a near pointer (**char near ***). If you want to read to or write from a buffer declared in your application as a far pointer or array, use the Windows functions **_lread** and **_lwrite**, which are particularly useful for reading into or writing out of dynamically allocated global memory objects. You can also use buffered file-input-and-output C functions, such as **fopen**, **fread**, and **fwrite**.

You can also use the Windows functions **_lopen** and **_lcreat** to create or open a file.

Since Windows is a multitasking system, other applications may attempt to access the same file that your application is reading to or writing from. You can control access by other applications when your application opens a file by setting the appropriate share bit in the *wStyle* parameter. Your application should leave files open only while it is reading to and writing from them, unless your application must control access to the file at other times.

Note If a dynamic-link library opens a file, the file handle belongs to the application that called the dynamic-link library. If the library opens more than one file on behalf of multiple applications, it is possible that MS-DOS will assign the same file-handle value more than once.

14.5.5 Using Console Input and Output

Your application must share the system console with other applications. Because of this, the Windows versions of the C run-time libraries exclude the following C run-time console-input-and-output functions:

- **cgets**
- **cprintf**
- **cputs**

- **getch**
- **getche**
- **kbhit**
- **putch**
- **ungetch**

Since it cannot use these functions, your application should accept console input through the WM_KEYDOWN, WM_KEYUP, and WM_CHAR messages to your window and dialog box procedures. If you require more advanced techniques, you can call the **PeekMessage** function to look ahead at keyboard input, or you can install a keyboard filter function in a dynamic-link library by calling the **Set-WindowsHook** function.

14.5.6 Using Graphics Functions

The Windows graphics device interface (GDI) provides device-independent graphics functions. Therefore, the C run-time library functions are not included in the Windows versions of the C run-time libraries.

14.5.7 Using Floating-Point Arithmetic

If your application uses floating-point variables, you must link your application by using the **/FPi**, **/FPc**, or **/FPa** option on the **link** command line.

An application compiled with the **/FPi** option will use a math coprocessor if one is present at run time. Otherwise, the application will use a floating-point emulator. An application compiled with the **/FPc** option compiles the same as an application compiled with the **/FPi** option, except that it can be linked with the alternate math library instead, if necessary. An application compiled with the **/FPa** option uses an alternative math library if no coprocessor is present at run time. This is the smallest and fastest option available without a coprocessor, but this option sacrifices some accuracy for speed, relative to the emulator library.

If you use the **/FPi** or **/FPc** option, you must include WIN87EM.LIB on the **link** command line, as shown:

```
link sample, , , slibcew win87EM libw, sample.def
```

The Windows retail **setup** command automatically installs WIN87EM.DLL in the user's Windows system directory.

You can use the SIGFPE (signal floating-point error) option of the C run-time **signal** function to trap floating-point run-time errors, such as overflow and division by zero.

Non-Windows applications typically use the C run-time **setjmp** and **longjmp** functions to isolate floating-point exceptions. A Windows application should call the Windows **Catch** and **Throw** functions instead.

14.5.8 Executing Other Applications

Windows provides the **WinExec** and **LoadModule** functions, which you can use in your application to run another application. **LoadModule** runs Windows applications only, but **WinExec** runs both Windows and non-Windows applications. Your application should call these functions instead of the C run-time **exec** and **spawn** family of functions. Like the **spawn** function family, **WinExec** and **Load-Module** are nonpreemptive; that is, they allow your application to continue running while the spawned application runs.

WinExec provides a simple interface for spawning a child process. **LoadModule** is more difficult to use because it requires a parameter block for the application you are running, but this also allows you greater control over the environment in which the application runs.

14.5.9 Using BIOS and MS-DOS Interface Functions

Do not use the C run-time BIOS interface routines with Windows.

You can use the C run-time Interrupt 21h routines **intdos**, **intdosx**, and some of the **_dos** functions such as **_dos_getdrive**. You can also use the **int86** and **int86x** routines to invoke interrupts other than Interrupt 21h. However, you should use interrupts with extreme caution and only if necessary.

14.5.10 Eliminating C Run-Time Startup Code

Usually, when you link a Windows application or dynamic-link library, the linker adds C run-time startup code to the _TEXT code segment. For Windows applications (but not dynamic-link libraries), this startup code in turn allocates memory for C run-time variables from the application's automatic data segment.

With Windows, you can eliminate this code and data overhead required by the C run-time libraries if all of the following conditions are true:

- Your application or dynamic-link library does not explicitly call any C run-time functions.

- Your application uses neither the **__argc** nor **__argv** command-line arguments nor the **environ** variable. For more information about how to retrieve the command line and the MS-DOS environment, see Section 14.3, "Using Command-Line Arguments and the MS-DOS Environment." Dynamic-link libraries cannot use **__argc**, **__argv**, and **environ** in any case.

- Your application or dynamic-link library does not implicitly call any C run-time functions, such as to perform stack checking or long division. Stack checking is enabled by default, but you can disable it by using the CL option **/Gs**.

14.5.10.1 Eliminating C Run-Time Startup Code from a Windows Application

To eliminate the C run-time startup code from a Windows application, link the library named xNOCRT.LIB instead of the usual C run-time library xLIBCEW.LIB (the x placeholder stands for the memory-model specifier S, M, L, or C).

The following example shows the **link** command line for an application named SAMPLE that does not make explicit or implicit calls to C run-time functions:

```
link /nod sample, , , snocrt libw, sample.def
```

The xNOCRT.LIB library includes the Windows startup code that ultimately calls your application's **WinMain** function.

If you link your application by using xNOCRT.LIB instead of xLIBCEW.LIB and the linker reports unresolved external symbols that do not belong to your application, your application is probably calling C run-time functions implicitly. In this case, you can still eliminate C run-time startup code and data required for explicit C run-time calls and for the use of the **__argc**, **__argv**, and **environ** variables. To do this, include xNOCRT.LIB on your linker command line before (rather than instead of) xLIBCEW.LIB. You must also specify the linker option **/noe**.

The following example shows the linker command line for an application named Sample if it makes implicit C run-time calls, but not explicit C run-time calls:

```
link /nod /noe sample, , , snocrt slibcew libw, sample.def
```

14.5.10.2 Eliminating C Run-Time Startup Code from a Windows Dynamic-Link Library

To eliminate the C run-time startup code from a Windows dynamic-link library, link the static library xNOCRTD.LIB in place of the usual C run-time library xDLLCEW.LIB.

The following example shows the linker command line for a dynamic-link library named SAMPDLL that does not make explicit or implicit calls to C run-time functions:

```
link /nod sampdll libentry,sampdll.dll,,snocrtd libw,sampdll.def
```

The *x*NOCRTD.LIB library includes the Windows startup code that ultimately calls your dynamic-link library's LibMain function.

As with an application, if the linker reports unresolved external references that do not belong to your dynamic-link library, the library is probably making implicit C run-time calls. In this case, you can eliminate the startup code required for explicit C run-time calls by linking *x*NOCRTD.LIB along with *x*DLLCEW.LIB, as follows:

```
link /nod /noe sampdll libentry,sampdll.dll,,snocrtd sdllcew,sampdll.def
```

Be sure to include the required **/noe** option.

14.6 Writing Assembly-Language Code

Assembly-language Windows applications are highly structured assembly-language programs that use high-level-language calling conventions in addition to Windows functions, data types, and programming conventions. Although you assemble assembly-language Windows applications by using the Microsoft Macro Assembler (ML), the goal is to generate object files that are similar to object files generated by using CL. Following are some guidelines designed to help you meet this goal and create assembly-language Windows applications:

1. Include the CMACROS.INC file in the application source files. This file contains high-level-language macros that define the segments, programming models, function interfaces, and data types needed to create Windows applications. For more information about Windows assembly-language macros, see the *Microsoft Windows Programmer's Reference, Volume 4*.

2. Define the programming model, setting one of the options **memS**, **memM**, **memC**, or **memL** to 1. One of these options must be set before you specify the statement that includes the CMACROS.INC file.

3. Set the calling convention to Pascal by setting the **?PLM** option to 1. This option must be set before you specify the statement that includes the CMACROS.INC file. Pascal calling conventions are required only for functions that Windows calls.

4. Set the Windows prolog and epilog option **?WIN** to 1. This option must be set before you specify the statement that includes the CMACROS.INC file. This option is required only for callback functions (or for exported functions in Windows libraries).

5. Create the application entry point, the **WinMain** function, and declare it as a public function. It should have the following form:

```
cProc WinMain, <PUBLIC>, <si,di>
             parmW hinst
             parmW hPrevInstance
             parmD lpCmdLine
             parmW nCmdShow
cBegin WinMain
                 .
                 .
                 .
cEnd WinMain
```

The **WinMain** function should be defined within the standard code segment **CODE**.

6. Make sure that your callback functions are declared:

```
cProc TestWndProc, <FAR,PUBLIC>, <si,di>
             parmW hWnd
             parmW message
             parmW wParam
             parmD lParam
cBegin TestWndProc
                 .
                 .
                 .
cEnd TestWndProc
```

Callback functions must be defined within a code segment.

7. Link your application with the appropriate C-language library for Windows and C run-time libraries. To link the application properly, you might need to add an external definition for the absolute symbol **__acrtused** in your application source file.

Note Windows functions destroy all registers except DI, SI, BP, and DS.

14.6.1 Modifying the Interrupt Flag

Windows in 386 enhanced mode runs at input and output (I/O) privilege level 0 (IOPL0). At this level, the **popf** and **iret** instructions will not change the state of the interrupt flag. (Other flags will still be saved and restored.) This means, for example, that the following code will leave interrupts disabled upon completion:

```
pushf       ; This is no longer valid code
cli
    .
    .
    .
popf        ; Leaves interrupts disabled
```

In this IOPL0 environment, **sti** and **cli** are the only instructions that will change the interrupt flag. Upon exiting a critical section of code in which you require interrupts to be disabled, you cannot rely on the **popf** instruction to restore the state of the interrupt flag. Instead, upon examining the interrupt flag, you should explicitly set it to its saved value (saved by a previous **pushf** instruction). The following example illustrates the proper method for restoring the interrupt flag:

```
pushf       ; This code illustrates the proper technique
        cli
            .
            .
            .

        pop ax
        test    ah,2
        jz SkipSTI
        sti
SkipSTI:
            .
            .
            .
```

If you have used a software interrupt hook that calls the next interrupt handler in the chain, you similarly cannot rely on the **iret** instruction of the next interrupt handler to return the state of the interrupt flag. The following code, for example, is incorrect:

```
My_SW_Int_Hook: ; The following is incorrect
    sti
    .
    .
    .

    pushf        ; Simulate interrupt call with a pushf
    cli          ; and a cli
```

```
call  [Next_Handler_In_Chain]
        ; The IRET of the next interrupt handler will not restore
        ; the interrupt flag, so it may be left cleared
        ; (interrupts disabled)
  .
  .
  .

    iret
```

The proper technique is to place an **sti** instruction immediately after the call to the next interrupt handler, to enable interrupts again in case the next interrupt handler leaves interrupts disabled. This technique is shown in the following example:

```
My_SW_Int_Hook: ; The following is correct
  sti
  .
  .
  .

  pushf ; Simulate interrupt call with a pushf
  cli   ; and a cli
  call [Next_Handler_In_Chain]
  sti   ; Enable interrupts again in case next handler disables them
  .
  .
  .

    iret
```

14.6.2 Writing Exported Functions in Assembly Language

When you write an exported function in assembly language, do not begin the function with the following code:

```
mov ax,xxxx
```

In this example, *xxxx* is any constant value.

This code at the beginning of an exported function is identical to the beginning of a library code segment that Windows has cached in extended memory. When Windows attempts to reload the code segment, it treats the constant value as if it were the address of the library's data segment and fixes up the constant value to the new address of the data segment.

To ensure that Windows does not treat your code segment as a cached library segment, simply precede the **mov ax** instruction with a **nop** instruction, as follows:

```
nop
mov ax,xxxx
```

14.6.3 Using the ES Register

You must take special care when using the ES register in an assembly-language application. Under certain circumstances, a selector that points to a discarded data object in the ES register can cause your application to produce a general-protection (GP) fault. Also, a rare combination of circumstances can cause Windows to enter an infinite loop.

A GP fault occurs when a program pops the ES stack and the selector in the ES register refers to a segment that has been discarded. For example, in the following example, ES refers to a global memory object. Freeing the object invalidates the selector that was temporarily pushed onto the stack.

```
push es
    .
    .
    .

cCall GlobalFree <es>
    .
    .
    .

pop es
```

Your application need not discard a segment explicitly for it to be discarded. The following example shows how a segment can be discarded indirectly:

```
push es        ; ES refers to a discardable data segment
    .
    .

call far Proc1 ; Proc1 directly or indirectly causes the memory
    .          ; object pointed to by ES to be discarded
    .
    .

pop es
```

Windows handles code-segment faults. It does not handle data-segment faults, however, so this example would result in a GP fault.

An unusual situation can arise that puts Windows in an infinite loop when the ES register holds the selector to a discardable code segment. In such cases, you should clear ES before making a call from one discardable segment to another. The following example shows how to make such a call:

```
mov es, _CODESEG1      ; CODESEG1 is discardable
    .
    .
    .

xor ax, ax             ; This sample clears the ES register before
mov es, ax             ; calling from a discardable segment to a
call far Proc1         ; discardable segment
```

If you fail to clear the ES register in this situation, the Windows segment fault handler can enter an infinite loop, discarding and reloading the three discardable code segments when memory is low. During this process, the ES stack is pushed and popped, forcing CODESEG1 to be unnecessarily reloaded when the "code fence" has room only for the other two segments.

14.7 Related Topics

For more information about managing memory, see Chapter 15, "Memory Management," and Chapter 16, "More Memory Management."

For more information about creating dynamic-link libraries, see Chapter 20, "Dynamic-Link Libraries."

For more information about Windows assembly-language macros, see the *Microsoft Windows Programmer's Reference, Volume 4*.

For more information about compiling and linking applications, see *Microsoft Windows Programming Tools*.

Memory Management

All applications must use memory in order to run. Because the Microsoft Windows 3.1 operating system is multitasking, several applications may use memory simultaneously. Windows manages the available memory to make sure all applications have access to it, and to make memory usage as efficient as possible.

This chapter provides a brief introduction to the Windows memory-management system and covers the following topics:

- Using memory in Windows
- Using code and data segments efficiently

This chapter also explains how to build a sample application, Memory, that illustrates these concepts.

15.1 Using Memory

In the Windows memory-management system, your application can allocate blocks of memory, called memory objects. You can allocate memory objects from either the global or the local heap. The global heap is a pool of free memory available to all applications. The local heap is a pool of free memory available to just your application. In managing the system memory, Windows also manages the code and data segments of your application.

In some memory-management systems, the memory you allocate remains fixed at a specific memory location until you free it. In Windows, allocated memory can be also be movable and discardable.

A movable memory object does not have a fixed address; Windows can move it at any time to a new address. Movable memory objects let Windows make the best use of free memory. For example, if a movable memory object separates two free memory objects, Windows can move the movable object to combine the free objects into one contiguous object.

Discardable memory is similar to movable memory in that Windows can move it, but Windows can also reallocate a discardable object to zero length if it must use the space to satisfy an allocation request. Reallocating a memory object to zero length destroys the data the object contains, but an application always has the option of reloading the discarded data whenever it is needed.

When you allocate a memory object, you receive a handle, rather than a pointer, to that memory object. The handle identifies the allocated object. You use it to retrieve the object's current address when you need to access the memory.

To access a memory object, you lock the memory handle. This temporarily fixes the memory object and returns a pointer to its beginning. While a memory handle is locked, Windows cannot move or discard the object. Therefore, after you have finished using the object, you should unlock the handle as soon as possible. Keeping a memory handle locked makes Windows memory management less efficient and can cause subsequent allocation requests to fail.

Windows lets you compact memory. By "squeezing" the free memory from between allocated memory objects, Windows collects the largest contiguous free memory object possible, from which you may allocate additional memory objects. This squeezing is a process of moving and (if necessary) discarding memory objects. You can also discard individual memory objects if you temporarily have no need for them.

15.1.1 Using the Global Heap

The global heap contains all of system memory. Windows allocates the memory it needs for code and data from the global heap when it first starts. Any remaining free memory in the global heap is available to applications and Windows libraries.

Applications typically use the global heap for large memory allocations (greater than a kilobyte or so). Although you can allocate larger memory objects from the global heap than you can from the local heap, there is a tradeoff: Because it is easier to manipulate local data than it is to manipulate global data, your application will be easier to write if you use only local data.

You can allocate any size of memory object from the global heap. Applications typically allocate large objects from the global heap; these objects can exceed 64K if the applications require that much contiguous space. Windows provides special services for accessing data past the first 64K segment. For more information about these services, see Chapter 16, "More Memory Management."

To allocate a global memory object, use the **GlobalAlloc** function. You specify the size and type (fixed, movable, or discardable); **GlobalAlloc** returns a handle of the memory object. Before you can use the memory object, you must lock it by using the **GlobalLock** function, which returns the full 32-bit address of the first byte in the memory object. You can then use this long pointer to access the bytes in the object.

In the following example, the **GlobalAlloc** function allocates 4096 bytes of movable memory, and the **GlobalLock** function locks it so that the first 256 bytes can be set to the address 0xFF:

```
HANDLE hMem;
LPSTR lpMem;
int i;
```

```
if ((hMem = GlobalAlloc(GMEM_MOVEABLE, 4096)) != NULL) {
    if ((lpMem = GlobalLock(hMem)) != (LPSTR) NULL) {
        for (i = 0; i < 256; i++)
            lpMem[i] = 0xFF;
        GlobalUnlock(hMem);
    }
}
```

In this example, the application unlocks the memory handle by using the **GlobalUnlock** function immediately after accessing the memory object. Once a movable or discardable memory object is locked, Windows guarantees that the object will remain fixed in memory until it is unlocked. This means the address remains valid as long as the object remains locked, but this also keeps Windows from making the best use of memory if other allocation requests are made. Cooperative applications unlock memory.

The **GlobalAlloc** function returns the value NULL if an allocation request fails. You should always check the return value to ensure that it is a valid handle. If you want to, you can determine how much memory is available in the global heap by using the **GlobalCompact** function. This function returns the number of bytes in the largest contiguous free memory object.

You should also check the address returned by the **GlobalLock** function. This function returns a NULL pointer if the memory handle was not valid or if the contents of the memory object have been discarded.

You can free any global memory you may no longer need by using the **GlobalFree** function. In general, you should free such memory so that other applications can use the space. You should always free global memory before your application terminates.

15.1.2 Using the Local Heap

The local heap contains free memory that may be allocated for private use by the application. The local heap is located in the application's data segment and is therefore accessible only to a specific instance of the application. You can allocate memory from the local heap in sizes of up to 64K and the memory can be fixed, movable, or discardable, as needed.

Windows does not automatically supply a local heap for an application. To request a local heap for your application, use the **HEAPSIZE** statement in the application's module-definition file. This statement sets the initial size, in bytes, of the local heap. If the local heap is in a fixed data segment, you may allocate up to the specified heap size. If the local heap is in a movable data segment, you may allocate beyond the initial heap size and up to 64K, since Windows will automatically allocate additional space for the local heap until the data segment reaches the 64K maximum. You should note, however, that if Windows allocates additional local memory to satisfy a local allocation, it may move the data segment, invalidating any long pointers to objects in local memory.

The maximum size of any local heap depends on the size of the application's stack, static data, and global data. The local heap shares the data segment with the stack and this data. Since a data segment can be no larger than 64K, an application's local heap can be no larger than 64K minus the size of the application's stack, global data, and static data. The application's stack size is defined by the **STACKSIZE** statement in the application's module-definition file. The global and static data sizes depend on how many strings and global or static variables are declared in the application. Windows enforces a minimum stack size of 5K, so if the module-definition file specifies a smaller stack size, Windows automatically sets the stack size to 5K.

You can allocate local memory by using the **LocalAlloc** function. This function allocates a memory object in the application's local heap and returns a handle of the memory. You lock the local memory object by using the **LocalLock** function. This returns a near address (a 16-bit offset) to the first byte in the memory object. The offset is relative to the beginning of your data segment. In the following example, the **LocalAlloc** function allocates 256 bytes of movable memory, and the **LocalLock** function locks it so that the first 256 bytes can be set to the address 0xFF:

```
HANDLE hMem;
PSTR pMem;
int i;

if ((hMem = LocalAlloc(LMEM_MOVEABLE, 256)) != NULL) {
    if ((pMem = LocalLock(hMem)) != NULL) {
        for (i = 0; i < 256; i++)
            pMem[i] = 0xFF;
        LocalUnlock(hMem);
    }
}
```

In this example, the application unlocks the memory handle by using the **Local-Unlock** function immediately after accessing the memory object. Once a movable or discardable memory object is locked, Windows guarantees that the object will remain fixed in memory until it is unlocked. This means the address remains valid as long as the object remains locked, but this also prevents Windows from making the best use of memory if other allocation requests are made. If you want to ensure that you are getting the best performance from your application's local heap, make sure you unlock memory after using it.

The **LocalAlloc** function returns the value NULL if an allocation request fails. You should always check the return value to ensure that a valid handle exists. If you want to, you can determine how much memory is available in the local heap by using the **LocalCompact** function. This function returns the number of bytes in the largest contiguous free memory object in the local heap.

You should also check the address returned by the **LocalLock** function. This function returns NULL if the memory handle was not valid or if the contents of the memory object have been discarded.

15.1.3 Working with Discardable Memory

You create a discardable memory object by combining the GMEM_DISCARDABLE and GMEM_MOVEABLE constants when allocating the object. The resulting object will be moved as necessary to make room for other allocation requests, or if there is not enough memory to satisfy the request, the object may be discarded. The following example allocates a discardable object from global memory:

```
hMem = GlobalAlloc(GMEM_MOVEABLE | GMEM_DISCARDABLE, 4096L);
```

When Windows discards a memory object, it empties the object by reallocating it, with zero bytes given as the new size. The contents of the object are lost, but the memory handle of the object remains valid. Any attempt to lock the handle and access the object will fail, however.

Windows determines which memory objects to discard by using a least-recently-used (LRU) algorithm. It continues to discard memory objects until there is enough memory to satisfy an allocation request. In general, if you have not accessed a discardable object in some time, it is a candidate for discarding. A locked object cannot be discarded.

You can discard your own memory objects by using the **GlobalDiscard** function. This function empties the object but preserves the memory handle. You can also discard other applications' memory objects by using the **GlobalCompact** function. This function moves and discards memory objects until the specified or largest possible amount of memory is available. One way to discard all discardable objects is to supply −1 as the argument. This is a request for every byte of memory. Although the request will fail, it will discard all discardable objects and leave the largest possible free memory object.

Since a discarded memory object's handle remains valid, you can still retrieve information about the object by using the **GlobalFlags** function. This is useful for verifying that the object has been discarded. **GlobalFlags** sets the GMEM_DISCARDED bit in its return value when the specified memory object has been discarded. Therefore, if you attempt to lock a discardable object and the lock fails, you can check the object's status by using **GlobalFlags**.

Once a discardable object has been discarded, its contents are lost. If you want to use the object again, you must reallocate it to its appropriate size and fill it with the data it previously contained. You can reallocate it by using the **GlobalReAlloc** function. The following example checks the object's status, and then fills it with data if it has been discarded:

```
lpMem = GlobalLock(hMem);

if (lpMem == NULL) {
    if (GlobalFlags(hMem) & GMEM_DISCARDED) {
        hMem = GlobalReAlloc(hMem, 4096L,
            GMEM_MOVEABLE | GMEM_DISCARDABLE);
        lpMem = GlobalLock(hMem);

        /* More program lines.... */
        /* Fill with data.       */

        GlobalUnlock(hMem);
    }
}
```

You can make a discardable object nondiscardable (or vice versa) by using the **GlobalReAlloc** function and the GMEM_MODIFY constant. The following example changes a movable object, identified by the hMem memory handle, to a movable, discardable object:

```
hMem = GlobalReAlloc(hMem, 0, GMEM_MODIFY | GMEM_DISCARDABLE);
```

The following example changes a discardable object to a nondiscardable one:

```
hMem = GlobalReAlloc(hMem, 0, GMEM_MODIFY);
```

When you specify GMEM_MODIFY in a call to the **GlobalReAlloc** function, the second parameter is ignored.

15.2 Using Segments

One of the principal features of Windows is that it lets the user run more than one application at a time. Because multiple applications place greater demands on memory than does a single application, the ability in Windows to run more than one application at a time significantly affects how you write applications. Although many computers have at least 640K of memory, this memory rapidly becomes limited as the user loads and runs more applications. With Windows, you must be aware of how your application uses memory and be prepared to minimize the amount of memory your application occupies at any given time.

To help you manage your application's use of memory, Windows uses the same memory-management system for your application's code and data segments that you use within your application to allocate and manage global memory objects. When the user starts your application, Windows allocates space for the code and data segments in global memory and then copies the segments from the executable file into memory. These segments can be fixed, movable, and even discardable. You specify their attributes in the application's module-definition file.

You can reduce the effect your application has on memory by using movable code and data segments. By using movable segments, you enable Windows to take advantage of free memory as the memory becomes available.

By using discardable code segments, you can further reduce the effect your application has on memory. If you make a code segment discardable, Windows discards it, if necessary, to satisfy requests for global memory. Unlike ordinary memory objects that you may allocate, discarded code segments are monitored by Windows, which automatically reloads them if your application attempts to execute code within them. This means that your application's code segments are in memory only when they are needed.

Discarding a segment destroys its contents. Windows does not save the current contents of a discarded segment. Instead, it treats the segment as if it were no different than when originally loaded and will load the segment directly from the executable file when it is needed.

15.2.1 Using Code Segments

A code segment is one or more bytes (but never more than 64K) of machine instructions. It represents all or part of an application's program instructions.

Important You must not store writable data in code segments; writing to a code segment causes a general-protection (GP) fault when your Windows version 3.1 application runs. Windows will, however, allow you to store read-only data, such as a jump table, in a code segment. For more information about running applications with Windows 3.1, see Chapter 16, "More Memory Management."

Every application has at least one code segment. For example, the sample applications described in previous chapters have one and only one code segment. You can also create an application that has multiple code segments. In fact, most Windows applications have multiple code segments. By using multiple code segments, you reduce the size of any given code segment to the number of instructions needed to carry out some task. If you also make these segments discardable, you effectively minimize the memory requirements of your application's code segments.

When you create medium- or large-model applications, you are creating applications that use multiple code segments. Medium- and large-model applications typically have one or more source files for each segment. When working with multiple source files, compile each source file separately and explicitly name the segment to which the compiled code will belong. Then link the application, defining the segments' attributes in the application's module-definition file.

To define a segment's attributes, use the **SEGMENTS** statement in the module-definition file. The following example shows definitions for three segments:

```
SEGMENTS
        PAINT_TEXT MOVEABLE DISCARDABLE
        INIT_TEXT MOVEABLE DISCARDABLE
        WNDPROC_TEXT MOVEABLE DISCARDABLE
```

You may also use the **CODE** statement in the module-definition file to define the default attributes for all code segments. The **CODE** statement also defines attributes for any segments that are not explicitly defined in the **SEGMENTS** statement. The following example shows how to make all segments not listed in the **SEGMENTS** statement discardable:

```
CODE MOVEABLE DISCARDABLE
```

If you use discardable code segments in your application, you must balance segment discarding with the number of times the segment may be accessed. For example, the segment containing your main window procedure should probably not be discardable, because Windows calls the procedure often. Typically, this segment is small (approximately 4K). Because a discarded segment has to be loaded from disk when needed, the memory savings you may realize by discarding the window procedure may be offset by the performance loss that comes with accessing the disk often. To optimize performance, you should ensure that the only things in the segment containing the main window procedure are called frequently by the system.

Note A code segment in a library can be fixed or movable. If it is movable, it is automatically made discardable.

15.2.2 The DATA Segment

Every application has a **DATA** segment. The **DATA** segment contains the application's stack, local heap, and static and global data. Like a code segment, the **DATA** segment cannot be larger than 64K.

A **DATA** segment can be fixed or movable, but not discardable. If the **DATA** segment is movable, Windows automatically locks the segment upon passing control to the application. Otherwise, a movable **DATA** segment may move if an application allocates global memory, or if the application attempts to allocate more memory than is currently available in the local heap. For this reason, it is important not to keep long pointers to variables in the **DATA** segment.

You define the attributes of the **DATA** segment by using the **DATA** statement in the module-definition file. The default attributes are **MOVEABLE** and **MULTIPLE**. The **MULTIPLE** attribute directs Windows to create one copy of an application's data segment for each instance of the application. This means the contents of the **DATA** segment are unique to each instance of the application.

A large-model application may have additional data segments, but only one **DATA** segment. Using large model with additional data segments is not recommended. If your application requires multiple segments of data, you can allocate them by using the **GlobalAlloc** function during the initialization of the application.

15.3 Sample Application: Memory

This sample application illustrates how to create a medium-model Windows application that uses discardable code segments. To create the Memory application, make the following modifications to the Generic application:

1. Split the C-language source file into four separate files.
2. Modify the header file.
3. Add new segment definitions to the module-definition file.
4. Modify the makefile.
5. Compile and link the application.

15.3.1 Splitting the C-Language Source File

So that the functions within the file are compiled as separate segments, you must split the C-language source file into separate files. For this application, you can split the source file into four parts, as described in the following list:

Source file	Content
MEMORY1.C	Contains the **WinMain** function. Because Windows executes the message loop in **WinMain** frequently, the segment created from this source file is not discardable. This prevents a situation in which the segment has to be loaded from the disk often. Because **WinMain** is relatively small anyway, keeping this segment in memory has little effect on available global memory.
MEMORY2.C	Contains the MemoryInit function. Since the MemoryInit function is used only when the application first starts, the segment created from this source file can be discardable.

Source file	Content
MEMORY3.C	Contains the MemoryWndProc function. Although the segment created from this source file can be discardable, the MemoryWnd-Proc function is likely to be called at least as often as the **WinMain** function receives control. In this case, the segment is movable but not discardable.
MEMORY4.C	Contains the About function. Since the About function is seldom called (only when the About dialog box is displayed), the code segment created from this source file can be discardable.

You must include the WINDOWS.H and MEMORY.H header files in each source file.

15.3.2 Modifying the Header File

You must move the declaration of the hInst variable into the MEMORY.H header file. This ensures that the variable is accessible in all segments. The hInst variable is used in the **WinMain** and MemoryWndProc functions.

15.3.3 Adding New Segment Definitions

To specify the attributes of each code segment, you must add segment definitions to the module-definition file. This means you must add a **SEGMENTS** statement to the file and list each segment by name in the application. After you have made the changes, the module-definition file should look like this:

```
NAME    Memory

DESCRIPTION 'Sample Microsoft Windows 3.1 Application'

EXETYPE WINDOWS

STUB    'WINSTUB.EXE'

SEGMENTS
    MEMORY_MAIN    PRELOAD    MOVEABLE
    MEMORY_INIT    LOADONCALL MOVEABLE DISCARDABLE
    MEMORY_WNDPROC LOADONCALL MOVEABLE
    MEMORY_ABOUT   LOADONCALL MOVEABLE DISCARDABLE

CODE    MOVEABLE DISCARDABLE

DATA    MOVEABLE MULTIPLE
```

```
HEAPSIZE  1024
STACKSIZE 8192

EXPORTS
   MainWndProc        @1
   About              @2
```

In this module-definition file, the **SEGMENTS** statement defines the attributes of each segment:

- The MEMORY_MAIN segment contains **WinMain**.
- The MEMORY_INIT segment contains the initialization functions.
- The MEMORY_WNDPROC segment contains the window procedure.
- The MEMORY_ABOUT segment contains the dialog box procedure.

Each segment has the **MOVEABLE** attribute, but only MEMORY_INIT and MEMORY_ABOUT have the **DISCARDABLE** attribute. Also, only the MEMORY_MAIN segment is loaded when the application starts. The other segments have the **LOADONCALL** attribute, which means they are loaded when needed.

Although each segment is explicitly defined, the **CODE** statement is still given. This statement specifies the attributes of any additional segments the linker may add to the application—for example, any segments containing C run-time functions called in the application source files.

15.3.4 Modifying the Makefile

To compile the new C-language source files separately, you must refer to each source file in the makefile. Since this application is a medium-model application, use the **/AM** option when compiling. For clarity, you should also name each segment by using the **/NT** option.

You will also need to change the **link** command line so that it refers to the medium-model library MLIBCEW.LIB rather than the small-model library SLIBCEW.LIB.

The makefile for the Memory application should look like this:

```
memory.res: memory.rc memory.h
    rc /r memory.rc

memory1.obj: memory1.c memory.h
    cl /c /AM /Gsw /Zp /NT MEMORY_MAIN memory1.c

memory2.obj: memory2.c memory.h
    cl /c /AM /Gsw /Zp /NT MEMORY_INIT memory2.c
```

```
memory3.obj: memory3.c memory.h
    cl /c /AM /Gsw /Zp /NT MEMORY_WNDPROC memory3.c

memory4.obj: memory4.c memory.h
    cl /c /AM /Gsw /Zp /NT MEMORY_ABOUT memory4.c

memory.exe: memory1.obj memory2.obj memory3.obj memory4.obj \
    memory.def
    link memory1 memory2 memory3 memory4,memory.exe,,mlibcew \
    libw,memory.def
    rc memory.res

memory.exe: memory.res
    rc memory.res
```

15.3.5 Compiling and Linking

After compiling and linking the Memory application, start Windows, Microsoft Windows Heap Walker (HEAPWALK.EXE), provided with the SDK, and Memory. Use Heap Walker to view the various segments of the Memory application.

15.4 Related Topics

For more information about managing memory, see Chapter 16, "More Memory Management."

For more information about memory-management functions, see the *Microsoft Windows Programmer's Reference, Volume 2*.

More Memory Management

Chapter 15, "Memory Management," presented the basic information you need to know about using memory in a Microsoft Windows 3.1 application. Some applications require more advanced memory-management techniques, however. This chapter provides more detailed information about how the Windows operating system manages memory and how you should write your application to make the best use of the Windows advanced memory features.

This chapter covers the following topics:

- Windows memory configurations
- Using data storage in Windows applications
- Using memory models
- Using huge data
- Managing program data
- Managing memory for program code

16.1 Memory Configurations

You should expect that your Windows application will be run in either of two memory configurations; most often, which configuration depends on the type of the system CPU and the amount and configuration of memory. Windows supports two memory configurations:

- Standard mode
- 386 enhanced mode

If the user started other programs before starting Windows, the amount of memory available to Windows will be less than that installed in the system.

Because Windows uses different memory configurations on different systems, your application should be able to run successfully with either memory configuration. The best way to ensure this is to write the application by following all the Windows memory-management rules. For a list of these rules, see Section 16.5, "Traps to Avoid When Managing Program Data."

Wherever possible, your application should not contain code that is dependent upon a particular memory configuration. In some instances, however, an application must be able to determine the memory configuration in which it is running. To do this, the application can call the **GetWinFlags** function. This function returns a 32-bit value containing flags that indicate the memory configuration in which Windows is running and other information about the user's system.

16.1.1 Standard Mode

Windows uses the standard-mode memory configuration by default on systems that meet the following criteria:

- An 80286-based system with at least 1 megabyte of memory.

- An 80386-based system with at least 1 megabyte of memory, but less than 2 megabytes. On 80386-based systems with 2 megabytes or more, Windows uses the 386 enhanced-mode memory configuration by default. For a description of this memory configuration, see Section 16.1.2, "386 Enhanced Mode."

The Windows heap is made up of at least two memory objects, one in conventional (MS-DOS) memory and one in extended memory. Additional conventional or extended memory objects may be present.

The memory object that Windows uses for the global heap is in conventional memory. This area begins above any terminate-and-stay-resident (TSR) programs, device drivers, MS-DOS, and so on, and extends to the top of conventional memory. This conventional memory is usually 640K, but can be less on some systems.

The second required memory object for the Windows standard-mode configuration is in extended memory. Windows allocates the object in extended memory through an extended-memory device driver and then accesses the object directly, without using the driver. The size and location of this object can vary, depending on what the user loaded into extended memory before starting Windows.

Windows links the two or more memory objects to form the Windows global heap. The beginning (bottom) of the conventional memory object is the beginning (bottom) of the global heap, and the end (top) of the extended-memory object is the end (top) of the global heap.

The following figure shows a typical Windows standard-mode memory configuration:

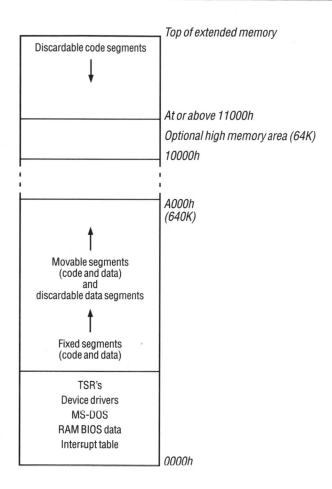

As with other memory configurations, Windows allocates discardable code segments from the top of the heap, fixed segments from the bottom of the heap, and movable code and data segments above fixed segments.

16.1.1.1 Using Huge Memory Objects in Standard Mode

A far address is created from 16-bit segment address and a 16-bit offset. The segment address is a selector, similar to a Windows handle, that points to an entry in a local or global descriptor table (LDT or GDT). The table entry indicates whether the segment referred to by the selector currently resides in memory. If the segment resides in memory, the table entry provides the linear address of the segment.

If you allocate a huge memory object (larger than 64K), the Microsoft C Optimizing Compiler (CL) generates huge-pointer code that performs segment arithmetic to advance a far pointer across segment 64K boundaries. However, CL does this only if the object is explicitly declared as huge or if the module was compiled with the huge memory model. Do not directly change the segment address portion of a far pointer. Attempting to increment the segment address with the intent of advancing the physical paragraph address will only result in an invalid selector. When the invalid selector is subsequently used to read or write to the memory location, either Windows will report a general-protection (GP) fault, or possibly worse, the invalid selector might inappropriately point to unintended data or code.

If you are programming in assembly language, the proper technique for incrementing a far pointer is to use the external variable **__ahincr**. Windows fixes up **__ahincr** with the correct constant to increment the segment selector. This is possible because when Windows allocates the huge memory object, it assigns related selector values to the related memory segments that are 64K (0x1000 paragraphs) in size. This is called selector tiling. The following example illustrates the proper method for incrementing a far pointer by 64K (the only increment provided):

```
extrn      __ahincr:abs
           .
           .
           .

mov     ax, es      ; es is the segment address you
                    ; wish to increment
add     ax, __ahincr
mov     es, ax
```

The largest memory object Windows can allocate on an 80286 processor is 1 megabyte less 16 bytes. The largest memory object on an 80386 is 16 megabytes less 64K. If your application requires a memory object larger than 16 megabytes less 64K, see the DOS Protected-Mode Interface (DPMI) specification in the Microsoft Windows Device Driver Kit. All parts of an application (code and data) are normally movable in linear memory.

16.1.1.2 Using Global Selectors

To perform memory-mapped input and output, you can use the following global-selector constants in an assembly-language application to access the corresponding locations in memory:

- __A000H
- __B000H
- __B800H
- __C000H

- __D000H
- __E000H
- __F000H

The following example illustrates how to use these selectors properly:

```
mov ax, __A000H
mov es,ax
```

Do not use these selectors except to support hardware devices that perform memory-mapped input and output.

16.1.1.3 Code-Segment and Data-Segment Aliasing

Usually, you cannot execute code stored in a data segment. In standard mode, an attempt to execute code in a data segment results in a GP fault. In rare cases, however, such execution may be necessary, and can be performed by aliasing the data segment in question. Aliasing involves copying a segment selector and then changing the TYPE field of the copy so that an operation that is not normally permitted can be performed on the segment.

Windows provides two functions that perform segment aliasing:

- **AllocDStoCSAlias**
- **ChangeSelector**

AllocDStoCSAlias accepts a data-segment selector and returns a code-segment selector. This permits you to write machine instructions on your data stack, create an alias for the stack segment, and then execute the code on the stack.

This function allocates a new selector; after calling **AllocDStoCSAlias**, you must call the **FreeSelector** function when you no longer need the selector.

You must be careful not to use a selector returned by **AllocDStoCSAlias** if it is possible that the segment has moved. The only way to prevent a segment from moving is by calling the **GlobalFix** function to fix it in linear address space before aliasing the segment.

You can also be sure that a segment has not moved if your application does not yield to another task and does not take any action that could result in memory being allocated. Typically, this would require you to allocate and free a new selector each time your application yields or allocates memory. To avoid allocating and freeing a selector so frequently, you can use a temporary selector. **Change-Selector** provides a convenient method for "aliasing" a temporary selector (generating a code selector corresponding to a given data selector, or vice versa). This function accepts two selectors: a temporary selector, and the selector you want to convert. To convert the selector repeatedly, you would perform the following steps:

1. Call **AllocateSelector** to create a temporary selector.

2. As often as necessary, call **ChangeSelector**, passing it the temporary selector and the selector you want to convert. Because **ChangeSelector** uses a previously allocated selector, you need not free the selector each time you convert it. Instead, you call **ChangeSelector** each time you need the converted selector after the converted segment might have moved.

3. When you no longer need the converted selector, call **FreeSelector** to free the temporary selector.

16.1.2 386 Enhanced Mode

If the user's system has at least 2 megabytes of extended memory available and an 80386 microprocessor, then Windows and Windows applications will run in 386 enhanced mode. In this mode, by taking advantage of certain features of the 80386 processor, Windows implements a virtual-memory management scheme using disk swapping. The result of this scheme is that the amount of memory available to all applications can be several times the amount of extended memory on the system. In this mode, Windows can theoretically address 4 gigabytes of memory, but is limited by the amount of RAM and disk space available for swapping.

Note Because 386 enhanced mode uses the protected-mode features of the 80386 processor, the restrictions for using memory in standard mode also apply to using memory in 386 enhanced mode.

The following describes the memory configuration of 386 enhanced mode:

- The global heap is essentially one large virtual address space shared by all applications.

- The size of the global heap's virtual address space is not bounded by the amount of extended memory. The disk serves as a secondary memory medium that extends the virtual address space.

16.1.2.1 Swapping Code and Data

The 386 enhanced-mode fixed code and data segments are located lower in memory than nondiscardable, movable code and data segments, and discardable data segments, which are allocated above the fixed code and data segments. Discardable code segments are allocated from the top of memory.

The 386 enhanced-mode memory configuration is distinct from standard mode, because Windows swaps code and data between physical memory and the disk. In standard mode, Windows may remove discardable data from memory, but it does not save the data to disk so that it may be read back into memory when needed.

In 386 enhanced mode, Windows continues allocating physical memory until it is used up, and then begins swapping 4K pages of code and data from physical memory to disk in order to make additional physical memory available. Windows swaps 4K objects (pages), rather than unequal-sized code and data segments. A swapped 4K object may be only part of a given code or data segment, or it may cross over two or more code or data segments.

This memory swapping, or paging, is transparent to the application. If the application attempts to access a code or data segment of which some part has been paged out to disk, the 80386 microprocessor issues an interrupt, called a page fault, to Windows. Windows then swaps other pages out of memory and restores the pages that the application needs. Windows chooses the pages that it swaps to disk based on a least-recently-used (LRU) algorithm.

This virtual-memory system provides as much additional memory as the size of the Windows swap file that is reserved on the user's disk. Windows determines the size of the swap file based on the total amount of physical memory on the system and the amount of disk space available. The user can modify the size of the swap file by changing an entry in the SYSTEM.INI file and can establish a permanent swap file by using the **swapfile** command.

The Windows demand-loading of code and data segments operates on top of the Windows virtual-memory paging scheme. That is, Windows treats virtual memory as though it were conventional memory for purposes of determining which code and data segments to discard. Windows, however, removes discardable code and data segments only when virtual memory is exhausted.

16.1.2.2 Preventing Memory from Being Paged to Disk

Occasionally, it is necessary to ensure that certain memory is always present in physical memory and is never paged to disk. For example, a dynamic-link library (DLL) function may be required to respond immediately to an interrupt instead of waiting for the system to generate a page fault and load the data from the disk. In such cases, a memory object can be page-locked to prevent it from being paged to disk.

To page-lock a memory object, call the **GlobalPageLock** function, passing it the global selector of the segment that is to be locked. This function increments (increases by one) a page-lock count for the segment; as long as the count for a given segment is nonzero, the segment will remain at the same physical address and will not be paged out to disk. When you no longer require the memory to be locked, call the **GlobalPageUnlock** to decrement (decrease by one) the page-lock count. In standard mode, these functions have no effect.

Note You should page-lock memory only in critical situations. Do not routinely page-lock memory to lock down a spreadsheet, for example. Page-locking memory adversely affects the performance of all applications, including yours.

16.2 Storing Data

Windows supports seven types of data storage, each of which is appropriate for different situations. The following list describes each type of storage, and suggests how to decide which type to use.

Type	Description
Static data	Includes all C-language variables that the application source code implicitly or explicitly declares by using the **static** keyword. Static data also includes all C-language variables declared as external, either explicitly (using the **extern** keyword) or by default (by declaring it outside the functions).
Automatic data	Includes all variables that are allocated in the stack at the time a function is called. The variables include the function parameters and any locally declared variables. For more information about automatic data, see Section 16.2.1, "Managing Automatic Data Segments."
Local dynamic data	Includes all data that is allocated by using the **LocalAlloc** function. Local dynamic data is allocated out of a local heap in the automatic data segment to which an application's DS register is set. Allocating memory objects from the local heap of a Windows application is similar to allocating memory by using the **malloc** C run-time library function in a non-Windows application that uses the small- or medium-memory model. For more information about local dynamic data, see Section 16.2.2, "Managing Local Dynamic-Data Objects."
Global dynamic data	Includes all data that is allocated out of the Windows global heap by using the **GlobalAlloc** function. The global heap is a system-wide memory resource. Allocating memory objects from the global heap is roughly equivalent to using the **malloc** function in a non-Windows application that uses the compact- or large-memory model. The difference is that in Windows, your application allocates memory objects out of a heap potentially shared by other applications, while a non-Windows application essentially has the whole heap to itself. For more information about global dynamic data, see Section 16.2.3, "Managing Global Memory Objects."

Type	Description
Window extra bytes	Specifies extra bytes that are allocated in the data structure that Windows maintains internally for a window created by your application. To create this kind of window, register a class for it (by calling the **RegisterClass** function) and request that extra bytes be allocated for each window that is a member of this class. You request the extra bytes by specifying a nonzero value for the **cbWndExtra** member of the **WNDCLASS** structure that you pass to **RegisterClass**. You can then store data in and retrieve data from this area by making calls to the **SetWindowWord**, **SetWindowLong**, **GetWindowWord**, and **GetWindowLong** functions. For more information about Window extra bytes, see Section 16.2.4, "Using Extra Bytes in Window and Class Data Structures."
Class extra bytes	Specifies extra bytes that are allocated at the end of the **WNDCLASS** structure created for a window class. When you register the window class, you specify a nonzero value for the **cbClsExtra** member. You can then store and retrieve data from this area by making calls to the functions **SetClassWord**, **SetClassLong**, **GetClassWord** and **GetClassLong**. For more information about using class extra bytes, see Section 16.2.4, "Using Extra Bytes in Window and Class Data Structures."
Resources	Specifies nonmodifiable collections of data stored in the resource portion of an executable file. This data can be loaded into memory where your application can use it conveniently. You can define private resources that contain whatever kind of read-only data you want to store. You compile a resource into your executable (.EXE) or .DLL file by using Microsoft Windows Resource Compiler (RC). At run time, you can then access the resource data by using various Windows library functions. For more information about resources, see Section 16.2.5, "Managing Resources."

16.2.1 Managing Automatic Data Segments

Each application has one data segment called the automatic data segment, which may contain up to 64K. The automatic data segment contains the following kinds of data:

Type	Description
Task header	Contains 16 bytes of information that Windows maintains for each application. The task header is always located in the first 16 bytes of the automatic data segment.

Type	Description
Static data	Includes all C-language variables that are declared as **static** or **extern**, either explicitly or by default.
Stack	Stores automatic data. The stack has a fixed size, but the active area within the stack grows and contracts as functions execute and return. Each time a function is called, the return address is pushed onto the active portion of the stack, along with the parameter values passed to the function.
Local heap	Contains all local dynamic data.

The following figure shows the layout of the application's automatic data segment:

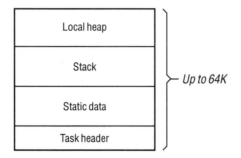

The size of the stack is always fixed for a given application. You specify the size, in bytes, of the stack by using the **STACKSIZE** statement in your application's module-definition (.DEF) file. Windows enforces a minimum stack size of 5K. You should experiment with your application to determine an optimum stack size, although keep in mind that the results of a stack overflow are unpredictable.

The size of the local heap is set to an initial value for the application according to the **HEAPSIZE** statement in your application's .DEF file. The local heap will grow as needed when you call the **LocalAlloc** function. For applications, the initial size of the local heap must be at least large enough to hold the current environment variables; a minimum heap size of 1K is recommended. If your application does not require access to environment information, you can link your application to an object file that will prevent this initialization information from being placed in the heap. For more information, see Chapter 14, "C and Assembly Language."

If your application requests memory from the local heap beyond what is available, the heap can grow until the total data segment reaches 64K. If some of the local heap objects are freed, however, the size of the heap does not automatically shrink. You can recover this area by calling the **LocalShrink** function. This function first compacts the local heap, and then truncates the automatic data segment to the specified number of bytes. **LocalShrink** will truncate below neither the highest currently allocated memory object, nor the originally specified heap size.

You can declare the automatic data segment to be fixed or movable in the application's .DEF file, just as you can any data or code segment. Unless you have a good reason to do otherwise, always declare the automatic data segment as movable and multiple. The automatic data segment is always preloaded. The following example shows how to declare the automatic data segment in the .DEF file:

```
DATA MOVEABLE MULTIPLE
```

By declaring the application's automatic data segment as movable, you allow Windows to relocate the data segment in memory as its size changes. If the automatic data segment is fixed, Windows increases the size of the local heap only if adjacent memory happens to be available. Consequently, if you declare the automatic data segment to be fixed, you should be careful to specify an adequate initial **HEAPSIZE** value in the .DEF file.

You should specify the **MULTIPLE** attribute for **DATA** to provide a separate automatic data segment for each instance of your application. Only dynamic-link libraries can be declared with the **SINGLE** attribute for **DATA**. In fact, dynamic-link libraries must be declared this way, since they can have only one instance each.

16.2.2 Managing Local Dynamic-Data Objects

In Windows, a local heap can be set up in any data segment. The application's automatic data segment, however, is by far the most common place a local heap is used.

The **LocalInit** function establishes a specified area within any data segment as a local heap. Calls to **LocalAlloc** and other local memory functions operate on the data segment currently referenced by the DS register. As long as this data segment has been initialized by **LocalInit**, the local memory functions will work.

If you are developing a dynamic-link library that requires a local heap, you should call **LocalInit** during the initialization of the library. If you are developing a Windows application, as opposed to a dynamic-link library, you should not call **LocalInit** for the application's automatic data segment. Based on the location of other data in the automatic data segment (the task header, static data, and stack) and the heap size specified in the application's .DEF file, Windows itself calls **LocalInit** with the correct values for the location and size of the local heap.

The organization of a local heap is similar to that of a global heap:

- Fixed objects are located at the bottom of the local heap.
- Nondiscardable, movable objects are allocated above the fixed objects.
- Discardable objects are allocated from the top of the local heap.

The following figure illustrates this organization:

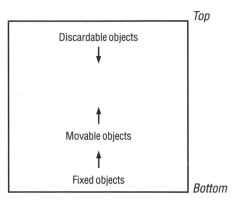

As Windows adds new objects to an application's local heap, movable objects may move as Windows compacts the heap. Also, Windows may discard some objects to make room for new ones. Windows never moves fixed objects when they are allocated in a local heap.

16.2.2.1 Allocating Memory in the Local Heap

By using the **LocalAlloc** function, you can allocate a specified size object in a local heap and can specify certain characteristics of the object. The most important characteristic is whether the object is fixed or movable, and if movable, whether it is discardable.

When you allocate an object in a local heap, other objects may be moved or discarded. In certain cases, you may not want the local heap to be reorganized as the new object is added. You may want to guarantee that pointers previously set to movable objects remain unchanged. To guarantee that no objects will be discarded from the local heap when you call **LocalAlloc**, set the LMEM_NODISCARD flag in the *wFlags* parameter. To guarantee that no objects in the local heap will be moved or discarded, specify the LMEM_NOCOMPACT flag.

LocalAlloc returns a handle to the allocated local memory object. If memory in the local heap is not available, **LocalAlloc** returns NULL. In managing an object using all other Windows memory functions described below, you should use the handle returned by **LocalAlloc**.

16.2.2.2 Locking and Unlocking Local Memory Objects

To many C programmers who are used to using the C run-time library function **malloc**, using memory handles may seem foreign at first. Because allocated objects in the local heap may move around as new objects are added, you cannot always expect a pointer to an allocated object to remain valid. The purpose of a local memory handle is to provide a constant reference to a movable object.

Since a memory handle is an indirect reference, you must dereference the handle to obtain the near address of the local object. You do this by calling the **Local-Lock** function. This function temporarily fixes the object at a constant location in the local heap. This means that the near address returned by **LocalLock** will remain valid until you subsequently call **LocalUnlock**. The following example shows how to use **LocalLock** to dereference the handle of a movable object.

```
HLOCAL hLocalObject;
char NEAR * pcLocalObject;

/* NEAR is not necessary in small and medium models. */

if (hLocalObject = LocalAlloc(LMEM_MOVEABLE, 32)) {
    if (pcLocalObject = LocalLock(hLocalObject)) {

        /*
         * Use pcLocalObject as the near address of the locally
         * allocated object.
         */
          .
          .
          .

        LocalUnlock(hLocalObject);
    }

    else {

        /* The lock failed. React accordingly. */

    }
}

else {

    /* The 32 bytes cannot be allocated. React accordingly. */

}
```

If you allocate a local memory object and specify the LMEM_FIXED attribute, the object is already guaranteed not to move in memory. Consequently, you need not call **LocalLock** to lock the object temporarily at a fixed address. Also, you need not dereference the handle, as you normally would by using **LocalLock**, because the 16-bit handle is simply the 16-bit near address of the local memory object. The following example illustrates this:

```
char NEAR * pcLocalObject;

/* NEAR is not necessary in small or medium models. */

if (pcLocalObject = LocalAlloc(LMEM_FIXED,32)) {

    /*
     * Use pcLocalObject as the near address of the locally
     * allocated object. It is not necessary to lock and unlock
     * the fixed local object.
     */
       .
       .
       .

}

else {

    /* The 32 bytes cannot be allocated. React accordingly. */

}
```

You should avoid leaving a movable object locked if your application needs to allocate other objects in the local heap. Otherwise, memory management in Windows is less efficient, since Windows has to work around the locked object while attempting to make room for another object in the movable area of the local heap.

16.2.2.3 Changing a Local Memory Object

You call the **LocalReAlloc** function to change the size of a local memory object but still preserve its contents. If you specify a smaller size, Windows truncates the object. If you specify a larger size, Windows fills the new area of the object with zeros if you specify LMEM_ZEROINIT; otherwise, the contents of the new area are undefined. Calling **LocalReAlloc** may cause objects in the local heap to be discarded or moved, just as when you call the **LocalAlloc** function. To prevent Windows from discarding objects, specify LMEM_NODISCARD; to prevent Windows from moving objects, specify LMEM_NOCOMPACT.

You can also call **LocalReAlloc** to change the object's attribute from LMEM_MOVEABLE to LMEM_DISCARDABLE or vice versa. To do so, you must also specify LMEM_MODIFY, as follows:

```
hLocalObject = LocalAlloc (32, LMEM_MOVEABLE);
     .
     .
     .

hLocalObject = LocalReAlloc(hLocalObject,
     32, LMEM_MODIFY | LMEM_DISCARDABLE);
```

You cannot use LMEM_MODIFY with **LocalReAlloc** to change the attribute of the local memory object to or from LMEM_FIXED.

16.2.2.4 Freeing and Discarding Local Memory Objects

The Windows functions **LocalDiscard** and **LocalFree** discard and free local objects, respectively.

There is a difference between freeing a local object and discarding it. When you discard a local object, its contents are removed from the local heap, but its handle remains valid. When you free a local object, not only are its contents removed from the local heap, but its handle is removed from the table of valid local memory handles. A local object can be discarded or freed only if there are no outstanding locks on it.

You may want to discard an object rather than free it, if you want to reuse its handle. To reuse the handle, call the **LocalReAlloc** function, specifying the handle and a nonzero size value. By reusing the handle in this way, you save Windows the time required to free an old handle and create a new one. Reusing a handle also allows you to determine how much local memory is available before attempting to allocate a local memory object.

16.2.2.5 Retrieving Information About a Local Memory Object

The **LocalSize** and **LocalFlags** functions provide you with information about a local memory object. **LocalSize** returns the size of the object. **LocalFlags** indicates whether the memory object is discardable and, if so, whether it has been discarded. **LocalFlags** also reports the lock count for the memory object.

16.2.3 Managing Global Memory Objects

The global heap is the Windows system-wide memory resource that is shared among applications. An application may request Windows to allocate memory objects out of the global heap by calling **GlobalAlloc**, the same function that Windows itself calls to allocate internally used memory objects. By using the global memory functions described in this section, you can take advantage of the same memory-management mechanisms Windows uses for its own purposes. In addition, by using these functions, your application can compete or cooperate with the system itself with essentially the same privileges. Misusing these privileges reduces your application's ability to cooperate with Windows and other applications.

The following considerations may help you determine whether to allocate memory for a given data object out of the global heap or the local heap:

- You should address a memory object allocated from the local heap by using a near pointer (after you dereference the handle by using **LocalLock**). On the other hand, you should address a memory object allocated from the global heap by using a far pointer (after you dereference the handle by using the **Global-Lock** function).

- An application's local heap is a relatively scarce memory resource, since it must fit in the application's automatic data segment (limited to 64K bytes) along with the stack and static data; the global heap is much larger.

If a memory object is in the current working set of your application, you should attempt to design it as a local object to take advantage of the more efficient near addressing. The current working set is data that you must frequently access during a fairly lengthy operation. Objects that are less frequently accessed belong in the global heap. For some applications, it might make sense to transfer data between the application's local heap and the global heap as the working set changes.

When designing the structure of global memory objects, you often have the choice of breaking them down into elementary objects or consolidating them into larger objects. In making this choice, you should consider the following:

- Each global memory object carries an overhead of at least 20 bytes.

- Global memory objects are aligned on 32-byte boundaries. The first 16 bytes are reserved for certain overhead information. In both standard-mode and 386 enhanced-mode memory configurations, there is a systemwide limit of 8192 global memory handles, only some of which are available to any given application.

In general, you should avoid allocating small global memory objects. A small object (128 bytes or less) carries at least a 15 percent space overhead, plus the memory that is wasted if the object's size (plus 16 bytes) is not a multiple of 32 bytes. This overhead may be justifiable in some cases, but you should weigh carefully the overhead involved. You should especially avoid allocating a large number (many hundreds) of small global objects if they can be consolidated into fewer, larger global objects. This consolidation not only eliminates space overhead but also avoids unnecessary use of the limited number of global memory handles.

With these considerations in mind, how you manage objects in the global heap is similar to how you manage memory objects in a local heap. For information about managing local memory, see Section 16.2.2, "Managing Local Dynamic-Data Objects."

16.2.3.1 Allocating Memory in the Global Heap

You call the **GlobalAlloc** function to allocate an object of specified size in the global heap. Windows manages memory objects in the global heap according to the same classifications used for memory objects in a local heap: fixed, movable, and discardable.

The same mechanisms for compacting memory that are applied in managing a local heap also apply to the global heap. Thus, you may specify GMEM_NODISCARD or GMEM_NOCOMPACT when you call the **Global-Alloc** function. For details, see the discussion of LMEM_NODISCARD and LMEM_NOCOMPACT under the description of the **LocalAlloc** function in Section 16.2.2.1, "Allocating Memory in the Local Heap."

GlobalAlloc returns a handle to the allocated global memory object. If memory in the global heap is not available, **GlobalAlloc** returns NULL. It is always important to check the return value from **GlobalAlloc**, since you have no guarantee that your allocation requests can be satisfied. Most of the functions that manage global memory require this handle to identify the memory object.

16.2.3.2 Locking and Unlocking a Global Memory Object

You can dereference the handle to a global memory object by calling the **Global-Lock** function. **GlobalLock** returns a far pointer that is guaranteed to remain valid until you subsequently call the **GlobalUnlock** function.

GlobalLock must lock the object by fixing it in memory to ensure that the pointer it returns will remain valid until you call **GlobalUnlock**. Because it has locked the object, **GlobalLock** increments a lock count for the object. This count helps prevent the object from being discarded or freed while it is still being used.

Windows need not fix the object in memory unless it is discardable. The pointer will always be valid whenever the object moves in linear memory. Because Windows does not lock the object in memory, **GlobalLock** does not increment the lock count for a nondiscardable object. **GlobalUnlock** decrements the lock count of an object only if **GlobalLock** incremented it for the object. However, you must still call **GlobalUnlock** when you no longer need the pointer returned by **Global-Lock**.

In addition to **GlobalLock** and **GlobalUnlock**, several other functions affect the lock count for an object:

Increments lock count	Decrements lock count
GlobalFix	**GlobalUnfix**
GlobalWire	**GlobalUnWire**
LockSegment	**UnlockSegment**

For more information about how these functions affect a global memory object and its lock count, see the *Microsoft Windows Programmer's Reference, Volume 2*. The **GlobalFlags** function returns the lock count of a global memory object as set by these functions.

As noted earlier, it is not necessary to call **LocalLock** to dereference a local handle if the object is allocated as LMEM_FIXED. There is no similar capability for fixed global objects. Even fixed global objects must always be locked to dereference the handle.

The following example uses **GlobalLock** to dereference the handle of a movable global object:

```
HGLOBAL hGlobalObject;
char FAR* lpGlobalObject;

if (hGlobalObject = GlobalAlloc(GMEM_MOVEABLE, 1024)) {
    if (lpGlobalObject = GlobalLock(hGlobalObject)) {

        /*
         * Use lpGlobalOBject as the far address of the
         * globally allocated object.
         */
         .
         .
         .

        GlobalUnlock(hGlobalObject);
    }

    else {

        /* The lock failed. React accordingly. */

    }
}

else {

    /* The 1024 bytes cannot be allocated. React accordingly. */

}
```

If you allocate an object whose size is 64K or larger, you should cast and save the pointer returned by **GlobalLock** as a huge pointer. The following example allocates a 128K global memory object:

```
HGLOBAL hGlobalObject;
char huge * hpGlobalObject;

if (hGlobalObject = GlobalAlloc(GMEM_MOVEABLE, 0x20000L)) {
```

```
        if (hpGlobalObject
                = (char huge *) GlobalLock(hGlobalObject)) {

            /*
             * Use hpGlobalOBject as the far address of the
             * globally allocated object.
             */
              .
              .
              .

            GlobalUnlock(hGlobalObject);
        }

        else {

        /* The lock failed. React accordingly. */

        }
    }

    else {

        /* The 128K cannot be allocated. React accordingly. */

    }
```

16.2.3.3 Changing a Global Memory Object

You can change the size or attributes of a global memory object while preserving its contents by calling **GlobalReAlloc**. If you specify a smaller size, Windows truncates the object. If you specify a larger size and also specify GMEM_ZEROINIT, Windows fills the new area of the object with zeros. By specifying GMEM_DISCARD or GMEM_NOCOMPACT, you ensure that Windows will not discard or move objects to satisfy the **GlobalReAlloc** request.

You can also call **GlobalReAlloc** to change the object's attribute from nondiscardable to discardable, or vice versa. Unlike **LocalReAlloc**, however, **GlobalReAlloc** can change a GMEM_FIXED object to GMEM_MOVEABLE or GMEM_DISCARDABLE. But it cannot change a movable or discardable object to a fixed object. To change the attribute of a global object, you must also specify the GMEM_MODIFY flag. For more information about doing this, see Section 16.2.2.3, "Changing a Local Memory Object."

Be careful when you are changing the size of a global memory object if its size increases across a multiple of 64K. Windows may return a new global handle for the reallocated memory object. For example, this applies if you change the size of the object from 50K to 70K, or 120K to 130K. In standard mode, this applies if you change the size of the object across a multiple of 65,519 bytes (64K less 17 bytes).

Because of the selector-tiling technique Windows uses, Windows might have to search for a larger set of related selectors when the size of a global object increases across a multiple of 64K. If so, Windows returns the first selector of the larger set as the global handle. For more information about selector tiling, see Section 16.1.1.1, "Using Huge Memory Objects in Standard Mode."

The following example reallocates a global memory object.

```
if (hTempHugeObject = GlobalReAlloc(hHugeObject,
        0x20000L,
        GMEM_MOVEABLE)) {
    hHugeObject = hTempObject;
}

else {

    /* The object could not be allocated. React accordingly. */

}
```

In this example, the temporary handle hTempHugeObject preserves the original handle in case **GlobalReAlloc** returns a NULL handle, indicating a failure to reallocate.

16.2.3.4 Freeing and Discarding Global Memory Objects

The **GlobalFree** and **GlobalDiscard** functions are identical to the **LocalFree** and **LocalDiscard** functions, except that they operate on global rather than local memory objects. For more information, see the discussion on **LocalFree** and **LocalDiscard** in Section 16.2.2.4, "Freeing and Discarding Local Memory Objects."

16.2.3.5 Retrieving Information About a Global Memory Object

The **GlobalSize** and **GlobalFlags** functions provide current information about a global memory object. **GlobalSize** returns the current size of the object. **GlobalFlags** indicates whether the object is discardable and, if so, whether it has been discarded. It also indicates whether the object was allocated with the GMEM_DDESHARE or GMEM_NOT_BANKED flag.

16.2.3.6 Locking a Global Memory Object for Extended Periods

When you call **GlobalLock** to prevent a movable object from moving as other objects are manipulated in the global heap, you can hinder the ability of Windows to manage these other objects efficiently. To lock a discardable memory object for an extended period, use the **GlobalWire** function. To lock a nondiscardable memory object for an extended period, use **GlobalLock**. **GlobalWire** relocates the movable object to the lower area of the global heap reserved for fixed objects and then locks it. By moving the locked object to low memory, Windows can compact upper memory more efficiently but will require additional CPU cycles to move the object. Call **GlobalUnWire** to unlock the object. After the object is unlocked, it can migrate out of the fixed portion of the global heap.

16.2.3.7 Being Notified When a Global Memory Object Is to Be Discarded

If you want your application to be notified whenever Windows is about to discard a global memory object, call the **GlobalNotify** function. **GlobalNotify** is useful if you are writing a custom virtual-memory-management system that swaps data to and from disk, for example. You specify the address of the notification callback function in your application.

16.2.3.8 Changing When a Global Memory Object Is Discarded

As Windows manages the global heap, it employs a least-recently-used (LRU) algorithm for determining which global memory objects should be discarded when memory must be freed. You can call the **GlobalLRUOldest** function to move an object to the oldest position in the LRU list. This means that this object will be the most likely object to be discarded if Windows subsequently requires more memory. Conversely, by calling the **GlobalLRUNewest** function, you ensure that an object is least likely to be discarded.

These functions are useful, for example, for discarding initialization code when it is no longer needed. You could also use these functions if you were writing a custom virtual-memory-management system that swaps data to and from disk. With these functions, you can influence which objects are least or most likely to be discarded by Windows, thus minimizing the amount of disk swapping.

16.2.3.9 Freeing Global Memory in Low-Memory Conditions

Global memory is a shared resource; the performance of all applications depends on the ability of all applications to share that resource. When system memory is low, your application should be prepared to free global memory that it has allocated.

Windows sends the WM_COMPACTING message to all top-level windows when Windows detects that more than 15 percent of system time over a 30- to 60-second interval is being spent compacting memory. This indicates that system memory is low.

When your application receives this message, it should free as much memory as possible, taking into account the current level of activity of the application and the total number of applications running in Windows. The application can call the **Get-NumTasks** function to determine how many applications are running.

16.2.4 Using Extra Bytes in Window and Class Data Structures

You can store extra, application-defined data by using the data structures that describe the attributes of a window or a window class. This extra data is known as window extra bytes and class extra bytes, respectively.

This private data is located at the end of a data structure that Windows maintains for the window. When you call the **RegisterClass** function, the **cbWndExtra** member of the **WNDCLASS** structure specifies the number of extra bytes of information that will be maintained for each window member of that class. The extra bytes are initialized to zero.

The technique of using the private data area of a window is particularly useful in cases where you have two or more windows that belong to the same class, and you want to associate different data with each window. Without the private data facility, you would have to maintain a list of private structures for each window. Then, each time you needed to access the data for a particular window, you would first have to locate the corresponding entry in the list. By using the private data facility, however, you can directly access the private data through the window handle rather than by using a separate list.

An additional advantage of using the window's private data area to store data is that you can encapsulate the data associated with each window better than if you were to store it as static data in the same module as, for example, the window procedure.

To write to the window's private data area, call the **SetWindowWord** and **SetWindowLong** functions. These two functions accept a byte offset within the area you set aside for private data. A zero offset refers to the first word or long value in the private area. An offset of 2 (bytes) refers to the second word value in the private area. An offset of 4 (bytes) refers to the third word value or the second long value in the private area. Note that **SetWindowWord** and **SetWindowLong** also accept constants such as GWW_STYLE and GWL_WNDPROC, which are defined in WINDOWS.H. These constants are negative offsets within the window's structure. The length of the structure (minus the private area) is thus added to the offset you provide in the call to **SetWindowWord** or **SetWindowLong** to determine the offset relative to the beginning of the structure.

To read from the private data area of a window, call the **GetWindowWord** and **GetWindowLong** functions. The offsets you specify work the same way as for **SetWindowWord** and **SetWindowLong**.

The structure for a window is allocated in USER's local heap. If you want to associate a large amount of data (more than 10 bytes) with the window, you should store a global handle in the window's private area instead of storing the actual data. The handle points to the data. This way, you increase the size of the window's structure only by the two bytes needed for the global handle, rather than by the large size of the private data itself.

Just as you can associate private data with a particular window, you can also associate private data with a window class. The functions that do this are **SetClassWord**, **SetClassLong**, **GetClassWord**, and **GetClassLong**. There are probably fewer occasions for associating private data with a window class than with a window. Using the private area for the window class is appropriate for data that is logically related to the window class as a whole and that is common among multiple windows of the same class.

16.2.5 Managing Resources

A resource is read-only data—stored in your application's .EXE file or your library's .DLL file—that Windows reads from disk on demand. Certain types of resources have prescribed formats recognized by Windows. These include bitmaps, icons, cursors, dialog boxes, and fonts. You can create these resources by using the resource editors included in the Microsoft Windows 3.1 Software Development Kit (SDK): Microsoft Image Editor (IMAGEDIT.EXE), Microsoft Dialog Editor (DLGEDIT.EXE), and Microsoft Windows Font Editor (FONTEDIT.EXE). You link these resources into your .EXE or .DLL file by using Microsoft Windows Resource Compiler (RC). You take advantage of Windows' ability to work with these resource formats by calling associated functions such as **LoadIcon** and **CreateDialog**.

A resource is read into memory by Windows as a single data segment. The resource may be declared in the resource-definition file to be fixed, movable, or discardable. When determining whether a resource should be fixed, movable, or discardable, you should take into account the same considerations as you would for a global memory object.

If you declare a resource by using the **PRELOAD** option, Windows loads the resource into memory during the startup of your application. Otherwise, Windows loads it when it is needed (the **LOADONCALL** option).

In addition to using resources whose formats Windows recognizes, you can also develop resources only your application recognizes. The data may be in any format that you design, including ASCII text, binary data, or a mixture of these.

When deciding whether to maintain data as a resource or as a separate file, consider the following:

- By compiling the resource into your application's .EXE file, you simplify the packaging of your application. You and your user need not worry about installing additional data files along with the application's .EXE file.

- On the other hand, maintaining the data as a resource means that you must re-compile your application's .EXE file if you change the data. If you plan to distribute updated data to several users, you may find it easier to distribute a new data file rather than a new .EXE file.

For more information about compiling a user-defined resource into an .EXE or .DLL file, see *Microsoft Windows Programming Tools*.

16.2.5.1 Locating a Custom Resource

The **FindResource** function determines the location of the resource according to the name specified in your resource-definition file. The function returns a handle, which you can then use in a call to the **LoadResource** function to load the resource. The resource handle returned by **FindResource** refers to information that describes the resource type declared in the resource-definition file, the position of the resource in the .EXE or .DLL file, and the size of the resource.

For example, suppose you want to maintain an ASCII text file as a resource. The source text file is named MYTEXT.TXT. You name the resource MyText, and you arbitrarily name the resource type TEXT. The resource-definition statement for this resource is as follows:

```
MyText TEXT MyText.txt
```

In your application, you retrieve the resource handle by calling **FindResource**, as follows:

```
HANDLE hMyTextResLoc;
    .
    .
    .

    hMyTextResLoc = FindResource(hinst, "MyText", "TEXT");
```

16.2.5.2 Loading a Custom Resource

The call to **FindResource** does not load the resource from the .EXE or .DLL file into memory. Rather, it finds only the location of the resource and returns the result of the search as a handle that points to the resource-location information. To load the resource into memory, you call the **LoadResource** function, as follows:

```
HRSRC hMyTextResLoc;
    HGLOBAL hMyTextRes;
    .
    .
    .

    hMyTextResLoc = FindResource(hinst, "MyText", "TEXT");
```

```
if (!hMyTextRes = LoadResource(hinst, hMyTextResLoc)) {

    /*
     * Handle the case that memory is not available
     * to load resource.
     */

}
```

LoadResource itself calls **GlobalAlloc** to allocate the memory object for the resource data, and then copies the data from disk to the memory object.

16.2.5.3 Locking and Unlocking a Custom Resource

To access the resource data now residing in a global memory object, you must call the **LockResource** function to lock the resource and retrieve a far pointer to the data. This is equivalent to using the **GlobalLock** function to retrieve the far pointer to a memory object allocated by the **GlobalAlloc** function. The following example continues the previous one:

```
LPSTR lpstrMyText;
    .
    .
    .

    lpstrMyText = LockResource(hMyTextRes);
```

Once you have the far address to the resource, you can read it as you would from a global memory object locked by **GlobalLock**.

If you have defined the resource as discardable and it has been discarded, **LockResource** will first load the resource back from disk. Unlike **GlobalLock**, **LockResource** saves you the trouble of calling **LoadResource** again if the resource has been discarded.

You should call **UnlockResource** when you are not in the process of accessing the resource data. This function is equivalent to **GlobalUnlock**. If you declare the resource as movable or discardable, this provides Windows the flexibility to move or discard the resource from memory as necessary to satisfy other memory-allocation requests.

16.2.5.4 Freeing a Custom Resource

The **FreeResource** function is similar to the **GlobalFree** function. It discards the memory used by the resource data as well as by the resource handle. If you need to load the resource again, you can call **LoadResource**, using the resource location handle returned by your initial call to **FindResource**.

16.3 Using Memory Models

A Windows application is like an MS-DOS application in that it may have one or more code segments and one or more data segments. The memory model, which you specify when you compile your source-code modules, determines whether compiler-generated instructions use near or far addresses. If you use a memory model that specifies only one code or data segment, the compiler generates instructions that employ near (16-bit) addresses for, respectively, code or data references. If you compile by using a memory model that specifies multiple code or data segments, the compiler generates instructions that use far (32-bit) addresses for code or data references. The following figure shows how the memory model affects the way an application addresses code and data:

Number of code segments

		One	Multiple
Number of data segments	One	Small memory model	Medium memory model
	Multiple	Compact memory model	Large memory model

There are two memory models, large and huge, for compiling a module that generates far addresses for both code and data references. In the large memory model, far pointers can be incremented only within the 64K offset range of a segment. In the huge memory model, far pointers can be incremented across 64K boundaries, causing both the segment address and the offset to be incremented. Also, if a module is compiled with the large memory model, Windows will be able to load only one instance of the module.

Ideally, a Windows application will use the medium model, and the size of its modules will be 8K or less. The module that initializes the application should be marked **PRELOAD** and **DISCARDABLE** in the .DEF file. The module that processes the message queue should be marked **PRELOAD**. All other modules should be marked **LOADONCALL** and **DISCARDABLE**. An application that follows these guidelines will start faster and consume fewer system resources.

If you are using CL, compile your Windows application's C-language source-code modules, using the **/AS** option for the small model or the **/AM** option for the medium model.

You can also use a mixed memory model. For a mixed model, you compile modules by using the **/AS** option, assign the same code-segment name to those modules whose code segments you want to group together, and assign different code-segment names to those modules for which you want to generate different code segments. To assign a code-segment name to a module, use the CL option **/NT**. A function that is called from a different code segment must be declared as a far function in the module where the call is made, as in the following example:

```
UINT FAR PASCAL FuncInAnotherCodeSeg(UINT, LONG);
UINT uReturn;
            .
            .
            .

uReturn = FuncInAnotherCodeSeg(0, 0L);
```

The advantage of using the mixed memory model is that you need only define calls made between code segments as **FAR**. Functions that are declared **FAR** increase code size and require more machine cycles to be called.

For another form of the mixed memory model, you can compile modules with the **/AM** option, which makes function calls **FAR** by default. Then, instead of declaring **FAR** functions, you prototype as **NEAR** those functions that are called only within the same segment. The disadvantage of this method is that all C run-time library functions will also be **FAR** functions.

16.4 Using Huge Data

You can declare data as huge in C-language modules. CL will correctly perform the arithmetic required to increment the pointer across segment boundaries. You can pass a huge pointer to Windows library functions or to your own functions that expect a far pointer, but only if the function is not expected to internally increment the far pointer so that it points to an object that straddles a 64K boundary. For example, the following code is acceptable, because 16 is a factor of 64K (65,356):

```
char huge Record[10000][16];
int i;

TextOut(hDC, x, y, (LPSTR) Record[i], 16);
```

The following example violates this limitation, because the pointer passed to the **TextOut** function will eventually point to an object that straddles a 64K boundary:

```
char huge Record[10000][15];
int i;

    /* DON'T DO THIS. */

TextOut(hDC, x, y, (LPSTR) Record[i], 15);
```

Since 15 is not a factor of 64K, the pointer would be incremented across a segment boundary.

16.5 Traps to Avoid When Managing Program Data

The previous sections in this chapter explained the basics of how Windows manages memory. They provided guidelines for choosing between methods for allocating program data and for effectively using a particular method.

This section focuses on common Windows programming errors that you should avoid when managing program data. Once you understand how Windows manages memory, the following guidelines will be quite clear.

Do not assume the privilege level in which your application is running.

Future versions of Windows may change the privilege-level ring in which applications will run.

Do not use DOS protected-mode interface (DPMI) services in a Windows application.

You can use DPMI services only in a dynamic-link library, and only the DPMI services not provided by Windows. Do not use DPMI services for hooking interrupts or faults. The DPMI specification does not provide for unhooking chained interrupts.

Avoid far pointers to static data in small and medium models.

Suppose a module contains the following declaration:

```
/* DO NOT FOLLOW THIS EXAMPLE. */

static LPSTR lpstrDlgName = "MyDlg";
    .
    .
    .

    hDlg = CreateDialog(hinst,
        lpstrDlgName,
        hWndParent,
        (DLGPROC) lpDialogProc);
```

The **LPSTR (char FAR *)** pointer initially set by the Windows loader will be made invalid if the automatic data segment that contains the literal MyDlg moves in memory (unless the automatic data segment is a fixed segment).

The proper way to write the preceding code is to declare the string with a near pointer, **PSTR** (**char NEAR ***), and cast it to the **LPSTR** data type required by the **CreateDialog** function, as shown in the following example:

```
/* FOLLOW THIS EXAMPLE. */

static PSTR pstrDlgName = "MyDlg";
    .
    .
    .

  hDlg = CreateDialog(hinst,
      (LPSTR) pstrDlgName,
      hWndParent,
      (DLGPROC) lpDialogProc);
```

The cast to **LPSTR** dynamically pushes the current value of the DS register instead of the value of DS at the time the module was loaded.

Do not pass data to other applications by means of a global handle.

You should not use a global handle to share data with another application, because you should assume that your application and other Windows applications have disjoint address spaces.

In future versions of Windows, the address spaces of applications may be disjoint.

The only methods supported by Windows to pass data between applications are the clipboard and the dynamic data exchange (DDE) protocol. If you pass a global handle through DDE to another application, the global object must have been allocated with the GMEM_DDESHARE flag. To share memory, you should always use DDE.

Do not assume any relationship between a handle and a far pointer in any mode.

When using global memory objects, you must always call the **GlobalLock** function to dereference a handle to a far pointer, regardless of the mode in which Windows is running.

Do not load a segment register with a value other than one provided by Windows or MS-DOS.

In Windows, segment registers are interpreted as selectors, not physical paragraph addresses. Therefore, you should not read the interrupt table by setting ES or DS to zero, for example. Use only the appropriate MS-DOS function to hook an interrupt vector.

Do not perform segment arithmetic.

Do not increment the segment address of a far pointer in an attempt to increment the pointer. This technique is not supported in Windows. For more information, see Section 16.2.3.2, "Locking and Unlocking a Global Memory Object."

Do not compare segment addresses.

Do not compare the selector values that Windows assigns to memory objects to determine which object is lower in memory. This technique is not supported in Windows.

Do not read or write past the ends of memory objects.

Do not read or write past the ends of memory objects under any circumstances. Although this may go undetected in other memory configurations, Windows will report this error as a GP fault.

16.6 Managing Memory for Program Code

You should plan how Windows will manage the code segments that make up the executable portion of your application or library. When planning, consider the following:

- Whether your code segments should be fixed, movable, or discardable
- Whether your application or library will contain one or more code segments
- How to maintain a balance of size and far calls between your code segments
- The order in which Windows loads the code segments

16.6.1 Using Code-Segment Attributes

Windows uses the same memory-management facilities for handling code segments as it does for handling data segments. You can, and generally should, partition your application into separate code segments. You can declare a particular code segment to be fixed, movable, or discardable, just as you can for the application's automatic data segment and global objects.

In your application's .DEF file, you can use the **CODE** statement to specify whether the code segments are by default fixed, movable, or discardable. For example, the following statement declares that the default attribute of all code segments will be **MOVEABLE**:

```
CODE MOVEABLE;
```

For information about overriding this default attribute for specific code segments, see Section 16.6.2, "Using Multiple Code Segments."

If you declare your code segments as discardable, Windows can free memory held by those code segments when it is necessary to allocate additional memory. Because a code segment is always unmodifiable, there is no risk that information will be lost when it is discarded. When your application makes a call to a code segment that is not currently in memory, Windows will first load it from the .EXE file. If a discardable code segment is not in memory, however, Windows requires extra time to load the segment from disk. On the other hand, this penalty is minimized because Windows uses a least-recently-used (LRU) algorithm for discarding segments, and so Windows does not discard frequently used segments.

16.6.2 Using Multiple Code Segments

Most Windows applications should be compiled by using the mixed memory model. The code should be partitioned into relatively small segments (8K or less). This allows Windows to move the code segments fluidly in memory. For more information about the mixed model, see Section 16.3, "Using Memory Models."

When you compile a C module, the code segment is assigned the name _TEXT by default. You can assign the code segment a different name, using the /NT option of CL. You partition the code by assigning different names to the code segments for different modules. The following command line produces a code segment named CODESEG1:

```
cl /u /c /AS /Gsw /Oas /Zpe /NT CODESEG1 module1.c
```

You can assign attributes in the application's .DEF file that override the values you specified for the default **CODE**. For example, the following .DEF file excerpt declares all code segments to be movable except the code segment named CODESEG1, which is discardable:

```
CODE LOADONCALL MOVEABLE

        SEGMENTS
                CODESEG1 MOVEABLE DISCARDABLE
```

16.6.3 Balancing Code Segments

Although it is a good idea to keep code segments small, compare the costs of a far call between code segments to a near call within a code segment. A far call costs more for Windows applications than it does for MS-DOS applications. Each far call carries the overhead of extra instructions, because Windows has to direct the call to a code segment that may have been moved or discarded.

The task of balancing code segments in an application is a matter of minimizing the frequency of far calls that must be made between segments, while maintaining roughly equal-sized segments whose sizes do not exceed 8K. Functions that frequently call each other should be grouped in the same code segment, subject to the code-size guideline.

16.7 Related Topics

For more information about using C and assembly language in your Windows applications, see Chapter 14, "C and Assembly Language."

For more information about memory-management functions, see the *Microsoft Windows Programmer's Reference, Volume 2*.

Print Settings

The Microsoft Windows 3.1 operating system provides common dialog boxes for many standard operations. (A common dialog box is a dialog box that a Windows-based application displays by calling a single function rather than by creating a dialog box procedure and a resource file containing a dialog box template.) An application can create a common dialog box for changing the print settings by calling the **PrintDlg** function. Common dialog boxes simplify the development of applications for Windows and assist users by providing a standard set of controls. Common dialog boxes can even be customized to meet the special requirements of an application. For more information about common dialog boxes, see the *Microsoft Windows Programmer's Reference, Volume 1*.

17.1 Overview

When a user prints from your Microsoft Windows 3.1 application, the resulting output depends not only on the data your application sends to the printer, it also depends on the current print settings for that printer. Print settings can include information such as page size, print orientation, or which paper bin to use.

The simplest way to print (illustrated in Chapter 12, "Printing") uses the current print settings without validating or changing them. This approach works as long as the settings are appropriate for your application's requirements. If the settings are not appropriate, your application's printed output could be less than ideal. For example, if your application prints a spreadsheet that requires a landscape print orientation on a printer that is set up for portrait orientation, your application's data will probably run off the right side of the paper.

With the Windows operating system, your application can change the print settings to fit the situation (for example, changing the print orientation to landscape, or specifying a different paper bin). After your application has tailored the print settings, it can print using those settings.

Because print settings differ from printer to printer, an application must interact with a printer's device driver in order to change the settings for that printer. Most printer drivers for Windows provide special functions that your application can use to control print settings easily.

This chapter explains how to use these printer-driver functions to control print settings. It covers the following topics:

- How Windows manages print settings
- Using device-driver functions
- Finding out the capabilities of a printer driver
- Controlling print settings
- Copying print settings from one driver to another

- Letting the user change the print settings
- Working with drivers written for previous versions of Windows

17.2 How Windows Manages Print Settings

When your application prints, it uses a printer device context that it created by using the **CreateDC** function. When creating a device context for a printer, the application specifies the printer driver and name, the output port, and, optionally, print settings for that driver. These settings are device-specific, applying to a specific printer and printer driver. Because the exact settings can differ from printer to printer, ensure that your application supplies the specific information that each printer driver requires.

When an application calls **CreateDC** to create a printer device context in preparation for printing, Windows creates the device context by using the first print settings it can find. It searches for print settings in the following order:

1. Windows first uses the print settings (if any) that the application passed by using the **DEVMODE** structure pointed to by the *lpvInitData* parameter of the **CreateDC** function.

2. If the application did not pass any print settings when calling **CreateDC**, Windows searches for the print settings that the printer driver stored most recently in memory.

3. If the printer driver has not yet stored any print settings in memory, the printer driver searches for the print settings in the WIN.INI file. If WIN.INI does not contain complete print settings for this printer and port, the printer driver fills any gaps by using its own built-in default settings.

Your application has the most control over print settings if you specify settings when calling the **CreateDC** function. If you do specify print settings by using **CreateDC**, Windows uses those settings instead of other settings that may be available from the driver or from WIN.INI.

17.2.1 Print Settings and the DEVMODE Structure

Usually, print settings are defined in the form of a **DEVMODE** structure. For example, when you pass print settings to the **CreateDC** function, you are passing a pointer to a **DEVMODE** structure. Printer drivers usually store print settings as strings in the WIN.INI file in order to retain the settings between Windows sessions. Typically, your application does not create the **DEVMODE** structure itself; instead, it gets a complete structure from the printer driver and modifies it, as necessary. This method ensures that the structure is complete and correct.

The **DEVMODE** structure includes three types of information:

Information	Description
Header information	The first five members in the **DEVMODE** structure make up the structure's header information. This information includes the model name (for example, "HP LaserJet Series II"), version information, and information about the size of the structure. You should always provide complete header information.
Device-independent settings	Most of the members in the **DEVMODE** structure are device-independent settings, such as print orientation, paper size, and number of copies. Although the complete structure always includes all the device-independent settings, some printers do not support all the settings. For example, many printers can print on one side of the paper only; printer drivers for those printers would therefore ignore the **DEVMODE** structure's **dmDuplex** member, which specifies two-sided printing.
Device-specific information	The optional **dmDriverData** member of **DEVMODE** contains device-specific information that is defined by each device driver. This information follows the **DEVMODE** structure in memory. Typically, an application would simply pass this information on without modifying it in any way.

The best way to supply a complete **DEVMODE** structure when calling **CreateDC** is to first use the **ExtDeviceMode** function (included in printer drivers written for Windows versions 3.0 and later). This function tells the printer driver to create a **DEVMODE** structure by using its current print settings. Because the driver itself creates the **DEVMODE** structure and includes its device-specific information, your application treats the structure as complete and correct. The application can then pass the resulting **DEVMODE** structure when calling the **CreateDC** function.

Your application can modify the members of the **DEVMODE** structure created by **ExtDeviceMode** to create a customized device context. For example, an application could change the value of the **dmOrientation** member of **DEVMODE** from DMORIENT_PORTRAIT to DMORIENT_LANDSCAPE before passing the structure to the **CreateDC** function. An application should never customize the device context in this manner without first using the **DeviceCapabilities** and **GetDeviceCaps** functions to verify that the printer supports the changes.

For more information about the **CreateDC** function and the **DEVMODE** structure, see the *Microsoft Windows Programmer's Reference*, *Volumes 2* and *3*, respectively.

17.2.2 Print Settings and the Printer Environment

A printer environment is a collection of print settings in memory. There can be one printer environment for each printer port. The current printer driver (whatever the user has installed for that port) creates and maintains the port's printer environment.

The settings in each port's environment are the same as those in the WIN.INI file, except that the WIN.INI information consists of character strings in a file, while the environment is the same information in the form of a **DEVMODE** structure in memory. Having the information in memory speeds up the process of creating a printer device context for that port.

When an application creates a printer device context without specifying its own customized print settings, Windows uses the settings in the printer environment. Because the printer environment is associated with a printer port, changes to the settings in a printer environment affect any application that does not provide its own print settings when creating a printer device context for that port.

When using printer drivers written for Windows versions 3.0 and later, an application can control the print settings to meet its own requirements; the changes need not affect other applications that are using the same port. (When using printer drivers written for earlier versions of Windows, applications can change the print settings only by changing the WIN.INI file and the printer environment; this affects all applications that use that port without providing their own print settings.)

17.3 Using Device-Driver Functions

Most printer drivers include special functions that an application can use to control print settings for that driver and printer port.

- Windows printer drivers (for versions 3.0 and later) include the **ExtDevice-Mode** function, which provides many ways for an application to alter print settings without affecting other applications. An application can also use this function to return a copy of the settings in a driver's **DEVMODE** structure; the application can then modify those settings, rather than creating a **DEVMODE** structure from scratch. (**ExtDeviceMode** also includes the functionality that the **DeviceMode** function provides in older drivers.)

- Windows drivers also include the **DeviceCapabilities** function. The application can use this function to determine which **DEVMODE** members a particular driver supports.

- Older printer drivers include the **DeviceMode** function. This function displays a dialog box from which the user can select print settings, such as page orientation and paper size, for the printer. The user's changes affect the WIN.INI file and the printer environment.

Because device-driver functions are part of the device driver and are not regular Windows functions, you must use the following procedure to call a device-driver function:

1. Load the device driver into memory by calling the **LoadLibrary** function.

2. Use the **GetProcAddress** function to retrieve the address of the function you want. (If **GetProcAddress** returns a NULL pointer, then that device driver does not provide the function you requested.)

3. Use the pointer returned by **GetProcAddress** to call the device-driver function.

4. After you have finished using the device-driver function, call the Windows **FreeLibrary** function to unload the device driver from the system.

The following example calls the **ExtDeviceMode** function of the PSCRIPT.DRV printer driver:

```
FARPROC lpfnExtDeviceMode;
FARPROC lpfnDeviceMode;
HINSTANCE hDriver;

if ((hDriver = LoadLibrary("PSCRIPT.DRV")) =< 32) {
    .
    . /* Handle the error. */
    .

}

lpfnExtDeviceMode = GetProcAddress(hDriver, "ExtDeviceMode");

if (lpfnExtDeviceMode != NULL) {

    /*
     * If the driver supports ExtDeviceMode, call the driver's
     * ExtDeviceMode function, using the procedure address in
     * lpfnExtDeviceMode.
     */

}

else {

    /*
     * The driver is not a Windows 3.x driver and does not support
     * the newer functions; use the DeviceMode function instead.
     */

    lpfnDeviceMode = GetProcAddress(hDriver, "DeviceMode");
```

```
        if (lpfnDeviceMode != NULL) {

        /*
         * If the driver supports DeviceMode, call the driver's
         * DeviceMode function by using the procedure address in
         * lpfnDeviceMode.
         */

        }
    }

    FreeLibrary(hDriver);   /* when finished, unloads driver from memory */
```

17.4 Determining the Capabilities of the Printer Driver

You can use the **DeviceCapabilities** function to determine the capabilities of a particular printer, including which **DEVMODE** members the driver supports. For example, if your application must print in landscape orientation, it might call **DeviceCapabilities** to determine whether the current printer supports landscape orientation.

For more information about the **DeviceCapabilities** function, see the *Microsoft Windows Programmer's Reference, Volume 2*.

17.5 Working with Print Settings

You can use the **ExtDeviceMode** function to perform one or more actions at a time—for example:

- Retrieve a **DEVMODE** structure containing the driver's current print settings.
- Change one or more of the driver's current print settings.
- Prompt the user for print settings.
- Reset the printer environment and the information in WIN.INI.

Because **ExtDeviceMode** provides so many different features, you will probably find that your application calls **ExtDeviceMode** repeatedly during the process of retrieving, altering, and maintaining print settings.

When calling the **ExtDeviceMode** function, your application should specify the following information:

- The module handle of the printer driver (returned by the **LoadLibrary** or **GetModuleHandle** function).
- The name of the printer model (for example, HP LaserJet Series II).

- The name of the port to which the printer is connected (for example, LPT2).

- The operation(s) that the device driver is to perform. Your application requests different operations by setting the values that make up the *fwMode* parameter. To request several operations at once, combine two or more values by using the OR operator.

- The input buffer (if any). The application can supply a partial or complete **DEVMODE** structure as input. (Unlike other functions that use **DEVMODE**, **ExtDeviceMode** does not require that the input **DEVMODE** structure be complete.)

- The output buffer (if any). At the application's request, the driver writes a complete **DEVMODE** structure to the output buffer.

Note   The **ExtDeviceMode** function requires eight parameters in all; the list above includes only parameters that are directly relevant to this discussion. For a complete list of parameters for the **ExtDeviceMode** function, see the *Microsoft Windows Programmer's Reference, Volume 2*.

17.5.1   Specifying ExtDeviceMode Input and Output

By setting the *fwMode* parameter, you specify how a driver's **ExtDeviceMode** function will receive input and where it will send output. The driver's response differs depending on the value(s) you use.

If you set *fwMode* to zero, **ExtDeviceMode** simply returns the size, in bytes, of the output **DEVMODE** structure. This is often the first call you will make to **ExtDeviceMode**, because it lets you know how large to make the output buffer.

You can set *fwMode* to one or more values other than zero. The following table describes the values for the **fwMode** parameter and notes whether a value controls input or output.

Value	Input/Output	Description
DM_MODIFY	Input	Directs the driver to change its current print settings to match those the application supplied as a **DEVMODE** structure in the input buffer.
DM_PROMPT	Input	Directs the driver to display its Print Setup dialog box, then change its current print settings to match those the user specifies.
DM_COPY	Output	Writes the driver's current print settings to the output buffer in the form of a **DEVMODE** structure.
DM_UPDATE	Output	Writes the driver's current print settings to the printer environment and the WIN.INI file.

You can use a combination of *fwMode* values to let both your application and the user control the print settings.

Important To change the settings, you must specify at least one input value and one output value. For example, you could use a combination of the input value DM_PROMPT and the output value DM_UPDATE to tell the driver to take input from the user and write the resulting settings to the current printer environment and WIN.INI. If you specify only an output value (DM_COPY or DM_UPDATE), the driver provides its current settings and ignores any input you provide. If you specify only an input value (DM_PROMPT or DM_MODIFY), calling **ExtDevice-Mode** generates no output, so your input has no real effect.

17.5.2 Retrieving a Copy of the Print Settings

It is often useful when working with print settings to determine a particular printer driver's current settings. This lets your application determine whether the settings are appropriate for its own printing requirements. Follow these steps to retrieve a copy of the driver's print settings:

1. Determine how much space the output **DEVMODE** structure will require. To do this, call **ExtDeviceMode** with the *fwMode* parameter set to zero. **Ext-DeviceMode** returns the size, in bytes, of the output **DEVMODE** structure (the one the driver would create if you set *fwMode* to DM_COPY).

2. Allocate a buffer of this size.

3. Call **ExtDeviceMode** again, including the following information in the parameters:

Parameter	Value
lpdmOutput	A pointer to the output buffer you just allocated
fwMode	DM_COPY

The printer driver then puts a **DEVMODE** structure containing its current print settings into the buffer you specified.

Because the output buffer contains a complete **DEVMODE** structure, you can easily pass that data to the **CreateDC** function.

17.5.3 Changing the Print Settings

Often, when printing, your application may have to change the print settings to suit its own printing requirements. To change the print settings, set the *fwMode* parameter of **ExtDeviceMode** to both an input value (DM_MODIFY or DM_PROMPT) and an output value (DM_COPY or DM_UPDATE). You can specify multiple values, as long as you use at least one input and one output value. (To change the settings without affecting other applications, do not specify the

DM_UPDATE output value; that value causes the driver to change the default print settings to those you specify.)

There are several different ways to provide new print settings as input. For each method, you set *fwMode* to a different combination of values. The input methods are as follows:

- Provide a partial **DEVMODE** structure with the new settings you want. (When calling **ExtDeviceMode**, specify the value DM_MODIFY.)
- Display the driver's Printer Setup dialog box so that the user can change the settings. (When calling **ExtDeviceMode**, specify the value DM_PROMPT.)
- Provide a partial **DEVMODE** structure and, in addition, display the driver's Printer Setup dialog box. This method lets both your application and the user change the settings. (When calling **ExtDeviceMode**, specify both the DM_MODIFY and DM_PROMPT values.)

When changing the print settings, you not only provide new print settings as input, you also specify where you want the driver to place the updated print settings. The driver provides as output a complete, valid **DEVMODE** structure that reflects the changes your application or the user (or both) has just made to the print settings. Your instructions tell the driver where to put this output structure. You determine the driver's output by specifying one or more output values for the *fwMode* parameter of the **ExtDeviceMode** function.

You can direct the driver to do one of the following:

- Place the updated **DEVMODE** structure in the output buffer. Your application can then pass this output structure to **CreateDC** and other Windows functions. (When calling **ExtDeviceMode**, specify the value DM_COPY in *fwMode*.)
- Write the updated **DEVMODE** structure to memory. When the printer driver does this, it resets the printer environment for that printer port and changes the relevant entries in WIN.INI. The new settings affect any application that uses that port and does not provide its own print settings. (When calling **ExtDevice-Mode**, specify the value DM_UPDATE in *fwMode*.)
- Place the updated **DEVMODE** structure in the output buffer, reset the printer environment, and update WIN.INI. (When calling **ExtDeviceMode**, specify both the DM_COPY and DM_UPDATE values in *fwMode*.)

17.5.4 Tailoring Print Settings for Use with the CreateDC Function

To use a printer, your application must first create a printer device context by using the **CreateDC** function. This function has an optional parameter, *lpvInit-Data*, which specifies the print settings to use when creating the printer device context. The simplest way to print is to set *lpvInitData* to NULL; Windows then creates the device context by using the current print settings for that printer port.

To print using your own settings instead of the current default settings, you can pass **CreateDC** a **DEVMODE** structure containing the print settings you want. Windows then creates the device context by using your customized print settings.

When calling the **CreateDC** function, you should provide only **DEVMODE** structures that you have received directly from the printer driver. Although it is possible to simply edit a **DEVMODE** structure and then pass it directly to **CreateDC**, it is not recommended. **CreateDC** requires a correct and complete **DEVMODE** structure. Therefore, any minor inconsistencies in the structure can result in an invalid device context. To ensure that a **DEVMODE** structure is valid, pass it to the printer driver as input. The driver then provides a complete, correct **DEVMODE** structure that incorporates your changes; you can safely pass this output structure to **CreateDC**.

To use particular print settings, you should provide, as input to **ExtDeviceMode**, a partial **DEVMODE** structure that contains the settings you want. The driver changes only those settings for which you supply a new value. This means that you can use this method to change a single print setting—for example, changing from portrait to landscape orientation—without affecting the driver's other print settings. In response to **ExtDeviceMode**, the driver provides as output a complete **DEVMODE** structure that includes your changes.

To change the print settings, follow these steps:

1. Set up a partial or complete **DEVMODE** structure that contains the members you want to change.

   If you are supplying a partial structure be sure to include all five header members (**dmDeviceName**, **dmSpecVersion**, **dmDriverVersion**, **dmSize**, and **dmDriverExtra**). Set the **dmDriverVersion** and **dmDriverExtra** members to zero if you are not passing any driver-specific information. Set the **dmFields** member to indicate which of the device-independent settings you are providing.

   For example, to request that a printer driver use landscape orientation with letter-sized paper, you could set up the following **DEVMODE** structure:

   ```
   DEVMODE dm;
   lstrcpy(dm.dmDeviceName, szDeviceName);
   /* Header information */
   dm.dmVersion = DM_SPECVERSION;
   dm.dmDriverVersion = 0;
   dm.dmSize = sizeof(DEVMODE);
   dm.dmDriverExtra = 0;
   /* Device-independent settings */
   dm.dmFields = DM_ORIENTATION | DM_PAPERSIZE;
   dm.dmOrientation = DMORIENT_LANDSCAPE;
   dm.dmPaperSize = DMPAPER_LETTER;
   ```

   The first five members make up the structure's header information. The szDeviceName value is a string that contains the name of the device, such as

HP LaserJet Series II. For information about how to retrieve this value from the WIN.INI file, see Chapter 12, "Printing."

2. Call **ExtDeviceMode**, including the following information in the parameters:

Parameter	Value
lpdmInput	A pointer to the buffer that contains the partial or complete **DEV-MODE** structure you are supplying
lpdmOutput	A pointer to the output buffer
fwMode	DM_MODIFY I DM_COPY

The driver then changes its settings to match those in your input structure and writes the resulting settings to the output buffer as a complete **DEVMODE** structure.

3. Pass the output **DEVMODE** structure to **CreateDC** to create a printer device context that uses the new settings.

After modifying its **DEVMODE** structure, the driver copies it to the output buffer. The output **DEVMODE** structure will be a complete structure and will include the changes you specified in your partial structure. Because the driver has just validated your changes, it is safe to pass this output structure to the **CreateDC** function.

17.5.5 Changing the Print Settings Without Affecting Other Applications

Your application can alter the print settings without affecting other applications. To make your application do this, follow these steps:

1. Call **ExtDeviceMode**, including the following information in the parameters:

Parameter	Value
lpdmInput	A pointer to the buffer that contains the partial or complete **DEV-MODE** structure you are supplying
lpdmOutput	A pointer to the output buffer
fwMode	DM_MODIFY I DM_COPY
	or
	DM_PROMPT I DM_COPY
	or
	DM_MODIFY I DM_PROMPT I DM_COPY

Note that you can specify either or both input values (DM_PROMPT and DM_MODIFY). This call to **ExtDeviceMode** saves a private copy of the print settings in a buffer that your application maintains. Since the call omits the DM_UPDATE output value, the driver does not copy the new print settings to the printer environment and WIN.INI. Therefore, other applications will not be affected by your private print settings.

2. Pass the output **DEVMODE** structure to **CreateDC** to create a printer device context that uses the new settings.

Note You can save the output **DEVMODE** structure to a permanent location such as a reserved area in your application's document file. Then, in a later session, your application can read the **DEVMODE** structure from the document file and pass it directly to **CreateDC** without having to first call **ExtDeviceMode**.

17.5.6 Prompting the User for Changes to the Print Settings

Your application can direct the printer driver to display its Print Setup dialog box, from which the user can specify changes to the print settings. The driver changes its current settings to reflect the user's preferences. The driver's output **DEV-MODE** structure (if any) then includes the user's changes.

To make you application prompt the user for print settings, follow these steps:

1. Call **ExtDeviceMode**, including the following information in the parameters:

Parameter	Value
lpdmOutput	A pointer to the output buffer
fwMode	DM_PROMPT I DM_COPY

The driver then displays its Print Setup dialog box, from which the user can select new print settings.

If the user clicks the OK button after changing the print settings, the **ExtDevice-Mode** function returns the value IDOK and the driver places a **DEVMODE** structure in the output buffer. This output structure includes the user's changes. If the user clicks the Cancel button instead, the function returns the value IDCANCEL and the driver's output structure will not include any of the user's selections.

2. To set up a printer device context that includes the user's changes, pass the output **DEVMODE** structure to **CreateDC**.

Setting the Values in the Print Setup Dialog Box   To preset the values that appear in the driver's Print Setup dialog box, your application can supply a **DEV-MODE** structure with its own settings and direct the driver to display its dialog box. The driver's Print Setup dialog box will appear with the settings you specified in the input **DEVMODE** structure. The user can then change some or all of the settings. After the user clicks the OK button, the driver provides an output **DEVMODE** structure that reflects the settings as they appeared when the user clicked OK. The output structure includes settings your application passed as input, with any changes the user made.

To prompt the user with a dialog box that reflects your application's print settings, follow these steps:

1. Set up a partial or complete **DEVMODE** structure that contains any settings you want to change. For information about setting up a partial **DEVMODE** structure, see Section 17.4.4, "Tailoring Print Settings for Use with the CreateDC Function."

2. Call **ExtDeviceMode**, including the following information in the parameters:

Parameter	Value
lpdmInput	A pointer to the buffer that contains the partial or complete **DEVMODE** structure you are supplying
lpdmOutput	A pointer to the output buffer
fwMode	DM_MODIFY I DM_PROMPT I DM_COPY

The driver first changes its current settings to reflect the settings you provided. It then displays its Print Setup dialog box with the new settings; the user can change some or all of the settings in the dialog box.

If the user clicks the OK button after changing the print settings, the **ExtDevice-Mode** function returns the value IDOK and the driver places in the output buffer a **DEVMODE** structure that includes your changes as updated by the user. If the user clicks the Cancel button instead, the function returns the value IDCANCEL and the driver's output **DEVMODE** structure includes only the changes your application provided.

3. To set up a printer device context that includes the new settings, pass the output **DEVMODE** structure to **CreateDC**.

17.6 Copying Print Settings Between Drivers

To copy print settings from one driver to another, follow these steps:

1. Copy the first driver's **DEVMODE** structure by using the steps outlined in Section 17.4.2, "Retrieving a Copy of the Print Settings."

2. Delete the device-specific information in the output **DEVMODE** structure by setting the **dmDriverVersion** and **dmDriverExtra** members to zero.

3. Determine the size of the buffer required for the **DEVMODE** structure for the second printer by calling the **ExtDeviceMode** function with the *fwMode* parameter set to zero and all other parameters set to information specific to the second printer.

4. Copy the **DEVMODE** structure produced in steps 1 and 2 to the buffer allocated in step 3. It is not necessary to copy the device-specific information to the buffer.

5. Free the buffer allocated in step 1.

6. Change the **dmDeviceName** member of the new **DEVMODE** structure to the name of the second device.

7. Call the second driver's **ExtDeviceMode** function, including the following information in the parameters:

Parameter	Value
lpdmInput	A pointer to the buffer that contains the altered **DEVMODE** structure
lpdmOutput	A pointer to the output buffer
fwMode	DM_MODIFY	DM_COPY

The second driver then places a valid, complete **DEVMODE** structure in the output buffer. The output structure reflects the device-independent settings your application copied from the first driver, but contains the second driver's device-specific information.

17.7 Maintaining Your Own Print Settings

With Windows, your application can maintain application-specific default print settings, or even settings specific to a particular document. So that your application can do this, store the **DEVMODE** structure that contains the settings you want to use as defaults. You can store the structure in an application setup file to provide application-wide defaults, or you can store it as part of a document, for document-specific setups.

17.8 Working with Older Printer Drivers

Printer drivers written for versions of Windows earlier than 3.0 provide only the **DeviceMode** function, which displays a dialog box from which the user can specify print settings, such as page orientation and paper size. With these printer drivers, changes made to the print settings affect the entire system, not just the calling application.

Like other device-driver functions, the **DeviceMode** function is part of the driver, not part of GDI. (For an explanation about how to call device-driver functions, see Section 17.2, "Using Device-Driver Functions.") When you call a driver's **Device-Mode** function, the driver displays its Printer Setup dialog box, from which the user can change the print settings for that printer and printer port.

The following example shows how to use the function's procedure address, lpfnDeviceMode, to call the **DeviceMode** function:

```
if (lpfnDeviceMode != NULL) /* if driver supports this function... */
{
    (*lpfnDeviceMode) ((HWND) hWnd,      /* handle of parent window */
        (HANDLE) hDriver,                /* handle of driver module */
        (LPSTR) "PSCRIPT",               /* printer name            */
        (LPSTR) "LPT1:");                /* port name               */
}
```

17.9 Related Topics

For more information about printing from your Windows application, see Chapter 12, "Printing."

For more information about functions and structures used for print settings, see the *Microsoft Windows Programmer's Reference, Volumes 2* and *3*.

For information about writing printer drivers, see the Microsoft Windows Device Driver Kit (DDK).

Fonts

This chapter describes the fonts an application can use with the Microsoft Windows 3.1 operating system and discusses how to use Windows font functions in applications. The information includes a description of TrueType font technology, which is new for Windows 3.1.

18.1 Font Fundamentals

The vocabulary used to describe fonts may be unfamiliar to application developers. This section defines some of the terms and concepts that a developer needs to use when describing a font.

18.1.1 Font Organization

A typeface is a collection of characters that share design characteristics; for example, Courier is a common typeface. A font is a collection of characters that have the same typeface and size.

The Windows graphics device interface (GDI) organizes fonts by family; each family consists of fonts that have a common design. Families are distinguished by stroke width and serif characteristics. A stroke is a horizontal or vertical line. A horizontal stroke is called a cross-stroke. The main vertical line in a character is called a stem.

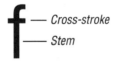

Serifs are short cross-lines drawn at the ends of the main strokes of a letter. Typefaces without serifs are called sans serif typefaces.

Within a font family, fonts are distinguished by stylistic variations that generally involve their weight and slant. Weights are described by adjectives such as "extra light," "light," "demi," "demi bold," "book," "bold," "heavy bold," "extra bold," and "black." The slant of a font is described by "roman," "italic," and "oblique." A roman font is the upright form of the font; an oblique font is slanted; and an italic font is both slanted and relatively cursive. Font families usually do not include both italic and oblique fonts.

GDI uses five family names to categorize typefaces and fonts. A sixth name (FF_DONTCARE) allows an application to use the default font. Following are the font-family names, each described briefly:

Font-family name	Description
FF_DECORATIVE	Specifies a novelty font. An example is Old English.
FF_DONTCARE	Specifies a generic family name. This name is used when information about a font does not exist or does not matter.
FF_MODERN	Specifies a font that has a constant stroke width, with or without serifs. Fixed-pitch fonts are usually modern; examples include Pica, Elite, and Courier New.
FF_ROMAN	Specifies a font that has a variable stroke width, with serifs. An example is Times New Roman®.
FF_SCRIPT	Specifies a font that is designed to look like handwriting; examples include Script and Cursive.
FF_SWISS	Specifies a font that has a variable stroke width, without serifs. An example is Arial®.

GDI family names do not always correspond to traditional typographic categories.

18.1.2 Measuring Characters

Both the visible and invisible parts of a character affect its measurement. The visible part of a character is called a glyph. The invisible part is a rectangular region that contains the character; this region is called a character cell. The origin of a character cell is its upper-left corner. When a text-output function specifies coordinates at which the text should appear, GDI places the origin of the first character cell at those coordinates. (This is the default behavior for GDI. An application can change this at any time by using the **SetTextAlign** function.)

The most common unit of measurement for measuring characters is the point. In the computer industry, a point is exactly 1/72 of an inch. Font heights in Windows can be specified in "twips," which are 1/20 of a point (that is, 1/1440 of an inch). Point size refers to the size of the character cell, but only loosely to the size of the visible characters; the glyphs from different 12-point fonts can have different heights. The following example shows the different font heights in alternating glyphs from Times New Roman, Palatino®, and Arial, each at 12 points:

AAAaaaBBBbbbCCCcccDDDddd

Following are some of the character-cell measurements an application can affect or query when it creates a font:

Measurement	Description
Ascent	Specifies the distance from the base line to the top of a character. The ascender of a character is the part of the character above the base line. In Windows, the value for the ascent is the distance from the base line to the top of the character cell; this can include white space. The typographic ascent, on the other hand, corresponds to the tallest character in a font. For TrueType fonts, this character is often the lowercase "f."
Base line	Specifies the line on which all characters stand. The base line is typically the lowest point of most of the capital letters in a font. (Though the tail of the "Q," for example, can extend below the base line.)
Descent	Specifies the distance from the base line to the bottom of a character. The descender of a character is the part of the character below the base line. For example, the tail of the letter "g" is a descender. In Windows, the value for the descent is the distance from the base line to the bottom of the character cell; this can include white space. The typographic descent, on the other hand, corresponds to the character in a font that extends farthest beneath the base line. For TrueType fonts, this character is often the lowercase "g."
Height	Specifies the vertical space required for a font. The height of a font is the sum of the ascent, descent, and internal leading for that font. (For a description of internal leading, see Section 18.1.3.)
Width	Specifies the horizontal space required for a character cell in a font. GDI returns widths for the average character cell in a font and for the widest character cell. The average width can be simple or weighted, depending on the font. An application can also retrieve the widths for individual characters. These widths include the empty space preceding and following the glyph.

18.1.3 Measuring Line and Intercharacter Spacing

Line spacing, like character size, is typically specified in points. If a 10-point font is displayed with 12-point line spacing, this is abbreviated as "10/12" and is called "ten on twelve" line spacing.

Following are some of the line and intercharacter measurements an application can affect or query when it creates a font:

Measurement	Description
External leading	Specifies the space between rows of text. External leading is not part of the character cell. When the internal leading for a font does not contain parts of characters, the apparent line spacing is the external leading plus the internal leading. Windows does not support negative values for external leading.

Measurement	Description
Internal leading	Specifies the difference between the height of the character glyphs for a font (the font's em square) and the height of the character cell for a font. Applications use internal leading to determine the point size for a font; the point size is the height of the character cell minus its internal leading. Some applications have used internal leading incorrectly; specifically, internal leading is not strictly reserved for diacritical marks, nor should it be used as the space to be removed from the first line on a page.
Overhang	Specifies a characteristic of some glyphs that occupy the same horizontal space as adjacent glyphs. All of the characters in most italic fonts use overhangs to keep the characters relatively close together—for example, in the italic word *Is*, the top part of the letter "I" is directly over the bottom of the letter "s."
Pitch	Specifies the general type of horizontal character spacing. A font can have either fixed or variable pitch. The character cells in a fixed-pitch font are all the same size, but in a variable-pitch font they vary depending on the width of the glyph. Another term for a fixed-pitch font is a monospace font.

The external leading for a font is specified by the designers of the font. The concept of internal leading is specific to Windows.

The following figure shows internal and external leading and their relationship to the height of a font. The names beginning with the letters "tm" are members of the **TEXTMETRIC** structure.

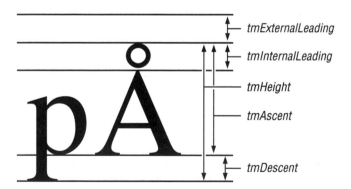

18.1.4 Character Sets

All fonts use a character set. A character set contains punctuation marks, numerals, uppercase and lowercase letters, and all other printable characters. Each element of a character set is identified by a number.

Most character sets used in Windows are supersets of the U.S. ASCII character set, which defines characters for the 96 numeric values from 32 through 127. There are four major groups of character sets:

- Windows
- OEM
- Symbol
- Vendor-specific

18.1.4.1 Windows Character Set

The Windows character set is the most commonly used character set in Windows programming. It is essentially equivalent to the ANSI character set. The blank character is the first character in the Windows character set. It has a hexadecimal value of 0x20 (decimal 32). The last character in the Windows character set has a hexadecimal value of 0xFF (decimal 255).

Many fonts specify a default character. Whenever a request is made for a character that is not in the font, GDI provides this default character. Many fonts using the Windows character set specify the period (.) as the default character. TrueType fonts typically use an open box as the default character.

Fonts use a break character to separate words and justify text. Most fonts using the Windows character set specify the blank character, whose hexadecimal value is 0x20 (decimal 32).

For Windows version 3.1, 24 characters have been added to the Windows code page:

Character	Name	Windows character code
,	base line single quote	130
ƒ	florin	131
„	base line double quote	132
…	ellipsis	133
†	dagger	134
‡	double dagger	135
	circumflex	136
‰	permille	137
Š	S Hacek	138
‹	left single guillemet	139
Œ	OE ligature	140
'	left single quote	145
'	right single quote	146

Character	Name	Windows character code
"	left double quote	147
"	right double quote	148
•	bullet	149
–	en dash	150
—	em dash	151
~	tilde	152
™	trademark ligature	153
š	s Hacek	154
›	right single guillemet	155
œ	oe ligature	156
Ÿ	Y Dieresis	159

The characters for left and right single quote were added to the character set for the release of Windows version 3.0.

18.1.4.2 OEM Character Set

The OEM character set is typically used in full-screen MS-DOS sessions for screen display. Characters 32 through 127 are usually the same in the OEM, U.S. ASCII, and Windows character sets. The other characters in the OEM character set (0 through 31 and 128 through 255) correspond to the characters that can be displayed in a full-screen MS-DOS session. These characters are generally different from the Windows characters.

18.1.4.3 Symbol Character Set

The Symbol character set contains special characters typically used to represent mathematical and scientific formulas.

18.1.4.4 Vendor-Specific Character Sets

Many printers and other output devices provide fonts based on character sets that differ from the Windows and OEM sets—for example, the EBCDIC character set. To use one of these character sets, the printer driver translates from the Windows character set to the vendor-specific character set.

18.2 Fonts in Windows

Windows applications can use three different kinds of font technologies to display and print text. This section discusses these font technologies and gives Windows-specific background information about fonts.

18.2.1 Raster, Vector, and TrueType Fonts

Previous versions of Windows had two types of fonts: raster and vector. Windows version 3.1 introduces a third type—TrueType fonts.

Raster fonts are stored as bitmaps. These bitmaps are designed for output devices of a particular resolution. GDI typically synthesizes bold, italic, underline, and strikeout characteristics for raster fonts; however, the results are not always attractive. When GDI must change the size of a raster font, aliasing problems can also reduce the attractiveness of the text. Raster fonts are useful for specialized applications in which TrueType fonts are not available. Another possible advantage to using raster fonts derives from the large number of raster fonts that are often present on a user's system; an application could look for the name of a particular specialized or decorative font and use a TrueType font if the specified font was not present.

When an application requests an italic or bold font that is not available, GDI synthesizes the font by transforming the character bitmaps. When an application using only raster fonts requests a point size that is not available, GDI also transforms the bitmaps to produce the font. Because TrueType font families include bold, italic, and bold italic fonts, and because TrueType fonts are scalable to any requested point size, GDI does not synthesize fonts as frequently as it did for earlier versions of Windows. For more information about this subject, see Section 18.2.5, "Font Mapper."

Windows version 3.1 contains a new set of raster fonts. This set, called Small Fonts, is for use at resolutions of less than 8 points. Although TrueType fonts can be scaled to less than 8 points, glyphs this small may not be legible enough for regular use. Because glyphs this small contain very little detail, it is more efficient to use the raster small fonts than to scale TrueType fonts to the small size. (GDI synthesizes bold and italic attributes for the raster small fonts, when necessary.)

Vector fonts are stored as collections of GDI calls. They are time-consuming to generate but are useful for such devices as plotters, on which bitmapped characters cannot be used. (By drawing lines, GDI can simulate vector fonts on a device that does not directly support them.) Prior to the introduction of TrueType fonts, vector fonts were also useful for applications that used very large or distorted characters or characters that needed to be perpendicular to a base line that was at an angle across the display surface.

TrueType fonts are stored as collections of points and hints that define character outlines. (Hints are algorithms that distort scaled font outlines to improve the appearance of the bitmaps at specific resolutions.) When an application requests a TrueType font, the TrueType rasterizer uses the outline and the hints to produce a bitmap of the size requested by the application.

The default font for a device context is the System font, a proportionally spaced raster font representing characters in the Windows character set. Its font name is System. Windows uses the System font for menus, window titles, and other text.

It is possible to have multiple fonts in the system that have the same name (for example, a Courier device font and a Courier GDI raster font). However, applications typically do not present a font name to the user more than once—instead, they discard duplicates. Applications can control which font is presented to the user when duplicate font names occur by using the **lfOutPrecision** member of the **LOGFONT** structure.

18.2.2 Font Resource Files

The SYSTEM subdirectory of a user's Windows directory (the directory in which Windows is installed) contains the system's font resource files. A font resource file is an empty Windows library; it contains no code or data but does contain resources.

Raster and vector font resource files are identified by the .FON filename extension. TrueType font resource files have the .FOT filename extension. Each .FOT file is a relatively short header that refers to a file containing TrueType font information. These TrueType font-information files have the same base filename as the .FOT files, but have the .TTF filename extension.

Some of the filenames for raster and vector fonts are followed by a lowercase letter that indicates the resolution for which the font was designed. This letter varies according to the type of display device that was specified when the fonts were installed. Following are the lowercase letters used to identify different resolutions:

Letter	Device
a	CGA
b	EGA
c	Okidata printers
d	IBM and Epson printers
e	VGA
f	IBM 8514/A

For information about defining and using a specialized font resource, see Section 18.4.9, "Creating Customized Fonts." For more information about the format of font resource files, see the *Microsoft Windows Programmer's Reference, Volume 4*.

18.2.3 Basics of TrueType Fonts

The TrueType fonts incorporated into Windows 3.1 are much more versatile than the fonts that were available in previous versions of Windows. TrueType fonts can be scaled and rotated; they allow the same fonts to be used on the screen as are used on printers; and they allow documents to be portable between printers, applications, and systems.

The following table lists the 13 core TrueType fonts distributed with Windows version 3.1. (Windows 3.1 may include additional TrueType fonts that supplement this core set.)

Font family	Font name	Type
Arial	Arial	Sans serif, variable pitch
	Arial Bold	Sans serif, variable pitch
	Arial Italic	Sans serif, variable pitch
	Arial Bold Italic	Sans serif, variable pitch
Courier New	Courier New	Serif, fixed pitch
	Courier New Bold	Serif, fixed pitch
	Courier New Italic	Serif, fixed pitch
	Courier New Bold Italic	Serif, fixed pitch
Symbol®	Symbol	N/A
Times New Roman	Times New Roman	Serif, variable pitch
	Times New Roman Bold	Serif, variable pitch
	Times New Roman Italic	Serif, variable pitch
	Times New Roman Bold Italic	Serif, variable pitch

TrueType font technology offers many benefits to application designers, at little or no cost. It is not necessary to revise an application written for Windows version 3.0 for that application to use TrueType fonts. If you want your application to take full advantage of the greater precision and versatility available with TrueType fonts, however, you can use the following new font functions:

Function	Description
CreateScalableFontResource	Creates a font resource file for a specified TrueType font.
EnumFontFamilies	Retrieves the fonts available on a specified device.
GetCharABCWidths	Retrieves the widths of consecutive TrueType characters.

Function	Description
GetFontData	Retrieves font-metric data (or the entire font) from a TrueType font file.
GetGlyphOutline	Retrieves data describing an individual character in a TrueType font.
GetOutlineTextMetrics	Retrieves font metrics for TrueType fonts.
GetRasterizerCaps	Determines whether TrueType is installed.

18.2.3.1 Benefits of TrueType

TrueType fonts offer many advantages over previous font technologies for Windows:

- What you see is what you get (WYSIWYG).

  Applications can scale and rotate TrueType fonts. TrueType fonts are attractive at all sizes. An application can use the same fonts on the screen and the printer.

- Printer portability.

  TrueType fonts work on different printers. Because detailed font metrics are available, an application can compose documents in a device-independent fashion.

- Document portability.

  Applications can embed TrueType fonts in documents. TrueType fonts work on different platforms. Applications can use the detailed font metrics to compose documents in a platform-independent fashion.

- Simplicity.

  The versatility of TrueType fonts reduces the number of required choices and compromises.

TrueType solves two important problems: matching fonts to the printer in use, and presenting high-quality fonts at any size on all devices.

The most obvious benefit of TrueType fonts is that they are scalable. Users can use TrueType to get virtually any point size they like. With TrueType, Windows users no longer need to think about the availability of point sizes on their printer or screen, about running a utility to create raster fonts, or about disk storage for these bitmaps.

TrueType fonts are presented to applications through the same enumeration and selection functions as the raster fonts. As a result, TrueType fonts work with every Windows application. Windows printer drivers have also been modified as required to support the use of TrueType.

18.2.3.2 Compatibility with Earlier Windows Versions

The introduction of TrueType fonts introduces a few issues that are important for applications developed for earlier versions of Windows.

Identifying TrueType Fonts for Users   Before TrueType fonts were introduced, some users had many different fonts to choose between; now, these users have still more choices. (Users can simplify their choices by selecting the "Enable TrueType Fonts" and "Show Only TrueType Fonts in Applications" check boxes in the Fonts dialog box from Control Panel.) Applications can use the standard font dialog box to make it easier for users to manage the fonts on their systems. (For more information about the standard font dialog box, see Section 18.2.6, "Standard Font Dialog Box.")

Character Widths   TrueType fonts use ABC character spacing, a spacing method that does not rely on the width of a character cell and any overhang (the method used for raster fonts). The extra accuracy of ABC spacing can introduce a problem for applications written prior to Windows version 3.1. Older applications that use character widths instead of ABC widths with TrueType fonts incorrectly calculate the end of the last glyph in the line. This calculation could be off by as much as several pixels. It is also possible that a line could start slightly to the left of the starting point specified by the application. These inaccuracies sometimes lead to problems when the screen is redrawn or when a selection of text is highlighted; pieces of glyphs can be handled incorrectly at either end of a line of text.

Many applications written before TrueType became available use the **ExtTextOut** function to clip or redraw lines of text that extend beyond the visible margins of the document.This method prevents any extra pieces of glyphs from being left behind because of incorrect character-width calculations.

For more information about ABC character widths, see Section 18.2.4.1, "Line and Character Spacing."

MS Serif and MS Sans Serif Fonts   In Windows version 3.1, the raster fonts Tms Rmn and Helv have been replaced by identical fonts named MS® Serif and MS Sans Serif, respectively. The Tms Rmn and Helv font names are mapped to their replacements in a new section of WIN.INI called [FontSubstitutes]. Whenever an application requests Helv or Tms Rmn, the font mapper checks this section and makes the appropriate substitution. The [FontSubstitutes] section also maps Helvetica® to Arial and Times® to Times New Roman.

A user could change the [FontSubstitutes] section to map any font name to any other font name. For example, a user could map Tms Rmn and Helv to the Times New Roman and Arial TrueType fonts. Entries in [FontSubstitutes] do not change the names of fonts, however; a user could not force Arial to appear as Helvetica in font menus.

The **EnumFonts** and **EnumFontFamilies** functions use the [FontSubstitutes] section of WIN.INI so that applications written prior to Windows version 3.1 do not fail unexpectedly when enumerating preexisting font names. If an application specifies Helv in a call to **EnumFontFamilies**, GDI enumerates the available MS Sans Serif fonts. When an application calls either of these functions with a NULL family name, GDI enumerates a representative font from each available family, returning the actual names of the fonts, not the remapped names.

Because most Windows applications display font menus that include only the fonts that can be printed on the current printer, this change in font names does not affect most users. Only users of dot-matrix printers see the new names in font menus and dialog boxes.

Font-Height Metrics Can Depend on Attributes   Because the members of a TrueType font family, such as bold and italic, come from different outlines, in some cases the font-height metrics could be different within a TrueType font family. For raster fonts this is not a problem, because when Windows simulates attributes, these metrics are preserved, and because hand-tuned bitmaps were made with matching heights. For the set of fonts shipped with Windows 3.1, most (but not all) of the height metrics match.

18.2.4 Text and Character Attributes

Character attributes are such features as whether a character is bold or italic and whether it has serifs. Text attributes are such features as line and character spacing and text justification. This section introduces some of these attribute categories. For descriptions of individual attributes, see the descriptions of the **LOGFONT**, **NEWTEXTMETRIC**, **TEXTMETRIC**, and **OUTLINETEXTMETRIC** structures in the *Microsoft Windows Programmer's Reference, Volume 3*.

18.2.4.1 Line and Character Spacing

Before the introduction of TrueType fonts, it was difficult for an application to position characters exactly, especially if the characters were in a string that included bold or italic text. Instead of the width of the character glyph, most Windows functions use the advance width of characters, which includes space on either side of the glyph, as in the following figure:

Character width

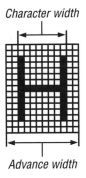

Advance width

Applications can control the spacing of TrueType characters accurately by using ABC character spacing. GDI constructs ABC spacing from information provided by the TrueType rasterizer. The "A" spacing is the width to add to the current position before placing the glyph. The "B" spacing is the width of the glyph itself. The "C" spacing is the white space to the right of the glyph. The total advance width is given by A+B+C.

Because either or both of the A and C increments can be negative, characters can overhang or underhang the character cell in a way that was not previously possible with GDI. For example, in the following figure the A, B, and C increments for the letter "g" are all positive, but the A and C increments for the letter "f" are negative.

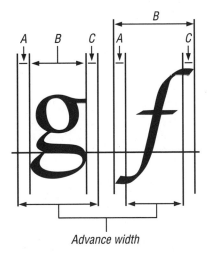

Advance width

An application can use the **GetCharABCWidths** function to retrieve the ABC spacing for characters in a TrueType font.

When an application using TrueType fonts calls a text-output function, GDI uses the font's complete set of ABC widths to provide character-placement information to the device driver.

Some applications determine the line spacing between text lines of different sizes by using a font's maximum ascender and descender. An application can retrieve these values by calling the **GetTextMetrics** function and then checking the **tmAscent** and **tmDescent** members of the **NEWTEXTMETRIC** structure.

The maximum ascent and descent are different from the typographic ascent and descent; in TrueType fonts, the typographic ascent and descent are typically the top of the "f" glyph and bottom of the "g" glyph. Rounded characters typically extend slightly beyond the limits of characters with straight edges, to overcome an optical illusion that would make them appear too small otherwise. An application can retrieve the typographic ascender and descender for a TrueType font by calling the **GetOutlineTextMetrics** function and checking the values in the **otmAscent** and **otmDescent** members of the **OUTLINETEXTMETRIC** structure.

Applications that use the HPPCL5A printer driver may experience problems with line spacing for the scalable fonts that are built into the HP LaserJet III printer. These fonts use external leading in the place of internal leading; accent marks for capital letters print outside the character cell reported by the **tmHeight** member of the **NEWTEXTMETRIC** structure.

TrueType font metrics do not correspond exactly to the metrics for Windows raster fonts, because TrueType font metrics have been designed by Apple Computer, Inc. TrueType metrics are required for any application that produces a document that is portable between Windows and an Apple Macintosh computer.

The following figure shows the difference between the vertical text metric values returned in the **NEWTEXTMETRIC** and **OUTLINETEXTMETRIC** structures. (The names beginning with "otm" are members of the **OUTLINETEXT-METRIC** structure.)

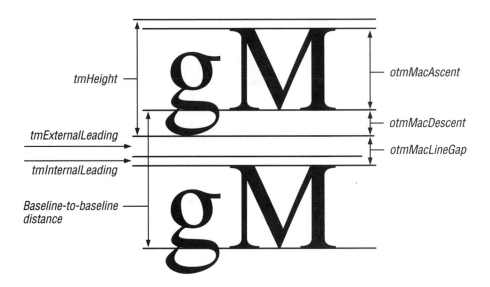

The overhang added by GDI when it synthesizes a bold or italic font is not taken into account by the **GetTextExtent** function. For more information about taking the overhang into account in character spacing, see Section 18.4.7.3, "Using Multiple Fonts in a Line."

18.2.4.2 Logical and Physical Inches

A logical inch is a measure Windows uses for presenting legible fonts on the screen; it is generally 30 to 40 percent larger than a physical inch. A 10-point font on a screen is larger than a 10-point font produced by a printer. Fonts on the screen are made larger because most screens do not have high enough resolutions to make a 10-point font legible. Furthermore, users generally read text on screens from a greater distance than they read text on paper.

Although logical inches solve the problem of legible fonts on the screen, they prevent a perfect match between the output of the screen and printer. The text on a screen is not simply a scaled version of the text that will appear on the page, particularly if graphics are incorporated into the text.

An application can retrieve the physical dimensions of a font by calling the **Get-OutlineTextMetrics** function. To determine the dimensions of an output device, an application can call the **GetDeviceCaps** function. **GetDeviceCaps** returns both physical and logical dimensions.

18.2.4.3 Font Sizes

Most Windows applications use the MM_TEXT mapping mode instead of MM_TWIPS, because MM_TEXT makes possible a relatively simple conversion from logical to physical font sizes. With MM_TEXT, each logical unit is mapped to one pixel.

To determine the point size for a font, an application must first convert the information returned in the **NEWTEXTMETRIC** or **OUTLINETEXTMETRIC** structure using the size of the logical inch for the output device. For example, an application using MM_TEXT units might use a font that has a cell height (**tmHeight**) of 12 and an internal leading (**tmInternalLeading**) of 2. The cell height minus the internal leading gives the point size in logical units; in this case, the point size of the font is 10 units (pixels).

To convert this value into a typographic point size (that is, a value in which one point equals 1/72 inch), the application should use the **GetDeviceCaps** function to determine the vertical size and resolution of the screen and the number of pixels per logical inch supported by that device. For example, if an application working in MM_TEXT mapping mode requires a 12-point font, it could use the value produced by the following algorithm in the **lfHeight** member of the **LOGFONT** structure:

$$-1 * ((LOGPIXELSY * 12) / 72)$$

Using a negative value in the **lfHeight** member causes GDI to use the value as the height of the character glyphs, not the height of the character cell. The LOGPIXELSY value is returned by a call to the **GetDeviceCaps** function. The point size of the requested font is 12, and the number of points in a physical inch is 72.

Similarly, an application could use the following algorithm to determine the point size of a font from information returned in the **NEWTEXTMETRIC** structure:

$$((\textbf{tmHeight} - \textbf{tmInternalLeading}) * 72) / LOGPIXELSY$$

For more information about setting a point size, see Section 18.4.4, "Creating a Logical Font." For more information about querying a point size, see Section 18.4.5, "Retrieving Information About the Selected Font."

18.2.5 Font Mapper

When calling a font-creation function, an application describes the font either by using a **LOGFONT** structure in a call to the **CreateFontIndirect** function or by using the parameters of the **CreateFont** function. The font returned by these functions is called a logical font, because a font matching the described characteristics is not necessarily available in the system. GDI uses the logical font to create a physical font, by finding the closest match to the logical font among the available TrueType, raster, vector, and device-dependent fonts.

The Windows font mapper determines which of the available fonts is the closest match to the requested logical font. The font mapper often chooses a TrueType font as the closest match; it will choose a raster or vector font only when the logical font matches the characteristics of the raster or vector font very closely or when the logical font specifies the name of the raster or vector font. Typically, a TrueType font is chosen when it is specifically requested or when GDI would otherwise have to synthesize the font. For example, if a font name is not specified in the logical font or if the specified name does not exist, the font mapper chooses a TrueType font that matches the requested point size, serif characteristics, and pitch.

When the font mapper determines that a TrueType font is the closest match for a requested logical font, the TrueType engine produces enhanced GDI raster characters that are presented to the raster device. (The characters are enhanced by the use of ABC character widths.) For devices that do not have raster font capabilities, the driver must request the TrueType engine to provide the glyphs in a form the driver can use.

When the font mapper chooses between raster fonts, it chooses the font that is closest to the requested size without being larger than that size.

When an application requests a very small font, the font mapper may choose one of the small fonts stored in the SMALL*X*.FON font resource file. TrueType fonts specify a suggested minimum size, which can be retrieved by calling the **GetOutlineTextMetrics** function and checking the **otmusMinimumPPEM** member of the **OUTLINETEXTMETRIC** structure. When an application requests a font smaller than this size, the font mapper typically chooses a small font instead of a TrueType font. If the requested size is not available as a small font, however, GDI scales the TrueType font instead. Microsoft's 13 core TrueType fonts are designed to be readable as small as 8 points on a VGA screen, although they can be used at smaller sizes.

18.2.6 Standard Font Dialog Box

Windows applications should take advantage of the standard font dialog box for Windows 3.1. Following are the advantages of this dialog box:

- It shows the user the font family name (for example, Times New Roman) along with the styles (for example, Regular, Bold Italic, and other combinations of italic and weight) for the installed fonts.

- It allows Windows version 3.0 simulations and effects to be applied, if the user wants them. When bold or italic simulations are applied, the user is warned that the font may not print as selected.

- It displays weights or styles outside the four standard styles (regular, bold, italic, bold italic).

- It clearly tells the user which fonts are TrueType and which are not.

The standard font dialog box also introduces a consistent user interface and frees applications from having to implement their own dialog boxes for fonts, while retaining enough flexibility for applications to add custom controls. The dialog box looks like this:

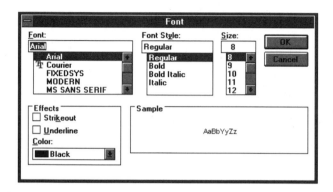

For more information about the standard font dialog box, see the *Microsoft Windows Programmer's Reference, Volume 1*.

18.3 TrueType Font Technology

With TrueType fonts, applications have much greater control over the final appearance of documents than was possible with previous Windows font technologies. Much of this added control is the result of the portability of TrueType fonts: An application can move them from the system to a printer, from a printer to the system, from one system to another system (by "embedding" them in documents), and even port them between incompatible operating systems.

Sophisticated desktop-publishing and word-processing applications go to great lengths to make the screen output mimic the printer output. Some applications even change the way the fonts appear on the screen, in an attempt to show users what the printer output will look like. This kind of application benefits greatly from exploiting the advantages of TrueType.

18.3.1 What You See Is What You Get: WYSIWYG

WYSIWYG means that the screen output matches the printer output. With perfect WYSIWYG, the user would be able to place a page of printed output over the same screen output and see every character and graphic element in exactly the same place. If the screen and printer have different resolutions, however, this degree of matching is impossible. Usually, WYSIWYG simply means that line breaks, paragraph breaks, and page breaks are the same on both devices and that justified paragraphs are presented properly. WYSIWYG does not mean the same document on two different printers will be formatted in exactly the same way. Because most applications make the best use of the available printer, WYSIWYG often applies only to the correspondence between the screen and printer for a given printer.

TrueType offers a higher level of WYSIWYG than was available with earlier versions of Windows, because it works on every device. Most Windows applications lay out the screen based on the target printer. The fonts they enumerate for the user are the fonts that can be printed. Because TrueType fonts work on the target printer, they are enumerated by the printer driver to the application and are typically displayed to the user as printer fonts. When the application and GDI match screen fonts to the printer fonts, the TrueType fonts are used on the screen as well.

If no screen font matches the widths of characters in the chosen printer font, WYSIWYG is difficult to achieve. When this happens, applications sometimes make the average width of the characters match, with as little variation in specific characters as possible. More exact matching is achieved with a technique known as metric coercion. There are two basic methods of coercing character metrics: width coercion and shape coercion. Width coercion simply adjusts the spacing between words and characters, and shape coercion applies a transformation to each character to force it into a bounding box. Because shape coercion can lead to unacceptably deformed characters, width coercion is typographically preferred.

Although Windows does not include a function to deform individual characters, the **lfWidth** member of the **LOGFONT** structure allows an application to scale the width of a TrueType font independently of its height. (Most applications do not scale TrueType fonts in this manner, however, because the results are usually unattractive.)

18.3.2 Embedded Fonts

Embedding a font is the technique of bundling the fonts used by a document into the document itself for transmission to another computer. Embedding a font guarantees that a font specified in a transmitted document will be present on the computer receiving the document. Not all fonts can be moved from computer to computer, however, since most fonts are licensed to only one computer at a time. In Windows, only TrueType fonts can be embedded.

Applications should embed a font in a document only on request from a user. An application cannot be distributed along with documents that contain embedded fonts, nor can an application itself contain an embedded font. Whenever an application distributes a font, in any format, the proprietary rights of the owner of the font must be acknowledged.

A font's license may not allow embedding; it may give read-write permission for a font to be installed and used on the destination computer; or it may give read-only permission. Read-only permission allows a document to be viewed and printed (but not modified) by the destination computer; documents with read-only embedded fonts are themselves read-only. Read-only embedded fonts may not be unbundled from the document and installed on the destination computer.

Applications that support embedded fonts determine the license status of a font by checking the **otmfsType** member of the **OUTLINETEXTMETRIC** structure. If bit 1 of **otmfsType** is set, embedding is not permitted for the font. If bit 1 is clear, the font can be embedded. If bit 2 is set, the embedding is read-only.

It may be a violation of a font vendor's proprietary rights and/or user license agreement to embed any fonts for which embedding is not permitted or to fail to observe the following guidelines on embedding fonts.

18.3.2.1 Embedding a Font in a Document

When an application has determined that a font can be embedded, it can use the **GetFontData** function to read the font file. (Setting the *dwTable* and *dwOffset* parameters of **GetFontData** to 0L and the *cbData* parameter to −1L ensures that the application will read the entire font file, starting at the beginning of the font).

After retrieving the font data, the application can store it with the document, using any applicable format. Most applications build a font directory in the document, listing which fonts are embedded and whether the embedding is read-write or read-only. (An application can use the **otmpStyleName** and **otmFamilyName** members of the **OUTLINETEXTMETRIC** structure to identify the font.)

If the read-only bit is set for the embedded font, applications must encrypt the font data before storing it with the document. The encryption method need not be complicated, for example, using the XOR operator to combine the font data with an application-specified constant is adequate and fast.

18.3.2.2 Installing and Using an Embedded Font

An embedded font must be separated from the containing document and installed in the user's system before Windows can use it. Although the exact procedure for separating the font from the document depends on the method the application uses to embed it, the following three steps are always taken:

1. Resolve name conflicts before installing the font.
2. Write the font data to a file, decoding read-only fonts as necessary.
3. Use the **CreateScalableFontResource** function to create a font resource file for the unembedded font.

An application should avoid installing a font with the same name as a preexisting font. To determine whether there is duplication in style names, an application could compare the information returned by **EnumFontFamilies** against the family name and style name stored with the embedded font.

Embedded fonts that have read-write permission (that is, that can be permanently installed on the user's system) should be written to a file that has the .TTF filename extension. Embedded fonts with read-only permission should not use the .TTF extension and should avoid the .FOT and .FON extensions. (A typical filename extension for read-only embedded fonts is .TTR.) Because files for read-only embedded fonts must be removed from the system and from storage as soon as the containing document is closed, their names do not need to be meaningful except to the application.

Most applications put the files for embedded fonts that have read-write permission into either the SYSTEM subdirectory of the user's Windows directory or into the application's working directory. Files for read-only embedded fonts are typically put into a temporary directory.

Before installing an embedded font, an application must use the **CreateScalable-FontResource** function to create a font resource file. Font resource files for fonts with read-write permission should use the .FOT filename extension. Font resource files for read-only fonts should use a different extension (for example, .FOR) and should be hidden from other applications in the system by specifying 1 for the first parameter of **CreateScalableFontResource**. The font resource files can be installed by using the **AddFontResource** function.

Applications should offer users the option of permanently installing embedded fonts that have read-write permission. To permanently install a font, applications should concatenate the family and style names and then use the **WriteProfile-String** function to insert this string along with the .FOT file name in the [Fonts] section of the WIN.INI file. A typical font entry in the [Fonts] section looks like this example:

Times New Roman Bold (TrueType)=TIMESBD.FOT

If a document contains one or more read-only embedded fonts, the user must not be permitted to edit the document. If the user is allowed to edit the document in any way, the application must first strip away and delete the read-only embedded fonts. As mentioned earlier, read-only embedded fonts must be removed from the system and storage immediately when the document in which they were bundled is closed.

To delete read-only embedded fonts, an application should follow these steps:

1. Call the **RemoveFontResource** function for each font to be deleted.
2. Delete the font resource file for each font.
3. Delete each TrueType font file for each font.

When an application creating a file for a read-only embedded font specifies 1 for the first parameter of the **CreateScalableFontResource** function, the **EnumFonts** and **EnumFontFamilies** functions will not enumerate this font. Hiding read-only embedded fonts in this manner makes it unlikely that another application could use them, even though Windows resources are theoretically available to all processes in Windows. If an application does use a read-only embedded font installed by another application, it could be difficult for the installing application to delete the font. The **RemoveFontResource** function will not delete a font that is currently in use. In this case, an application should delete the resource file and the TrueType font file when the user closes the document that contained the read-only fonts.

It is very important that applications delete the TrueType font file for read-only embedded fonts. If the delete operation fails when the user closes the document, the application should periodically attempt to delete the file as the application runs, when it closes, and the next time it starts.

In some cases, an application could be unable to delete a TrueType font file for a read-only embedded font because of external events (such as a system failure). There is no legal liability for events that are out of the control of the application.

18.3.3 Printer Portability

A document with printer portability is formatted identically on all output devices under Windows—all monitors and all printers. Although TrueType allows the same font to be used on all output devices, this does not guarantee that line breaks will be the same on all devices. For line breaks to match, applications must take advantage of TrueType design metrics. These design metrics allow an application to compute the fractional portion of the spacing at the ends of lines and make up the difference in the interword spacing. This computation reduces the round-off error from a half-pixel per character to a half-pixel per line, preserving line breaks in all cases.

18.3.3.1 Line Breaks and Justification

Applications must cooperate in order to guarantee the printer portability enabled by TrueType technology, because different devices may have different resolutions. Even when fonts are portable across printers, glyphs designed or rasterized for different resolutions must have different pixel widths. For applications that use the

TextOut function, for example, different character widths can lead to accumulated round-off errors that change line breaks and paragraph placement.

Applications that lay out a document at the highest printer resolution attempt to distribute any difference in character resolutions in white spaces. This method is not always successful; for example, it fails when all glyphs are one pixel larger at 600 dots per inch (DPI) than at 300 DPI. In this case, fonts with a width of 45 at 600 DPI would have a width of 23 at 300 DPI, a width of 11 at 150 DPI, and so on. There could easily be insufficient white space to absorb the glyphs at the lower resolutions if line breaks were being preserved, because the glyphs become larger in relation to the resolution of the device. In this case, the characters would have to overlap to preserve the line breaks. Even if all the character widths exactly doubled when changing from a resolution of 300 DPI to 600 DPI, the line breaks might not be the same if an application justified text—that is, aligned it on both the left and right. It is possible that another half-pixel of white space at the lower resolution would allow one more word on the line. At the higher resolution, the half-pixel would become a full pixel and the line breaks would change. (Similar device resolution problems occur in the vertical direction.) TrueType exposes the design width of characters to help applications maintain line breaks. For information about design widths, see Section 18.4.8.2, "Design Widths."

Different printers, or even different production runs of the same printer, can have different limits for their printable areas. If a document has been laid out up to the margins of one printer, it may not format identically on a different printer. If glyphs are in contact with the margins on the first printer, parts of the glyph may be beyond the printable area on the second printer. Depending on the printer, the glyph will either be clipped or dropped completely.

Prior to the introduction of TrueType, sophisticated desktop-publishing and word-processing applications were forced to "reflow" the entire document whenever a user selected a different printer. Applications can now use TrueType font metrics to solve this problem. For a description of using these metrics, see Section 18.4.8.2, "Using Portable TrueType Metrics."

18.3.3.2 Performance and Printer Portability

Printer portability can potentially downgrade font performance, quality, or both, depending on such factors as the type of connection between the computer and printer, the speed of the computer, the memory in the printer and the computer, the number of fonts being used, differing resolutions between the screen and printer, and the number of characters used in each font. Documents that are fully portable between printers necessarily cannot take advantage of the specialized features of a particular printer.

GDI cannot perform text operations to printer-compatible memory device contexts. This means that it is not possible to build a bitmap describing a page to be printed and then send the completed bitmap to the printer.

18.3.4 Document Portability

A portable document appears the same on different operating systems. In the case of TrueType, documents can be portable between Windows and the Apple Macintosh computer; this could also be called platform portability. If a document appears the same on the Macintosh and with Windows, it can also look the same imported into different applications on either platform.

Since the same TrueType fonts work on the Macintosh, in Windows, and on all devices supported by both systems, the same characters and metrics could be exposed for all applications. Currently, however, fully portable documents are not possible. Windows and the Macintosh computer have slightly different character sets. Even though TrueType fonts contain the default Macintosh and PostScript character sets, Windows does not give applications access to the Macintosh characters. Likewise, a Macintosh application cannot gain access to the Windows characters present in TrueType fonts. Document portability is also a problem with international document exchange. Localized versions of TrueType fonts will still be in use for both the Apple System 7 and Windows version 3.1, leading to further character-set incompatibilities when documents that use these fonts are transmitted to a system that does not have them.

18.3.5 Disk Space, Memory Usage, and Speed

An application's overall font performance could decrease if a large font cache forced the paging of more segments to the disk. With previous font technologies, this could occur even in situations that were not "low memory." Because fonts are cached glyph by glyph as they are used, however, less memory is used for the cache than would be required to keep the corresponding raster fonts in memory; this leads to a net performance gain. The only time the font cache uses more memory than fonts required in earlier versions of Windows is when multiple logical fonts would have been mapped to the same raster font. Typically, however, any additional swapping to disk caused by these larger caches is still faster overall than discarding and subsequently re-rendering bitmaps.

Hard-disk space is not a large problem for TrueType fonts, although more disk space is required for fonts with the introduction of TrueType. The two reasons for this increased space requirement are that raster fonts are shipped with TrueType fonts, for backward-compatibility reasons, and that users may have preexisting soft fonts on their hard disks.

Hard-disk space is not the only limitation imposed on TrueType fonts. GDI imposes an internal limit to the number of TrueType fonts that can exist simultaneously on a system. The maximum number of physical fonts is 1170. (The maximum number of logical fonts that can exist simultaneously on a system is 253.)

18.3.6 Font Design and Scaling

Raster fonts are designed to be attractive and readable at a particular aspect ratio. (The aspect ratio is the ratio of the width and height of a pixel.) The digitized aspect of a font is the ideal x-aspect and y-aspect of that font. Windows provides an aspect-ratio filter to select fonts designed for a particular aspect ratio from all of the available fonts. The **GetAspectRatioFilter** function retrieves the setting for the current aspect-ratio filter. An application can use the **SetMapperFlags** function to change the algorithm the font mapper uses when it maps physical fonts to logical fonts.

The aspect ratio of the screen is not as critical for scalable fonts as it is for raster fonts. The dimensions of the em square for a TrueType font are used when scaling the font to a specified point size. (An em square is a square whose width is approximately equal to the width of the uppercase M.) Because the height of the em square is given in pixels, it can be thought of as the point size in device units. For example, a font could be referred to as a 50-ppem (pixels per em square) font. The pixel size determines the physical point size. For example, a 75-ppem font on a 300-DPI device is an 18-point font, while on a 150-DPI device it would be a 36-point font. The number of pixels required for the desired point size is computed by using the resolution of the output device and the em square size, according to the following formula:

ppem = $(PointSize/72) * DeviceResolution$

According to this formula, a 12-point font on a 72-DPI screen is at 12 ppem, while on a 300-DPI device it is at 50 ppem.

TrueType fonts can be scaled linearly, nonlinearly, or optically, depending on their design. Linear scaling means that the character width is scaled and rounded to the appropriate ppem. Nonlinear scaling means that hinted character widths can be larger or smaller than the scaled widths. Optical scaling is a superset of nonlinear scaling; it includes the preservation of the color and contrast of a font across point sizes. Optical scaling can involve changing the proportions of the stroke widths to preserve their perceived width and color.

The TrueType fonts shipped with Windows 3.1 scale nonlinearly. Windows applications can also support linearly and optically scaled TrueType fonts.

18.3.7 Designing Portable Fonts

Most application developers need not be concerned with font-portability issues. This discussion is included here with other portability issues for those developers who need to create fonts that are portable between systems. Microsoft currently publishes a TrueType Font Files Specification, which teaches font vendors how to create a single TrueType font that will work in Windows, on the Macintosh computer, and in TrueImage.

Microsoft uses the same byte ordering in TrueType font files as Apple uses in its font files, to help make the fonts portable between the systems. As a result, Windows fonts can be moved directly to the Macintosh computer, where they can quickly be converted into font suitcases for installation. (The format of TrueType font files precisely follows the format of the Apple "sfnt" resource. To convert an MS-DOS binary TrueType font into an sfnt resource requires editing the file information, setting Type to sfnt and Creator to bass. The sfnt resource can then be integrated into a standard Macintosh font suitcase. To move a font suitcase to Windows, an application need only extract the sfnt portion from the data fork and move the suitcase, unaltered, to Windows. After the suitcase has been moved to Windows, it can be installed by using Control Panel or the **CreateScalableFontResource** and **AddFontResource** functions.

If a Macintosh font is installed that does not contain the Windows "cmap" mapping table, the system maps text fonts (for example, Times or ITC Zapf Chancery®) from the Macintosh character set onto the Windows character set. Novelty fonts (like ITC Zapf Dingbats®), which have no formal character set, are not mapped; these fonts are taken along with the Macintosh character encodings. The decision whether to remap is based on a test that looks at the "post" table (which contains PostScript names). Whenever necessary, Windows compensates for missing metric tables based on other metric data in the font; anything that cannot be computed in a reasonable manner is given a default value.

The creation of portable fonts requires more than just the right characters and the right character-mapping tables. All the metrics needed by all systems must be included and must yield the same results. Matching metrics for the individual characters is not a problem; since the characters and their hints and metrics appear only once in the TrueType font, the same metrics are available across platforms. The more difficult problems in the creation of portable fonts have to do with line-spacing metrics, the determination of font styles, and making these factors match across systems.

The Apple System 7 core TrueType fonts ship with metrics designed to be compatible with the raster fonts in System 6. The "hdmx" table will be used to force widths onto TrueType fonts that match those for the bitmaps at bitmap sizes. The "name" table (and its ability to group fonts by separating the family and subfamily names) is not used. (The name used comes from the FOND Macintosh font resource.) Only the macStyle bits (from the "head" table) denoting regular, bold, italic, or bold italic are used.

Apple's line spacing recommendations are less robust than the line-spacing used by Microsoft. The following formula defines the default recommended line spacing for a Macintosh font:

line spacing = ascent − descent + leading

The values for ascent, descent and leading come directly from TrueType values:

Macintosh	TrueType
ascent	**otmMacAscent**
descent	**otmMacDescent**
leading	**otmMacLineGap**

For its TrueType fonts, Apple recommends that Ascender – Descender = unitsPerEm, and LineGap = 0. This recommendation is based on the definition of point size for Macintosh raster fonts. Macintosh documentation defines the point size of a font as being equal to the line spacing (ascent – descent + leading). Although this definition is compatible with previous Apple font metrics, it ties line spacing to the size of the em square. Because some fonts (for example, Palatino) have ascenders and descenders that extend beyond the em square, the line-spacing definition is inconsistent for these fonts.

Windows and the Macintosh have the same default line spacing for a font only if the following formula is true:

otmMacLineGap >= (tmAscent + tmDescent) – (otmMacAscent – otmMacDescent)

Microsoft TrueType fonts follow this formula to ensure that default line spacing is preserved between the Macintosh and Windows. The core fonts and all fonts from vendors that follow the Microsoft specification will have the same character widths, the same default line spacing, and the same character forms.

Unless the Windows and Macintosh font heights are equal, a font with a line gap of zero will yield different default line spacings in Windows and on the Macintosh.

Despite some incompatibilities, TrueType and GDI accept Macintosh-only fonts. Metrics that are not present in Macintosh-only fonts are set to default values. Although these default values are imperfect, using them allows Macintosh-only fonts to work in Windows.

18.4   Using Fonts in Applications

The remainder of this chapter discusses the implementation of font functions in Windows applications.

18.4.1   Using Stock Fonts

GDI offers a variety of stock fonts that an application can retrieve and use. For many applications, the stock fonts provide all the functionality required for basic text output. To use stock fonts, an application specifies the type of font in the **GetStockObject** function. **GetStockObject** creates a handle to a logical font. When the application selects that handle into a device context, the font mapper uses the logical font to create a physical font. The application can select and use this physical font for text output.

GDI offers the following stock fonts:

Font	Description
ANSI_FIXED_FONT	Specifies a fixed-pitch font based on the Windows character set. A Courier font is typically used.
ANSI_VAR_FONT	Specifies a variable-pitch font based on the Windows character set. MS Sans Serif is typically used.
DEVICE_DEFAULT_FONT	Specifies a font preferred by the given device. Because this font depends on how the GDI font mapper interprets font requests, the font may vary widely from device to device.
OEM_FIXED_FONT	Specifies a fixed-pitch font based on an OEM character set. OEM character sets vary from system to system. For IBM computers and compatibles, the OEM font is based on the IBM PC character set.
SYSTEM_FONT	Specifies the System font. This is a variable-pitch font based on the Windows character set, and is used by the system to display window titles, menu names, and text in dialog boxes. The System font is always available. Other fonts are available only if they have been installed.

The following example retrieves a handle of the Windows variable stock font, selects it into a device context, and then writes a string using that font:

```
HFONT hfnt, hOldFont;

    hfnt = GetStockObject(ANSI_VAR_FONT);
    if (hOldFont = SelectObject(hdc, hfnt)) {
        TextOut(hdc, 10, 50, "Sample ANSI_VAR_FONT text.", 26);
        SelectObject(hdc, hOldFont);
    }
```

If no other stock fonts are available, **GetStockObject** returns a handle to the System font (SYSTEM_FONT).

Applications that use the **GetStockObject** function to retrieve the handle of a logical font should work in MM_TEXT units. The logical font identified by the handle returned by **GetStockObject** may specify a height that does not match the height of the requested logical font when the application works in mapping modes other than MM_TEXT.

18.4.2 Enumerating Fonts

An application can discover which fonts are available for a given device by using the **EnumFonts** or **EnumFontFamilies** function. These functions send information about the available fonts to a callback function that the application supplies. The callback function receives information in **LOGFONT** and **NEWTEXT-METRIC** structures. (The **NEWTEXTMETRIC** structure contains information about a TrueType font. When the callback function receives information about a non-TrueType font, the information is contained in a **TEXTMETRIC** structure.) By using this information, an application can allow the user to choose among only those fonts that are available.

The **EnumFontFamilies** function is similar to the **EnumFonts** function but includes some extra functionality. New and upgrading applications should use **EnumFontFamilies** instead of **EnumFonts**. **EnumFontFamilies** allows an application to take advantage of the style name that is available with TrueType fonts.

In previous versions of Windows, the only style attributes were weight and italic; any other styles were specified in the family name for the font. If an application used the **EnumFonts** function to query the available Courier fonts, for example, **EnumFonts** might return information for Courier, Courier Bold, Courier Bold Italic, and Courier Italic, but it would not return information about any other Courier fonts that might be installed, because any other Courier fonts would typically have a different family name.

TrueType fonts are organized around a family name (for example, Courier New) and style names (for example, italic, bold, and extra-bold). The **EnumFont-Families** function enumerates all the styles associated with a given family name, not simply the bold and italic attributes; if the system included a TrueType font called Courier New Extra-Bold, **EnumFontFamilies** would list it with the other Courier New fonts. The capabilities of **EnumFontFamilies** are helpful for fonts with many or unusual styles and for fonts that cross international borders. (Because a style name often changes with the language spoken in a country, an application that depends on the **EnumFonts** function could enumerate fonts whose names would change from country to country, while **EnumFontFamilies** would continue to enumerate the font families correctly.)

If an application does not supply a typeface name, the **EnumFonts** and **Enum-FontFamilies** functions supply information about one font in each available family. To enumerate all the fonts in a device context, an application can specify NULL for the typeface name, compile a list of the available typefaces, and then enumerate each font in each typeface.

The following example uses the **EnumFontFamilies** function to retrieve the number of available raster, vector, and TrueType fonts:

```
FONTENUMPROC lpEnumFamCallBack;
UINT uAlignPrev;
int aFontCount[] = { 0, 0, 0 };
char szCount[8];

lpEnumFamCallBack = (FONTENUMPROC) MakeProcInstance(
    (FARPROC) EnumFamCallBack, hinstApp);
EnumFontFamilies(hdc, NULL, lpEnumFamCallBack,
    (LPARAM) aFontCount);
FreeProcInstance((FARPROC) lpEnumFamCallBack);

uAlignPrev = SetTextAlign(hdc, TA_UPDATECP);

MoveTo(hdc, 10, 50);
TextOut(hdc, 0, 0, "Number of raster fonts: ", 24);
itoa(aFontCount[0], szCount, 10);
TextOut(hdc, 0, 0, szCount, strlen(szCount));

MoveTo(hdc, 10, 75);
TextOut(hdc, 0, 0, "Number of vector fonts: ", 24);
itoa(aFontCount[1], szCount, 10);
TextOut(hdc, 0, 0, szCount, strlen(szCount));

MoveTo(hdc, 10, 100);
TextOut(hdc, 0, 0, "Number of TrueType fonts: ", 26);
itoa(aFontCount[2], szCount, 10);
TextOut(hdc, 0, 0, szCount, strlen(szCount));

SetTextAlign(hdc, uAlignPrev);
    .
    .
    .

BOOL FAR PASCAL EnumFamCallBack(lplf, lpntm, FontType, aFontCount)
LPLOGFONT lplf;
LPNEWTEXTMETRIC lpntm;
short FontType;
LPSTR aFontCount;
{
    int far * aiFontCount = (int far *) aFontCount;

    if (FontType & RASTER_FONTTYPE)
        aiFontCount[0]++;
    else if (FontType & TRUETYPE_FONTTYPE)
        aiFontCount[2]++;
    else
        aiFontCount[1]++;
```

```
        if (aiFontCount[0] || aiFontCount[1] || aiFontCount[2])
            return TRUE;
        else
            return FALSE;
}
```

This example uses two masks, RASTER_FONTTYPE and TRUETYPE_FONTTYPE, to determine the type of font being enumerated. If the RASTER_FONTTYPE bit is set, the font is a raster font. If the TRUETYPE_FONTTYPE bit is set, the font is a TrueType font. If neither bit is set, the font is a vector font. A third mask, DEVICE_FONTTYPE, is set when a device (for example, a laser printer) supports downloading TrueType fonts; it is zero if the device is a display adapter, dot-matrix printer, or other raster device. An application can also use the DEVICE_FONTTYPE mask to distinguish GDI-supplied raster fonts from device-supplied fonts. GDI can simulate bold, italic, underline, and strikeout attributes for GDI-supplied raster fonts, but not for device supplied fonts.

An application can also check bit 1 and 2 in the **tmPitchandFamily** member of the **NEWTEXTMETRIC** structure to identify a TrueType font. If bit 1 is zero and bit 2 is 1, the font is a TrueType font.

Vector fonts are categorized as OEM_CHARSET instead of ANSI_CHARSET. Some applications identify vector fonts by using this information, checking the **tmCharSet** member of the **NEWTEXTMETRIC** structure. This categorization usually prevents the font mapper from choosing vector fonts unless they are specifically requested. (Most applications do not use vector fonts, because they are slow and generally unattractive, and because TrueType fonts offer many of the same scaling and rotation features that required the use of vector fonts in earlier versions of Windows.)

18.4.3 Checking a Device's Text Capabilities

Applications can use the **EnumFonts** and **EnumFontFamilies** functions to enumerate the fonts in a printer-compatible memory device context. An application can also use the **GetDeviceCaps** function to retrieve information about the text capabilities of a device. By calling the **GetDeviceCaps** function with the NUMFONTS index, an application can determine the minimum number of fonts supported by a printer. (An individual printer may support more fonts than specified in the return value from **GetDeviceCaps** with the NUMFONTS index.) By using the TEXTCAPS index, an application can identify many of the text capabilities of the specified device.

The following example uses the **GetDeviceCaps** function to determine whether a device supports text rotation:

```
    int result;

    result = GetDeviceCaps(hdc, TEXTCAPS);
    if (result & TC_CR_90)
        TextOut(hdc, 10, 100, "Device can rotate text 90 degrees", 33);
    if (result & TC_CR_ANY)
        TextOut(hdc, 10, 120, "Device can rotate text at any angle", 35);
    else if ((result & TC_CR_90) == 0 && (result & TC_CR_ANY) == 0)
        TextOut(hdc, 10, 100, "Device cannot rotate text", 25);
```

18.4.4 Creating a Logical Font

A logical font is a list of font attributes, such as height, width, character set, and typeface. An application creates a logical font to describe the font that is best suited for a given task; the font mapper uses this logical font to choose the available physical font that best matches the specified characteristics. For more information about the font mapper, see Section 18.2.5, "Font Mapper."

An application can use either the **CreateFont** or the **CreateFontIndirect** function to create a logical font. Most applications use **CreateFontIndirect**, assigning values to a **LOGFONT** structure. These functions return a handle of a logical font, which can then be selected into a device context and used.

The following example is a function that takes a handle of a device context, the name of a font, and a nominal point size as input. It creates a logical font of the requested size and face name and selects that font into the specified device context.

```
BOOL FAR PASCAL CreateLogFont(hdc, pszFace, PointSize)
HDC hdc;
PSTR pszFace;
int PointSize;
{
    HFONT hfnt, hfntOld;
    PLOGFONT plf = (PLOGFONT) LocalAlloc(GPTR, sizeof(LOGFONT));

    if (GetMapMode(hdc) != MM_TEXT) {
        TextOut(hdc, 100, -200, "Mapping mode must be MM_TEXT",
            28);
        return FALSE;
    }

    plf->lfHeight = -MulDiv(PointSize,
        GetDeviceCaps(hdc, LOGPIXELSY), 72);
    lstrcpy(plf->lfFaceName, pszFace);

    hfnt = CreateFontIndirect(plf);
```

```
        hfntOld = SelectObject(hdc, hfnt);

            .
            . /* Use font for text output. */
            .
    LocalFree((LOCALHANDLE) plf);
    SelectObject(hdc, hfntOld);
    if (DeleteObject(hfnt))
        return TRUE;
    else
        return FALSE;
}
```

Memory for the logical font in this example is allocated and initialized to zero (by using the **LocalAlloc** function with the GPTR constant); this means the logical font created by the **CreateFontIndirect** function uses default values for all members except **lfHeight** and **lfFaceName**. (Applications should always specify values for at least these two members.) For a description of all of the members of the **LOGFONT** structure, see the *Microsoft Windows Programmer's Reference, Volume 3*.

The function in this example uses the Windows **MulDiv** function to convert the specified point size into a different negative value and then assigns that value to the **lfHeight** member. This conversion is required because logical inches are larger than physical inches. (For a description of logical inches, see Section 18.2.4.2, "Logical and Physical Inches.") The **MulDiv** function multiplies the requested point size by the result of dividing the number of pixels per logical inch by the number of points in a physical inch (72). A negative value is specified for **lfHeight** to indicate that the system should interpret this value as the height of the character glyphs in the font; when a positive value is specified, GDI interprets it as the height of a font's character cells, including internal leading.

An application would use a positive value for the **lfHeight** member to choose a font that fits within a specific height. For example, to display a page in "print preview" mode, an application would retrieve the height of the printer font from the **tmHeight** member of the **NEWTEXTMETRIC** structure, scale that height to the screen resolution, and use this value for the **lfHeight** member. The formula in this case would look like this:

$$\textbf{lfHeight} = \frac{\textbf{tmHeight} * \text{DPI of screen}}{\text{DPI of printer}}$$

The results of this calculation should always be rounded down to the nearest whole number.

When an application specifies the handle of a logical font in a call to the **SelectObject** function, the font mapper returns a handle of the physical font that is the best match for the requested attributes.

An application that requires a raster font can identify the available raster fonts by calling the **EnumFontFamilies** function and checking the RASTER_FONTTYPE bit. The application can then specify the typeface name in a **LOGFONT** structure. Similarly, vector fonts can be selected by checking the RASTER_FONTTYPE and TRUETYPE_FONTTYPE bits. An application can also specify a vector font by specifying OEM_CHARSET in the **lfCharSet** member of the **LOGFONT** structure, as discussed in Section 18.4.2, "Enumerating Fonts."

An application can use TrueType fonts exclusively by specifying OUT_TT_ONLY_PRECIS in the **lfOutPrecision** member of the **LOGFONT** structure. This is important for applications that use object linking and embedding (OLE), because metafiles can be scaled much better when they use only TrueType fonts.

18.4.5 Retrieving Information About the Selected Font

Applications can retrieve font information from a device context by using the **GetTextMetrics**, **GetTextFace**, and **GetOutlineTextMetrics** functions.

The **GetTextMetrics** function copies a **TEXTMETRIC** structure into a buffer. The **TEXTMETRIC** structure contains a description of the physical font, including the average dimensions of the character cells within the font, the spacing between lines of text, the number of characters in the font, and the character set on which the font is based. An application working with TrueType fonts can call the **GetOutlineTextMetrics** function to retrieve information in an **OUTLINETEXT-METRIC** structure.

Applications often use the **TEXTMETRIC** structure to determine how much space to specify between lines of text. For example, to compute an appropriate value for single-line spacing, an application could add the values of the **tmHeight** and **tmExternalLeading** members. The **tmHeight** member specifies the height of each character cell, and **tmExternalLeading** specifies the font designer's recommended spacing between the bottom of one character cell and the top of the next. (More accurate information can be retrieved for TrueType fonts from the **OUTLINETEXTMETRIC** structure; in this case, applications can add the values of the **otmAscent**, **otmDescent**, and **otmLineGap** members.) The following example writes several lines of single-spaced text:

```
TEXTMETRIC tm;
int LineSpacing, i, YIncrement;

GetTextMetrics(hdc, &tm);
LineSpacing = tm.tmHeight + tm.tmExternalLeading;
```

```
YIncrement = 50;
for (i = 0; i < 4; i++) {
    TextOut(hdc, 10, YIncrement, "Single-line spacing", 19);
    YIncrement += LineSpacing;
}
```

The **GetTextFace** function copies a name identifying the typeface of the selected font into a buffer. An application can use this information in dialog boxes and menus.

18.4.6 Retrieving Information About a Logical Font

An application can retrieve information about a font by specifying the font handle in a call to the **GetObject** function. The **GetObject** function copies logical-font information to a **LOGFONT** structure.

The following example uses the **GetObject** function to retrieve logical-font information for a font and then checks whether the font is italic:

```
LOGFONT lf;

GetObject(hfnt, sizeof(LOGFONT), &lf);
if (lf.lfItalic)
    return TRUE;
else
    return FALSE;
```

18.4.7 Drawing Text

An application can use the following functions to draw text:

Function	Description
DrawText	Draws formatted text in a rectangle. **DrawText** formats text by expanding tabs into appropriate spaces, aligning text to the left, right, or center of the given rectangle, and breaking text into lines that fit within the given rectangle. This is not a GDI function; it is in USER.EXE.
ExtTextOut	Writes a character string within a rectangular region. The rectangular region can be opaque (filled with the current background color), and it can be a clipping region.
GrayString	Draws gray text by writing the text in a memory bitmap, graying the bitmap, and then copying the bitmap to the device. **GrayString** grays the text regardless of the selected brush and background. This is not a GDI function; it is in USER.EXE.
TabbedTextOut	Writes a character string, expanding tabs to the values specified in an array of tab-stop positions.

Function	Description
TextOut	Writes a character string at a specified location.

The **ExtTextOut** function is the fastest Windows text-output function. The **DrawText** function is the slowest (although it offers the richest formatting options).

Instead of using the **GrayString** function, an application could simply set the text color to gray, as follows:

```
dwColorPrevious = SetTextColor(hdc, GetSysColor(COLOR_GRAYTEXT));
```

18.4.7.1 Setting the Text Alignment

An application can query and set the text alignment for a device context by using the **GetTextAlign** and **SetTextAlign** functions. The text-alignment settings determine how text is positioned relative to a given location. Text can be aligned to the right or left of the position or centered over it; it can also be aligned above or below the point. In addition, an application can use the **SetTextAlign** function to update the current position when a text-output function is called.

For example, the following example uses the **SetTextAlign** function to update the current position when the **TextOut** function is called. In this example, cArial is an integer that specifies the number of Arial fonts:

```
UINT uAlignPrev;
char szCount[8];

uAlignPrev = SetTextAlign(hdc, TA_UPDATECP);
MoveTo(hdc, 10, 50);
TextOut(hdc, 0, 0, "Number of Arial fonts: ", 23);
itoa(cArial, szCount, 10);
TextOut(hdc, 0, 0, (LPSTR) szCount, strlen(szCount));
SetTextAlign(hdc, uAlignPrev);
```

18.4.7.2 Using Color

When an application first creates a device context, the text color is black and the background color is white. An application can add color to text by setting the text and background colors of the device context. The text color determines the color of the character to be written; the background color determines the color of everything in the character cell except the character.

An application can set the text and background colors by using the **SetTextColor** and **SetBkColor** functions. The following example sets the text color to red and the background color to green:

```
SetTextColor(hdc, RGB(255,0,0));
SetBkColor(hdc, RGB(0,255,0));
```

The background color applies only when the background mode is opaque. The background mode determines whether the background color in the character cell has any effect on what is already on the screen. If the mode is opaque, the background color overwrites anything already on the screen; if the mode is transparent, anything on the screen that would otherwise be overwritten by the background is preserved. The background color for an italic string that GDI has synthesized is sheared along with the characters; this can lead to unexpected results when the text background color is different from the window background color. An application can set and retrieve the background mode by using the **SetBkMode** function and **GetBkMode** functions. Similarly, an application can retrieve the current text and background color by using the **GetTextColor** and **GetBkColor** functions.

18.4.7.3 Using Multiple Fonts in a Line

Different type styles within a font family can have different widths. For example, bold and italic styles of a family are always wider than the roman style for a given point size. An application that can display or print several type styles on a single line must keep track of the width of the line to avoid having characters print on top of one another.

An application can use the following functions to retrieve the width (or extent) of text in the current font:

Function	Description
GetTabbedTextExtent	Computes the width and height of a character string. If the string contains one or more tab characters, the width of the string is based upon a specified array of tab-stop positions.
GetTextExtent	Computes the width and height of a line of text.

When necessary, GDI synthesizes a font by changing the character bitmaps. To synthesize a character in a bold font, GDI draws the character twice: once at the starting point, and again one pixel to the right of the starting point. To synthesize a character in an italic font, GDI draws the two rows of pixels at the bottom of the character cell, moves the starting point one pixel to the right, draws the next two rows, and continues until the character has been drawn. The base line of a synthesized italic character is shifted to the right by an amount determined by the height of the character cell. To determine the amount a base line is shifted to the right, an application can perform the following calculation, using values retrieved by a call to the **GetTextMetrics** function:

units base line shifted right = (**tmDescent** * **tmOverhang**) / **tmAscent**

One way to write a line of text that contains multiple fonts is to use the **GetText-Extent** function after each call to **TextOut** and add the length to a current position. The following example writes the line "This is a sample string.", using bold characters for the words "This is a", italic characters for the word "sample", and system default characters for "string.":

```
int XIncrement;
TEXTMETRIC tm;
HFONT hfntDefault, hfntItalic, hfntBold;

XIncrement = 10;
hfntDefault = SelectObject(hdc, hfntBold);
TextOut(hdc, XIncrement, 50, "This is a ", 10);

XIncrement += LOWORD(GetTextExtent(hdc, "This is a ", 10));
GetTextMetrics(hdc, &tm);
XIncrement -= tm.tmOverhang;
SelectObject(hdc, hfntItalic);
GetTextMetrics(hdc, &tm);
XIncrement -= tm.tmOverhang;
TextOut(hdc, XIncrement, 50, "sample ", 7);

XIncrement += LOWORD(GetTextExtent(hdc, "sample ", 7));
SelectObject(hdc, hfntDefault);
TextOut(hdc, XIncrement - tm.tmOverhang, 50, "string.", 7);
```

In this example, the **GetTextExtent** function returns a 32-bit value (of type **DWORD**) containing both the length and height of the specified string. The **LOWORD** macro then retrieves the length of the string, which is added to the current position. The **GetTextMetrics** function retrieves the overhang for the current font. Because the overhang is zero if the font is a TrueType font, the overhang value does not change the string placement in that case. For raster fonts, however, it is important to use the overhang value. (For more information about overhangs, see Section 18.1.3, "Measuring Line and Intercharacter Spacing.") The overhang is subtracted from the bold string once, to bring subsequent characters closer to the end of the string if the font is a raster font. Because overhang affects both the beginning and end of the italic string in a raster font, the glyphs begin to the right of the specified location and end to the left of the endpoint of the last character cell. (The **GetTextExtent** function retrieves the extent of the character cells, not the extent of the glyphs.) To account for the overhang for the raster italic string, this example subtracts the overhang before placing the string and subtracts it again before placing subsequent characters.

An application that must place characters with greater precision can use the **Get-CharWidth** or **GetCharABCWidths** function to retrieve the widths of individual characters in a font. The **GetCharABCWidths** function is more accurate than the **GetCharWidth** function, but only when it is used with TrueType fonts; when **Get-CharABCWidths** is used with non-TrueType fonts, it retrieves the same information as **GetCharWidth**.

The **SetTextJustification** function adds extra space to the break characters in a line of text. An application can use the **GetTextExtent** function to determine the extent of a string, subtract the extent from the total amount of space the line should occupy, and use the **SetTextJustification** function to distribute the extra space among the break characters in the string. The **SetTextCharacterExtra** function adds extra space to every character cell in the selected font, including the break character. (An application can use the **GetTextCharacterExtra** function to determine the current amount of extra space being added to the character cells; the default setting is zero.)

ABC spacing also allows an application to perform very accurate text alignment. For example, when an application right aligns a raster roman font without using ABC spacing, the advance width is calculated as the character width. This means the white space to the right of the glyph in the bitmap is aligned, not the glyph itself. By using ABC widths, applications have more flexibility in the placement and removal of white space when aligning text, because they have information that allows them to finely control intercharacter spacing.

18.4.7.4 Rotating Text

Applications can rotate TrueType fonts at any angle. This is useful for labeling charts and other illustrations. The following example rotates a string in 10-degree increments around the center of the client area by changing the value of the **lfEscapement** member of the **LOGFONT** structure used to create the font:

```
RECT rc;
int angle;
HFONT hfnt, hfntPrev;
LPSTR lpszRotate = "String to be rotated.";
PLOGFONT plf = (PLOGFONT) LocalAlloc(LPTR, sizeof(LOGFONT));

lstrcpy(plf->lfFaceName, "Arial");
plf->lfWeight = 700;

GetClientRect(hwnd, &rc);
SetBkMode(hdc, TRANSPARENT);

for (angle = 0; angle < 3600; angle += 100) {
    plf->lfEscapement = angle;
    hfnt = CreateFontIndirect(plf);
    hfntPrev = SelectObject(hdc, hfnt);
    TextOut(hdc, rc.right / 2, rc.bottom / 2,
        lpszRotate, lstrlen(lpszRotate));
    SelectObject(hdc, hfntPrev);
    DeleteObject(hfnt);
}

SetBkMode(hdc, OPAQUE);
LocalFree((LOCALHANDLE) plf);
```

This example produces the following pattern:

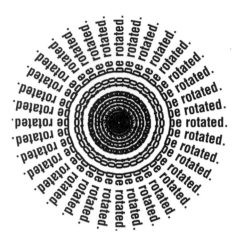

The **lfOrientation** member of the **LOGFONT** structure is ignored by GDI, which currently, assumes that the values for **lfEscapement** and **lfOrientation** are identical.

18.4.8 TrueType Font Functions and Structures

Some of the functions and structures that allow an application to take advantage of the extra functionality of TrueType are discussed elsewhere in this chapter. This section describes some of the TrueType functions that are useful for applications that must take full advantage of the new font technology.

18.4.8.1 Retrieving Character Outlines

Applications can use the **GetGlyphOutline** function to retrieve the outline of a glyph from a TrueType font. **GetGlyphOutline** returns the outline as a bitmap or as a series of polylines and splines.

When an application retrieves a glyph outline as a series of polylines and splines, the information is returned in a **TTPOLYGONHEADER** structure followed by as many **TTPOLYCURVE** structures as are required to describe the glyph. All points are returned as **POINTFX** structures and represent absolute positions, not relative moves. The starting point given by the **pfxStart** member of the **TTPOLYGONHEADER** structure is the point at which the outline for a contour begins. The **TTPOLYCURVE** structures that follow can be either polyline records or spline records. Polyline records are a series of points; lines drawn between the points describe the outline of the character. Spline records represent the quadratic curves used by TrueType (that is, quadratic b-splines).

Each polyline and spline record contains as many sequential points as possible, to minimize the number of records returned.

The starting point given in the **TTPOLYGONHEADER** structure is always on the outline of the glyph. The specified point is both the starting point and the ending point for the contour.

A polyline record begins with the last point in the previous record (or with the starting point, for the first record in the contour). Each point in the record is on the glyph outline and can be connected simply by using straight lines.

A spline record begins with the last point in the previous record (or with the starting point, for the first record in the contour). For the first spline record, the starting point and the last point in the record are on the glyph outline. For all other spline records, only the last point is on the glyph outline. All other points in the spline records are off the glyph outline and must be rendered as the control points of b-splines.

The last spline or polyline record in a contour always ends with the contour's starting point. This ensures that every contour is closed.

Because b-splines require three points (one point that is off the glyph outline between two that are on the outline), applications must perform some calculations when a spline record contains more than one off-curve point.

For example, if a spline record contains three points (A, B, and C) and it is not the first record, points A and B are off the glyph outline. To interpret point A, an application can use the current position (which is always on the glyph outline) and the point on the glyph outline between points A and B. To find this point between A and B, the application can perform the following calculation:

$$M = A + (B - A) / 2$$

The midpoint between consecutive off-outline points in a spline record is a point that is on the glyph outline, according to the definition of the spline format used in TrueType fonts. In preceding formula, M is the midpoint on the line between points A and B.

If the current position is designated by P, the two quadratic splines defined by this spline record are (P, A, M) and (M, B, C).

To render a TrueType character outline in GDI, an application must use both the polyline and the spline records. GDI can render polylines easily, but it does not support any spline formats. To use the spline records, an application must convert them into a series of polylines that approximate the spline.

The glyph outline returned by the **GetGlyphOutline** function is for a grid-fitted glyph. (A grid-fitted glyph has been modified so that its bitmap image conforms as closely as possible to the original design of the glyph.) If an application requires an unmodified glyph outline, it should request the glyph outline for a character in a font whose size is equal to the font's em units. (To create a font with this size, an application can set the **lfHeight** member of the **LOGFONT** structure to the negative of the value of the **ntmSizeEM** member of the **NEWTEXTMETRIC** structure.)

18.4.8.2 Using Portable TrueType Metrics

Applications that use the TrueType font metrics can achieve a high degree of printer and document portability. Applications that must maintain compatibility with earlier versions of Windows can use the TrueType metrics, as can applications that are written specifically for Windows version 3.1.

Design Widths   Design widths overcome most of the problems of device-dependent text introduced by physical devices. Design widths are a kind of logical width. Independent of any rasterization problems or scaling transformations, each glyph has a logical width and height. Composed to a logical page, each character in a string has a place independent of the physical device widths. Although a logical width implies that widths can be scaled linearly at all point sizes, this is not necessarily true for either nonportable or most TrueType fonts. At smaller point sizes, some glyphs are made wider relative to their height for better readability.

The characters in TrueType core fonts are designed against a 2048-by-2048 grid. The design width is the width of a character in these grid units. (TrueType supports any integer grid size up to 16,384 by 16,384; grid sizes that are integer powers of 2 scale faster than other grid sizes.)

The outline of a font is designed in notional units. The em square is the notional grid against which the font outline is fitted. (The **otmEMSquare** member of **OUTLINETEXTMETRIC** and the **ntmSizeEM** member of **NEWTEXT-METRIC** give the size of the em square in notional units.) When a font is created that has a point size (in device units) equal to the size of its em square, the ABC widths for this font are the desired design widths. For example, if the size of an em square is 1000 and the ABC widths of a character in the font are 150, 400, and 150, a character in this font that has a height of 10 in device units would have ABC widths of 1.5, 4, and 1.5, respectively. Since the MM_TEXT mapping mode is most commonly used with fonts (and MM_TEXT is equivalent to device units), this is a simple calculation.

Because of the high resolution of TrueType design widths, applications that use them must take into account the large numeric values that can be created.

Device vs. Design Units   Portable metrics in fonts are known as design units. To apply to a given device, design units must be converted to device units. An application can use the following formula to convert design units to device units:

$$DeviceUnits = (DesignUnits/unitsPerEm) * (PointSize/72) * DeviceResolution$$

The variables in this formula have the following meanings:

Variable	Description
DeviceUnits	Specifies the *DesignUnits* font metric converted to device units. This value is in the same units as the value given for *Device-Resolution*.
DesignUnits	Specifies the font metric to be converted to device units. This value could be any font metric, including the width of a character or the ascender value for an entire font.
unitsPerEm	Specifies the em square size for the font.
PointSize	Specifies size of the font in points. (One point equals 1/72 of an inch.)
DeviceResolution	Specifies number of device units (pixels) per inch. Typical values might be 300 for a laser printer or 96 for a VGA screen.

Note   This formula should not be used to convert device units back to design units. Device units are always rounded to the nearest pixel. The propagated round-off error can become very large, especially when an application is working with screen sizes.

Requesting Design-Unit Metrics .   Font metrics for a physical font can be retrieved only after a font has been selected into a device context. When a font is selected into a device context, it is scaled for the device, which makes the font metrics specific to the device. To request design units, an application should create a logical font whose height is specified as *–unitsPerEm*. Applications can retrieve the value for *unitsPerEm* by calling the **EnumFontFamilies** function and checking the **ntmSizeEM** member of the **NEWTEXTMETRIC** structure.

Metrics for Portable Documents   The following table specifies the most important font metrics for applications that require portable documents and the functions that allow an application to retrieve them:

Function	Metric	Use
EnumFontFamilies	**ntmSizeEM**	Retrieving design metrics; conversion to device metrics

Function	Metric	Use
GetCharABCWidths	**ABCWidths**	Accurate placement of characters at the start and end of margins, picture boundaries, and other text breaks
GetCharWidth	**AdvanceWidths**	Placement of characters on a line. (This function is not new for Windows 3.1.)
GetOutlineTextMetrics	**otmfsType**	Font-embedding bits
	otmsCharSlopeRise	Y-component for slope of cursor for italic fonts
	otmsCharSlopeRun	X-component for slope of cursor for italic fonts
	otmAscent	Line spacing
	otmDescent	Line spacing
	otmLineGap	Line spacing
	otmpFamilyName	Font identification
	otmpStyleName	Font identification
	otmpFullName	Font identification (typically, family and style name)

The **otmsCharSlopeRise**, **otmsCharSlopeRun**, **otmAscent**, **otmDescent**, and **otmLineGap** members of the **OUTLINETEXTMETRIC** structure are scaled or transformed to correspond to the current device mode and physical height (as given in the **tmHeight** member of the **NEWTEXTMETRIC** structure).

Font identification is important if the same font must be selected when a document is reopened or moved to a different system. The font mapper always selects the correct font when it is asked for by full name. The family and style names are needed in order to provide input to the standard font dialog box for proper placement of the selection bars.

The **otmsCharSlopeRise** and **otmsCharSlopeRun** values are used to produce a close approximation of the main italic angle of the font. For typical roman fonts, **otmsCharSlopeRise** is 1 and **otmsCharSlopeRun** is 0. For italic fonts, the values attempt to approximate the sine and cosine of the main italic angle of the font (in counterclockwise degrees past vertical); note that the italic angle for upright fonts is 0. Because these values are not expressed in design units, they should not be converted into device units.

The character placement and line spacing metrics allow an application to compute device-independent line breaks that are portable across screens, printers, typesetters, and even platforms. If all applications adopt these techniques, documents moved from one application to another will not reflow.

Device-independent page layout requires seven basic steps:

1. Normalize all design metrics to a common ultra-high resolution (UHR) value (for example, 65,536 DPI); this prevents round-off errors.

2. Compute line breaks based on UHR metrics and physical page width; this yields a starting point and an ending point of a line within the text stream.

3. Compute the device page width in device units (for example, pixels).

4. Fit each line of text into the device page width, using the line breaks computed in step 2.

5. Compute page breaks by using UHR metrics and the physical page length; this yields the number of lines per page.

6. Compute the line heights in device units.

7. Fit the lines of text onto the page, using the lines per page from step 5 and the line heights from step 6.

18.4.8.3 Panose Numbers

TrueType font files include Panose numbers, which applications can use to choose a font that closely matches their specifications. The Panose system classifies faces by 10 different attributes. These attributes are each rated on a scale. The resulting values are concatenated to produce a number. Given this number for a font and a mathematical metric to measure distances in the Panose space, an application can determine nearest neighbors. A **PANOSE** structure is part of the **OUTLINE-TEXTMETRIC** structure (whose values are filled in by calling the **GetOutline-TextMetrics** function).

18.4.9 Creating Customized Fonts

GDI keeps a system font table containing all the fonts that applications can use. GDI chooses a font from this table when an application calls the **CreateFont** or **CreateFontIndirect** function. There can be up to 253 entries in the system font table.

A font resource is a group of individual fonts representing characters in a given character set that have various combinations of heights, widths, and pitches. Applications can load font resources and add the fonts in the resource to the system font table by using the **AddFontResource** function. After a font resource has been added, the application can use the individual fonts in the resource. In other words, the **CreateFont** function takes the fonts into account when it tries to match a physical font with the specified logical font. (Fonts in the system font table are never directly accessible to an application. They are available only through the **CreateFontIndirect** and **CreateFont** functions, which return handles of the fonts, not memory addresses.)

An application can add a font resource to the system font table by using the **Add-FontResource** function. To remove a font resource, an application can use the **RemoveFontResource** function.

Whenever an application adds or removes a font resource, it should inform all other applications of the change by sending a WM_FONTCHANGE message to them. An application can use the following call to the **SendMessage** function to send the message to all windows:

```
SendMessage(HWND_BROADCAST, WM_FONTCHANGE, 0, 0);
```

An application can use the **GetProfileString** function to retrieve a list of any fonts the user has used Control Panel to install. The application would use **GetProfile-String** to search the [Fonts] section of the WIN.INI file.

An application can create font resources by creating font files and adding them as resources to a font resource file. To create a font resource file, an application should follow these steps:

1. Create the font files.
2. Create a resource-definition file for the font.
3. Create a dummy code module.
4. Create a module-definition file that describes the fonts and the devices that use the fonts.
5. Compile and link the sources.

A font resource file is an empty Windows dynamic-link library; it contains no code or data, but does contain resources. An application can add a font file to an empty library, along with such resources as icons, cursors, and menus, by using Microsoft Windows Resource Compiler (RC).

18.4.9.1 Creating Font Files

An application can create raster font files by using Microsoft Windows Font Editor (FONTEDIT.EXE), as described in *Microsoft Windows Programming Tools*. (Font Editor cannot be used to generate vector or TrueType fonts.) The application can use any number, size, and type of font files in a font resource. In most cases, enough fonts should be included to reasonably satisfy most logical-font requests for the target device.

GDI can scale device-independent raster fonts by 1 to 8 times vertically and 1 to 5 times horizontally. GDI can also simulate bold, underlined, strikeout, and italic fonts. Font designers may choose to allow GDI to synthesize some sizes and properties of a font, rather than providing separate font files.

Font Editor modifies existing .FNT files; it cannot create font files from scratch. The Microsoft Windows 3.1 Software Development Kit (SDK) includes two .FNT files that font designers can load into Font Editor, modify, and save as customized fonts. The file named ATRM1111.FNT is a fixed-width font. The file named VGASYS.FNT is a variable-width font.

The Save As dialog box in Font Editor includes two File Format radio buttons. Font files saved in Font Editor 3.0 format can be used only in 386 enhanced mode. Font files saved in Font Editor 2.0 format can be used in all modes.

18.4.9.2 Creating the Resource-Definition File for a Font

An application can add resources to a font file by adding one or more **FONT** statements to the resource-definition file. The resource-definition file can add .FNT files to a Windows library, a device driver, or a resource-only file that contains only icons, cursor, fonts, and other resources. Because font resources are available to all applications, they should not be added to application modules.

The **FONT** statement has the following form:

number **FONT** *filename*

One statement is required for each font file to be placed in the resource. The *number* must be unique, because it is used to identify the font later. The following is a typical resource-definition file for a font resource:

```
1   FONT FNTFIL01.FNT
2   FONT FNTFIL02.FNT
3   FONT FNTFIL03.FNT
4   FONT FNTFIL04.FNT
5   FONT FNTFIL05.FNT
6   FONT FNTFIL06.FNT
```

You can add fonts to modules that contain other resources by adding them to the existing resource-definition file. An application can have icon, menu, cursor, and dialog box definitions in the resource-definition file, as well as **FONT** statements.

18.4.9.3 Creating a Dummy Code Module

A dummy code module provides the object file from which the font resource file is made. A developer can create the dummy code module by using the assembler and the Cmacros. The module's source file could look like this:

```
TITLE   FONTRES - Stub file to build a .FON resource file

.xlist
include cmacros.inc
.list
```

```
sBegin CODE
db 0
sEnd    CODE
end
```

Microsoft Segmented Executable Linker LINK version 4 allows empty code segments, but LINK versions 5.12 and later does not. The inclusion of "db 0" between sBegin and sEnd in the preceding example prevents an empty code segment.

The developer can assemble this source file by using the **masm** command. The object file that will be created will contain no code and no data, but it can be linked to an empty Windows library to which the font resources can be added.

Developers who build font files using version 6.0 of Microsoft Macro Assembler (ML) should use version 5.3 of the CMACROS.INC file (included with ML) instead of version 5.2 of the file, which is included with the SDK.

18.4.9.4 Creating a Module-Definition File

The module-definition file for the font resource must contain a **LIBRARY** statement that defines the resource name, a **DESCRIPTION** statement that describes the font resource characteristics, and a **DATA** statement. The module-definition file for a font resource should look like this:

```
LIBRARY FONTRES

DESCRIPTION 'FONTRES 133,96,72 : System, Terminal (Set #3)'

EXETYPE WINDOWS

STUB 'WINSTUB.EXE'
DATA NONE
```

The **DESCRIPTION** statement provides device-specific information about the font that is used to match a font with a given screen or printer. The following are the three possible formats for the **DESCRIPTION** statement in a font resource. In each case, the first characters in the description must be a single quote and the name of the library module (FONTRES):

DESCRIPTION 'FONTRES *Aspect*, *LogPixelsX*, *LogPixelsY*: *Cmt*'
DESCRIPTION 'FONTRES CONTINUOUSSCALING: *Cmt*'
DESCRIPTION 'FONTRES DEVICESPECIFIC *DeviceTypeGroup*: *Cmt*'

The first format specifies a font that was designed for a specific aspect ratio and logical pixel width and height, and can be used with any device having the same aspect and logical pixel dimensions. *Aspect* is the value $(100*AspectY)/AspectX$ rounded to an integer. The *AspectX*, *AspectY*, *LogPixelsX*, and *LogPixelsY* values are the same as the values given in the corresponding device's **GDIINFO** structure (values that are accessible by using the **GetDeviceCaps** function). You can specify more than one set of *Aspect*, *LogPixelsX*, and *LogPixelsY* values. The *Cmt* value is a comment. The following statements are examples:

```
DESCRIPTION 'FONTRES 133,96,72: System, Terminal (Set #3)'
DESCRIPTION 'FONTRES 200,96,48; 133,96,72; 83,60,72; 167,120,72: \
    MS Sans Serif'
```

The second format specifies a continuous scaling font. This typically corresponds to vector fonts that can be drawn to any size and that do not depend on the aspect or logical pixel width of the output device. The following statement is an example:

```
DESCRIPTION 'FONTRES CONTINUOUSSCALING : Modern, Roman, Script'
```

The third format specifies a font that is specific to a particular device or group of devices. The *DeviceTypeGroup* can be **DISPLAY** or a list of device-type names— the same names an application might specify as the second parameter in a call to the **CreateDC** function. Following is an example of the third format:

```
DESCRIPTION 'FONTRES DISPLAY: HP 7470 plotters'
DESCRIPTION 'FONTRES DEVICESPECIFIC HP 7470A, HP 7475A: \
    HP 7470 plotters'
```

Note The maximum length of a **DESCRIPTION** line is 127 characters. Because GDI is capable of synthesizing attributes, such as bold, italic, and underline, the font designer need not create separate .FNT files for fonts with these attributes. Windows may use other fonts that do not correspond to the user's screen aspect ratio. These are generic raster fonts that are intended for output devices such as bit-map printers, which rely on the display driver to draw text.

18.4.9.5 Compiling and Linking a Font Resource File

The following makefile lists the commands required to compile and link a font re-source file:

```
fontres.obj: fontres.asm
    masm fontres;

fontres.exe: fontres.def fontres.obj fontres.rc fontres.exe \
            fntfil01.fnt fntfil02.fnt fntfil03.fnt \
            fntfil04.fnt fntfil05.fnt fntfil06.fnt
    link fontres.obj, fontres.exe, NUL, /nod, fontres.def
    rc fontres.rc
    rename fontres.exe custom.fon
```

By convention, all raster font resource files have the .FON filename extension. The last line in the makefile renames the executable file to CUSTOM.FON.

18.4.9.6 Adding TrueType Fonts

Because Windows cannot directly interpret the native TrueType font file format, a file that mimics the standard .FON file (called a .FOT file) is required to make internal bookkeeping and enumeration easier. The **CreateScalableFontResource** function produces a .FOT file that points to the TrueType font file. Once this .FOT file is produced, Windows applications can use TrueType fonts transparently by using the **AddFontResource** and **RemoveFontResource** functions. Applications could also use the **CreateScalableFontResource** function to install special fonts for logos, icons, and other graphics.

18.5 Related Topics

For more information about functions used with TrueType fonts, see the *Microsoft Windows Programmer's Reference, Volume 2*.

Color Palettes

Color palettes in the Microsoft Windows operating system provide an interface between an application and a color output device (such as a display device). Through this interface the application can take full advantage of the color capabilities of the output device without severely interfering with the colors displayed by other applications. Windows takes color information contained in an application's logical palette (a graphics object that is essentially a list of colors needed by the application) and applies it to a system palette (the list of colors that is available on the system and that is shared by all Windows applications). When more than one application displays colors from a logical palette, Windows intervenes, controlling which application has primary access to the system palette and maintaining a high level of color quality for the remaining applications.

This chapter covers the following topics:

- Creating a logical palette for your application and preparing it for use
- Using colors in the palette for painting in a window's client area
- Making changes in your logical palette and controlling when Windows displays those changes
- Responding to changes in the system palette made by other applications

19.1 What a Color Palette Does

Many color graphics adapters (screens) are capable of displaying a wide range of colors. In most cases, however, the number of colors that the screen can render at any given time is more limited. For example, a screen that is potentially able to produce 26,000 different colors may be able to show only 256 of those colors simultaneously, because of hardware limitations. When such a limitation exists, the device often maintains a palette of colors. When an application requests a color that is not currently displayed, the device adds the requested color to the palette. However, when the number of requested colors exceeds the maximum number for the device, it maps the requested color to an existing color; this means the colors displayed are different from the colors requested. When this happens, the system attempts to replace requested colors with similar existing colors, so the difference between the requested colors and the displayed colors is often small.

Windows color palettes provide a buffer between a color-intensive application and the system. A color palette allows an application to use as many colors as are necessary without interfering with colors displayed by other windows. When a window uses a color palette and has the input focus, Windows ensures that it will display all the colors it requests, up to the maximum number available simultaneously on the screen, and displays additional colors by matching them to available colors. In addition, Windows matches the colors requested by inactive windows as closely as possible to the available colors. This reduces undesirable changes in what colors are displayed in inactive windows.

19.2 How a Color Palette Works

Windows provides a device-independent method for accessing the color capabilities of a display device by managing the device's system palette, if the device has one.

As noted previously, your application employs the system palette by creating and using one or more logical palettes. A logical palette is a graphics device interface (GDI) object that specifies the colors to be drawn in the device context. Each entry in the palette contains a specific color. When performing graphics operations, the application does not indicate which color is to be displayed by supplying an explicit red, green, blue (RGB) value. Instead, the application accesses the palette either directly or indirectly. Using the direct method, it indicates which color to use in your logical palette by specifying an index into the palette entries. Using the indirect method, you specify a palette-relative RGB value similar to an explicit RGB value. For a more complete description of these two methods, see Sections 19.4.1, "Directly Specifying Palette Colors," and 19.4.2, "Indirectly Specifying Palette Colors."

When a window requests that the system use the colors in the window's logical palette (a process known as realizing the window's palette), Windows first exactly matches entries in the logical palette to current entries in the system palette.

If it cannot make an exact match for a given logical-palette entry, Windows sets the entry in the logical palette into an unused entry in the system palette.

Finally, when all entries in the system palette have been used, Windows matches logical-palette entries as closely as possible to entries in the system palette. Windows sets aside 20 static colors (called the default palette) in the system palette to aid this color matching.

Windows always satisfies the color requests of the foreground window first; this ensures that the active window will have the best color display. For the remaining windows, Windows satisfies the color requests of the window that most recently received the input focus, and so on. This process is shown in the following figure:

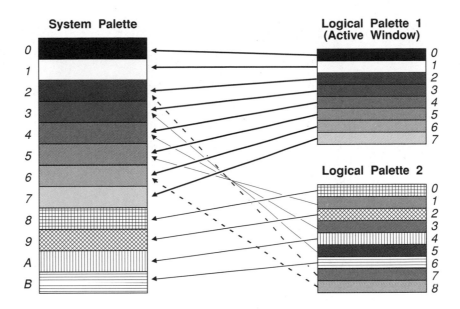

In this figure, a hypothetical screen has a system palette capable of containing 12 colors. The application that created Logical Palette 1, which contains 8 colors, owns the active window and was the first to realize its logical palette. Logical Palette 2, which contains 9 colors, is owned by a window that realized its logical palette while it was inactive. Because the active window was active when it realized its palette, Windows mapped all of the colors in Logical Palette 1 directly to the system palette.

Colors 1, 3, and 5 in Logical Palette 2 are identical to colors in the system palette. When the second application realized its logical palette, Windows simply matched those colors to the existing system colors to save space in the palette. Colors 0, 2, 4, and 6 of Logical Palette 2 were not already in the system palette, however, so Windows mapped those colors into the system palette.

Colors 7 and 8 in Logical Palette 2 do not exactly match colors in the system palette. Because the system palette was full, Windows could not map these 2 colors into the system palette. Instead, it matched them to the closest colors in the system palette.

19.3 Creating and Using a Logical Palette

To use a logical palette, your application must first perform four steps:

1. Create a **LOGPALETTE** structure that describes the palette.
2. Create the palette itself.
3. Select the palette into a device context.
4. Realize the palette.

19.3.1 Creating a LOGPALETTE Structure

The **LOGPALETTE** structure describes the logical palette you plan to use. It contains the following information:

- A Windows version number (for Windows versions 3.0 and 3.1, this value should be 0x300)
- The number of entries in the palette
- An array of **PALETTEENTRY** structures, each of which contains 1-byte values for red, green, and blue, and a flags member named **peFlags**. The **peFlags** member can be set to one of the following values:
  - NULL
  - PC_EXPLICIT
  - PC_NOCOLLAPSE
  - PC_RESERVED

Specifying NULL for the **peFlags** member informs Windows that the palette entry contains an RGB value and that it should be mapped normally.

Setting the PC_EXPLICIT flag indicates to Windows that the palette entry does not contain color values; instead, the low-order word of the entry specifies an index into the system palette.

Setting the PC_NOCOLLAPSE flag indicates to Windows that the color will be placed in an unused entry in the system palette instead of being matched to an existing color in the system palette. Once this color is in the system palette, colors in other logical palettes can be matched to this color. If there are no unused entries in the system palette, the color is matched normally.

An application sets PC_RESERVED in a palette entry when it is going to animate the entry (that is, change it dynamically by using the **AnimatePalette** function). Setting this flag prevents Windows from attempting to match colors from other logical palettes to this color while the entry is mapped to the system palette.

The ShowDIB code sample creates its **LOGPALETTE** structure as follows:

```
#define PALETTESIZE        256
        .
        .
        .

/* Make space for the logical palette. */

pLogPal = (NPLOGPALETTE) LocalAlloc(LMEM_FIXED,
    (sizeof(LOGPALETTE) + (sizeof(PALETTEENTRY) * (PALETTESIZE)))));
```

ShowDIB initializes the palette structure with 256 entries; however, you can make a palette any size you need.

ShowDIB fills in the palette entries by opening a bitmap (.BMP) file and copying the color values in the **BITMAPINFO** structure's color table to the corresponding palette entries:

```
HPALETTE CreateBIPalette(lpbi)
LPBITMAPINFOHEADER lpbi;
{
    LOGPALETTE  *pPal;
    HPALETTE    hpal = NULL;
    WORD        nNumColors;
    BYTE        red;
    BYTE        green;
    BYTE        blue;
    int         i;
    RGBQUAD     FAR *pRgb;

    if (!lpbi)
        return NULL;

    if (lpbi->biSize != sizeof(BITMAPINFOHEADER))
        return NULL;

    /*
     * Retrieve a pointer to the color table, and retrieve the
     * number of colors in the table.
     */

    pRgb = (RGBQUAD FAR *) ((LPSTR) lpbi + (WORD) lpbi->biSize);
    nNumColors = DibNumColors(lpbi);

    if (nNumColors) {

        /* Allocate memory for the logical-palette structure. */

        pPal = (LOGPALETTE*) LocalAlloc(LPTR, sizeof(LOGPALETTE) +
            nNumColors * sizeof(PALETTEENTRY));
```

```
        if (!pPal)
            return NULL;

        pPal->palNumEntries = nNumColors;
        pPal->palVersion = 0x300;

/*
 * Fill in the palette entries from the DIB color table and
 * create a logical color palette.
 */

        for (i = 0; i < nNumColors; i++) {
            pPal->palPalEntry[i].peRed   = pRgb[i].rgbRed;
            pPal->palPalEntry[i].peGreen = pRgb[i].rgbGreen;
            pPal->palPalEntry[i].peBlue  = pRgb[i].rgbBlue;
            pPal->palPalEntry[i].peFlags = (BYTE) 0;
        }
        hpal = CreatePalette(pPal);
        LocalFree((HANDLE) pPal);
    }
    else if (lpbi->biBitCount == 24) {

        /*
         * A 24-bitcount DIB has no color-table entries, so set
         * the number of entries to the maximum value (256).
         */

        nNumColors = MAXPALETTE;
        pPal = (LOGPALETTE*) LocalAlloc(LPTR, sizeof(LOGPALETTE) +
            nNumColors * sizeof(PALETTEENTRY));
        if (!pPal)
            return NULL;

        pPal->palNumEntries = nNumColors;
        pPal->palVersion = 0x300;

        red = green = blue = 0;

        /*
         * Generate 256 (= 8*8*4) RGB combinations to fill the
         * palette entries.
         */

        for (i = 0; i < pPal->palNumEntries; i++) {
            pPal->palPalEntry[i].peRed   = red;
            pPal->palPalEntry[i].peGreen = green;
            pPal->palPalEntry[i].peBlue  = blue;
            pPal->palPalEntry[i].peFlags = (BYTE) 0;
```

```
                    if (!(red += 32))
                        if (!(green += 32))
                            blue += 64;
            }
            hpal = CreatePalette(pPal);
            LocalFree((HANDLE) pPal);
        }
        return hpal;
}
```

ShowDIB first calls the DibNumColors function to determine the number of colors in the color table. If there is a color table (that is, the **biBitCount** member is not 24), it copies the **RGBQUAD** values in each **bmiColors** member in the **BITMAPINFO** structure to the corresponding palette entry. If there is no color table, ShowDIB creates a palette of 256 entries containing a spread of colors. When ShowDIB displays the bitmap, Windows matches the colors in the bitmap to the colors in this spread.

19.3.2 Creating a Logical Palette

After the application has created the **LOGPALETTE** structure, the next step is to create a logical palette by calling the **CreatePalette** function:

```
hPal = CreatePalette((LPSTR) pLogPal);
```

CreatePalette accepts a long pointer to the **LOGPALETTE** structure as its only parameter and returns a handle of the palette (**HPALETTE**).

19.3.3 Selecting the Palette into a Device Context

As you would any other GDI object, you must select the palette into the device context in which it is to be used. The usual way to do this is by calling the **Select-Object** function. However, because **SelectObject** does not recognize a palette object, you must instead call **SelectPalette** to select the palette into the device context:

```
hDC = GetDC(hWnd);
SelectPalette(hDC, hPal, 0);
```

These statements associate the palette with the device context so that any reference to a palette (such as a palette index passed to a GDI function instead of a color) will be to the selected palette.

To delete a logical-palette object, you use the **DeleteObject** function.

Since the palette is independent of any particular device context, several windows can share it. However, Windows does not make a copy of the palette object when an application selects the palette into a device context; consequently, any change to the palette affects all device contexts using the same palette. Also, if an application selects a palette object into more than one device context, the device contexts must all belong to the same physical device (such as a screen or printer). In other respects, however, a palette object is like other Windows objects.

19.3.4 Realizing the Palette

After your application has selected its palette into a device context, it must realize the palette before using it, as follows:

```
RealizePalette(hDC);
```

When your application calls the **RealizePalette** function, Windows compares the system palette with your logical palette and matches identical colors. If there is room in the system palette, Windows then maps unmatched colors in the logical palette to the system palette. Finally, if there are unmatched colors that it could not map to the system palette, Windows matches the remaining colors to the nearest color in the system palette.

19.4 Drawing with Palette Colors

Once your application has created a logical palette, selected it into a device context, and realized it, you can use the palette to control the colors used by GDI functions that draw within the client area of the screen. For functions that require a color (such as **CreatePen** and **CreateSolidBrush**), you specify, directly or indirectly, which palette color you want to use.

19.4.1 Directly Specifying Palette Colors

Use the direct method to specify a palette color by supplying an index into your logical palette instead of an explicit RGB value to functions that expect a color. The **PALETTEINDEX** macro accepts an integer representing an index into your logical palette and returns a palette-index **COLORREF** value, which you would use as the color specifier for such functions. For example, to fill a region bounded by pure green with a solid brush consisting of pure red, you could use a sequence similar to the following:

```
pLogPal->palPalEntry[5].pRed = 0xFF;
pLogPal->palPalEntry[5].pGreen = 0x00;
pLogPal->palPalEntry[5].pBlue = 0x00;
pLogPal->palPalEntry[5].pFlags = (BYTE) 0;
pLogPal->palPalEntry[6].pRed = 0x00;
pLogPal->palPalEntry[6].pGreen = 0xFF;
pLogPal->palPalEntry[6].pBlue = 0x00;
pLogPal->palPalEntry[6].pFlags = (BYTE) 0;
        .
        .
        .

hPal = CreatePalette((LPSTR) pLogPal);
hDC = GetDC(hWnd);
SelectPalette(hDC, hPal, 0);
RealizePalette(hDC);
lSolidBrushColor = PALETTEINDEX(5);
lBoundaryColor = PALETTEINDEX(6);
hSolidBrush = CreateSolidBrush(lSolidBrushColor);
hOldSolidBrush = SelectObject(hDC, hSolidBrush);
hPen = CreatePen(lBoundaryColor);
hOldPen = SelectObject(hDC, hPen);
Rectangle(hDC, x1, y1, x2, y2);
```

This example indicates to Windows that it should draw a rectangle bounded by the color in the palette entry at index 6 (green) and filled with the color located in the entry at index 5 (red).

Note that the brush created by **CreateSolidBrush** is independent of any device context. As a result, the color specified in the lSolidBrushColor parameter is the color in the sixth entry of the palette that was current when the brush was selected into the device context (not when the application created the brush). Selecting and realizing a different palette and selecting the brush again would change the color drawn by the brush. Thus, when using a logical palette, you need only create a brush for each type required (such as solid or vertical hatch). You can then change the color of the brush by using different palettes or by changing the color in the palette entry to which the brush refers.

19.4.2 Indirectly Specifying Palette Colors

Using an index into a logical palette allows your application greater control over the colors displayed. This method becomes impractical, however, when dealing with a device that has 2^{24} colors with no system palette. On a device capable of supporting full 24-bit color, this limits your application to displaying only the colors in your logical palette. By specifying palette colors indirectly, you can avoid this limitation.

You specify a palette color indirectly by using a palette-relative RGB **COLOR-REF** value instead of a palette index. A palette-relative RGB value is a 32-bit value that has the second bit in the high-order byte set to 1 and one-byte values for red, green, and blue in the remaining bytes. The **PALETTERGB** macro accepts three values that indicate the relative intensity of red, green, and blue, and returns a palette-relative RGB **COLORREF** value, which, like a palette-index **COLOR-REF** value, you can use in place of an explicit RGB **COLORREF** value for functions that require a color.

By specifying a palette-relative RGB value instead of a palette index, your application can draw to an output device by using palette colors, without having to determine first whether the device supports a system palette. The following table shows how Windows interprets a palette-relative RGB value.

Device supports a system palette?	How Windows uses a palette-relative RGB value
Yes	Windows matches the RGB information to the nearest color in the currently selected logical palette and uses that palette entry as though the application had directly specified the entry.
No	Windows uses the RGB information as though the palette-relative RGB were an explicit RGB value.

For example, assume your application includes the following statements:

```
pLogPal->palPalEntry[5].pRed = 0xFF;
pLogPal->palPalEntry[5].pGreen = 0x00;
pLogPal->palPalEntry[5].pBlue = 0x00;
CreatePalette((LPSTR) &pa);
crRed = PALETTERGB(0xFF, 0x00, 0x00);
```

If the target output device supports a system palette, crRed would be equivalent to this:

```
crRed = PALETTEINDEX(5);
```

If the output device does not support a system palette, however, crRed would be equivalent to this:

```
crRed = RGB(0xFF, 0x00, 0x00);
```

Even when using a logical palette, an application can use an explicit RGB value to specify color. In such cases, Windows displays the color as it would for an application that does not use a color palette, by displaying the nearest color in the default palette. If an application creates a solid brush by using an explicit RGB value, Windows simulates the color by dithering—that is, producing a pattern of pixels made up of colors in the default palette.

19.4.3 Using a Palette When Drawing Bitmaps

A device-independent bitmap's color table can contain indices into the currently selected logical palette instead of explicit RGB values. (For more information, see Section 19.3.1, "Creating a LOGPALETTE Structure.") This allows Windows to avoid color matching and can significantly increase the speed with which images are rendered. The ShowDIB code sample demonstrates this by converting its DIB color table into palette indices, as shown in the following example:

```
lpbi = (VOID FAR *) GlobalLock(hbiCurrent);
if (lpbi->biBitCount != 24) {
    fPalColors = TRUE;

    pw = (WORD FAR *) ((LPSTR) lpbi + lpbi->biSize);

    for (i = 0; i<(int) lpbi->biClrUsed; i++)
        *pw++ = (WORD) i;
}
GlobalUnlock(hbiCurrent);
```

Note that ShowDIB had already set the **biClrUsed** member of the **BITMAP-INFOHEADER** structure to the number of colors in the color table.

After converting the DIB color table into palette indices, ShowDIB calls the **SetDIBits** function with the DIB_PAL_COLORS flag, as shown in the following example:

```
/* Set the DIB bits to a device-dependent format */

if (lpbi->biHeight != (LONG) SetDIBits(hMemDC,
        hBitmap,
        0,
        (WORD) lpbi->biHeight,
        pBuf,
        (LPBITMAPINFO) lpbi,
        fPalColors ?
        DIB_PAL_COLORS :
        DIB_RGB_COLORS)) {
    ErrMsg("Could not draw DIB scans!");
    GlobalUnlock(hBuf);
    GlobalFree(hBuf);
    GlobalUnlock(hbiCurrent);
    _lclose(fh);
    return;
}
```

Depending on whether the original device-independent bitmap used 24-bit pixels, ShowDIB sets the *wUsage* parameter of **SetDIBits** to DIB_RGB_COLORS (for a 24-bit bitmap) or DIB_PAL_COLORS (for all other bitmaps). DIB_RGB_COLORS instructs Windows to use the color values in the **BITMAP-INFO** color table when setting the bits in the device-dependent memory bitmap. If the *wUsage* parameter is set to DIB_PAL_COLORS, however, Windows interprets the color table as 16-bit indices into a logical palette and sets the bits in the memory bitmap by using the indicated color values in the logical palette of the current device context.

If the **BITMAPINFO** color table contains explicit RGB values instead of palette indices, Windows matches those values to the nearest colors in the currently selected logical palette, as though they were palette-relative RGB values.

Note If the source and destination device contexts have selected and realized different palettes, the **BitBlt** function does not properly move bitmap bits to or from a memory device context. In such a case, you must call the **GetDIBits** function with the *wUsage* parameter set to DIB_RGB_COLORS to retrieve the bitmap bits from the source bitmap in a device-independent format. You then use the **SetDIBits** function to set the retrieved bits in the destination bitmap. This ensures that Windows will properly match colors between the two device contexts. **BitBlt** can successfully move bitmap bits between two screen display contexts, even if they have selected and realized different palettes. The **StretchBlt** function properly moves bitmap bits between device contexts whether or not they use different palettes.

19.5 Changing a Logical Palette

You can change one or more entries in a logical palette by calling the **SetPalette-Entries** function. This function accepts the following parameters:

- The handle of the palette to be changed and an integer specifying the first palette entry to be changed
- An integer specifying the number of entries to be changed
- An array of **PALETTEENTRY** structures, each of which contains the red, green, and blue intensities and flags for each entry

Windows does not map changes made to the palette until the application calls **RealizePalette** for any device context in which the palette is selected. Because this changes the system palette, colors displayed in the client area will likewise change. For more information about how to respond when Windows changes the system palette, see Section 19.6, "Responding to Changes in the System Palette."

A second method of updating a logical palette is by animating it. In most cases, an application animates its logical palette when it is necessary to change the palette rapidly and to make those changes immediately apparent.

To animate a palette, the application must first set the flags in the affected palette entries to PC_RESERVED. This flag has two functions:

- It enables animation for the palette entry.
- It prevents Windows from matching colors displayed in other device contexts to the corresponding color in the system palette.

The following example shows how ShowDIB sets the PC_RESERVED flag in all the entries in an existing logical palette:

```
for (i = 0; i < pLogPal->palNumEntries; i++) {
    pLogPal->palPalEntry[i].peFlags = (BYTE) PC_RESERVED;
}

SetPaletteEntries(hpalCurrent, 0, pLogPal->palNumEntries,
    pLogPal->palPalEntry);
```

The **AnimatePalette** function accepts the same parameters as **SetPaletteEntries**. Unlike **SetPaletteEntries**, however, **AnimatePalette** changes only those palette entries in which the PC_RESERVED flag is set.

When an application calls **AnimatePalette**, Windows immediately maps the changed entries to the system palette, but it does not rematch the colors displayed in the device contexts by using the palette for which the application called **AnimatePalette**. In other words, if a pixel was displaying the color in the fifth entry in the system palette before the application called **AnimatePalette**, it will continue to display the color in that entry after **AnimatePalette** is called, even if the fifth entry now contains a different color.

To demonstrate palette animation, ShowDIB sets a system timer and then calls **AnimatePalette** to shift each entry in the palette each time its window receives a WM_TIMER message:

```
case WM_TIMER:

        /* WM_TIMER is the signal for palette animation. */

        hDC = GetDC(hWnd);
        hOldPal = SelectPalette(hDC, hpalCurrent, 0); {
            PALETTEENTRY peTemp;

            /*
             * Shift all palette entries left by one
             * position and wrap around the first entry.
             */
```

```
                    peTemp = pLogPal->palPalEntry[0];
                    for (i = 0; i < (pLogPal->palNumEntries - 1); i++)
                        pLogPal->palPalEntry[i] =
                        pLogPal->palPalEntry[i + 1];
                    pLogPal->palPalEntry[i] = peTemp;
            }

            /* Replace entries in logical palette with new entries. */

            AnimatePalette(hpalCurrent, 0, pLogPal->palNumEntries,
                pLogPal->palPalEntry);

            SelectPalette(hDC, hOldPal, 0);
            ReleaseDC(hWnd, hDC);

            /*
             * Decrement animation count and terminate
             * animation if it reaches zero.
             */

            if (!(--nAnimating))
                PostMessage(hWnd, WM_COMMAND, IDM_ANIMATE0, 0L);
            break;
```

Animating an entire logical palette will degrade colors displayed by other applications' windows if the active window is using the animated palette, particularly if the animated palette is large enough to "take over" the system palette. For this reason, your application should animate no more entries than it requires.

19.6 Responding to Changes in the System Palette

Whenever an application realizes a logical palette for a particular device context, Windows maps colors in that logical palette into the system palette if the system palette does not already contain those colors and if there are available entries in the system palette. Because the system palette has changed, many or all of the colors displayed in the client areas of all windows using palettes likewise change. So that applications can respond appropriately to these changes, Windows sends the following two messages to overlapped and pop-up windows to deal with the changes:

- WM_QUERYNEWPALETTE
- WM_PALETTECHANGED

19.6.1 Responding to the WM_QUERYNEWPALETTE Message

Windows sends the WM_QUERYNEWPALETTE message to the window that is about to become active. When a window receives this message, the application that owns the window should realize its logical palette, invalidate the contents of the window's client area, and then return TRUE to inform Windows that it has changed the system palette.

ShowDIB responds to the WM_QUERYNEWPALETTE message as follows:

```
case WM_QUERYNEWPALETTE:

        /* If palette realization causes a palette change, redraw. */

        if (fLegitDraw) {
            hDC = GetDC(hWnd);
            hOldPal = SelectPalette(hDC, hpalCurrent, 0);

            i = RealizePalette(hDC);

            SelectPalette(hDC, hOldPal, 0);
            ReleaseDC(hWnd, hDC);

            if (i) {
                InvalidateRect(hWnd, (RECT FAR*) NULL, 1);
                UpdateCount = 0;
                return 1;
            } else
                return FALSE;
        }
        else
            return FALSE;
        break;
```

19.6.2 Responding to the WM_PALETTECHANGED Message

Windows sends the WM_PALETTECHANGED message to all overlapped and pop-up windows when any window changes the system palette by realizing its logical palette. The *wParam* parameter of this message contains the handle of the window that realized its palette. If your window responds to this message by realizing its own palette, to avoid creating a loop you should first determine that this handle is not the handle of your window.

When an inactive window receives the WM_PALETTECHANGED message, it has three options:

- It can do nothing. In this case, the colors displayed in the window's client area potentially will be incorrect until the window updates its client area. Consider this option only if color quality is unimportant to your application when its windows are inactive or if your application does not use a palette.

- It can realize its logical palette and redraw its client area. This option ensures that the colors displayed in the window's client area will be as correct as possible, because Windows updates the colors in the client area by using the window's logical palette. This accuracy does increase the time required to redraw the client area, however. So if the quality of the colors displayed by your inactive window is crucial to your application, or if the image contained in your window's client area can be redrawn quickly, choose this option.

- It can realize its logical palette and directly update the colors in its client area. This option provides a reasonable compromise between performance and color quality. A window directly updates the colors in its client area by realizing its palette and then calling the **UpdateColors** function. When an application calls **UpdateColors**, Windows quickly updates the client area by matching the current colors in the client area pixel by pixel to the system palette. Since the match is made based on the color of the pixel before the system palette changed rather than on the contents of the window's logical palette, the accuracy of the match decreases each time the window calls **UpdateColors**. Consequently, if color accuracy is of any importance to your application when your windows are inactive, limit the number of times the application calls **UpdateColors** for a window before repainting the window's client area.

The following demonstrates how ShowDIB updates its client area in response to the WM_PALETTECHANGED message:

```
case WM_PALETTECHANGED:

        /*
         * If SHOWDIB was not responsible for palette
         * change and if palette realization causes a
         * palette change, redraw.
         */

        if (wParam != (WPARAM) hWnd) {
            if (fLegitDraw) {
                hDC = GetDC(hWnd);
                hOldPal = SelectPalette(hDC, hpalCurrent, 0);

                i = RealizePalette(hDC);
```

```
                        if (i) {
                            if (fUpdateColors) {
                                UpdateColors(hDC);
                                UpdateCount++;
                            }
                            else
                                InvalidateRect(hWnd, (RECT FAR*) NULL, 1);
                        }

                        SelectPalette(hDC, hOldPal, 0);
                        ReleaseDC(hWnd, hDC);
                    }
                }
                break;
```

When ShowDIB receives the WM_PALETTECHANGED message, it first determines whether the *wParam* parameter contains its own window handle. This would indicate that it was the window that had realized its logical palette and so no response is needed. After selecting and realizing its logical palette, the window determines whether a flag was set indicating that the user had chosen the Update Colors command from the Options menu. If the user had done so, the window calls **UpdateColors** to update its client area and sets a flag to indicate that it has directly updated its colors. Otherwise, the window invalidates its client area, forcing it to be redrawn.

19.7 Related Topics

For more information about displaying bitmaps, see Chapter 11, "Bitmaps."

For more information about color-palette and GDI functions and about data types, messages, and structures used by logical palettes, see the *Microsoft Windows Programmer's Reference, Volumes 2* and *3*.

Dynamic-Link Libraries

The Microsoft Windows operating system provides special libraries, called dynamic-link libraries, (DLLs) that applications can use to share code and resources. In addition, you can create your own dynamic-link libraries to share code and resources among your applications.

This chapter covers the following topics:

- What a dynamic-link library is
- When to use a dynamic-link library
- How to build a dynamic-link library

This chapter also explains how to build a sample library, SELECT.DLL, that illustrates the concepts this chapter covers.

20.1 What Is a Dynamic-Link Library?

A dynamic-link library is an executable module containing functions that Windows applications can call to perform useful tasks. Dynamic-link libraries exist primarily to provide services to application modules. These libraries play an important role in Windows, which uses them to make its functions and resources available to Windows applications. All Windows libraries are dynamic-link libraries.

Dynamic-link libraries are similar to run-time libraries, such as the C run-time libraries. The main difference is that dynamic-link libraries are linked with the application at run time, not when you link the application files by using Microsoft Segmented Executable Linker (LINK). Linking a library with an application at run time is called dynamic linking; linking the library with an application by using the linker is called static linking.

One way to understand dynamic-link libraries is to compare them to static-link libraries. An example of a static-link library is MLIBCEW.LIB, the medium-model Windows C run-time library. MLIBCEW.LIB contains the executable code for C run-time functions such as **strcpy** and **strlen**. You use C run-time functions in your application without having to include the source code for those functions. When you link your C application, the linker incorporates information from the appropriate static-link library. Wherever the application's code uses a C run-time function, the linker copies that function to the application's executable (.EXE) file.

The primary advantage of static-link libraries is that they make a standard set of functions available to applications, and do not require the applications to include the original source code for those functions. Static-link libraries, however, can be inefficient in a multitasking system such as Windows. If two applications are running simultaneously and they use the same static-library function, there will be two copies of that function present in the system. This is an inefficient use of memory. It would be more efficient for both applications to share a single copy of the function, but static-link libraries provide no facility for sharing code between applications.

With dynamic-link libraries, on the other hand, several applications can share a single copy of a function. Every standard Windows function, such as **GetMessage**, **CreateWindow**, or **TextOut**, is in one of three dynamic-link libraries: either KRNL286.EXE or KRNL386.EXE, USER.EXE, and GDI.EXE. If two Windows applications are running at the same time and both use a particular Windows function, both share a single copy of the source code for that function.

In addition to being able to share code, applications using dynamic-link libraries can share other resources, such as data and hardware. For example, Windows fonts are text-drawing data that applications can share by means of dynamic-link libraries. Likewise, Windows device drivers are dynamic-link libraries that applications can use to share hardware resources.

20.1.1 Import and Dynamic-Link Libraries

Thus far, we have described two types of libraries: static-link and dynamic-link libraries. There is a third type of library that is important when working with dynamic-link libraries: import libraries. An import library contains information that Windows uses to locate code in a dynamic-link library.

During linking, the linker uses static-link libraries and import libraries to resolve references to external functions. When an application uses a function from a static-link library, the linker copies the code for that function into the application's .EXE file. When the application uses a function from a dynamic-link library, however, the linker does not copy any code. Instead, it copies information from the import library—information that indicates where to find the necessary code in the dynamic-link library at run time. While the application is running, this relocation information creates a dynamic link between the executing application and the dynamic-link library.

The following table summarizes the uses of each of the three types of libraries.

Library type	Linked at link time	Linked at run time	Example library	Example function
Static	Yes	No	MLIBCEW.LIB	**strcpy**
Import	Yes	No	LIBW.LIB	**TextOut**
Dynamic	No	Yes	GDI.EXE	**TextOut**

As this table indicates, when an application calls the **strcpy** function in the C run-time library the linker links the application to the library by copying the code of the function from the MLIBCEW.LIB run-time library into the application's .EXE file. But when the application calls the **TextOut** GDI function, the linker copies location information for **TextOut** from the LIBW.LIB import library into the .EXE file. It does not copy the code of the function itself. Then, at run time, when the application makes the call to **TextOut**, Windows uses the location information in the .EXE file to locate **TextOut** in the dynamic-link library GDI.EXE. It then executes the **TextOut** function in GDI.EXE. In other words, import libraries provide the connection between application modules and dynamic-link library modules.

20.1.2 Application and Dynamic-Link Modules

Modules are a fundamental structural unit in Windows. There are two types of modules: application modules and dynamic-link modules. You should already be familiar with application modules; the .EXE file for every Windows application is considered a module. Examples of dynamic-link modules include any Windows system file with an extension of .DLL, .DRV, or .FON. (Some Windows system modules have a filename extension of .EXE instead of .DLL.)

Application and dynamic-link modules have the same file format. This format, which is sometimes called the New EXE Header Format, allows dynamic linking to take place. You can use the Microsoft EXE File Header Utility (EXEHDR) to read the header of a module file. EXEHDR provides information about the functions that the module imports or exports. EXEHDR is included with Microsoft C Optimizing Compiler (CL); for information about how to run EXEHDR, see your C compiler documentation.

A module exports a function to make the function available to other modules. Thus, dynamic-link modules export functions for use by applications and other dynamic-link libraries. For example, the Windows dynamic-link library GDI.EXE exports all the graphics device interface (GDI) functions. Unlike dynamic-link modules, however, application modules cannot export functions for use by other applications.

A module imports a function contained in another module if it must use that function. Importing a function creates a dynamic link to the code for that function.

There are two ways to import a function into a module:

- By linking the module with an import library that contains information for that function
- By listing the individual function in the **IMPORTS** section of the module-definition file

Although both application and dynamic-link modules can import and export functions, they differ in one important respect: Unlike applications modules, dynamic-link modules are not tasks.

20.1.3 Dynamic-Link Libraries and Tasks

One of the basic differences between an application module and a dynamic-link module is in the notion of the task. A task is the fundamental unit of scheduling in Windows. An application module is said to be a tasked executable module. When an application module is loaded, a call is made to its entry point, the **WinMain** function, which typically contains the message loop. As the application module creates windows and begins to interact with the user, the message loop connects the application module to the Windows scheduler. As long as the user is interacting with the application's windows, messages are fed to the application module and the module retains control of the processor.

A dynamic-link library is sometimes said to be a nontasked executable module. Like the application module, a dynamic-link module may contain an entry point. When the module is loaded, the entry point for the library is called but, typically, performs only minor initialization. Unlike the application module, a dynamic-link module does not interact with the Windows scheduler by means of a message loop; instead, the dynamic-link module waits for tasks to request its services.

Application modules are the active components of Windows. They receive system- and user-generated messages and, when necessary, call library modules for specific data and services. Library modules exist to provide services to application modules.

Note Some dynamic-link libraries are not completely passive; for example, some are device drivers for interrupt-driven devices such as the keyboard, mouse, and communication ports. However, the interaction of such libraries is carefully controlled to avoid disrupting the Windows scheduler. If you require a dynamic-link library to take an active role, you should write it according to the guidelines described in Section 20.2.4, "Device Drivers."

20.1.4 Dynamic-Link Libraries and Stacks

Unlike a task module, a dynamic-link module does not have its own stack. Instead, it uses the stack segment of the task that called it. This can create problems when a library calls a function that treats the DS and SS registers as if they hold the same address. This problem is most likely to occur in small- and medium-model dynamic-link libraries, since pointers in these models are, by default, near pointers. Many C run-time library functions, for example, treat DS and SS as equal. You must take care when you call these functions from within your dynamic-link library.

Your library can also encounter difficulties when calling user-written functions. Consider, for example, a dynamic-link library containing a function that declares a variable within the body of the function. The address of this function will be relative to the stack of the task that called the library. If this function passes the variable to a second function that expects a near pointer, the second function will assume that the address it receives is relative to the dynamic-link library's data segment rather than to the stack segment of the task that called it.

The following example shows a function in a dynamic-link library passing a variable from the stack, rather than from its data segment:

```
void DLLFunction(WORD wMyWord)
{
    char szMyString[10];
    .
    .
    .

    AnotherFunction(szMyString);
}
```

In this example, if AnotherFunction was declared as accepting a near pointer to a character array (**char NEAR ***), it will interpret the address it receives as being an offset of the data segment, rather than of the stack segment of the task that called the library.

To ensure that your dynamic-link library does not attempt to pass stack variables to functions that expect near pointers, you should compile your library modules by using the CL /Aw option. This will produce warning messages that indicate when the library is making a call to a function that treats DS and SS as equal. When you receive a warning for a particular function, you can either remove that function call from your library, or rewrite the library source module so that it does not pass a stack variable to that function.

20.1.5 How Windows Locates Dynamic-Link Libraries

Windows locates a dynamic-link library by searching the same directories it searches to find an application module. For Windows to the find the library, it must be in one of the following directories, which Windows searches in the order listed:

1. The current directory.

2. The Windows directory (the directory containing WIN.COM); use the **Get-WindowsDirectory** function to retrieve the path of this directory.

3. The Windows system directory (the directory containing such system files as GDI.EXE); use the **GetSystemDirectory** function to retrieve the path of this directory.

4. Any of the directories listed in the PATH environment variable.

5. Any directory in the list of directories mapped in a network.

Implicitly loaded libraries must be named with the .DLL extension.

20.2 When to Use a Custom Dynamic-Link Library

Although dynamic-link libraries are central to the architecture of Windows, they are not necessary components of most Windows applications. Your application does not have to use a dynamic-link library simply to maximize memory management in Windows. If you split your application into multiple code segments, Windows provides a type of dynamic linking between code segments that allows for optimal memory usage. For more information about using multiple code segments, see Chapter 16, "More Memory Management."

Among other purposes, however, dynamic-link libraries are useful for the following tasks:

- Sharing code and resources among applications
- Easily customizing your application for different markets
- Filtering messages on a systemwide basis
- Creating device drivers
- Allowing Microsoft Dialog Editor (DLGEDIT.EXE) to support your custom-designed controls
- Facilitating the development of a complex application

20.2.1 Sharing Objects Between Applications

By using dynamic-link libraries, applications can share certain types of objects, including code and resources. Sharing other types of objects, including data and file handles, is much more limited. This is because file handles and data are created in an application's private address space. Attempts to share file handles, or to share data (outside of dynamic data exchange, the clipboard, and the library's data segment) will lead to unpredictable results, and could be incompatible with future versions of Windows.

20.2.1.1 Sharing Code

If you are developing a family of applications, you may want to consider using one or more dynamic-link libraries. This saves memory when two or more applications that use a common set of DLL functions are running at the same time. With these libraries, multiple applications can share common routines that would be duplicated for each application if static-link libraries were used.

Suppose, for example, that you are creating two graphics applications, one a vector (draw) program and the other a bitmap (paint) application. A common requirement for both programs is the ability to import drawings created by other applications. For these applications, you could create dynamic-link libraries for each supported "foreign" file format that would convert it into an intermediate format. Your paint and draw applications could then convert this intermediate data into their own formats. The applications themselves would be required to contain only the code to convert from a single format to their own format. To support the importing of a new file type, you would simply develop a new library module and distribute it to the user, instead of modifying, recompiling, and distributing the application modules themselves.

20.2.1.2 Sharing Resources

Resources are read-only data objects that are bound into an executable file by Microsoft Windows Resource Compiler (RC). You can bind resources into an application's .EXE file, as well as into a library's .DLL file. Applications can share a dynamic-link library's resources; this saves memory when multiple applications are running. Windows has built-in support for eight resource types:

- Accelerator tables
- Bitmaps
- Cursors
- Dialog box templates
- Fonts
- Icons
- Menu templates
- String tables

In addition to using the standard Windows resources, you can create custom resources and install them in an executable file. For more information about resources, see Chapter 16, "More Memory Management."

Any application can freely use resources that reside in a dynamic-link library. However, each application must explicitly request each resource object it requires.

For example, if an application uses a menu resource called MainMenu in a library named MENULIB.DLL, it would have to contain code similar to the following:

```
HINSTANCE hLibrary;
HMENU   hMenu;

hLibrary = LoadLibrary("MENULIB.DLL");

hMenu = LoadMenu(hLibrary, "MainMenu");
```

20.2.2 Customizing an Application for Different Markets

You can use dynamic-link libraries for customizing your application for different markets. For each market, you would create a library containing code, data, and resources that would make your application more appropriate for that market. You need not design and compile a completely separate application module for each market. Instead, you need only create a general-purpose application that would draw upon the market-specific information contained in the library.

Dynamic-link libraries are often used to customize applications for international markets. The libraries can supply language- and culture-specific data for applications that are to be marketed in different countries. For example, an application could be shipped with its application module, APPFILE.EXE, and with three language-specific libraries: ENGLISH.DLL, FRENCH.DLL, and GERMAN.DLL.

When the product is installed, the correct language library could be selected and used for all dialog box templates, menus, string information, and other language-specific information.

When you use the resources of a library, you use the library's instance handle to identify it. You obtain the library instance handle by calling the **LoadLibrary** function:

```
HINSTANCE hLibrary;

hLibrary = LoadLibrary("FRENCH.DLL");
```

The hLibrary value could be used anywhere that an hinst value is requested for normal resource loading. For example, if the FRENCH.DLL library contains a menu template named MAINMENU, the application loads the library and then accesses the menu with the following call:

```
HMENU hMenu;

hMenu = LoadMenu(hLibrary, "MAINMENU");
```

20.2.3 Windows Hooks

With Windows, applications can use hooks to filter messages on a systemwide basis. A Windows hook is a function that receives and processes events before they are sent to an application's message loop. For example, a function that provides special-purpose processing of keystrokes before passing them to an application is a Windows hook function.

There are seven types of Windows hooks, which are explained more fully in the *Microsoft Windows Programmer's Reference*, *Volume 2*.

20.2.4 Device Drivers

Standard Windows device drivers are implemented as dynamic-link libraries. Following are the standard Windows device drivers:

Device driver	Purpose
COMM.DRV	Serial communication
DISPLAY.DRV	Video display
KEYBOARD.DRV	Keyboard input
MOUSE.DRV	Mouse input
SOUND.DRV	Sound output
SYSTEM.DRV	Timer

The SYSTEM.INI file identifies the drivers that are to be installed when Windows starts.

A device driver for a nonstandard device also must be implemented by using custom dynamic-link libraries. Different applications can then access the device, and the device driver provides the necessary synchronization to prevent conflicts between the applications.

Because interrupts can occur at any time, not just during the execution of the application that is using the device, device interrupt-handling code must be in a fixed code segment.

Interrupt-handling code in a device driver should not call client applications directly. In addition, such a device driver must not call application code using the **SendMessage** function, because there is no mechanism to synchronize such calls with an application's normal message processing. Such calls can lead to race conditions, data corruption, and indeterminate results.

Instead, interrupt-handling code must wait to be polled by the client applications, in much the same way that the communication driver must be polled by its client applications. Alternatively, a device driver can use the **PostMessage** function to place a message in the application's message queue.

20.2.5 Custom Controls

If you have developed custom controls, you can place the code for the controls in a dynamic-link library. You can then use Dialog Editor to access the library to display your custom control during a dialog box editing session. For more information about Dialog Editor, see its online help file.

For your control library to be used by Dialog Editor and other applications, you will need to define and export the functions described in this section.

In the following function descriptions, *Class* is used as a placeholder for the class name of your control. The name of your custom control is the same name a user of Dialog Editor specifies for the control. The control name is typically the same as the module name of the dynamic-link library, but not necessarily.

Structure definitions, such as for **CTLINFO**, and constants that define the interface of a custom control by using Dialog Editor, are provided in the CUSTCNTL.H header file.

This section describes six functions that your custom-control library must export. The library should export these functions by ordinal value, as shown in the following list:

Exported function	Ordinal value
WEP	Any number except 2 through 6
*Class***Init** or LibMain	Not required
*Class***Info**	2
*Class***Style**	3
*Class***Flags**	4
*Class***WndFn**	5
*Class***DlgFn**	6

For example, the functions exported by the Rainbow custom-control example are declared in the RAINBOW.DEF file as follows:

```
EXPORTS
    WEP             @1  RESIDENTNAME
    RAINBOWINFO     @2
    RAINBOWSTYLE    @3
    RAINBOWFLAGS    @4
    RAINBOWWNDFN    @5
    RAINBOWDLGFN    @6
```

For more information about the LibMain function, see Section 20.3.1.1, "Initializing a Dynamic-Link Library." For more information about the **WEP** function, see Section 20.3.1.2, "Terminating a Dynamic-Link Library."

Following are descriptions of the custom-control functions:

HANDLE FAR PASCAL *Class***Init**(*hinst*, *wDataSegment*, *wHeapSize*, *lpszCmdLine*)

The *Class***Init** function takes care of all the initialization necessary to use the dynamic-link control library. Your assembly-language entry point to the library usually calls this function. In addition to saving the library instance handle by using a global static variable, this function should register the control window class and initialize the local heap by calling the **LocalInit** function, if your assembly-language entry routine does not initialize the local heap. If you link the custom-control dynamic-link library with LIBENTRY.OBJ instead of providing your own assembly-language entry point, this function is named LibMain. For more information about dynamic-link-library entry points and initialization, see Section 20.3.1.1, "Initializing a Dynamic-Link Library."

Parameter	Type	Description
hinst	**HANDLE**	Identifies the instance of the library.
wDataSegment	**WORD**	Specifies the library data segment.
wHeapSize	**WORD**	Specifies the default library heap size.
lpszCmdLine	**LPSTR**	Specifies the initial command-line arguments.

The return value is a library-instance handle if the function registers the control class and completes the initialization. Otherwise, the return value is NULL.

HANDLE FAR PASCAL *Class***Info**( )

The *Class***Info** function provides the calling process with basic information about the control library. Based on the information returned, the application can create instances of the control by using one of the supported styles. For example, Dialog Editor calls this function to query a library about the different control styles it can display.

This function has no parameters.

The return value identifies a **CTLINFO** structure if the function is successful. This information becomes the property of the caller, which must explicitly release it by using the **GlobalFree** function when the structure is no longer needed. If there was insufficient memory to allocate and define this structure, the return value is NULL.

The **CTLINFO** structure defines the class name and version number. The **CTLINFO** structure also contains an array of **CTLTYPE** structures, each of which lists commonly used combinations of control styles (called variants) with a short description and suggested size information.

Following are the structure definitions and their related values:

```
/* general style & size definitions */

#define CTLTYPES 12
#define CTLDESCR 22
#define CTLCLASS 20
#define CTLTITLE 94

/* control information structure */

typedef struct {
    UINT        wType;
    UINT        wWidth;
    UINT        wHeight;
    DWORD       dwStyle;
    char        szDescr[CTLDESCR];
} CTLTYPE;

typedef struct {
    UINT        wVersion;
    UINT        wCtlTypes;
    char        szClass[CTLCLASS];
    char        szTitle[CTLTITLE];
    char        szReserved[10];
    CTLTYPE     Type[CTLTYPES];
} CTLINFO;

typedef CTLINFO *    PCTLINFO;
typedef CTLINFO FAR *LPCTLINFO;
```

For full descriptions of the **CTLTYPE** and **CTLINFO** structures, see the *Microsoft Windows Programmer's Reference, Volume 3*.

BOOL FAR PASCAL *Class***Style**(*hWnd*, *hCtlStyle*, *lpfnStrToId*, *lpfnIdToStr*)

Dialog Editor calls the *Class*Style function to display a dialog box to edit the style of the selected control. When this function is called, it should display a modal dialog box in which the user can edit the **CTLSTYLE** members. The user interface of this dialog box should be consistent with that of the predefined controls that Dialog Editor supports.

Parameter	Type	Description
hWnd	**HWND**	Identifies the parent window of the dialog box.
hCtlStyle	**HANDLE**	Identifies the **CTLSTYLE** structure.

Parameter	Type	Description
lpfnStrToId	**LPFNSTRTOID**	Points to a function supplied by Dialog Editor that converts a string to a numeric identifier.
lpfnIdToStr	**LPFNIDTOSTR**	Points to a function supplied by Dialog Editor that converts a numeric identifier to a string.

The return value is nonzero if the **CTLSTYLE** structure was changed. Otherwise, it is zero.

The **CTLSTYLE** structure specifies the attributes of the selected control, including the current style flags, location, dimensions, and associated text. The **CTLSTYLE** structure has the following format:

```
/* control style structure */

typedef struct {
    UINT        wX;
    UINT        wY;
    UINT        wCx;
    UINT        wCy;
    UINT        wId;
    DWORD       dwStyle;
    char        szClass[CTLCLASS];
    char        szTitle[CTLTITLE];
} CTLSTYLE;

typedef CTLSTYLE *     PCTLSTYLE;
typedef CTLSTYLE FAR * LPCTLSTYLE;
```

For a full description of the **CTLSTYLE** structure, see the *Microsoft Windows Programmer's Reference, Volume 3*.

Dialog Editor keeps track of user-specified control identifiers and their corresponding symbolic-constant names, maintaining them in a header file that is included when the application is compiled. The control-style function accesses this information by using the functions pointed to by the *lpfnStrToId* and *lpfnIdToStr* parameters. The parameters point to two function entry points within Dialog Editor itself. To call these functions, you should prototype them as follows:

```
/* ID to string translation function prototypes */

typedef WORD   (FAR PASCAL *LPFNIDTOSTR) (WORD, LPSTR, WORD);
typedef DWORD  (FAR PASCAL *LPFNSTRTOID) (LPSTR);
```

The Dialog Editor entry-point function pointed to by the *lpfnIdToStr* parameter allows you to translate the numeric identifier provided in the **CTLSTYLE** structure into a text string containing the symbolic-constant name defined in the header file. This text string can then be displayed in place of a numeric value in your custom control's style dialog box. The first parameter is the control identifier. The second parameter is a long pointer to a buffer that receives the string, and the third parameter is the maximum length of that buffer. The function pointed to by *lpfnIdToStr* returns the number of characters copied to the string. If the function returns zero, it failed.

The function pointed to by *lpfnStrToId* works in reverse, translating a string to a numeric identifier. The function accepts the string containing a symbolic-constant name and returns the corresponding control identifier. If the low-order word of the return value is nonzero, the high-order word contains the control identifier, which you can use to update the **wId** member of the **CTLSTYLE** structure. If the low-order word of the return value is zero, the constant name was undefined and the *Class***Style** function should generate an error message.

Typically, whenever *Class***Style** is called it will call the function pointed to by *lpfnIdToStr*, passing it the value contained in the **CTLSTYLE** member **wId**. If the function pointed to by *lpfnIdToStr* returns a value greater than zero, *Class***Style** displays the resulting string in an edit control so the user can change it. Otherwise, it displays the numeric value of the control identifier. If the user changes the edit field, *Class***Style** calls the function pointed to by *lpfnStrToId* to verify that the string contains a valid symbolic-constant name and replaces the **CTLSTYLE** member **wId** with the high-order word of the return value.

BOOL FAR PASCAL *Class***DlgFn**(*hDlg*, *wMessage*, *wParam*, *lParam*)

The *Class***DlgFn** function is the dialog box procedure responsible for processing all the messages sent to the style dialog box. The style dialog box is invoked when the *Class***Style** function is called. The *Class***DlgFn** function should enable the user to edit selected portions of the **CTLSTYLE** structure passed to the *Class***Style** function.

Parameter	Type	Description
hDlg	**HWND**	Identifies the window that will receive the message.
wMessage	**WORD**	Specifies the message.
wParam	**WORD**	Specifies 16 bits of additional message-dependent information.
lParam	**LONG**	Specifies 32 bits of additional message-dependent information.

The return value is nonzero if the function is successful. Otherwise, it is zero.

WORD FAR PASCAL *Class***Flags**(*dwFlags*, *lpStyle*, *wMaxString*)

The *Class***Flags** function translates the specified class style flags into a corresponding text string for output to a resource-definition (.RC) file. This function should not interpret the flags contained in the high word, since these are managed by

Dialog Editor. Note that you should use the same control style definitions that are specified in your control header file.

Parameter	Type	Description
dwFlags	**DWORD**	Specifies the current control flags.
lpStyle	**LPSTR**	Points to a buffer that will receive the style string.
wMaxString	**WORD**	Specifies the maximum length, in bytes, of the style string.

The return value is the number of characters copied to the buffer identified by the *lpStyle* parameter, if the function is successful. Otherwise, the return value is zero.

LONG FAR PASCAL *Class***WndFn**(*hWnd*, *wMessage*, *wParam*, *lParam*)

The *Class***WndFn** function is the window procedure responsible for processing all the messages sent to the control.

Parameter	Type	Description
hWnd	**HWND**	Identifies the window that will receive the message.
wMessage	**WORD**	Specifies the message.
wParam	**WORD**	Specifies 16 bits of additional message-dependent information.
lParam	**LONG**	Specifies 32 bits of additional message-dependent information.

The return value indicates the result of the message processing and depends on the message sent.

20.2.6 Project Management

If you are developing a large or complex application, dynamic-link libraries can make your task easier. By splitting an application into clearly defined subsystems, you can logically divide work between different groups of developers. Each subsystem can then be developed as a separate dynamic-link library.

One of the challenges in such a project is defining the interface between each two subsystems. Since dynamic-link code can freely call functions in other dynamic-link modules, Windows imposes no constraints on subsystem definitions. In addition, Windows manages the movement and discarding of code segments to minimize the problems that memory limitations often cause for MS-DOS development projects. To take advantage of this feature, you should define code segments as **MOVEABLE**, or **MOVEABLE** and **DISCARDABLE**, in the module-definition (.DEF) file.

One benefit of using multiple dynamic-link libraries is that, because each library has its own data segment, data corruption between subsystems is minimized. This type of encapsulation is useful in developing large applications.

There is another type of encapsulation, however, that might cause problems in large projects that require multiple applications to run simultaneously. Because each application is treated as if it has its own private address space, applications can move global data to other applications only by using dynamic data exchange (DDE). For more information on using DDE, see Chapter 22, "Dynamic Data Exchange."

20.3 Creating a Dynamic-Link Library

This section provides sample code that you can use as a basis for creating a dynamic-link library. To create the library, you must have at least three files:

- A C-language source file
- A module-definition (.DEF) file
- A makefile

Once you have created these files, you run the Microsoft Program Maintenance Utility (NMAKE) to compile and link the source file.

20.3.1 Creating the C-Language Source File

Like any other type of C application, dynamic-link libraries can contain multiple functions. Each function that other applications or libraries will use must be declared as **FAR** and must be listed in the **EXPORTS** section of the library's module-definition (.DEF) file. The module-definition file for this sample library is discussed further in Section 20.3.2, "Creating the Module-Definition File."

```
/* MINDLL.C -- Sample DLL code to demonstrate minimum code */
/*             needed to create a dynamic-link library.     */

#include <windows.h>

int FAR PASCAL LibMain(HINSTANCE hinst,
    WORD    wDataSeg,
    WORD    cbHeapSize,
    LPSTR   lpszCmdLine)
{
        .
        . /* Perform DLL initialization. */
        .
```

```
        if (cbHeapSize != 0)      /* if DLL data seg is MOVEABLE */
            UnlockData(0);

        return 1;                 /* initialization successful    */
}

VOID FAR PASCAL MinRoutine(int iParam1,
    LPSTR lpszParam2)
{
    char  cLocalVariable;   /* local variables on stack      */
        .
        . /*  MinRoutine code goes here. */
        .
}

int FAR PASCAL WEP(int nParameter)
{
    if (nParameter == WEP_SYSTEM_EXIT) {

        /*  System shutdown is in progress. Respond accordingly. */

        return 1;
    }
    else {
        if (nParameter == WEP_FREE_DLL) {

            /*
             * DLL usage count is zero. Every application that had
             * loaded the DLL has freed it.
             */

            return 1;
        }
        else {

            /* Value is undefined. Ignore it. */

            return 1;
        }
    }
}
```

Source code for a dynamic-link library uses the WINDOWS.H header file in the same way application source code does. WINDOWS.H contains data-type definitions, application programming interface (API) entry-point definitions, and other useful parameter information.

The **PASCAL** declaration defines the parameter-passing and stack-cleanup convention for this function. This declaration is not required for dynamic-link functions, but its use results in slightly smaller and faster code and, therefore, is recommended. You cannot use the Pascal calling convention for functions with a variable number of parameters, or for calling C run-time functions. In such cases, the **CDECL** calling convention is required.

There are two parameters shown on the MinRoutine parameter list, but dynamic-link functions can have as few or as many parameters as are required. The only requirement is that pointers passed from outside the dynamic-link module must be long pointers.

20.3.1.1 Initializing a Dynamic-Link Library

You must include an automatic initialization function in your dynamic-link library. The initialization function performs one-time startup processing. Windows calls the function once, when the library is initially loaded. When subsequent applications load the library to use it, Windows does not call the initialization function; instead, it increments the library's usage count.

Windows maintains a library in memory as long as its usage count is greater than zero. If the count becomes zero, it is removed from memory. When an application reloads the library into memory, Windows will call the initialization function again.

Following are some typical tasks a library's initialization function might perform:

- Registering window classes for window procedures contained in the library
- Initializing the library's local heap
- Setting initial values for the library's global variables

This initialization function is required in order to allocate the library's local heap. The local heap must be created before the library calls any local heap functions, such as **LocalAlloc**. While Windows automatically initializes the local heap for Windows applications, dynamic-link libraries must explicitly initialize the local heap by calling the **LocalInit** function.

In addition, you should include the following declaration in the initialization function:

```
extrn __acrtused:abs
```

This ensures that, if the library does not call any C run-time functions, it will be linked with the dynamic-link startup code in the Windows dynamic-link C run-time libraries (*x*DLLC*y*W.LIB).

Initialization information is passed in hardware registers to a library when it is loaded. Since hardware registers are not accessible from the C language, you must provide an assembly-language routine to obtain these values. The location and value of the heap information are as follows:

Register	Value
DI	Identifies the library's instance handle.
DS	Identifies the library's data segment, if any.
CX	Contains the heap size specified in the library's .DEF file.
ES:SI	Points to the command line (in the **lpCmdLine** member of the **Load-Module** function's *lpvParameterBlock* parameter).

The Microsoft Windows 3.1 Software Development Kit (SDK) includes an assembly-language file, LIBENTRY.ASM, that you can use to create an initialization function for your dynamic-link library. The LibEntry function in this file is defined as follows:

```
;;;;;;;;;;;;;;;;;;;;;;;;;;;;;;;;;;;;;;;;;;;;;;;;;;;;;;;;;;;;;;;;;
;
;       LIBENTRY.ASM
;
;       Windows dynamic-link library entry routine
;
; This module generates a code segment called INIT_TEXT.
; It initializes the local heap if one exists and then calls
; the LibMain function, which should have the following form:
;
; BOOL FAR PASCAL LibMain(HANDLE hinst,
;       WORD    wDataSeg,
;       WORD    cbHeap,
;       DWORD   ignore);  /* Always NULL - ignore   */
;
; The result of the call to LibMain is returned to Windows.
; The C function should return TRUE if it completes initialization
; successfully; it should return FALSE if some error occurs.
;
; Note - The last parameter to LibMain is included for compatibility
; reasons.  Applications that need to modify this file and remove
; the parameter from LibMain can do so by simply removing the two
; instructions marked with "****" in the following code.
;
;;;;;;;;;;;;;;;;;;;;;;;;;;;;;;;;;;;;;;;;;;;;;;;;;;;;;;;;;;;;;;;;;

include cmacros.inc

externFP <LibMain>              ; the C routine to be called

createSeg INIT_TEXT, INIT_TEXT, BYTE, PUBLIC, CODE
sBegin  INIT_TEXT
assumes CS,INIT_TEXT
```

```
            ?PLM=0                          ; 'C'naming
            externA  <_acrtused>           ; ensures that Win DLL startup code
                                            ; is linked

            ?PLM=1                          ; 'PASCAL' naming
            externFP <LocalInit>           ; Windows heap initialization routine

            cProc   LibEntry, <PUBLIC,FAR>   ; entry point into DLL

            include CONVDLL.INC

            cBegin
                    push    di              ; handle of the module instance
                    push    ds              ; library data segment
                    push    cx              ; heap size
                    push    es              ; always NULL; may remove  ****
                    push    si              ; always NULL; may remove  ****

                    ; If we have some heap, then initialize it.
                    jcxz    callc           ; Jump if no heap specified

                    ; Call the Windows function LocalInit to set up the heap.
                    ; LocalInit((LPSTR)start, WORD cbHeap);

                    xor     ax,ax
                    cCall   LocalInit <ds, ax, cx>
                    or      ax,ax           ; Did it do it ok ?
                    jz      error           ; Quit if it failed

                    ; Invoke the C routine to do any special initialization.

            callc:
                    call    LibMain         ; Invoke the 'C' routine (result in AX)
                    jmp short exit          ; LibMain is responsible for stack cleanup

            error:
                    pop     si              ; Clean up stack on a LocalInit error
                    pop     es
                    pop     cx
                    pop     ds
                    pop     di

            exit:

            cEnd

            sEnd    INIT_TEXT

            end LibEntry
```

You can find an assembled copy of this function in the file LIBENTRY.OBJ. You
can use the LibEntry function to create a C-language initialization function. To use

the LibEntry function unchanged, just add its filename, LIBENTRY.OBJ, to your
link command line as follows:

```
link mindll.obj libentry.obj, mindll.dll,mindll.map /map,
    mdllcew.lib libw.lib/noe/nod,mindll.def
```

LibEntry calls a **FAR PASCAL** function named LibMain. Your dynamic-link
library must contain the LibMain function if you link the library with the file
LIBENTRY.OBJ.

Following is a sample LibMain function:

```
int FAR PASCAL LibMain(HINSTANCE hinst,
    WORD    wDataSeg,
    WORD    cbHeapSize,
    LPSTR   lpszCmdLine)
{
    .
    . /*  Perform DLL initialization. */
    .

    if (cbHeapSize != 0)            /* if DLL data seg is MOVEABLE */
        UnlockData(0);

    return 1;  /* successful installation; otherwise, return 0 */
}
```

LibMain takes four parameters: *hinst*, *wDataSeg*, *cbHeapSize*, and *lpszCmdLine*.
The first parameter, *hinst*, is the instance handle of the dynamic-link library. The
wDataSeg parameter is the value of the data-segment (DS) register. The *cbHeap-
Size* parameter is the size of the heap defined in the module-definition file.
LibEntry uses this value to initialize the local heap. The *lpszCmdLine* parameter
contains command-line information and is rarely used by dynamic-link libraries.

If you do not want the dynamic-link data segment to be locked, the call to **Unlock-
Data** is necessary, because the **LocalInit** function leaves the data segment locked.
UnlockData restores the data segment to its normal unlocked state.

If the dynamic-link library's initialization is successful, the library returns a value
of 1. If the initialization is not successful, the library returns a value of 0 and is unloaded from system memory.

Note If you are writing the dynamic-link library entirely in assembly language,
you must reserve the first 16 bytes of the dynamic-link data segment and initialize
the area with zeros. If the dynamic-link module contains any C-language code,
however, the C Optimizing Compiler automatically reserves and initializes this
area.

20.3.1.2 Terminating a Dynamic-Link Library

Windows dynamic-link libraries typically include a termination function. A termination function, sometimes called an exit procedure, performs cleanup operations for a library before it is unloaded.

Libraries that contain window procedures that have been registered (by using the **RegisterClass** function) are not required to remove the class registration (by using the **UnRegisterClass** function); Windows does this automatically when the library terminates.

You should define the termination function as shown in the following example. In this example, a single argument is passed, *nParameter*, which indicates whether all of Windows is shutting down (nParameter==WEP_SYSTEM_EXIT), or just the individual library (WEP_FREE_DLL). This function always returns 1 to indicate success.

```
int FAR PASCAL WEP(int nParameter)
{
    if (nParameter == WEP_SYSTEM_EXIT) {

        /* System shutdown is in progress. Respond accordingly. */

        return 1;
    }
    else {
        if (nParameter == WEP_FREE_DLL) {

            /*
             * The DLL use count is zero. Every application that
             * had loaded the DLL has freed it.
             */

            return 1;
        }
        else {

            /* Value is undefined. Ignore it. */

            return 1;
        }
    }
}
```

The name of the termination function must be **WEP**, and it must be included in the **EXPORTS** section of the dynamic-link library's module-definition file. It is strongly recommended, for performance reasons, that the ordinal entry value and the **RESIDENTNAME** keyword be used, to minimize the time used to find this function. Since using the **RESIDENTNAME** keyword causes the export information for this function to stay in memory at all times, it is not recommended for use with other exported functions.

20.3.2 Creating the Module-Definition File

This section contains the module-definition file for a minimum dynamic-link library. This file provides input to LINK to define various attributes of the library. Note that there is no **STACKSIZE** statement, because dynamic-link libraries make use of the calling application's stack.

```
LIBRARY MinDLL

DESCRIPTION 'MinDLL -- Minimum Code Required for DLL.'

EXETYPE WINDOWS

STUB  'WINSTUB.EXE'

CODE  MOVEABLE DISCARDABLE

DATA  MOVEABLE SINGLE

HEAPSIZE 0

EXPORTS
    MinRoutine @1
    WEP        @2 RESIDENTNAME
```

The **LIBRARY** keyword identifies this module as a dynamic-link library. The name of the library, MinDLL, follows this keyword and must be the same as the name of the library's .DLL file.

The **EXETYPE WINDOWS** statement is required for every Windows application and dynamic-link library.

The **DESCRIPTION** statement takes a string that can be up to 128 characters in length. It is typically used to hold module description information and perhaps a copyright notice. This statement is optional in a dynamic-link library.

The **STUB** statement defines an MS-DOS 2.*x* application that is copied into the body of the library's .DLL file. The purpose of the stub is to provide information to users who attempt to run Windows modules from the MS-DOS command prompt. If you do not provide a **STUB** statement, the linker inserts one automatically.

The **CODE** statement defines the default memory attributes of the library's code segments. Movable and discardable code segments offer the most freedom to the Windows memory manager, which ensures that the proper code segment is available when it is needed. You can also use the **SEGMENTS** statement, which is not included in this example, to define the attributes for individual code segments.

The **DATA** statement is required. It defines memory attributes of the library's data segment. The **MOVEABLE** keyword allows the memory manager to move the segment if needed. The **SINGLE** keyword is required for dynamic-link libraries, because they always have a single data segment, regardless of the number of applications that access it.

The **HEAPSIZE** statement defines the initial (and minimum) size of a library's local heap. Libraries that allocate local memory (by using the **LocalAlloc** function) must initialize the heap at library startup time. The heap size is passed to the library's LibEntry routine, which, in turn, can call the **LocalInit** function to initialize the library's local heap, using that heap size. For more information, see Section 20.3.1.1, "Initializing a Dynamic-Link Library." In the example, the heap size is set to zero because the local heap is not used.

The **EXPORTS** statement defines the functions that will be used as entry points from applications or from other dynamic-link libraries. Windows uses this information to establish the proper data segment to be used by each library function. Each function should have a unique ordinal entry value, which, in this example, is specified after the @ as the value 1. The ordinal entry value is an optimization that allows the dynamic-link mechanism to operate faster and to use less memory.

20.3.3 Creating the Makefile

The NMAKE utility controls the creation of executable files to ensure that only the minimum required processing is performed. Four utilities are used in creating a dynamic-link library:

- Microsoft C Optimizing Compiler (CL)
- Microsoft Segmented Executable Linker (LINK)
- Microsoft Import Library Manager (IMPLIB)
- Microsoft Windows Resource Compiler (RC)

A fifth (optional) utility, the Microsoft Symbol File Generator (MAPSYM), is also used but only with the debugging version of Windows.

The makefile for creating the sample library is as follows.

```
mindll.obj: mindll.c
    cl /ASw /c /Gsw /Os /W3 mindll.c
```

```
mindll.dll: mindll.obj
    link mindll.obj libentry.obj, mindll.dll,mindll.map/map, \
        mdllcew.lib libw.lib/noe/nod,mindll.def
    mapsym mindll.map
    implib mindll.lib mindll.def
    rc mindll.dll
```

For more information about NMAKE see the CL documentation.

20.3.3.1 Compiler Options

CL uses five sets of options, which are briefly described following. For more information, see the CL documentation. The following example shows the options used to compile the sample dynamic-link library:

```
cl /ASw /c /Gsw /Os /W3 mindll.c
```

The **/ASw** option controls the default addressing to be created by the compiler. The **S** option specifies the small model, which uses short data pointers and near code pointers. The **w** option tells the compiler that the stack is not part of the default data segment (that is, SS != DS). This causes the compiler to generate an error message when it detects the improper creation of a near pointer to an automatic variable.

The **/c** option requests compile-only operation. This is required if your dynamic-link library has multiple C-language source-code modules.

The **/Gsw** option consists of two parts. The **s** option disables normal CL stack checking. This is required because the stack checking is incompatible with Windows. The **w** option requests that Windows prolog and epilog code be attached to every **FAR** function. This code is used for two purposes: to assist in establishing the correct data segment, and to allow the memory manager to move code segments at any time during system operation.

The **/Os** option tells CL to optimize for size rather than for speed. This option is not required, but is recommended.

The **/W3** option sets the warning level to 3 (the highest warning level is 4). It is a good idea to use this option during the development process to allow CL to perform various checks on data types and function prototypes, among others. This option is not required, but it is recommended.

20.3.3.2 Linker Command Line

The **link** command takes five arguments, each separated by a comma:

```
link mindll.obj libentry.obj, mindll.dll,mindll.map/map,
    mdllcew.lib libw.lib/noe/nod,mindll.def
```

The first argument lists the object (.OBJ) files that are to be used to create the dynamic-link library. If you use the standard dynamic-link initialization function, include the LIBENTRY.OBJ file as an object.

The second argument specifies the name of the final executable file. The linker uses the .DLL extension for dynamic-link libraries. Implicitly loaded libraries must be named with the .DLL extension. An implicitly loaded library is imported in the application's module-definition file rather than explicitly loaded by the **LoadLibrary** function. For more information about loading a dynamic-link library, see Section 20.4, "Application Access to Dynamic-Link Code."

The third argument is the name of the .MAP file, which is created when you specify the **/map** option. This file contains symbol information for the global variables and functions. It is used as input to MAPSYM, described in the following section.

The fourth argument lists the import libraries and the static-link libraries required to create the dynamic-link library. There are two listed in this example: MDLLCEW.LIB and LIBW.LIB. MDLLCEW.LIB is a C run-time library that contains some dynamic-link startup code and C run-time library functions and math support. LIBW.LIB contains import information for the Windows API functions. The fourth argument also includes two linker options, **/nod** and **/noe**. The **/nod** option disables default library searches based on memory-model selection. If you use C run-time functions, you must also include the appropriate C run-time library in this library list. The **/noe** option disables extended library searches. This inhibits the error messages created by the linker when a symbol is identified in multiple libraries.

The fifth argument is the name of the module-definition file, described in Section 20.3.2, "Creating the Module-Definition File."

20.3.3.3 Symbol File Generator: MAPSYM

MAPSYM reads the .MAP file created by the linker and creates a symbol file having the .SYM extension. The symbol file is used by the debugging version of Windows to create stack trace information when a fatal error occurs.

20.3.3.4 Import Library Manager: IMPLIB

IMPLIB creates an import library with the .LIB extension from a dynamic-link library's module-definition file. An import library is listed on the linker command line of applications that will use the functions in the library. Because of this, references to library functions in an application can be properly resolved.

20.3.3.5 Resource Compiler: RC

All dynamic-link libraries must be compiled by using RC, to mark them as compatible with Windows version 3.1. You can compile the library by using the RC option **/p**. This marks the library as private to the calling application and means that no other applications should attempt to use the library.

20.4 Application Access to Dynamic-Link Code

This section describes the three steps you must follow for an application to access a function in a dynamic-link library:

1. Create a prototype for the library function.
2. Call the library function.
3. Import the library function.

20.4.1 Creating a Prototype for the Library Function

A prototype statement should be used to define each library function in each application source file. The prototype statement for the sample function is as follows:

```
VOID FAR PASCAL MinRoutine (int, LPSTR);
```

The purpose of a prototype statement is to define a function's parameters and return value to the compiler. The compiler is then able to create the proper code for the library function. In addition, the compiler is able to issue warning messages when a function's prototype differs from its usage and when the **/W2** compiler option has been selected. It is strongly recommended that you create prototypes for application functions as well, to minimize the problems that can occur from errors of this type. For example, a warning message would be generated if MinRoutine, as defined previously, were used with the wrong number of parameters, as in the following example:

```
MinRoutine (5);
```

Calling the Library Function   The call to a dynamic-link library function is indistinguishable from a call to a static-link library function, or to other functions in the application itself. Once you have made the proper prototype definition, the exported functions can be called by using normal C syntax.

20.4.2 Importing the Library Function

There are three ways an application can import dynamic-link library functions:

- Import implicitly at link time
- Import explicitly at link time
- Import dynamically at run time

In each case, dynamic-link information contained in the application identifies the name of the library and the function name or function's ordinal entry value. The implicit import is the most commonly used method.

20.4.2.1 Implicit Link-Time Import

An implicit import is performed by listing the import library for the dynamic-link library on the linker command line for an application. You create the import library by using IMPLIB, as discussed in Section 20.3.3, "Creating the Makefile."

The SDK contains a set of import libraries to allow linking to Windows DLLs. The following table lists these files and the purpose of each.

Filename	Purpose
LIBW.LIB	Import information for Windows dynamic-link libraries.
SDLLCEW.LIB	Startup code for Windows dynamic-link libraries, C run-time library functions, and emulated math packages for small-model dynamic-link libraries.
MDLLCEW.LIB	Startup code for Windows dynamic-link libraries, C run-time library functions, and emulated math packages for medium-model dynamic-link libraries.
CDLLCEW.LIB	Startup code for Windows dynamic-link libraries, C run-time library functions, and emulated math packages for compact-model dynamic-link libraries.
LDLLCEW.LIB	Startup code for Windows dynamic-link libraries, C run-time library functions, and emulated math packages for large-model dynamic-link libraries.

Filename	Purpose
SLIBCEW.LIB	Startup code for Windows applications, C run-time library functions, and emulated math packages for small-model applications.
MLIBCEW.LIB	Startup code for Windows applications, C run-time library functions, and emulated math packages for medium-model applications.
CLIBCEW.LIB	Startup code for Windows applications, C run-time library functions, and emulated math packages for compact-model applications.
LLIBCEW.LIB	Startup code for Windows applications, C run-time library functions, and emulated math packages for large-model applications.
WIN87EM.LIB	Import information for the Windows floating-point dynamic-link library.

20.4.2.2 Explicit Link-Time Import

Like an implicit import, an explicit import is performed at link time. You perform an explicit import by listing each function in the **IMPORTS** section of the application's module-definition file. In the following example, there are three parts: the imported function name (MinRoutine), the dynamic-link library name (MinDLL), and the ordinal entry value of the function in the library (1).

```
IMPORTS
   MinRoutine=MinDLL.1
```

Due to performance and size considerations, it is strongly advised that application developers define ordinal entry values for all exported dynamic-link library functions. If you do not assign an ordinal entry value, however, you perform the explicit import as in the following example:

```
IMPORTS
   MinDLL.MinRoutine
```

20.4.2.3 Dynamic Run-Time Import

For dynamic run-time imports, the application must first load the library and explicitly ask for the address of the necessary function. After this is done, the application can call the function. In the following example, an application links dynamically with the CreateInfo function in the Windows library INFO.DLL.

```
HINSTANCE hLibrary;
FARPROC lpFunc;

hLibrary = LoadLibrary("INFO.DLL");
if (hLibrary >= 32) {
    lpFunc = GetProcAddress(hLibrary, "CreateInfo");
```

```
      if (lpFunc != (FARPROC) NULL)
          (*lpFunc) ((LPSTR) Buffer, 512);

      FreeLibrary(hLibrary);
      }
```

In this example, the **LoadLibrary** function loads the necessary Windows library and returns a module handle of it. The **GetProcAddress** function retrieves the address of the CreateInfo function by using the function's name, CreateInfo. The function address can then be used to call the function. The following statement is an indirect function call that passes two arguments (Buffer and the integer 512) to the function:

```
*(lpFunc) ((LPSTR) Buffer, 512);
```

Finally, the **FreeLibrary** function decrements (decreases by 1) the library's usage count. When the usage count becomes zero (that is, when no application is using the library), the library is removed from memory.

You could gain slightly better performance if the CreateInfo function had an ordinal value assigned in the library's module-definition file. Following is an example of such a .DEF file entry:

```
EXPORTS
    CreateInfo @27
```

This statement defines the ordinal value of CreateInfo as 27. Using this value involves changing the call to the **GetProcAddress** function to the following:

```
GetProcAddress(hLibrary, MAKEINTRESOURCE(27));
```

20.5 Rules for Windows Object Ownership

Windows memory objects can be in global or local memory. Windows objects include the following:

- Bitmaps
- Metafiles
- Application code segments
- Resources (except fonts)

Windows treats memory objects as follows:

- An application that allocates memory owns that memory.

- When a dynamic-link library allocates a global object, the application that called the library owns that object.

- When an application or dynamic-link library terminates, Windows purges the system of all objects and window classes owned by that application or library.

- Data sharing should be performed by using the clipboard or dynamic data exchange (DDE), although you can also share data by using the data segment of a dynamic-link library. When using the clipboard or DDE, Windows copies the data into the private address space of the receiving application.

- GDI objects (pens, brushes, device contexts, and regions) are not typical Windows objects in that they are not purged when the owning application terminates. For this reason, an application or dynamic-link library must explicitly destroy any GDI objects it created before terminating.

20.6 Sample Dynamic-Link Library: Select

This sample dynamic-link library contains functions that you can use to carry out selections by using the mouse. The functions are based on the graphics selection method described in Chapter 6, "Cursors." These functions provide two kinds of selection feedback: a box that shows the outline of the selection, and a block that shows the entire selection inverted. The library exports the following functions:

Function	Action
StartSelection	Starts the selection and initializes the selection rectangle. When selecting with the mouse, you call this function when you receive a WM_LBUTTONDOWN message.
UpdateSelection	Updates the selection box or block. When selecting with the mouse, you call this function when you receive a WM_MOUSEMOVE message.
EndSelection	Ends the selection and fills in the selection rectangle with the final selection dimensions. When selecting with the mouse, you call this function when you receive a WM_LBUTTONUP message.
ClearSelection	Clears the selection box or block from the screen and empties the selection rectangle.

The selection rectangle is a **RECT** structure that the application supplies and that the library functions fill in. The coordinates given in the rectangle are client coordinates.

To create this library you need to create several files:

File	Contents
SELECT.C	The C-language source for selection functions
SELECT.DEF	The module-definition file for the Select library

File	Contents
SELECT.H	The header file for the Select library
SELECT	The makefile for the Select library
SELECT.LIB	The import library for the Select library

The Select library does not have an initialization file because the functions do not use a local heap and because no other initialization is necessary.

20.6.1 Creating the Functions

You can create the library functions by following the description given in Chapter 6, "Cursors." Simply copy the statements used to make the graphics selection into the corresponding functions. Also, to make the selection functions more flexible, add the additional block capability.

After you change it, the StartSelection function should look like this:

```
void FAR PASCAL StartSelection(hWnd, ptCurrent, lpSelectRect, fFlags)
HWND hWnd;
POINT ptCurrent;
LPRECT lpSelectRect;
int fFlags;
{
    if (lpSelectRect->left != lpSelectRect->right ||
            lpSelectRect->top != lpSelectRect->bottom)
        ClearSelection(hWnd, lpSelectRect, fFlags);

    lpSelectRect->right = ptCurrent.x;
    lpSelectRect->bottom = ptCurrent.y;

    /* If you are extending the box, invert the current rectangle. */

    if ((fFlags & SL_SPECIAL) == SL_EXTEND)
        ClearSelection(hWnd, lpSelectRect, fFlags);

    /* Otherwise, set origin to current location. */

    else {
        lpSelectRect->left = ptCurrent.x;
        lpSelectRect->top = ptCurrent.y;
    }
    SetCapture(hWnd);
}
```

This function receives four parameters: a window handle, *hWnd*; the current mouse location, *ptCurrent*; a long pointer to the selection rectangle, *lpSelectRect*; and the selection flags, *fFlags*.

The first step is to clear the selection if the selection rectangle is not empty. The **IsRectEmpty** function returns TRUE if the rectangle is empty. The StartSelection function clears the selection by calling the ClearSelection function, which is also in this library.

The next step is to initialize the selection rectangle. The StartSelection function extends the selection (leaving the upper-left corner of the selection unchanged), if the SS_EXTEND bit in the *fFlags* argument is set. Otherwise, it sets the upper-left and lower-right corners of the selection rectangle to the current mouse location. The **SetCapture** function directs all subsequent mouse input to the window even if the cursor moves outside of the window. This is to ensure that the selection process continues uninterrupted. To call this function, an application would use the following statements:

```
case WM_LBUTTONDOWN:

    fTrack = TRUE;    /* User has pressed the left button. */
    StartSelection(hWnd, MAKEPOINT(lParam), &Rect,
        (wParam & MK_SHIFT) ? SL_EXTEND | Shape : Shape);
    break;
```

After you change it, the UpdateSelection function should look like this:

```
void FAR PASCAL UpdateSelection(hWnd, ptCurrent, lpSelectRect, fFlags)
HWND hWnd;
POINT ptCurrent;
LPRECT lpSelectRect;
int fFlags;
{
    HDC hDC;
    short OldROP;

    hDC = GetDC(hWnd);

    switch (fFlags & SL_TYPE) {

        case SL_BOX:

            OldROP = SetROP2(hDC, R2_NOTXORPEN);
            MoveTo(hDC, lpSelectRect->left, lpSelectRect->top);
            LineTo(hDC, lpSelectRect->right, lpSelectRect->top);
            LineTo(hDC, lpSelectRect->right, lpSelectRect->bottom);
            LineTo(hDC, lpSelectRect->left, lpSelectRect->bottom);
            LineTo(hDC, lpSelectRect->left, lpSelectRect->top);
            LineTo(hDC, ptCurrent.x, lpSelectRect->top);
            LineTo(hDC, ptCurrent.x, ptCurrent.y);
            LineTo(hDC, lpSelectRect->left, ptCurrent.y);
            LineTo(hDC, lpSelectRect->left, lpSelectRect->top);
            SetROP2(hDC, OldROP);
            break;
```

```
     case SL_BLOCK:

         PatBlt(hDC,
             lpSelectRect->left,
             lpSelectRect->bottom,
             lpSelectRect->right - lpSelectRect->left,
             ptCurrent.y - lpSelectRect->bottom,
             DSTINVERT);
         PatBlt(hDC,
             lpSelectRect->right,
             lpSelectRect->top,
             ptCurrent.x - lpSelectRect->right,
             ptCurrent.y - lpSelectRect->top,
             DSTINVERT);
         break;
    }
    lpSelectRect->right = ptCurrent.x;
    lpSelectRect->bottom = ptCurrent.y;
    ReleaseDC(hWnd, hDC);
}
```

As the user makes the selection, the UpdateSelection function provides feedback about the user's progress. For the box selection, the function first clears the current box by drawing over it, and then draws the new box. This requires eight calls to the **LineTo** function.

To update a block selection, the UpdateSelection function inverts the rectangle by using the **PatBlt** function. To avoid flicker while the user selects, UpdateSelection inverts only the portions of the rectangle that are different from the previous selection rectangle. This means the function inverts two separate pieces of the screen. It "assumes" that the only area that needs inverting is the area between the previous and current mouse locations. The following figure shows the typical coordinates for describing the areas being inverted:

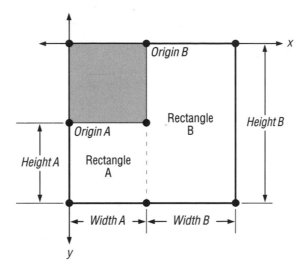

To set the origin of the area to be inverted, the first **PatBlt** call inverts the leftmost rectangle by using lpSelectRect->left (the location of the x-coordinate of the mouse when its button was first pressed) and lpSelectRect->bottom (the most recent update of the y-coordinate location). The width of the first area is determined by subtracting lpSelectRect->left from lpSelectRect->right (the most recent update of the x-coordinate location). The height of this area is determined by subtracting lpSelectRect->bottom from ptCurrent.y (the current y-coordinate location).

The second **PatBlt** call inverts the rightmost rectangle by using lpSelectRect->right and lpSelectRect->top to set the origin of the area to be inverted. The width of this second area is determined by subtracting lpSelectRect->bottom from ptCurrent.x. The height of the area is determined by subtracting lpSelectRect->top from ptCurrent.y.

When the selection updating is complete, the values lpSelectRect->right and lpSelectRect->bottom are updated by assigning them the current values contained in ptCurrent.

To update a box selection, the application should call the UpdateSelection function as follows:

```
case WM_MOUSEMOVE:

    if (fTrack)
        UpdateSelection(hWnd, MAKEPOINT(lParam), &Rect, Shape);
    break;
```

After you change it, the EndSelection function should look like this:

```
void FAR PASCAL EndSelection(ptCurrent, lpSelectRect)
POINT ptCurrent;
LPRECT lpSelectRect;
{
    lpSelectRect->right = ptCurrent.x;
    lpSelectRect->bottom = ptCurrent.y;
    ReleaseCapture();
}
```

The EndSelection function saves the current mouse position in the selection rectangle. The **ReleaseCapture** function is required because a corresponding **Set-Capture** function was called. In general, you should release the mouse immediately after mouse capture is no longer needed.

Finally, when the user releases the left mouse button, the application should call the EndSelection function to save the final point:

```
case WM_LBUTTONUP:

    if (fTrack)
        EndSelection(MAKEPOINT(lParam), &Rect);
    fTrack = FALSE;
    break;
```

After you change it, the ClearSelection function should look like this:

```
void FAR PASCAL ClearSelection(hWnd, lpSelectRect, fFlags)
HWND hWnd;
LPRECT lpSelectRect;
int fFlags;
{
    HDC hDC;
    short OldROP;

    hDC = GetDC(hWnd);
    switch (fFlags & SL_TYPE) {

        case SL_BOX:

            OldROP = SetROP2(hDC, R2_NOTXORPEN);
            MoveTo(hDC, lpSelectRect->left, lpSelectRect->top);
            LineTo(hDC, lpSelectRect->right, lpSelectRect->top);
            LineTo(hDC, lpSelectRect->right, lpSelectRect->bottom);
            LineTo(hDC, lpSelectRect->left, lpSelectRect->bottom);
            LineTo(hDC, lpSelectRect->left, lpSelectRect->top);
            SetROP2(hDC, OldROP);
            break;
```

```
        case SL_BLOCK:

            PatBlt(hDC,
                lpSelectRect->left,
                lpSelectRect->top,
                lpSelectRect->right - lpSelectRect->left,
                lpSelectRect->bottom - lpSelectRect->top,
                DSTINVERT);
            break;
    }
    ReleaseDC(hWnd, hDC);
}
```

Clearing a box selection means removing it from the screen. You can remove the outline by drawing over it with the XOR pen. Clearing a block selection means restoring the inverted screen to its previous state. You can restore the inverted screen by inverting the entire selection.

20.6.2 Creating the Initialization Function

Select uses the standard LibEntry function contained in the LIBENTRY.OBJ file. This function in turn calls a function named LibMain, which should be defined in the source code of the dynamic-link library and which performs library-specific initialization. Since Select does not require initialization beyond that provided by LibEntry, it simply returns a value of 1 to indicate success. The LibMain function of the Select library is defined as follows:

```
int FAR PASCAL LibMain(hinst, wDataSeg, cbHeapSize, lpszCmdLine)
HINSTANCE hinst;
WORD        wDataSeg,
WORD        cbHeapSize;
LPSTR       lpszCmdLine;
{
    return 1;
}
```

20.6.3 Creating the Exit Routine

Like every DLL, Select must include the standard exit dynamic-link library, **WEP**. Again, since Select does not require any cleanup tasks, the **WEP** function simply returns:

```
int FAR PASCAL WEP(nParameter)
int nParameter;
{
    return;
}
```

20.6.4 Creating the Module-Definition File

To link the Select library, you must create a module-definition file containing the following:

```
LIBRARY Select

CODE MOVEABLE DISCARDABLE
DATA SINGLE

EXPORTS
    WEP                     @1 RESIDENTNAME
    StartSelection          @2
    UpdateSelection         @3
    EndSelection            @4
    ClearSelection          @5
```

Because the selection functions do not use global or static variables and there is no local heap, the **DATA** statement is used to specify no data segment. The default heap size is zero.

20.6.5 Creating the Header File

You must also create the SELECT.H header file for the Select library. This file contains the definitions for the constants used in the functions, as well as function definitions. The header file should look like this:

```
void FAR PASCAL StartSelection(HWND, POINT, LPRECT, int);
void FAR PASCAL UpdateSelection(HWND, POINT, LPRECT, int);
void FAR PASCAL EndSelection(POINT, LPRECT);
void FAR PASCAL ClearSelection(HWND, LPRECT, int);
```

You should also use the header file in applications that use the selection functions. This will ensure that proper parameter and return types are used with the functions.

20.6.6 Compiling and Linking

To compile and link the Select library, you must create the makefile, as follows:

```
select.obj: select.c select.h
    cl /c /Asnw /Gsw /W3 /Os /Zp select.c

select.dll: select.obj
    link select libentry,select.dll,,/noe /nod sdllcew libw,select.def
    rc select.dll
    implib select.lib select.def
```

After you have compiled and linked the Select library, you can create a small test application to confirm that it is working properly. For a description of an application that uses the selection functions, see Chapter 11, "Bitmaps," or Chapter 13, "Clipboard."

20.7 Related Topics

For information about using the C language to create a dynamic-link library, see Chapter 14, "C and Assembly Language."

For information about managing memory in a dynamic-link library, see Chapter 16, "More Memory Management."

Multiple Document Interface

The multiple document interface (MDI) in the Microsoft Windows operating system is a user-interface standard for presenting and manipulating multiple documents within a single Windows application. An MDI application has one main window, in which the user can open and work with several documents. Each document appears in its own child window in the main application window. Because each child window has a frame, System menu, Maximize and Minimize buttons, and an icon, the user can control it just as if it were a normal, independent window. The difference is that the child windows cannot move outside the main application window.

This chapter covers the following topics:

- The structure of an MDI application
- Writing procedures for an MDI application
- Controlling the child windows of an MDI application

21.1 Elements of a Multiple Document Interface Application

Like most Windows applications, an MDI application contains a message loop for dispatching messages to the application's various windows. The MDI message loop is similar to normal message loops, except for the way it handles menu accelerator keys.

The main window of an MDI application is similar to that of most Windows applications. In an MDI application, the main window is called the frame window and differs from a normal main window in that its client area is filled by a special child window called the client window. Because Windows maintains the MDI client window and controls the MDI interface, the application need not store a lot of information about the MDI user interface. (In this sense, the MDI client window is similar to a standard control, such as a radio button; it has a standard behavior that Windows provides automatically. The application can use the client window but need not provide code that defines how the window appears or behaves.)

Visually, an MDI client window is simply a large monochromatic rectangle. To the user, the client window is part of the main window; it provides a background upon which the child windows appear. The application defines the child windows; usually, there is one child window per document. The MDI child windows look much like the main window: They have window frames, System menus, and Minimize and Maximize buttons. The main difference to the user is that each child window contains a separate document. Also, the child windows cannot move outside the client window.

The following figure shows the sample application Multipad, a typical MDI application:

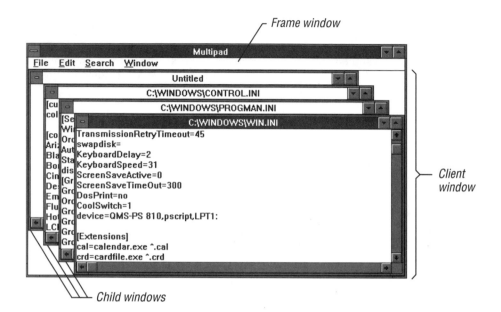

In general, an application controls the MDI interface by passing messages up and down the hierarchy of MDI windows. The MDI client window, which Windows controls, carries out many operations on behalf of the application.

21.2 Initializing a Multiple Document Interface Application

The first place in which an MDI application differs from a normal Windows application is in the initialization process. Although the overall process is the same, an MDI application requires that you set certain values in the window class structure.

To initialize an MDI application, you first register its window classes (if there is no previous instance of the application) just as you would for a normal application. You then create and display any windows that will be initially visible.

21.2.1 Registering the Window Classes

In general, a typical MDI application must register two window classes: one for its frame window and one for its child window. The class structure for the frame window is similar to the class structure for the main window in non-MDI applications.

The class structure for the MDI child windows differs slightly from the structure for child windows in non-MDI applications; following are the differences:

- The class structure should have an icon, because the user can minimize an MDI child window as if it were a normal application window.

- The menu name should be NULL, because MDI child windows cannot have their own menus.

- The class structure should reserve extra space in the window structure. With this space, the application can associate data, such as a filename, with a particular child window.

An application may have more than one window class for its MDI child windows, if there is more than one type of document available in the application.

Note that the application does not register a class for the MDI client window, which Windows defines.

In the Multipad application, the locally defined function InitializeApplication registers the MDI window classes.

21.2.2 Creating the Windows

After registering its window classes, your MDI application can create its windows. It first creates its frame window, again by using the **CreateWindow** function. After creating its frame window, the application creates its client window by using **CreateWindow**. It should specify MDICLIENT as the client window's class name. MDICLIENT is a preregistered window class, defined by Windows. The *lParam* parameter of **CreateWindow** should point to a **CLIENTCREATE-STRUCT** structure. This structure contains the following members:

Member	Description
hWindowMenu	Identifies a pop-up menu used for controlling MDI child windows. As child windows are created, the application adds their titles to the pop-up menu as menu items. The user can then activate a child window by choosing its title from the window menu. Multipad places this pop-up menu in its Window menu and retrieves a handle of the pop-up menu by using the **GetSubMenu** function.
idFirstChild	Specifies the window identifier of the first MDI child window. The first MDI child window created will be assigned this identifier. Additional windows will be created with subsequent window identifiers. When a child window is destroyed, Windows immediately reassigns the window identifiers to keep their range continuous.

When a child window's title is added to the window menu, the menu item is assigned the child window's identifier, which means that the frame window will receive WM_COMMAND messages with these identifiers in the *wParam* parameter. Thus, you should choose the value for the **idFirstChild** member so that it does not conflict with menu-item identifiers in the frame window's menu.

The titles of child windows are added to the end of the window menu. If the application adds strings to the window menu by using the **AppendMenu** function, these strings can be overwritten by the titles of the child windows when the window menu is repainted. (The window menu is repainted whenever a child window is created or destroyed.) Applications that add strings to the window menu of MDI applications should use the **InsertMenu** function and verify that the titles of child windows have not overwritten these new strings.

The MDI client window is created with the WS_CLIPCHILDREN style bit set, since the window must not paint over its child windows.

In Multipad, the locally defined InitializeInstance function creates the frame window. However, Multipad does not create its client window at this point. Instead, it does this as part of the frame window's WM_CREATE message processing. Multipad handles the WM_CREATE message in its MPFrameWndProc function. After creating the frame window and the client window, Multipad carries out any additional initialization, such as loading the accelerator table and checking a printer driver.

Multipad then creates its first MDI child window, either empty or containing a file appearing on the command line. (For information about creating MDI child windows, see Section 21.7.1, "Creating a Child Window.")

21.3 Writing the Main Message Loop

The main message loop for an MDI application is similar to a normal message loop, except that the MDI application uses the **TranslateMDISysAccel** function to translate child-window accelerator keys.

The System-menu accelerator keys for an MDI child window are similar to those in a normal window's System menu. The difference is that child-window accelerator keys respond to the CTRL key rather than the ALT (Menu) key.

A typical MDI application's message loop looks like this:

```
while (GetMessage(&msg, NULL, 0, 0)) {
    if (!TranslateMDISysAccel(hwndMDIClient, &msg)
            && !TranslateAccelerator(hwndFrame, hAccel, &msg)) {
        TranslateMessage(&msg);
        DispatchMessage(&msg);
    }
}
```

This loop is similar to a normal message loop that handles accelerator keys. The difference is that the MDI message loop calls **TranslateMDISysAccel** before checking for application-defined accelerator keys or dispatching the message as usual.

The **TranslateMDISysAccel** function translates WM_KEYDOWN messages into WM_SYSCOMMAND messages to the active MDI child window. The function returns FALSE if the message is not an MDI accelerator message; in that case, the application uses the **TranslateAccelerator** function to determine whether any of the application-defined accelerator keys were pressed. If not, the loop dispatches the message to the appropriate window procedure.

21.4 Writing the Frame Window Procedure

The frame window procedure for an MDI application is similar to a normal application's main window procedure, with a few differences:

- Usually, a window procedure passes all messages it does not handle to the **DefWindowProc** function. The window procedure for an MDI frame window passes such messages to the **DefFrameProc** function instead.

- The frame window procedure passes **DefFrameProc** all messages it does not handle; in addition, it also passes some messages that the application does handle. For a list of messages your application must pass to **DefFrameProc**, see the *Microsoft Windows Programmer's Reference, Volume 2*.

DefFrameProc also handles WM_SIZE messages by resizing the MDI client window to fit into the new client area. The application can calculate a smaller area for the MDI client window, if necessary (for example, to allow room for status or ribbon windows).

DefFrameProc will also set the focus to the client window upon receiving a WM_SETFOCUS message. The client window sets the focus to the active child window, if there is one. As noted previously, the WM_CREATE message causes the frame window to create its MDI client window.

The frame window procedure in Multipad is called MPFrameWndProc. The handling of other messages by MPFrameWndProc is similar to that of non-MDI applications. WM_COMMAND messages in Multipad are handled by the locally defined CommandHandler function, which calls **DefFrameProc** for command messages Multipad does not handle. If Multipad did not do this, the user would not be able to activate a child window from the Window menu, because the WM_COMMAND message sent by choosing the window's item (command) would be lost.

21.5 Writing the Child Window Procedure

Like the frame window procedure, an MDI child window procedure uses a special function for processing messages by default. All messages the child window procedure does not handle must be passed to the **DefMDIChildProc** function rather than to the **DefWindowProc** function. In addition, some window-management messages (such as WM_SIZE, WM_MOVE, and WM_GETMINMAXINFO) must be passed to **DefMDIChildProc** even if the application handles the message, in order for MDI to function correctly. For a complete list of messages the application must pass to **DefMDIChildProc**, see the *Microsoft Windows Programmer's Reference, Volume 2*.

The child window procedure in Multipad is named MPChildWndProc.

21.6 Associating Data with Child Windows

Because the number of child windows varies depending on how many documents the user opens, an MDI application must be able to associate data (for example, the name of the current file) with each child window. There are two ways to do this:

- Storing data in the window structure
- Using window properties

21.6.1 Storing Data in the Window Structure

When the application registers the window class, it may reserve extra space in the window structure for application data specific to this particular class of windows. To store and retrieve data in this extra space, the application uses the functions **GetWindowWord**, **SetWindowWord**, **GetWindowLong**, and **SetWindowLong**.

If the application must maintain a large amount of data for a document window, the application can allocate memory for a data structure and then store the handle of the structure in the extra space of the window structure.

Multipad uses this technique. For example, the WM_CREATE message processing in the Multipad window procedure MPChildWndProc creates a multiline edit control used as the text-editor window. Multipad stores the handle to this edit control in its child window structure by using the **SetWindowWord** function. Whenever Multipad must use the edit control, it calls the **GetWindowWord** function to retrieve the handle of the edit control. Multipad maintains several per-document variables this way.

21.6.2 Using Window Properties

Your MDI application can also store per-document data by using window properties. Properties are different from extra space in the window structure in that you need not allocate extra space when registering the window class. A window can have any number of properties. Also, where offsets are used to access the extra space in window structures, properties are referred to by string names.

Associated with each property is a handle. For example, Multipad could have used a property called EditCntl to store the edit control window handle discussed previously. The handle could be any 2-byte value and could be a handle of a data structure. Properties are often more convenient than extra space in the window structure. This is because, when using properties, the application is not required to reserve extra space in advance or to calculate offsets to variables. On the other hand, accessing extra space by offset is generally faster than accessing properties.

21.7 Controlling Child Windows

To control its child windows, an MDI application sends messages to its MDI client window. This type of control includes creating, destroying, activating, or changing the state of a child window.

Generally, an application will work only with the active child window. For example, in Multipad, most of the File menu commands and all of the Edit and Search menu commands refer to the active window. Thus, Multipad maintains the hwndActive and hwndActiveEdit variables, because only the windows identified by those variables will receive messages.

There are exceptions. For example, the application might send messages to all child windows in order to determine each window's state. Multipad does this when closing, to ensure that all files have been saved.

Because MDI child windows may be minimized, the application must be careful to avoid manipulating icon title windows as if they were normal MDI child windows. Icon title windows appear when the application enumerates child windows of the MDI client window. Icon titles differ from other child windows, however, in that they are owned by an MDI child window. Thus, you can use the **GetWindow** function with the GW_OWNER index to detect whether a child window is an icon title. Non-title windows will return NULL. Note that this test is insufficient for top-level windows, because pop-up menus and dialog boxes are owned windows as well.

21.7.1 Creating a Child Window

To create an MDI child window, the application sends a WM_MDICREATE message to the MDI client. (The application must not use the **CreateWindow** function to create MDI child windows.) The *lParam* parameter of a WM_MDICREATE message is a far pointer to a structure called **MDICREATESTRUCT**, which contains members similar to **CreateWindow** function parameters.

Multipad creates its MDI child windows by using its locally defined AddFile function (located in the source file MPFILE.C). The AddFile function sets the title of the child window by assigning the **szTitle** member of the window's **MDICREATESTRUCT** structure to either the name of the file being edited or to "Untitled." The **szClass** member is set to the name of the MDI child-window class registered in the Multipad InitializeApplication function. The owner **hOwner** member is set to the application's instance handle.

The **MDICREATESTRUCT** structure contains four dimension members: **x** and **y**, which are the position of the window, and **cx** and **cy**, the horizontal and vertical extents of the window. Any of these may be assigned explicitly by the application or may be set to CW_USEDEFAULT, in which case Windows picks a position or size or both according to a cascading algorithm. All four fields must be initialized in all cases. Multipad uses CW_USEDEFAULT for all dimensions.

The last member is the **style** member, which may contain style bits for the window. To create an MDI child window that can have any combination of window styles, specify MDIS_ALLCHILDSTYLES for the window style. When this style is not specified, an MDI child window has the WS_MINIMIZE, WS_MAXIMIZE, WS_HSCROLL, and WS_VSCROLL styles as default settings.

You can use the WS_MINIMIZE or WS_MAXIMIZE bit to set the original state of the window.

The pointer passed in the *lParam* parameter of the WM_MDICREATE message is passed to **CreateWindow** and appears as the first member in the **CREATE-STRUCT** structure passed in the WM_CREATE message. In Multipad, the child window initializes itself during WM_CREATE message processing by initializing document variables in its extra data and by creating the edit control's child window.

21.7.2 Destroying a Child Window

To destroy an MDI child window, use the WM_MDIDESTROY message. Pass the child window's handle in the message's *wParam* parameter.

21.7.3 Activating and Deactivating a Child Window

You can activate or deactivate a child window by using the WM_MDINEXT and WM_MDIACTIVATE messages. WM_MDINEXT activates the next MDI child window in the window list, and WM_MDIACTIVATE activates the child window specified by the message's *wParam* parameter. The user usually controls child window activation by using the MDI user interface. Multipad does not use either of these messages directly.

A more common use of WM_MDIACTIVATE is tracking activation changes. WM_MDIACTIVATE is also sent to the MDI child windows being activated and deactivated, so by monitoring WM_MDIACTIVATE messages sent to child windows, the application can track the active window.

Multipad maintains two global variables, hwndActive and hwndActiveEdit, which are the window handles of the active MDI child window and its edit control, respectively. Maintaining these variables simplifies sending messages to these windows.

You can retrieve the active MDI child window at any time by using the WM_MDIGETACTIVE message, which returns a handle of the active child window in its low-order word. The application could then use the **GetWindowWord** function to retrieve a window handle of the document's edit control. To explicitly maximize and restore a child window, the application could use the WM_MDIMAXIMIZE and WM_MDIRESTORE messages, with the *wParam* parameter of each message set to the handle of the child window the application wants to change. Again, these are messages that an application will not normally use, since Windows manages the MDI user interface on behalf of the application.

21.7.4 Arranging Child Windows on the Screen

Windows provides three utility messages that you can use to arrange MDI child windows:

Message	Description
WM_MDICASCADE	Arranges in order all the child windows that are not minimized, diagonally from upper-left to lower-right. (This message also arranges child window icons.)
WM_MDIICONARRANGE	Arranges all child window icons along the bottom of the MDI client window.
WM_MDITILE	Arranges all child windows that are not minimized so that they are tiled within the MDI client window. (This message also arranges child window icons.)

21.8 Related Topics

For more information about creating and managing windows, see the *Microsoft Windows Programmer's Reference, Volume 1*.

For more information about MDI functions, see the *Microsoft Windows Programmer's Reference, Volume 2*.

For more information about the window class structure, see the *Microsoft Windows Programmer's Reference, Volume 3*.

Dynamic Data Exchange

The Microsoft Windows operating system provides several methods for transferring data between applications. One way to transfer data is to use Windows dynamic data exchange (DDE). DDE is a message protocol that developers can use for data exchanging between Windows applications. When used in an application, DDE offers the user a more integrated Windows work environment.

Windows version 3.1 includes the Dynamic Data Exchange Management Library (DDEML). The DDEML is a dynamic-link library (DLL) that applications running with Windows can use to share data. The DDEML provides an application programming interface (API) that simplifies the task of adding DDE capability to a Windows application. Instead of sending, posting, and processing DDE messages directly, an application uses the functions provided by the DDEML to manage DDE conversations. (A DDE conversation is the interaction between client and server applications.) The DDEML also provides a facility for managing the strings and data that are shared among DDE applications. Instead of using atoms and pointers to shared memory objects, DDE applications create and exchange string handles, which identify strings, and data handles, which identify global memory objects. DDEML provides a service that makes it possible for a server application to register the service names that it supports. The names are broadcast to other applications in the system, which can then use the names to connect to the server. The DDEML also ensures compatibility among DDE applications by forcing them to implement the DDE protocol in a consistent manner.

Existing applications that use the message-based DDE protocol are fully compatible with those that use the DDEML. That is, an application that uses message-based DDE can establish conversations and perform transactions with applications that use the DDEML. Because of the many advantages of the DDEML, new applications should use it rather than the DDE messages.

The DDEML can run on systems that have Windows version 3.0 or later installed. The DDEML does not support real mode. To use the API elements of the DDE management library, you must include the DDEML.H header file in your source files, link with DDEML.LIB, and ensure that DDEML.DLL resides in the system's path.

This chapter provides guidelines for implementing dynamic data exchange for applications that cannot use the DDEML. For more information about the DDEML, see the *Microsoft Windows Programmer's Reference, Volume 1*.

This chapter covers the following topics:

- Data exchange in Windows
- DDE concepts
- DDE messages
- DDE message flow

22.1 Data Exchange in Windows

In general, Windows supports three mechanisms that applications can use to exchange data with one another:

- Clipboard transfers
- Dynamic-link libraries
- Dynamic data exchange

Windows does not support sharing global memory handles directly. Because of expanded memory considerations, as well as compatibility with future versions of Windows, you should not dereference (by using the **GlobalUnlock** function), or otherwise manipulate, global memory handles created by another application. DDE is the only Windows mechanism that supports passing of global-memory handles between applications.

22.1.1 Clipboard Transfers

With the Windows clipboard, a user can transfer data between applications in the system. The user issues a command in an application to copy selected data to the clipboard. Then, in another application, the user issues a command to paste the data from the clipboard into the second application's workspace. In general, the clipboard is a temporary repository of information that requires direct involvement of the user to initiate and complete the transfer.

22.1.2 Dynamic-Link Libraries

You can design a dynamic-link library (DLL) to serve as a repository for data shared between applications. This dynamic-link library offers an application interface for storing and retrieving data. The data itself is stored in the library's local heap or in the static data area of its data segment. Handles or addresses of this data can be passed to applications only as logical identifiers, never to be deferenced by the applications themselves. Only the dynamic-link library can dereference its handles or address, using the **GlobalUnlock** or **LocalUnlock** function or address indirection. In general, you can use only the dynamic-link library's data segment for data exchange.

22.1.3 Dynamic Data Exchange

The Windows DDE protocol is a standard for cooperating applications. By using the protocol, applications exchange data and carry out remote commands by means of Windows messages.

Because Windows has a message-based architecture, passing messages is the most appropriate method for automatically transferring information between applications. However, Windows messages contain only two parameters (*wParam* and *lParam*) for passing data. As a result, these parameters must refer indirectly to other pieces of data if more than a few words of information are to be passed between applications.

The DDE protocol defines exactly how *wParam* and *lParam* are used to pass larger pieces of data by means of global atoms and global shared-memory handles.

A global atom is a reference to a character string. In the DDE protocol, atoms identify the applications exchanging data, the nature of the data being exchanged, and the data items themselves.

A global shared-memory handle is a handle of a memory object allocated by **GlobalAlloc**, using the GMEM_DDESHARE option. In the DDE protocol, global shared-memory objects store data items passed between applications, protocol options, and remote command execution strings.

The DDE protocol has specific rules for applications involved in a DDE exchange. These rules apply to allocating and deleting global atoms and shared memory objects.

22.1.4 Uses for Windows Dynamic Data Exchange

DDE is most appropriate for data exchanges that do not require ongoing user interaction. Usually, application provides a method for the user to establish the link between the applications exchanging data. Once that link is established, however, the applications exchange data without further user involvement.

DDE can be used to implement a broad range of application features:

- Linking to real-time data, such as to stock market updates, scientific instruments, or process control.

- Creating compound documents, such as a word-processing document that includes a chart produced by a graphics program. Using DDE, the chart will change when the source data is changed, while the rest of the document remains the same.

- Performing data queries between applications, such as a spreadsheet querying a database application for accounts past due.

22.1.5 Dynamic Data Exchange from the User's Point of View

The following example illustrates two cooperating Windows DDE applications, as seen from the user's point of view.

A Microsoft Excel spreadsheet user wants to track the price of a particular stock on the New York Stock Exchange. The user has a Windows application called Quote that in turn has access to NYSE data. The DDE conversation between Microsoft Excel and Quote takes place as follows:

■ The user initiates the conversation by supplying the name of the application (Quote) that will supply the data and the particular topic of interest (NYSE). The resulting DDE conversation is used to request quotes on specific stocks.

■ Microsoft Excel broadcasts the application and topic names to all DDE applications currently running in the system. Quote responds, establishing a conversation with Excel about the NYSE topic.

■ The user can then create a spreadsheet formula in a cell that requests that the spreadsheet be automatically updated whenever a particular stock quotation changes. For example, the user could request an automatic update whenever a change in the selling price of ZAXX stock occurs, by specifying the following Microsoft Excel formula:

```
='Quote'|'NYSE'!ZAXX
```

■ The user can terminate the automatic updating of the ZAXX stock quotation at any time. Other data links that were established separately (such as for quotations for other stocks) still will remain active under the same NYSE conversation.

■ The user can also terminate the entire conversation between Excel and Quote on the NYSE topic, so that no specific data links may be subsequently established on that topic without initiating a new conversation.

22.2 Dynamic-Data-Exchange Concepts

Certain concepts and terminology are key to understanding dynamic data exchange. The following sections explain the most important of these.

22.2.1 Client, Server, and Conversation

Two applications participating in dynamic data exchange are engaged in a DDE conversation. The application that initiates the conversation is the client application; the application responding to the client is the server application. An application can be engaged in several conversations at the same time, acting as the client in some and as the server in others.

A DDE conversation takes place between two windows, one for each of the participating applications. The window may be the main window of the application; a window associated with a specific document, as in a multiple document interface

(MDI) application; or a hidden (invisible) window whose only purpose is to process DDE messages.

Since a DDE conversation is identified by the pair of handles of the windows engaged in the conversation, no window should be engaged in more than one conversation with another window. Either the client application or the server application must provide a different window for each of its conversations with a particular server or client application.

An application can ensure that a pair of client and server windows is never involved in more than one conversation by creating a hidden window for each conversation. The sole purpose of this window is to process DDE messages.

22.2.2 Application, Topic, and Item Names

DDE identifies the units of data passed between the client and server with a three-level hierarchy of application, topic, and item names.

Each DDE conversation is uniquely defined by the application name and topic. At the beginning of a DDE conversation, the client and server determine the application name and topic. The application name is usually the name of the server application. For example, in a conversation in which Microsoft Excel acts as the server, the conversation application name is Excel.

The DDE topic is a general classification of data within which multiple data items may be "discussed" (exchanged) during the conversation. For applications that operate on file-based documents, the topic is usually a filename. For other applications, the topic is an application-specific name.

Because the client and server window handles together identify a DDE conversation, the application name and topic that define a conversation cannot be changed during the course of the conversation.

A DDE data item is information related to the conversation topic that is exchanged between the applications. Values for the data item can be passed from the server to the client, or from the client to the server. Data can be passed with any of the standard clipboard formats or with a registered clipboard format. For more information about standard clipboard formats, see the description of the **SetClipboardData** function in *Microsoft Windows Programmer's Reference*, *Volume 2*. For more information about registering clipboard formats, see the description of the **RegisterClipboardFormat** function. A special, registered format named Link is used to identify an item in a DDE conversation.

22.2.3 Permanent Data Links

Once a DDE conversation has begun, the client can establish one or more permanent data links with the server. A data link is a communication mechanism by which the server notifies the client whenever the value of a given data item changes. The data link is permanent in the sense that this notification process continues until the data link or the DDE conversation itself is terminated.

There are two kinds of permanent DDE data links: warm and hot. In a warm data link, the server notifies the client that the value of the data item has changed, but the server does not send the data value to the client until the client requests it. In a hot data link, the server immediately sends the changed data value to the client.

Applications that support hot or warm data links typically provide a Copy or Paste Link command in their Edit menu to permit the user to establish links between applications. For more information, see Section 22.4.3.2, "Initiating a Data Link with the Paste Link Command."

22.2.4 Atoms and Shared Memory Objects

Certain arguments of DDE messages are global atoms. Applications using these atoms must follow explicit rules about when to to allocate and delete these atoms. In all cases, the sender of a message must delete any atom which the intended receiver will not receive due to an error condition, such as failure of the **Post-Message** function.

DDE uses shared memory objects for three purposes:

- To carry a data item value to be exchanged. This is an item referenced by the *hData* argument in the WM_DDE_DATA and WM_DDE_POKE messages.

- To carry options in a message. This is an item referenced by the *hOptions* argument in a WM_DDE_ADVISE message.

- To carry an execution-command string. This is an item referenced by the *hCommands* argument in the WM_DDE_EXECUTE message and its corresponding WM_DDE_ACK message.

Applications that receive a DDE shared memory object must treat it as read only. It must not be used as a mutual read-write area for the free exchange of data.

As with a DDE atom, a shared memory object should be freed properly to provide for effective memory management. Shared memory objects should be properly locked and unlocked. In all cases, the sender of a message must delete any shared memory object which the intended receiver will not receive due to an error condition, such as failure of the **PostMessage** function.

For information about how the DDE messages allocate and delete atoms and shared memory objects, see the *Microsoft Windows Programmer's Reference*, *Volume 3*.

22.3 Dynamic-Data-Exchange Messages

Because DDE is a message-based protocol, it employs no special Windows functions or libraries. All DDE transactions are conducted by passing certain defined DDE messages between the client and server windows.

There are nine DDE messages; the symbolic constants for these messages are defined in the Microsoft Windows 3.1 Software Development Kit (SDK) header file DDE.H, not WINDOWS.H. Certain data structures for the various DDE messages are also defined in DDE.H.

The nine DDE messages are summarized as follows. For a detailed description of each DDE message, see the *Microsoft Windows Programmer's Reference*, *Volume 3*.

Message	Description
WM_DDE_ACK	Acknowledges receiving or not receiving a message.
WM_DDE_ADVISE	Requests the server application to supply an update or notification for a data item whenever it changes. This establishes a permanent data link.
WM_DDE_DATA	Sends a data-item value to the client application.
WM_DDE_EXECUTE	Sends a string to the server application, which is expected to process it as a series of commands.
WM_DDE_INITIATE	Initiates a conversation between the client and server applications.
WM_DDE_POKE	Sends a data-item value to the server application.
WM_DDE_REQUEST	Requests the server application to provide the value of a data item.
WM_DDE_TERMINATE	Terminates a conversation.
WM_DDE_UNADVISE	Terminates a permanent data link.

An application calls the **SendMessage** function to issue the WM_DDE_INITIATE message or a WM_DDE_ACK message sent in response to WM_DDE_INITIATE. All other messages are sent by the **PostMessage** function. The window handle of the receiving window appears as the first parameter of these calls. The second parameter contains the message to be sent, the third parameter identifies the sending window, and the fourth parameter contains the message-specific arguments.

22.4 Dynamic-Data-Exchange Message Flow

A typical DDE conversation consists of the following events:

1. The client application initiates the conversation, and the server application responds.

2. The applications exchange data by any or all of the following methods:

   - The server application sends data to the client at the client's request.

   - The client application sends unsolicited data to the server application.

   - The client application requests the server application to send data whenever the data changes (hot data link).

   - The client application requests the server application to notify the client whenever a data item changes (warm data link).

   - The server application carries out a command at the client's request.

3. Either the client or server application terminates the conversation.

An application window that processes requests from a client or server must process them strictly in the order in which they are received.

A client can establish conversations with more than one server; a server can have conversations with more than one client. When handling messages from more than one source, a client or server must process the messages of a given conversation synchronously, but need not process all messages synchronously. In other words, it can shift from one conversation to another as needed.

If an application is unable to process an incoming request because it is waiting for a DDE response, it must post a WM_DDE_ACK message with the **fBusy** flag set to 1 to prevent deadlock. An application can also send a busy WM_DDE_ACK message if it, for any reason, cannot process an incoming request within a reasonable amount of time.

An application should be able to handle, in some way, the failure of a client or server to respond with a message within a certain time. Since the length of the time-out interval may vary depending on the nature of the application and the configuration of the user's system (including whether it is on a network), the application should provide a way for the user to specify the interval.

22.4.1 Initiating a Conversation

To initiate a DDE conversation, the client sends a WM_DDE_INITIATE message. Usually, the client broadcasts this message by calling the **SendMessage** function, with −1 as the first parameter. If the application already has the window handle of the server application, however, it can send the message directly to that window. The client prepares atoms for the application and topic names by calling the **GlobalAddAtom** function. The client may request conversations with any potential server application and for any potential topic by supplying NULL (wildcard) atoms for, respectively, the application and topic.

The following example illustrates how the client initiates a conversation, where both the application and topic are specified:

```
atomApplication = *szApplication == 0 ?
    NULL : GlobalAddAtom((LPSTR)szApplication);
atomTopic = *szTopic == 0 ?
    NULL : GlobalAddAtom((LPSTR)szTopic);

fInInitiate = TRUE;
SendMessage(-1,
    WM_DDE_INITIATE,
    hwndClientDDE,
    MAKELONG(atomApplication, atomTopic));
fInInitiate = FALSE;
if (atomApplication != NULL)
    GlobalDeleteAtom(atomApplication);
if (atomTopic != NULL)
    GlobalDeleteAtom(atomTopic);
```

Note that if your application uses NULL atoms, you need not use the **GlobalAddAtom** and **GlobalDeleteAtom** functions. In this example, the client application creates two global atoms containing the name of the server and the name of the topic, respectively.

The client application sends a WM_DDE_INITIATE message with these two atoms in the *lParam* parameter of the message. The special window handle −1 in the call to the **SendMessage** function directs Windows to send this message to all other active applications. **SendMessage** does not return to the client application until all applications that receive the message have, in turn, returned control to Windows. This means that all WM_DDE_ACK messages sent in reply by the server applications are guaranteed to have been processed by the client by the time the **SendMessage** call has returned.

After **SendMessage** returns, the client application deletes the global atoms.

Server applications respond according to the following logic:

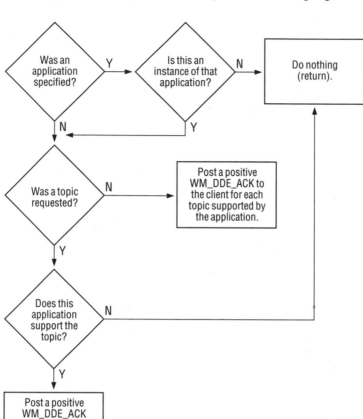

To acknowledge one or more topics, the server must create atoms for each conversation (requiring duplicate application-name atoms if there are multiple topics) and send a WM_DDE_ACK message for each conversation, as follows:

```
if ((atomApplication = GlobalAddAtom("Server")) != 0) {
    if ((atomTopic = GlobalAddAtom(szTopic)) != 0) {
        SendMessage(hwndClientDDE,
            WM_DDE_ACK,
            hwndServerDDE,
            MAKELONG(atomApplication, atomTopic));
        GlobalDeleteAtom(atomApplication);
    }
    GlobalDeleteAtom(atomTopic);
}
```

```
if ((atomApplication == 0) || (atomTopic == 0)) {

    .  /* error handling */
    .
    .

}
```

When a server responds with a WM_DDE_ACK message, the client application should save the handle of the server window. The client application receives this handle as the *wParam* parameter of the WM_DDE_ACK message. The client application then sends all subsequent DDE messages to the server window identified by this handle.

If your client application uses NULL atoms for the application or topic, you should expect that it will receive acknowledgments from more than one server application. As stated in Section 22.2.1, "Client, Server, and Conversation," creating a unique, hidden window for each DDE conversation ensures that a pair of client and server windows is never involved in more than one conversation. To follow this practice, however, the client application must terminate conversations with all but one of the server applications that respond to the same WM_DDE_INITIATE message from the client.

22.4.2 Transferring a Single Item

Once a DDE conversation has been established, the client can retrieve the value of a data item from the server by issuing the WM_DDE_REQUEST message, or the client can submit a data-item value to the server by issuing the WM_DDE_POKE message.

22.4.2.1 Retrieving an Item from the Server

To retrieve an item from the server, the client sends the server a WM_DDE_REQUEST message specifying the item and format to retrieve, as follows:

```
if ((atomItem = GlobalAddAtom(szItemName)) != 0) {
    if (!PostMessage(hwndServerDDE,
            WM_DDE_REQUEST,
            hwndClientDDE,
            MAKELONG(CF_TEXT, atomItem)))
        GlobalDeleteAtom(atomItem);
}
if (atomItem == 0) {

    .  /* error handling */
    .
    .

}
```

In this example, the client specifies the clipboard format CF_TEXT as the preferred format for the requested data item.

The receiver (server) of the WM_DDE_REQUEST message typically must delete the item atom, but if the **PostMessage** call itself fails, the client must delete the atom.

If the server has access to the requested item and can render it in the requested format, the server copies the item value as a global shared-memory object and sends the client a WM_DDE_DATA message, as follows:

```
/*
 * Allocate the size of the DDE data header, plus the data: a
 * string,<CR><LF><NULL>. The byte for the string's terminating
 * null character is counted by DDEDATA.Value[1].
 */

if (!(hData = GlobalAlloc(GMEM_MOVEABLE | GMEM_DDESHARE,
        (LONG) sizeof(DDEDATA) + strlen(szItemValue) + 2)))
    return;
if (!(lpData = (DDEDATA FAR*) GlobalLock(hData)))  {
    GlobalFree(hData);
    return;
}
    .
    .
    .


lpData->cfFormat = CF_TEXT;
lstrcpy((LPSTR) lpData->Value, (LPSTR) szItemValue);

/* Each line of CF_TEXT data is terminated by CR/LF.*/

lstrcat((LPSTR) lpData->Value, (LPSTR) "\r\n");
GlobalUnlock(hData);
if ((atomItem = GlobalAddAtom((LPSTR) szItemName)) != 0) {
    if (!PostMessage(hwndClientDDE,
            WM_DDE_DATA,
            hwndServerDDE,
            MAKELONG(hData, atomItem))) {
        GlobalFree(hData);
        GlobalDeleteAtom(atomItem);
    }
}

if (atomItem == 0) {

    .
    . /* error handling */
    .


}
```

In this example, the server application allocates a memory object to contain the data item. The memory is allocated with the GMEM_DDESHARE option, so that the server and client applications can share the memory. After allocating the memory object, the server application locks the object so it can obtain the object's address. The data object is initialized as a **DDEDATA** structure.

The server application then sets the **cfFormat** member of the structure to CF_TEXT to inform the client application that the data is in text format. In response, the client copies the value of the requested data into the **Value** member of the **DDEDATA** structure.

After the server has filled the data object, the server unlocks the data. It then creates a global atom containing the name of the data item.

Finally, the server issues the WM_DDE_DATA message by calling the **Post-Message** function. The handle of the data object and the atom containing the item name are contained in the *lParam* parameter of the message.

If the server cannot satisfy the request, it sends the client a negative WM_DDE_ACK message, as follows:

```
/* negative acknowledgment */

PostMessage(hwndClientDDE,
    WM_DDE_ACK,
    hwndServerDDE,
    MAKELONG(0, atomItem));
```

Upon receiving a WM_DDE_DATA message, the client processes the data-item value as appropriate. Then, if the **fAckReq** bit specified in the WM_DDE_DATA message is 1, the client must send the server a positive WM_DDE_ACK message, as follows:

```
hData = LOWORD(lParam);    /* of WM_DDE_DATA message */
atomItem = HIWORD(lParam);
if (!(lpDDEData = (DDEDATA FAR*) GlobalLock(hData))
        || (lpDDEData->cfFormat != CF_TEXT)) {
    PostMessage(hwndServerDDE,
        WM_DDE_ACK,
        hwndClientDDE,
        MAKELONG(0, atomItem));    /* negative ACK */
}

/* Copy data from lpDDEData here.*/
```

```
if (lpDDEData->fAckReq) {
    PostMessage(hwndServerDDE,
        WM_DDE_ACK,
        hwndClientDDE,
        MAKELONG(0x8000, atomItem)); /* positive ACK */
}
bRelease = lpDDEData->fRelease;
GlobalUnlock(hData);
if (bRelease)
    GlobalFree(hData);
```

In this example, the client examines the format of the data; if the format is not CF_TEXT (or if the client cannot lock the memory for the data), the client sends a negative WM_DDE_ACK message to indicate that it cannot process the data.

If it can process the data, the client examines the **fAckReq** member of the **DDE-DATA** structure to determine whether the server requested that it be informed that the client received and processed the data successfully. If the server did request this information, the client sends the server a positive WM_DDE_ACK message.

The client saves the value of the **fRelease** member before unlocking the data object, because unlocking the data invalidates the pointer to the data. The client then examines the flag value to determine whether the server application requested the client to free the global memory containing the data; the client acts accordingly.

Upon receiving a negative WM_DDE_ACK message, the client may ask for the same item value again, specifying a different clipboard format. Typically, a client will first ask for the most complex format it can support, and then step down if necessary through progressively simpler formats until it finds one the server can provide.

If the server supports the Formats item of the System topic, the client can determine once what clipboard formats the server supports, instead of determining them each time the client requests an item. For more information about the System topic, see Section 22.5, "The System Topic."

22.4.2.2 Submitting an Item to the Server

The client may send an item value to the server by using the WM_DDE_POKE message. The client renders the item to be sent and sends the WM_DDE_POKE message, as follows:

```
if (!(hPokeData
        = GlobalAlloc(GMEM_MOVEABLE | GMEM_DDESHARE,
        (LONG) sizeof(DDEPOKE) + lstrlen(szValue) + 2)))
    return;
```

```
if (!(lpPokeData
        = (DDEPOKE FAR*) GlobalLock(hPokeData))) {
    GlobalFree(hPokeData);
    return;
}
lpPokeData->fRelease = TRUE;
lpPokeData->cfFormat = CF_TEXT;
lstrcpy((LPSTR) lpPokeData->Value, (LPSTR) szValue);

/* Each line of CF_TEXT data is terminated by CR/LF.*/

lstrcat((LPSTR) lpPokeData->Value, (LPSTR) "\r\n");
GlobalUnlock(hPokeData);
if ((atomItem = GlobalAddAtom((LPSTR) szItem)) != 0) {

    .
    .
    .


    if (!PostMessage(hwndServerDDE,
            WM_DDE_POKE,
            hwndClientDDE,
            MAKELONG(hPokeData, atomItem))) {
        GlobalDeleteAtom(atomItem);
        GlobalFree(hPokeData);
    }
}

if (atomItem == 0) {

    .
    . /* error handling */
    .

}
```

Note that sending data by using a WM_DDE_POKE message is essentially the same as sending it by using a WM_DDE_DATA message, except that WM_DDE_POKE is sent from the client to the server.

If the server is able to accept the data-item value in the format in which it was rendered by the client, the server processes the item value as appropriate and sends the client a positive WM_DDE_ACK message. If it is unable to process the item value, because of format or other reasons, the server sends the client a negative WM_DDE_ACK message.

```
hPokeData = LOWORD(lParam);
atomItem = HIWORD(lParam);
GlobalGetAtomName(atomItem, szItemName, ITEM_NAME_MAX_SIZE);
```

```
if (!(lpPokeData = (DDEPOKE FAR*) GlobalLock(hPokeData))
        || lpPokeData->cfFormat != CF_TEXT
        || !IsItemSupportedByServer(szItemName))) {
    PostMessage(hwndClientDDE,
        WM_DDE_ACK,
        hwndServerDDE,
        MAKELONG(0, atomItem));              /* neg ACK      */
}
lstrcpy(szItemValue, lpPokeData->Value); /* copies value */
bRelease = lpPokeData->fRelease;
GlobalUnlock(hPokeData);
if (bRelease) {
    GlobalFree(hPokeData);
}
PostMessage(hwndClientDDE,
    WM_DDE_ACK,
    hwndServerDDE,
    MAKELONG(0x8000, atomItem));            /* positive ACK */
```

In this example, the server calls the **GlobalGetAtomName** function to retrieve the name of the item sent by the client. The server then determines whether it supports the item and whether the item is rendered in the correct format (CF_TEXT). If not, or if the server cannot lock the memory for the data, it sends a negative acknowledgment back to the client application.

22.4.3 Establishing a Permanent Data Link

A client application can use DDE to establish a link to an item in a server application. Once such a link is established, the server sends periodic updates of the linked item to the client (typically, whenever the value of the item changes). Thus, a permanent data stream is established between the two applications; this data stream remains in place until it is explicitly disconnected.

22.4.3.1 Initiating a Data Link

The client initiates a data link by sending a WM_DDE_ADVISE message, as follows:

```
if (!hOptions = GlobalAlloc(GMEM_MOVEABLE | GMEM_DDESHARE,
        sizeof(DDEADVISE))))
    return;
if (!(lpOptions = (DDEADVISE FAR*) GlobalLock(hOptions))) {
    GlobalFree(hOptions);
    return;
}
lpOptions->cfFormat = CF_TEXT;
lpOptions->fAckReq = TRUE;
lpOptions->fDeferUpd = FALSE;
GlobalUnlock(hOptions);
```

```
if ((atomItem = GlobalAddAtom(szItemName)) != 0) {
    if (!(PostMessage(hwndServerDDE,
            WM_DDE_ADVISE,
            hwndClientDDE,
            MAKELONG(hOptions, atomItem)))) {
        GlobalDeleteAtom(atomItem);
        GlobalFree(hOptions);
    }
}

if (atomItem == 0) {
    .
    . /* error handling */
    .
}
```

In this example, the client application sets the **fDeferUpd** flag of the WM_DDE_ADVISE message to FALSE. This directs the server application to send the data to the client whenever the data changes.

If the server has access to the item and can render it in the requested format, the server notes the new link (recalling the flags specified in hOptions) and sends the client a positive WM_DDE_ACK message. From then on, until the client issues a matching WM_DDE_UNADVISE message, the server sends the new data to the client every time the value of the item changes in the server application.

If the server is unable to service the WM_DDE_ADVISE request, it sends the client a negative WM_DDE_ACK message.

22.4.3.2 Initiating a Data Link with the Paste Link Command

Applications that support hot or warm data links typically support a registered clipboard format named Link. When associated with the application's Copy and Paste Link commands, this clipboard format allows the user to establish DDE conversations between applications simply by copying a data item in the server application and pasting it into the client application.

A server application supports the Link clipboard format by placing in the clipboard a string containing the application, topic, and item names when the user chooses the Copy command from the Edit menu. Following is the standard Link format:

*application***\0***topic***\0***item***\0\0**

A single null character separates the names, and two null characters terminate the entire string.

Both the client and server applications must register the Link clipboard format, as shown:

```
cfLink = RegisterClipboardFormat("Link");
```

A client application supports the Link clipboard format by means of a Paste Link command on its Edit menu. When the user chooses this command, the client application parses the application, topic, and item names from the Link-format clipboard data. Using these names, the client application initiates a conversation for the application and topic, if such a conversation does not already exist. The client application then sends a WM_DDE_ADVISE message to the server application, specifying the item name contained in the Link-format clipboard data.

Following is an example of a client application's response to the Paste Link command being chosen:

```
void DoPasteLink(hwndClientDDE)
HWND hwndClientDDE;
{

    HANDLE hData;
    LPSTR  lpData;
    HWND   hwndServerDDE;
    char   szApplication[APP_MAX_SIZE + 1];
    char   szTopic[TOPIC_MAX_SIZE + 1];
    char   szItem[ITEM_MAX_SIZE + 1];
    int    nBufLen;

    if (OpenClipboard(hwndClientDDE)) {
        if (!(hData = GetClipboardData(cfLink)) ||
                !(lpData = GlobalLock(hData))) {
            CloseClipboard();
            return;
        }

        /* Parse the clipboard data.*/

        if ((nBufLen = lstrlen(lpData)) >= APP_MAX_SIZE) {
            CloseClipboard();
            GlobalUnlock(hData);
            return;
        }
        lstrcpy(szApplication, lpData);
        lpData += (nBufLen + 1); /* skips over null */
        if ((nBufLen = lstrlen(lpData)) >= TOPIC_MAX_SIZE) {
            CloseClipboard();
            GlobalUnlock(hData);
            return;
        }
        lstrcpy(szTopic, lpData);
        lpData += (nBufLen + 1); /* skips over null */
```

```
            if ((nBufLen = lstrlen(lpData)) >= ITEM_MAX_SIZE) {
                CloseClipboard();
                GlobalUnlock(hData);
                return;
            }
            lstrcpy(szItem, lpData);
            GlobalUnlock(hData);
            CloseClipboard();

            if (hwndServerDDE =
                    FindServerGivenAppTopic(sszApplication, zTopic)) {

                /* App/topic conversation is already started. */

                if (DoesAdviseAlreadyExist(hwndServerDDE, szItem))
                    MessageBox(hwndMain,
                        "Advisory already established",
                        "Client", MB_ICONEXCLAMATION | MB_OK);
                else
                    SendAdvise(hwndClientDDE, hwndServerDDE, szItem);
            }
            else {

                /* Must initiate a new conversation first. */

                SendInitiate(szApplication, szTopic);
                if (hwndServerDDE =
                        FindServerGivenAppTopic(szApplication, szTopic))
                    SendAdvise(hwndServerDDE, szItem);
            }
        }
    }
    return;
}
```

In this example, the client application opens the clipboard and determines whether the clipboard contains data in the Link format (cfLink) that it had previously registered. If not, or if it cannot lock the data in the clipboard, the client returns.

After the client application has retrieved a pointer to the clipboard data, it parses the data to extract the application, topic, and item names.

The client application determines whether a conversation on the topic already exists between it and the server application. If a conversation does exist, the client application checks whether a link already exists for the data item. If such a link exists, the client displays a message box to the user; otherwise, it calls its own SendAdvise function to send a WM_DDE_ADVISE message to the server for the item.

If a conversation on the topic does not exist already between the client and the server, the client first calls its own SendInitiate function to broadcast the WM_DDE_INITIATE message to request a conversation and, second, calls its own FindServerGivenAppTopic function to establish the conversation with the window that responds on behalf of the server application. Once the conversation has begun, the client application calls SendAdvise to request the link.

22.4.3.3 Notifying the Client That Data Has Changed

When the client establishes a link by using the WM_DDE_ADVISE message—with the **fDeferUpd** flag not set (that is, equal to zero), the client has requested the server to send the data item each time the item's value changes. In such cases, the server renders the new value of the data item in the previously specified format and sends the client a WM_DDE_DATA message, as follows:

```
/*
 * Allocate the size of a DDE data header, plus data (a string),
 * plus a <CR><LF><NULL>
 */

if (!(hData = GlobalAlloc(GMEM_MOVEABLE | GMEM_DDESHARE),
        sizeof(DDEDATA) + strlen(szItemValue) + 3)))
    return;
if (!(lpData = (DDEDATA FAR*) GlobalLock(hData))) {
    GlobalFree(hData);
    return;
}
lpData->fAckReq = bAckRequest;  /* as specified in original   */
                                /* WM_DDE_ADVISE message       */
lpData->cfFormat = CF_TEXT;
lstrcpy(lpData->Value, szItemValue); /* copies value to be sent */
lstrcat(lpData->Value, "\r\n"); /* CR/LF for CF_TEXT format    */
GlobalUnlock(hData);
if ((atomItem = GlobalAddAtom(szItemName)) != 0) {
    if (!PostMessage(hwndClientDDE,
            WM_DDE_DATA,
            hwndServerDDE,
            MAKELONG(hData, atomItem))) {
        GlobalFree(hData);
        GlobalDeleteAtom(atomItem);
    }
}

if (atomItem == 0) {
    .
    . /* error handling */
    .
}
```

The client processes the item value as appropriate. If the **fAckReq** bit for the item is set, the client sends the server a positive WM_DDE_ACK message.

When the client establishes the link with the **fDeferUpd** flag set (that is, equal to 1), the client has requested that only a notification, not the data itself, be sent each time the data changes. In such cases, when the item value changes, the server does not render the value but simply sends the client a WM_DDE_DATA message with a null data handle, as follows:

```
if (bDeferUpd) {          /* checking whether the flag was originally */
                          /* set in the WM_DDE_ADVISE message         */

    if ((atomItem = GlobalAddAtom(szItemName)) != 0) {
        if (!PostMessage(hwndClientDDE,
                WM_DDE_DATA,
                hwndServerDDE,
                MAKELONG(0, atomItem))) { /* NULL data             */
            GlobalDeleteAtom(atomItem);
        }
    }
}

if (atomItem == 0) {
    .
    . /* error handling */
    .

}
```

As necessary, the client can then request the latest value of the data item by issuing a normal WM_DDE_REQUEST message, or it can simply ignore the notice from the server that the data has changed. In either case, if **fAckReq** is equal to 1, the client is expected to send a positive WM_DDE_ACK message to the server.

22.4.3.4 Terminating a Data Link

If the client requests that a specific data link be terminated, the client sends the server a WM_DDE_UNADVISE message, as follows:

```
if ((atomItem = GlobalAddAtom(szItemName)) != 0) {
    if (!PostMessage(hwndServerDDE,
            WM_DDE_UNADVISE,
            hwndClientDDE,
            MAKELONG(0, atomItem))) {
        GlobalDeleteAtom(atomItem);
    }
}
if (atomItem == 0) {
    .
    . /* error handling */
    .

}
```

The server checks whether the client currently has a link to the specific item in this conversation. If it does, the server sends the client a positive WM_DDE_ACK message; the server is then no longer required to send updates about the item. If the server has no such link, it sends a negative WM_DDE_ACK message.

To terminate all links for a conversation, the client sends the server a WM_DDE_UNADVISE message with a null item atom. The server determines whether the conversation has at least one link currently established. If it does, the server sends the client a positive WM_DDE_ACK message; the server then no longer has to send any updates in the conversation. If the server has no links in the conversation, it sends the client a negative WM_DDE_ACK message.

22.4.4 Carrying Out Commands in a Remote Application

A Windows application can use the WM_DDE_EXECUTE message to cause a certain command or series of commands to be carried out in another application. The client sends the server a WM_DDE_EXECUTE message containing a handle of a command string, as follows:

```
if (!(hCommand = GlobalAlloc(GMEM_MOVEABLE | GMEM_DDESHARE,
        sizeof(szCommandString) + 1)))
    return;
if (!(lpCommand = GlobalLock(hCommand))) {
    GlobalFree(hCommand);
    return;
}
lstrcpy(lpCommand, szCommandString);
GlobalUnlock(hCommand);
if (!PostMessage(hwndServerDDE,
        WM_DDE_EXECUTE,
        hwndClientDDE,
        MAKELONG(0, hCommand))) {
    GlobalFree(hCommand);
}
```

The server attempts to carry out the specified command string. If the server is successful, it sends the client a positive WM_DDE_ACK message; otherwise, it sends a negative WM_DDE_ACK message. This WM_DDE_ACK message re-uses the hCommand handle passed in the original WM_DDE_EXECUTE message.

22.4.5 Terminating a Conversation

Either the client or the server can issue a WM_DDE_TERMINATE message to terminate a conversation at any time. Similarly, both the client and server applications should be prepared to receive this message at any time. An application must terminate all of its conversations before shutting down.

The application terminating the conversation sends a WM_DDE_TERMINATE message, as follows:

```
PostMessage(hwndServerDDE, WM_DDE_TERMINATE, hwndClientDDE, 0L);
```

This informs the other application that the sending application will send no further messages and that the recipient can close its window. The recipient is expected in all cases to send a WM_DDE_TERMINATE message promptly in response. It is not permissible to send a negative, busy, or positive WM_DDE_ACK message.

After an application has sent the WM_DDE_TERMINATE message to the partner in a DDE conversation, it must not respond to any messages from that partner, since the partner might already have destroyed the window to which the response would be sent.

When an application is about to terminate, it should end all active DDE conversations before completing processing of the WM_DESTROY message. Your application should include timeout logic to allow for the possibility that one of its DDE partners is unable to respond to the WM_DDE_TERMINATE message. The following example shows how a server application terminates all DDE conversations:

```
void TerminateConversations(hwndServerDDE)
HWND   hwndServerDDE;
{
    HWND   hwndClientDDE;
    LONG   lTimeOut;
    MSG    msg;

    /* Terminate each active conversation.*/

    hwndClientDDE = NULL;
    while (hwndClientDDE = GetNextLink(hwndClientDDE)) {
        SendTerminate(hwndServerDDE, hwndClientDDE);
    }

    /* Wait for all conversations to terminate; wait for timeout. */

    lTimeOut = GetTickCount() + (LONG) nAckTimeOut;
    while (PeekMessage(&msg, NULL, WM_DDE_FIRST, WM_DDE_LAST,
            PM_REMOVE)) {
        DispatchMessage (&msg);
        if (msg.message == WM_DDE_TERMINATE) {
            if (!AtLeastOneLinkActive())
            break;
        }
        if (GetTickCount() > lTimeOut)
            break;
    }
    return;
}
```

22.5 The System Topic

Applications are encouraged to support the System topic at all times. This topic provides a context for items of information that may be of general interest to another application.

Data-item values should be rendered in CF_TEXT format. Individual elements of item values for a System topic should be delimited by tab characters. Suggested items for the System topic include:

Item	Description
SysItems	List of System-topic items supported by the application.
Topics	List of topics supported by the application at the current time; this list can vary from moment to moment.
ReturnMessage	Supporting detail for the most recently used WM_DDE_ACK message. This item is useful when more than eight bits of application-specific return data are required.
Status	Indication of the current status of the application. When a server receives a WM_DDE_REQUEST message for this System-topic item, it should respond by posting a WM_DDE_DATA message with a string containing either Busy or Ready, as appropriate.
Formats	List of clipboard format numbers that the application can render.

22.6 Related Topics

For more information about using the clipboard to exchange data, see Chapter 13, "Clipboard."

For more information about allocating and using memory objects for dynamic data exchange, see Chapter 15, "Memory Management," and Chapter 16, "More Memory Management."

For more information about DDE functions and about sending messages to other applications, see the *Microsoft Windows Programmer's Reference*, *Volumes 2* and *3*.

Index